Legalines

T3-BPD-315

Editorial Advisors:
Gloria A. Aluise
Attorney at Law
David H. Barber
Attorney at Law
Jonathan Neville
Attorney at Law
Robert A. Wyler
Attorney at Law

Authors:
Gloria A. Aluise
Attorney at Law
David H. Barber
Attorney at Law
Daniel O. Bernstine
Professor of Law
D. Steven Brewster
C.P.A.
Roy L. Brooks
Professor of Law
Frank L. Bruno
Attorney at Law
Scott M. Burbank
C.P.A.
Jonathan C. Carlson
Professor of Law
Charles N. Carnes
Professor of Law
Paul S. Dempsey
Professor of Law
Jerome A. Hoffman
Professor of Law
Mark R. Lee
Professor of Law
Jonathan Neville
Attorney at Law
Laurence C. Nolan
Professor of Law
Arpiar Saunders
Professor of Law
Robert A. Wyler
Attorney at Law

CONSTITUTIONAL LAW

Adaptable to Second Edition of Stone Casebook

By Jonathan Neville
Attorney at Law

Third Edition
Supplement
in Back of Book

THE
barbri
GROUP

HARCOURT BRACE LEGAL AND PROFESSIONAL PUBLICATIONS, INC.
EDITORIAL OFFICES: 176 W. Adams, Suite 2100, Chicago, IL 60603

Legalines

REGIONAL OFFICES: New York, Chicago, Los Angeles, Washington, D.C.
Distributed by: **Harcourt Brace & Company** 6277 Sea Harbor Drive, Orlando, FL 32887 (800)787-8717

SERIES EDITOR
John P. King, J.D.

PRODUCTION COORDINATOR
Sanetta Hister

THIRD PRINTING—1997

Copyright © 1991 by Harcourt Brace Legal and Professional Publications, Inc.

All rights reserved. No part of this publication may be reproduced or transmitted in any form or by any means, electronic or mechanical, including photocopy, recording, or any information storage and retrieval system, without permission in writing from the publisher.

Printed in the United States of America.

Legalines™

Features Detailed Briefs of Every Major Case, Plus Summaries of the Black Letter Law.

Titles Available

Administrative Law . . . . .Keyed to Breyer
Administrative Law . . . . .Keyed to Gellhorn
Administrative Law . . . . .Keyed to Schwartz
Antitrust . . . . .Keyed to Areeda
Antitrust . . . . .Keyed to Handler
Civil Procedure . . . . .Keyed to Cound
Civil Procedure . . . . .Keyed to Field
Civil Procedure . . . . .Keyed to Hazard
Civil Procedure . . . . .Keyed to Rosenberg
Civil Procedure . . . . .Keyed to Yeazell
Commercial Law . . . . .Keyed to Farnsworth
Conflict of Laws . . . . .Keyed to Cramton
Conflict of Laws . . . . .Keyed to Reese
Constitutional Law . . . . .Keyed to Brest
Constitutional Law . . . . .Keyed to Cohen
Constitutional Law . . . . .Keyed to Gunther
Constitutional Law . . . . .Keyed to Lockhart
Constitutional Law . . . . .Keyed to Rotunda
Constitutional Law . . . . .Keyed to Stone
Contracts . . . . .Keyed to Calamari
Contracts . . . . .Keyed to Dawson
Contracts . . . . .Keyed to Farnsworth
Contracts . . . . .Keyed to Fuller
Contracts . . . . .Keyed to Kessler
Contracts . . . . .Keyed to Knapp/Crystal
Contracts . . . . .Keyed to Murphy
Corporations . . . . .Keyed to Cary
Corporations . . . . .Keyed to Choper
Corporations . . . . .Keyed to Hamilton
Corporations . . . . .Keyed to Vagts
Criminal Law . . . . .Keyed to Boyce
Criminal Law . . . . .Keyed to Dix
Criminal Law . . . . .Keyed to Johnson
Criminal Law . . . . .Keyed to Kadish
Criminal Law . . . . .Keyed to LaFave
Criminal Procedure . . . . .Keyed to Kamisar
Decedents' Estates & Trusts . . . . .Keyed to Ritchie

Domestic Relations . . . . .Keyed to Clark
Domestic Relations . . . . .Keyed to Wadlington
Enterprise Organizations . . . . .Keyed to Conard
Estate & Gift Tax . . . . .Keyed to Surrey
Evidence . . . . .Keyed to Sutton
Evidence . . . . .Keyed to Waltz
Evidence . . . . .Keyed to Weinstein
Family Law . . . . .Keyed to Areen
Federal Courts . . . . .Keyed to McCormick
Income Tax . . . . .Keyed to Andrews
Income Tax . . . . .Keyed to Freeland
Income Tax . . . . .Keyed to Klein
Labor Law . . . . .Keyed to Cox
Labor Law . . . . .Keyed to Merrifield
Partnership & Corporate Tax . . . . .Keyed to Surrey
Property . . . . .Keyed to Browder
Property . . . . .Keyed to Casner
Property . . . . .Keyed to Cribbet
Property . . . . .Keyed to Dukeminier
Real Property . . . . .Keyed to Rabin
Remedies . . . . .Keyed to Re
Remedies . . . . .Keyed to York
Sales & Secured Transactions . . . . .Keyed to Speidel
Securities Regulation . . . . .Keyed to Jennings
Torts . . . . .Keyed to Dobbs
Torts . . . . .Keyed to Epstein
Torts . . . . .Keyed to Franklin
Torts . . . . .Keyed to Henderson
Torts . . . . .Keyed to Keeton
Torts . . . . .Keyed to Prosser
Wills, Trusts & Estates . . . . .Keyed to Dukeminier

Other Titles Available:
Accounting For Lawyers
Criminal Law Questions & Answers
Excelling on Exams/How to Study
Torts Questions & Answers

All Titles Available at Your Law School Bookstore,
or Call to Order: 1-800-787-8717

Harcourt Brace Legal and Professional Publications, Inc.
176 West Adams, Suite 2100
Chicago, IL 60603

There are two things BAR/BRI will do for you:

1 # Get you through LAW SCHOOL

2 # Get you through the BAR EXAM

O.K. we'll throw in a highlighter*

*Available at your local BAR/BRI office.

gilbert LAW SUMMARIES

Over 4 Million Copies Sold!

- Gilbert Law Summaries
- Legalines
- Law School Legends Audio Tapes
- Employment Guides
- Casebriefs Interactive Software

barbri BAR REVIEW

Relied On By Over 600,000 Students!

- Lectures, Outlines & Mini Review
- Innovative Computer Software
- Multistate, Essay & Performance Workshop
- Complete MPRE Preparation
- First Year Review Program

THE **barbri** GROUP

Our <u>Only</u> Mission Is Test Preparation

BAR/BRI Bar Review 1-888-3BARBRI

GILBERT LAW SUMMARIES 1-800-787-8717

SHORT SUMMARY OF CONTENTS

TABLE OF CONTENTS AND SHORT REVIEW OUTLINE

I. INTRODUCTION TO THE CONSTITUTION

A. BASIC DOCUMENT

The Constitution of the United States currently consists of seven articles and 26 amendments. It was created in response to the inadequacies of the Articles of Confederation and was ratified by the nine states necessary in 1788. The Constitution separates the powers of the national government into three branches: executive, legislative, and judicial. Each branch was intended to remain independent yet subject to restraint by the other branches through a system of checks and balances. The Constitution also establishes the federal/state framework of government. The study of constitutional law is essentially an examination of the sources of governmental power and the limitations imposed on its exercise. Through the system of judicial review, the United States Supreme Court has the final say in interpreting the Constitution; hence the heavy reliance on studying decisions of that Court.

B. SIGNIFICANT AMENDMENTS

The articles of the Constitution contain important protections of individual liberty, including the writ of habeas corpus, prohibition of ex post facto laws, and the Privileges and Immunities Clause. Two groups of amendments, however, provide the majority of the civil liberties enjoyed in the United States today.

1. **The Bill of Rights.** Many of the states included a bill of rights in their constitutions, but none was included in the original Constitution. Adoption of the first 10 amendments, or Bill of Rights, was prompted largely by the concerns expressed during the state ratification conventions. These amendments did not affect state power; they were only limitations on the power of the federal government.

2. **Civil War Amendments.** The abolition of slavery during the Civil War presented serious social problems. The thirteenth amendment, which was ratified in 1865, provided legal support to eradicate slavery, which had been recognized in the original Constitution. In 1866 Congress enacted the Civil Rights Act to prohibit racial discrimination practiced by the states. The President vetoed the act on grounds that it was unconstitutional, and although Congress overrode the veto, the fourteenth amendment was proposed to overcome constitutional objections to the Civil Rights Act. It was ratified largely because Congress made ratification a condition for the rebel states to be represented in Congress. The fifteenth amendment prohibited denial of the right to vote for racial reasons.

C. THE PROCESS OF CONSTITUTIONAL INTERPRETATION

Effective study of the Constitution requires more than just learning what "the law is." Many of the currently prevailing constitutional doctrines are relative newcomers; some are even the exact opposite of the doctrines that prevailed in earlier times. To be an effective constitutional advocate, a lawyer must understand various approaches to an issue. Often there is no "correct" interpretation of the Constitution; the interpretation that persuades a majority of the Supreme Court Justices is the one which becomes the law.

II. THE SUPREME COURT'S CONSTITUTIONAL ROLE—JUDICIAL REVIEW

A. JUDICIAL REVIEW OF THE CONSTITUTIONALITY OF LEGISLATION

1. **Origins of Judicial Review.** Although there was some debate at the Constitutional Convention about the role of the judiciary in reviewing legislative acts, nothing in the Constitution expressly gives the Supreme Court power to rule on the constitutionality of acts of Congress or state statutes, nor the power to review decisions of state courts. Article III merely creates the Supreme Court and extends the judicial power to "all Cases, in Law and Equity, arising under this Constitution, the Laws of the United States, and Treaties made . . . under their authority." However, section 2 spells out those cases in which the Supreme Court has original jurisdiction and specifies that in all other cases, the Court shall have appellate jurisdiction.

2. **Judiciary Act of 1789.** In the Judiciary Act of 1789, Congress created lower federal courts as permitted by the Constitution, but did not give them general jurisdiction in civil cases arising under federal law. The state courts were to exercise jurisdiction over such cases. The Supreme Court was authorized to hear three types of cases on appeal, all essentially involving state court rejection of claims made under federal law.

3. **Review of Acts of Congress.** The authority of the Supreme Court to review acts of Congress is not set forth in the Constitution. In the early days of the Marshall Court there was a considerable dispute about the propriety of this doctrine.

   a. **Hamilton.** The Federalist No. 78, written by Alexander Hamilton, argues that the judiciary is the least powerful of the branches of government in that it controls neither public funds nor the military. The independence of the judiciary allows it to guard the Constitution and the rights of individuals from improper actions of the other branches. Judicial decisions must be governed by the Constitution rather than by any contrary statute.

   b. **Jefferson.** Thomas Jefferson argued that each branch was responsible to determine for itself the constitutionality of its actions, and that the judges should not be the ultimate arbiters of all constitutional questions, although he recognized that the courts would face constitutional questions more often than the other branches.

   c. **The Judiciary Act.** In the Judiciary Act of 1789, Congress also gave the Supreme Court power to issue writs of mandamus to United States officials. This grant of original jurisdiction arguably violated the specific provisions of article III, section 2, setting the stage for the following case.

Marbury
v. Madison

4.   Assertion of Judicial Review Power--Marbury v. Madison, 5 U.S. (1 Cranch) 137 (1803).

    a.   Facts. Marbury (P) and others were appointed justices of the peace for the District of Columbia by President Adams and confirmed by the Senate on Adams's last day in office. Their formal commissions were signed but not delivered. Madison (D), as Secretary of State, was directed by the new President, Thomas Jefferson, to withhold the commissions. P brought a writ of mandamus directly to the Supreme Court under the Judiciary Act of 1789, which established United States courts and authorized the Supreme Court to issue writs of mandamus to public officers.

    b.   Issue. Is the Supreme Court empowered to review acts of Congress and void those which it finds to be repugnant to the Constitution?

    c.   Held. Yes. P's action is discharged because the Court does not have original jurisdiction; the Judiciary Act is unconstitutional.

        1)   The facts demonstrate a plain case for mandamus action, and under the Judiciary Act this Court could so act.

        2)   P claims that since the constitutional grant of jurisdiction is general and the clause assigning original jurisdiction to the Supreme Court (article III, section 2, clause 2) contains no negative or restrictive words, the legislature may assign original jurisdiction to this Court in addition to that specified in the Constitution. But the clause specifies in what cases this Court is to have original jurisdiction, and that in all other cases its jurisdiction is appellate. P's contention would render the clause ineffectual, an impermissible construction. Therefore, the Judiciary Act's grant of original mandamus jurisdiction is unconstitutional and void.

        3)   The grant of judicial power extends to all cases arising under the Constitution and laws of the United States. Since the Constitution is superior to any ordinary legislative act, it must govern a case to which both apply.

        4)   The Supremacy Clause (article VI, section 2) declares that the Constitution and those acts of Congress made in pursuance thereof shall be the supreme law of the land. Thus, the Court must determine when such acts are actually made in pursuance of the Constitution. The power of judicial review is implicit in the Constitution.

d. **Comment.** In more recent times, the Court has asserted a broad judicial review power, claiming the responsibility of being the ultimate interpreter of the Constitution. Once a law is declared unconstitutional, the courts simply decline to enforce it.

5. **Review of State Legislation--Martin v. Hunter's Lessee,** 14 U.S. (1 Wheat.) 304 (1816).

a. **Facts.** British subject Martin (D) was heir to the Virginia estates of Lord Fairfax, who died in England in 1781. Through state legislation confiscating the property of British loyalists, Virginia had conveyed title to Hunter. Hunter's lessee (P) brought an action of ejectment. D defended his title by virtue of two treaties between the United States and Britain that protected such British-owned property. The Virginia Court of Appeals sustained P's claim but was reversed by the United States Supreme Court. The Virginia court refused to comply with the reversal, and D again appealed.

b. **Issue.** Does the United States Supreme Court have appellate jurisdiction over the highest state courts on issues involving the Federal Constitution, laws, and treaties?

c. **Held.** Yes. The Virginia court must obey the United States Supreme Court's rulings.

1) The Judiciary Act of 1789, section 25, provided for review by the United States Supreme Court of final state court decisions rejecting claims under the Federal Constitution and laws. The outcome of this case depends on the constitutionality of that section.

2) Appellate jurisdiction is given by the Constitution to the Supreme Court in all cases where it does not have original jurisdiction, subject to congressional regulations.

3) All cases involving the Constitution, laws, and treaties of the United States are included in the judicial power granted by the Constitution to the Supreme Court; hence all such cases are properly subject to that Court's appellate jurisdiction, and section 25 of the Judiciary Act is valid.

4) Such power is necessary for uniformity of decisions throughout the whole United States, upon all subjects within the purview of the Constitution.

d. **Comment.** In *Cohens v. Virginia,* 19 U.S. (6 Wheat.) 264 (1821), a case involving the illegal sale in Virginia of lottery tickets issued with congressional authority in the District of

Columbia, the Court extended the *Martin* decision to permit review of state court criminal judgments.

e. **Comment**. When the Supreme Court reverses a state court judgment, it normally remands for "proceedings not inconsistent with this opinion." This allows the state court to both review previously undecided issues and to reconsider its decision on matters of state law.

B. SOURCES OF CONSTITUTIONAL DOCTRINE

1. **Introduction**. The Constitution itself is a relatively brief document and cannot include all the various legal doctrines a court must use to decide cases. The text of the Constitution is often merely the starting point for the court to determine what constitutional law is. Other sources of constitutional doctrine include concepts of natural law and natural rights, and notions about "public policy," or what would promote the principles and values behind our representative form of government.

2. **The Necessary and Proper Clause**. A good example of the need for constitutional doctrine to illuminate the text of the Constitution is the Necessary and Proper Clause. Article I, section 1, grants legislative powers to Congress. This is the power to make laws and to do all things that are necessary to enact them, such as to conduct investigations, hold hearings, etc. Because the federal government has only such power as is granted by the people, the powers of Congress are specifically enumerated in section 8; every federal statute must be based on one of the enumerated powers. The Necessary and Proper Clause, however, gives Congress authority to "make all laws which shall be necessary and proper for carrying into execution the foregoing powers." The interpretation of this clause was a critical issue because, if narrowly construed, it could severely limit the federal government's ability to function, while if broadly construed, it could undermine the notion of federalism by removing any limits on the power of the federal government vis-a-vis the states.

3. **The Bank of the United States**. The meaning of federalism was initially clarified by the outcome of the controversy over the Bank of the United States. Nothing in the Constitution specifically granted Congress power to organize a Bank of the United States. However, Congress did create such a bank, as proposed by Secretary of the Treasury Alexander Hamilton, despite the objections of Thomas Jefferson and James Madison that Congress lacked power to do so. The original bank's charter expired after 20 years. Four years later, Congress established a second Bank of the United States. Many of the states objected to the bank and imposed stiff taxes on it. Maryland's tax on the Bank became the basis for the first important Supreme Court opinion on federalism.

a. **Scope of federal authority--McCulloch v. Maryland**, 17 U.S. (4 Wheat.) 316 (1819).

   1) **Facts**. The state of Maryland (P) imposed a tax requiring all banks chartered outside the state to print their bank notes on stamped paper if they established any branch or office within P's boundaries. The tax was similar to those passed in other states during a period of strong state sentiment against the Bank of the United States. The taxes were aimed at excluding the Bank of the United States from operating branches within those states. The Bank fell within the statutory definition but issued notes on unstamped paper. Accordingly, P brought an action for debt collection against McCulloch (D), the cashier of the Baltimore branch of the Bank of the United States. The state courts imposed penalties on D, and D appeals.

   2) **Issue**. Even though the Constitution does not expressly grant Congress the power to incorporate a bank, can it do so under a doctrine of implied powers?

   3) **Held**. Yes. Judgment reversed.

      a) Under the Necessary and Proper Clause, any appropriate means which Congress uses to attain legitimate ends that are within the scope of the Constitution and not prohibited by it, but are consistent with the letter and spirit of the Constitution, are constitutional.

      b) The federal government is one of enumerated powers, which are found in the Constitution. However, the Constitution cannot contain an accurate detail of all the subdivisions of governmental powers and of all the means by which they may be carried into execution. Otherwise, the Constitution would become nothing more than a legal code. The government must have the ability to execute the powers entrusted to it through the best available means.

      c) Any means that directly executes a power enumerated in the Constitution may be considered incidental to the enumerated power. The word "necessary" in the Necessary and Proper Clause does not limit Congress to indispensable means; rather, the term enlarges the powers vested in the federal government. Congress has discretion in choosing the best means to perform its duties in the manner most beneficial to the people.

      d) The creation of a corporation is one of those powers that can be implied as incidental to other powers or used as a means of executing them. The incorporation of the Bank of the United States is a convenient, useful, and essential instrument in the performance of the fiscal operations of the federal government. The United

States is a sovereign and thus has the power to create a corporation.

4) **Comment.** This case is one of the most important in the history of the Court because it established the doctrine of implied powers and emphatically articulated the supremacy of the federal government. The opinion went far beyond the needs of the specific case to promote a powerful federal government. Many commentators at the time objected that the idea of the nation as a union of sovereign states was being undermined. Instead of giving Congress only those additional powers that were needful or indispensable, the Necessary and Proper Clause was now a grant of discretionary power. However, exercise of this discretion must be based on powers granted by the Constitution.

b. **Subsequent history of the bank.** In 1832 Congress extended the charter of the bank, but President Andrew Jackson vetoed the legislation. Among other things, he objected to the windfall that the original private stockholders would have received upon extension of the charter. He also objected that many of these stockholders were foreigners. He found insufficient precedent to sustain the act, because Congress had been inconsistent over the years in its support and because the states were primarily against it. The Supreme Court's opinion was not determinative; President Jackson felt that each branch of the government had to determine for itself the constitutionality of a proposal, and he did not view the bank as necessary and proper.

C. EXTERNAL REGULATION OF JUDICIAL POWER

1. **Introduction.** The power of judicial review gives the courts significant power over the other branches of government. By declaring what the Constitution means, the Supreme Court can establish the binding law for the entire government. This power is not unchecked, however.

2. **Amendments.** A decision of the Supreme Court may be overturned through the cumbersome and difficult constitutional amendment procedure. This procedure has been used in the past to overturn four Supreme Court decisions.

3. **Appointment Power.** Because the President appoints the Supreme Court Justices, subject to the advice and consent of the Senate, there is some political control over the court. Of course, the President has no control over the Justice after the appointment is approved.

4. **Impeachment and Public Opinion.** The Constitution provides for removal of Justices upon impeachment for and conviction

of treason, bribery, or other high crimes and misdemeanors, but this procedure has never been successfully used against a Supreme Court Justice. Public opinion may have some influence on the Court, although the Court has made decisions in highly controversial areas.

5. **Supreme Court Jurisdiction.** The Supreme Court's original jurisdiction, codified in 28 U.S.C. section 1251, mainly concerns controversies between two or more states. Congress cannot alter this jurisdiction. However, under article III, section 2, clause 2, Congress has the power to regulate and limit the appellate jurisdiction of the Supreme Court. This power arguably applies at any time and at any stage of proceedings and may even allow Congress to withdraw particular classes of cases from the Court's appellate review. Congress has codified the Court's appellate jurisdiction in 28 U.S.C. sections 1254 and 1257.

   a. **Review of courts of appeals.** Under section 1254, the Court may review cases in the courts of appeals by writ of certiorari or by certification from a court of appeals.

   b. **Review of final judgments of the highest state courts.** Under section 1257, the Court may review final judgments of the highest state courts by writ of certiorari where the validity of a federal treaty or statute is drawn in question or where the validity of a state statute is drawn in question on the grounds of its being repugnant to the Federal Constitution, treaties, or laws; or where any title, right, privilege, or immunity is specially set up or claimed under the United States Constitution, laws, or treaties.

6. **Withdrawal of Jurisdiction During Consideration of Case--Ex parte McCardle,** 74 U.S. (7 Wall.) 506 (1869).

   a. **Facts.** After the Civil War, Congress imposed military government on many of the former Confederate states. McCardle (P), a newspaper editor in Mississippi, was held in military custody. P sought a writ of habeas corpus pursuant to an 1867 act of Congress, but the federal court denied the petition. P appealed to the Supreme Court as provided by the 1867 act. After a hearing but before the final decision, Congress repealed the portions of the act that permitted the appeal.

   b. **Issue.** Does congressional negation of previously granted jurisdiction preclude further consideration of matters brought to the Supreme Court based on that jurisdiction?

   c. **Held.** Yes. Case dismissed.

      1) The Supreme Court's jurisdiction is conferred by the Constitution subject to such exceptions and under such regulations as Congress shall make. The First Congress established the federal courts and prescribed regulations

for jurisdiction. Congressional affirmation of appellate jurisdiction implies the negation of all jurisdiction not so affirmed.

2) Here Congress has expressly removed jurisdiction previously granted. The Court may not inquire into the motives of Congress; without jurisdiction, the Court cannot proceed to consider the case.

3) No judgment can be rendered in a suit after the repeal of the act under which it was brought and prosecuted. Judicial duty requires rejection of ungranted jurisdiction as much as it requires exercise of valid jurisdiction.

d. **Comment.** This case represented the third major attempt to have the Court review the Reconstruction Acts, which had been passed over President Johnson's veto. The *McCardle* decision has never been directly reexamined by the Court, although Justice Douglas doubted that its rationale would prevail today.

7. **Limits on Congress's Authority.** There are two basic theoretical limits on congressional authority over the Court's jurisdiction. First, Congress should not be able to interfere with the essential role of the Court in the constitutional scheme. This would include interference with the Court's independence, as by altering appellate jurisdiction in response to specific Court opinions. Second, Congress should not curtail jurisdiction in a manner that impairs the rights of litigants; i.e., limits on jurisdiction should not violate litigants' due process and equal protection rights.

8. **Modern Attempts to Limit the Court's Jurisdiction.** In modern times, legislation to limit the Court's jurisdiction has been introduced in response to particularly controversial decisions, such as the *Miranda* decision, the busing decisions, the school prayer decisions, and the abortion decisions. To date, these proposals have not succeeded.

9. **Limitation of Jurisdiction of Lower Federal Courts.** Because Congress has power to create lower federal courts, it can limit their jurisdiction. Only in 1875 did the lower federal courts receive general jurisdiction to decide federal questions. At various times, Congress has removed certain types of cases from the jurisdiction of these courts.

D. CASE OR CONTROVERSY

1. **Introduction.** In addition to the congressional power over Supreme Court jurisdiction, the Court has itself imposed certain limits on the exercise of federal jurisdiction to avoid nonessential interpretation of the Constitution.

a. **Cases and controversies.** Article III, section 2 limits the jurisdiction of all federal courts to "cases and controversies," requiring federal courts to deal only with real and substantial disputes that affect the legal rights and obligations of parties having adverse interests, and that allow specific relief through a conclusive judicial decree.

b. **Justiciability.** Justiciability is the term of art expressing this limitation placed on federal courts by the case and controversy doctrine. Justiciability is a highly flexible concept, construed narrowly by activist courts, broadly by more conservative courts. The limits of justiciability also preclude rendering advisory opinions (opinions based on assumed or hypothetical facts that are not part of an existing, actual controversy), deciding moot cases (ones already decided by circumstances) or collusive or friendly suits, or adjudicating purely political questions.

c. **Common scenarios.** Problems of case and controversy and justiciability arise most frequently when a plaintiff seeks an injunction or a declaratory judgment as to the constitutionality of a statute.

2. **Advisory Opinions.** The Supreme Court has an established policy against providing advisory opinions, even though some state supreme courts do provide such opinions. While it may appear that the use of advisory opinions would prevent considerable litigation, the Court has determined that preservation of the system of checks and balances, as well as the Court's status as the court of last resort in the nation, outweigh any advantages to be gained. This policy was first articulated when President George Washington requested advice pertaining to legal aspects of foreign relations.

3. **Standing.** The requirement of article III that federal courts adjudicate actual cases and controversies has been interpreted to require that litigants have "standing." This means that each litigant must be entitled to have the court decide the merits of the dispute or of particular issues.

a. **Aspects of standing.** The concept of standing has two aspects—one constitutional, the other self-imposed. First, the Court will not pass upon constitutional questions unless the party raising the claim is actually injured by the statute or act complained of. If the claimant does not show such injury, she has no standing to raise the issue; thus there is not justiciable controversy as required by article III, and the appeal will be dismissed. Second, even if the claimant is injured, the Court must deem it prudent to resolve the issues presented by that party. This latter issue of judicial "self-governance" arises primarily when a litigant seeks to assert the constitutional rights of a third party (e.g., a doctor asserting his patient's right to purchase contraceptives).

Allen v.
Wright

b. Application--Allen v. Wright, 468 U.S. 737 (1984).

   1) Facts. The Wrights (Ps) brought a class action on behalf of
        black school children, claiming that the failure of the IRS to
        deny tax-exempt status to private schools that practice racial
        discrimination constituted federal support for such schools
        and interfered with efforts to desegregate public schools. Ps
        sought declaratory and injunctive relief to force the IRS to
        deny tax exemptions to discriminatory private schools. The
        court of appeals held for Ps. The Supreme Court granted
        certiorari.

   2) Issue. Does a private person have standing to force the
        government to comply in accordance with law when the per-
        son can show no direct personal injury resulting from the
        alleged failure of the government to obey the law?

   3) Held. No. Judgment reversed.

      a) Under article III, Ps must have standing in order to
          obtain their requested relief. The standing requirement
          prevents a litigant from raising another person's legal
          rights, prevents adjudication in courts of generalized
          grievances better suited to representative branches, and
          precludes consideration of complaints that do not fall
          within the zone of interests protected by the law in-
          voked.

      b) Although the standing doctrine may not be precisely
          defined, it fundamentally requires Ps to allege personal
          injuries fairly traceable to the defendant's allegedly
          unlawful conduct and likely to be redressed by the
          requested relief. Ps' injury must be distinct and palpa-
          ble. It cannot be abstract or hypothetical.

      c) The first injury alleged by Ps is that of direct injury
          due to the mere fact of government financial assistance
          to racially discriminatory private schools. To the extent
          this claim is for a violation of the right to have the
          government abide by its laws, the claim is not sufficient
          to confer jurisdiction on the federal courts. To the
          extent the claim is for the stigma of being a member of
          a group that is discriminated against, the claim is cog-
          nizable only as to those persons who are personally
          discriminated against. However, Ps were not personally
          victims of discrimination.

      d) The second injury Ps alleged is that the federal tax
          exemptions granted to racially discriminatory private
          schools make desegregation of public schools more diffi-
          cult and thus give their children a diminished ability to
          receive an education in a racially integrated school.
          This type of injury is serious. However, the injury is

not fairly traceable to the government conduct Ps challenge.

  e) The only way the tax exemptions could possibly cause the harm Ps complain of would be if there were enough racially discriminatory private schools receiving the exemptions in Ps' community that withdrawal of the exemptions would make an appreciable difference in public school integration. Ps have not alleged such a causal connection, and there is no evidence of the number of such schools in Ps' community. One can only speculate whether withdrawal of the exemption would cause a school to change its policies, or whether a parent would transfer his or her child to public school as a result of those changes, or whether enough private schools and parents would react to make a difference. Because Ps' claimed injury cannot be fairly traced to the challenged action, Ps have no standing.

4) Dissenting (Brennan, J.). Ps' injury is clear, and the causal connection they allege is sufficient. They have identified 14 elementary schools in their own community that receive the tax exemption despite racially discriminatory policies.

5) Dissenting (Stevens, Blackmun, JJ.). The actual wrong Ps complain of is that the government subsidizes the exodus of white children from public schools that would otherwise be racially integrated. Clearly D's tax exemption policy causes the wrong complained of. The standing requirement measures the plaintiff's stake in the outcome, not whether the court is authorized to provide the plaintiff with the outcome sought. The Court should examine the justiciability of Ps' case, not their standing.

4. Political Questions.

a. Constitutional decision-making by other branches. The requirement of a justiciable article III controversy is deemed to carry with it a limitation against the deciding of purely "political questions." Hence, the Court will leave the resolution of such questions to the other departments of government. In determining whether there is a political question, the primary criteria are:

  1) A "textually demonstrable" constitutional commitment of the issue to the political branches for resolution;

  2) The appropriateness of attributing finality to the action of the political branches;

3) The lack of adequate standards for judicial resolution of the issue; and

4) The lack of adequate judicial remedies.

b. **Legislative districting.** In early decisions, the Supreme Court consistently refused to review questions arising from a state's distribution of electoral strength among its political or geographical subdivisions. In *Baker v. Carr, infra*, the Court decided that federal courts had jurisdiction over challenges to apportionment plans. The modern approach to federal elections requires that representation must reflect the total population as precisely as possible. More flexibility is permitted in apportionment of state legislatures, but grossly disproportionate districts are not allowed. State apportionment may not be used to further discrimination, but numerical deviations resulting from political considerations may be allowed.

Baker
v. Carr

c. **Justiciability of apportionment challenges--Baker v. Carr**, 369 U.S. 186 (1962).

1) **Facts.** The state of Tennessee continued to base the apportionment of voting districts on the 1901 census. In the intervening years, the population had grown at different rates in different voting districts. Baker (P) sought to force reapportionment through the courts because the unequal representation was unconstitutional and because the legislature in its present composition would not pass a state constitutional amendment. The lower federal courts denied relief on grounds of nonjusticiability; P appeals.

2) **Issue.** Do federal courts possess jurisdiction over a constitutional challenge to a legislative apportionment?

3) **Held.** Yes. Judgment reversed and remanded.

a) The relationship between the judiciary and the coordinate branches of the federal government gives rise to political questions, not the federal judiciary's relationship to the states. This case involves none of the types of problems normally identified as involving political questions.

b) The issue here is whether the state's activity is consistent with the Federal Constitution. Case remanded for consideration of that issue.

4) **Concurring** (Clark, J.). P and his fellow citizens have no other recourse than to federal courts.

5) **Concurring** (Stewart, J.). The Court properly does not decide the merits.

6) **Dissenting** (Frankfurter, Harlan, JJ.). The Court improperly hears a hypothetical claim based on abstract assumptions. The Court now permits federal courts to devise what they feel to be the proper composition of state legislatures.

7) **Dissenting** (Harlan, Frankfurter, JJ.). P has not asserted any right assured by the fourteenth amendment, and should not be granted standing.

E.   JURISDICTION

1.   Discretionary Review. Most of the cases on the Court's docket are discretionary. Petitions for certiorari are granted on a discretionary basis. The Supreme Court accepts cases brought to it on a writ of certiorari if at least four of the Justices want to grant the writ. United States Supreme Court Rule 10 sets forth the type of cases the Court will likely hear by granting certiorari. These are:

a.   Supervision of federal courts. When a federal court of appeals renders a decision in conflict with another circuit or a state court of last resort, or has departed from the usual course of judicial proceedings, the Court will likely exercise its supervisory power.

b.   Control over federal law. When a state court of last resort decides a federal question in conflict with a federal circuit or another state court of last resort, the Court will likely review the decision.

c.   Important cases. Whenever a lower court decides an important question which the Supreme Court has not settled, or whenever the lower court decides a federal question in conflict with a Supreme Court decision, the Court will likely review the decision.

2.   Jurisdiction over State Courts. The Supreme Court's only power over state judgments is to correct them where they incorrectly adjudge federal rights. The Court will not review severable state issues also decided in the case. To avoid advisory opinions, review is denied where an adequate and independent state ground supports the judgment, since a reversal of the federal law interpretation would not change the outcome. Whether adequate and independent state grounds exist is a federal question, however. If a decision appears to rest primarily on federal law, the Court assumes that the state court felt bound by federal law unless it clearly states that its decision rests on an adequate and independent state ground. [Michigan v. Long, 463 U.S. 1032 (1983)]

III. CONGRESSIONAL POWERS

A. SOURCES AND NATURE OF NATIONAL LEGISLATIVE POWER

Much of the Constitution deals with the allocation of governmental powers among the branches of government and between the federal and state governments. From an early date, the Supreme Court has had to determine the scope of these powers. It is useful to classify governmental powers as follows.

1. **Exclusive Federal Powers.** Certain federal powers specifically enumerated in the Constitution are exclusive by the terms of the granting provisions. Others are deemed exclusive because of the nature of the power itself, or because the power is denied to the states, e.g., the powers to enter treaties, to coin money, and to collect duties on imports. Many of the early constitutional cases involved disputes over the scope of the enumerated powers, especially when Congress acted under the Necessary and Proper Clause of section 8, clause 18.

2. **Exclusive State Powers.** Under the tenth amendment, the federal government may not exercise power in a fashion that impairs the states' integrity or their ability to function effectively in the federal system. The states are sovereign within their spheres.

3. **Concurrent Powers.** Most of the enumerated federal powers do not specifically deny state power in the areas covered. Under the Supremacy Clause, however, federal law prevails over any conflicting or inconsistent state law. Hence, Congress may preempt an area when uniform national laws are deemed necessary. Many of the disputes between the states and the federal government arise from differing views as to the application of the Supremacy Clause.

4. **Denied Powers.** In addition to the specific limitations on state powers contained in article I, section 10, the Bill of Rights and other amendments deny powers to the federal and state governments; e.g., Congress cannot establish a religion or abridge the freedom of speech.

5. **Necessary and Proper Powers.** The Necessary and Proper Clause of article I, section 8, gives Congress authority to make all laws necessary and proper to execute the enumerated powers and all other powers given by the Constitution to the federal government. The clause provoked controversy as the states met to ratify the Constitution. It allows Congress to take action not specifically authorized by the Constitution and has provided the basis for many decisions upholding federal laws. The Court has consistently held that this clause does not grant a new and independent power, however; it simply makes effective the enumerated powers.

6. **Scope of the Federal Legislative Power.** Article I, section 1, lodges all legislative power in Congress. This is the power to make laws and to do all things that are necessary to enact them, such as to conduct investigations and hold hearings. Article I enumerates many specific powers, but it also contains a broad provision in section 8, clause 18, which permits Congress to "make all laws which shall be necessary and proper for carrying into execution the foregoing powers, and all other powers vested by this Constitution in the government of the United States, or in any department or officer thereof." The scope of the Necessary and Proper Clause has been a subject of intense debate.

B. NATIONAL COMMERCE POWER

1. **Basic Commerce Clause Concepts.** Among the most important powers of government are its powers to regulate commerce and to tax goods and instrumentalities in commerce.

   a. **Overlapping nature of commercial regulation.** The states granted power to Congress to regulate commerce with foreign nations, and among the several states, and with the Indian tribes; if they had not done so, they could have erected trade barriers among themselves which would have destroyed the political union. [*See* U.S. Const. art. I, §8, cl. 3] In effect, the United States was intended to be a "common market," made up of individual states. The federal power to regulate commerce among the several states overlaps with each state's power to regulate commerce within its boundaries.

   b. **Relationship between state and federal authority over "commerce"--Gibbons v. Ogden,** 22 U.S. (9 Wheat.) 1 (1824).

   Gibbons
v. Ogden

      1) **Facts.** A New York statute granted the exclusive right to navigate by steamboat between New York City and Elizabethtown, New Jersey, to Livingston and Fulton, who in turn conveyed the right to Ogden (P). Gibbons (D) also operated boats along P's route. D's boats were licensed in the coasting trade under the federal Coasting Act. P sought and obtained a state court injunction prohibiting D's operation. D appeals, claiming that the power of Congress to regulate interstate commerce under the Commerce Clause is exclusive.

      2) **Issue.** Is state regulation of commercial navigation that excludes federally licensed operators constitutional?

      3) **Held.** No. Judgment reversed.

a) P admits that Congress has the power to regulate commerce with foreign nations and among the several states, but would limit the meaning of commerce to traffic (buying and selling) or the interchange of commodities, and would exclude navigation. But one of the primary objects of the creation of the federal government was to grant the power over commerce, including navigation.

b) The commerce power of Congress must be exercised within the territorial jurisdiction of the states, even though it cannot reach solely intrastate commerce. The power of Congress does not stop at the boundary lines of a state; it follows interstate commerce into the territory of a state.

c) P attempts to analogize between the taxing power and the commerce power, claiming that since the taxing power is concurrent, the commerce power should be. But regulation of interstate commerce is an exclusive federal power. When a state regulates commerce with foreign nations or among the several states, it exercises the very power granted to Congress, and the analogy fails.

d) State inspection laws are recognized in the Constitution, but do not derive from a power to regulate commerce. They act upon the subject before it becomes an article of foreign commerce.

e) D has been granted, through a federal license, the privilege of employment in the coasting trade. P would restrict such trade to property transport, excluding passengers. Such a narrow interpretation would eventually "explain away the Constitution." Instead, safe and fundamental principles must be followed, and coasting trade includes transport of both property and persons for hire.

f) For these reasons, the federal license must be recognized, and state laws prohibiting exercise of such licenses are void.

4) **Concurring.** Creation of a federal power over commerce was one of the main purposes of adopting the Constitution. This power must be exclusive.

5) **Comment.** Just five years after *Gibbons*, the Court decided *Willson v. Black Bird Creek Marsh Co.*, 27 U.S. (2 Pet.) 244 (1829). The state had permitted a private party to build a dam across a navigable creek, and Willson, whose vessel was licensed under federal law, broke the dam. The Court upheld the state law against Willson's challenge, emphasizing that the state regulation affected only a small, navigable creek concerning which Congress had not acted. The law was intended to preserve property values and protect the public health, and was therefore a permissible exercise of state police power.

6)   Comment. The *Gibbons* case illustrates the difficulty in interpreting the language of the Constitution. The entire case revolved around the proper definition of the term "commerce." Some commentators look to the dictionary for definitions, others look to the context in which the term is used, and others attempt to determine the intent of the framers as expressed in letters and other writings. The most commonly used expression of the framers' intent is the Federalist Papers. In *Gibbons*, Chief Justice Marshall stated that the only limits on congressional power to regulate interstate commerce are political, not judicial. His broad definition included as commerce any commercial intercourse among the states.

c.   Development of Commerce Clause jurisprudence. Most early cases dealing with the Commerce Clause involved challenges against state action that allegedly discriminated against or burdened interstate commerce. The Commerce Clause acted primarily as a restraint upon state regulation. It was not until 1887 and the enactment of the first Interstate Commerce Act that the Commerce Clause was relied on as the basis for the affirmative exercise of federal power. This occurred when Congress attempted to solve certain national economic problems. After the Interstate Commerce Act, Congress enacted several other regulatory statutes, including the Sherman Antitrust Act of 1890. The primary issue faced by the Court in deciding commerce cases was the definition of "interstate commerce." Recall that states have power over commerce within their boundaries. Thus federal power is concurrent with state power to some extent.

d.   Manufacturing not considered commerce. When the American Sugar Refining Company acquired four competing sugar refineries, effectively monopolizing the production of sugar, the United States sought to break up the company under the Sherman Antitrust Act. However, the Court held that Congress did not have authority to regulate manufacturing, which it held was not commerce. The fact that interstate commerce could ultimately be affected by the monopoly was not a sufficient basis for the exercise of congressional power. [United States v. E.C. Knight Co., 156 U.S. 1 (1895)]

e.   Rate-setting as commerce--Houston, East & West Railway v. United States (Shreveport Rate Case), 234 U.S. 342 (1914).

Houston, East & West Railway v. United States

1)   Facts. The Houston, East & West Railway (P) charged lower rates on its intrastate lines from Dallas and Houston to points eastward than on its interstate lines from Shreveport, Louisiana (near the Texas border), to points westward. All three cities competed for the same trade within Texas. The difference between the intrastate and interstate rates was so substantial that the ability of Shreveport merchants to compete in the east Texas markets was significantly impaired. The Interstate Commerce Commission (ICC) found that the interstate rates charged out of Shreveport to points in Texas were unreasonable because conditions on both the interstate and the intrastate lines were similar. The ICC ordered P to desist from charging higher rates on its interstate lines. P unsuccessfully challenged the ICC order. P appeals.

2) **Issue.** Does Congress have the power under the Commerce Clause to control intrastate charges of an interstate carrier in order to end injurious discrimination against interstate commerce?

3) **Held.** Yes. Judgment affirmed.

   a) The Commerce Clause gives Congress power to protect interstate commerce from impediments of local control that could destroy such commerce in violation of the policy behind the Constitution.

   b) Congressional power over interstate commerce necessarily extends to all other operations which have a close and substantial relation to interstate traffic. In order to foster and protect interstate commerce, Congress may take all measures necessary or appropriate to that end, including control of intrastate commercial activities that substantially affect the interstate commerce.

   c) Here the intrastate rates discriminated against interstate commerce. This constitutes sufficient grounds for federal intervention to protect the interstate commerce by regulating rates.

4) **Comment.** One of the chief problems that the Court struggled with during the rapid industrialization after the Civil War was the extent of congressional power under the Commerce Clause over intrastate commerce. The creation of a truly national market increased the tensions between local and interstate commerce as states tried to protect their industries against those of the sister states. The Shreveport case set forth the substantial economic impact test, which guided many of the Court's decisions in this area.

Champion
v. Ames

f. **Using the commerce power to regulate undesirable activity--Champion v. Ames** (the Lottery Case), 188 U.S. 321 (1903).

1) **Facts.** Champion (D) was arrested for shipping a box of lottery tickets by express from Texas to California in violation of the Federal Lottery Act, which prohibited importation, mailing, or causing interstate carriage of lottery tickets. Claiming that the Act was unconstitutional, D obtained a writ of habeas corpus. D appeals from a dismissal of the writ.

2) **Issue.** Does Congress have power under the Commerce Clause to regulate undesirable activity?

3) **Held.** Yes. Judgment affirmed.

a) Lottery tickets are subjects of commerce. They can be sold and transported. Hence, they can be regulated when trafficked from state to state. The power to regulate includes the power to prohibit.

b) This statute does not interfere with traffic or commerce carried on exclusively within the limits of a state. A state could prohibit sales of lottery tickets within its boundaries; so also Congress, for the purpose of guarding the people of the United States against the "widespread pestilence of lotteries," and to protect the commerce which concerns all the states, may prohibit the carrying of lottery tickets from one state to another.

c) Congress has the complete power to prohibit such commerce because it is the only governmental power capable of protecting the public from the evils of interstate traffic of lottery tickets.

4) **Dissenting.** Congress does not have power to suppress lotteries. Use of the police power has been reserved to the states by the tenth amendment. Furthermore, lottery tickets are not objects of commerce. This decision attempts to transform a noncommercial article into a commercial one simply because it is transported.

5) **Comment.** This is but one of several decisions that treat the commerce power almost as a federal police power. The rationale is simple; since Congress has plenary power over the channels or facilities of interstate commerce, it may prohibit their use for any activity that it deems adverse to the public health and welfare. Congress may prohibit entry into interstate commerce of:

a) Goods harmful to interstate commerce itself, such as diseased animals which might spread the disease;

b) Commercial items that are harmful, such as adulterated or misbranded articles; and

c) Noncommercial items that constitute an evil activity, such as stolen goods.

2. **Regulation of Economic Problems Through 1936.**

a. **Introduction.** Industrialization and the Depression presented many new social and economic problems for the nation to address. Congress and the President initiated new kinds of legislative programs to deal with these problems, often bringing government into the private sector through increased economic regulation. Although the Commerce Clause was raised as the constitutional basis for many of these laws, the Court narrowly construed the clause through 1936.

Hammer v. Dagenhart

b.   Promotion of social values--Hammer v. Dagenhart, 247 U.S. 251 (1918).

1)   **Facts.** Dagenhart (P) sought to enjoin Hammer (D), the United States Attorney General, from enforcing the Child Labor Act, which prohibited the shipment in interstate commerce of any product produced or mined by child labor. P was the father of two children who were to be discharged in compliance with the law by the company for which they worked. The district court enjoined enforcement; D appeals.

2)   **Issue.** May Congress prohibit the transportation in interstate commerce of goods manufactured by child labor?

3)   **Held.** No. Judgment affirmed.

a)   Congress does not have general police power. Unlike the *Lottery Case*, this case involves goods that are themselves harmless. Congress does not have power to prohibit movement of ordinary commodities.

b)   Manufacturing is purely a local activity, not subject to the congressional commerce power. The Constitutional scheme must be respected; only the states may regulate purely local matters.

c)   Even though this result leaves those states without their own child labor laws with an advantage in interstate competition, Congress simply has no power to force states to exercise their police power or to equalize conditions among the states.

4)   **Dissenting** (Holmes, J.). The Child Labor Act does not meddle with state rights. When products are sent across state lines, the states are no longer within their rights. If there were no Constitution and no Congress, their power to cross the line would depend on their neighbors. Under the Constitution, control of such commerce belongs to Congress and not the states. Congress may carry out its views of public policy, whatever the indirect effect on the states. Instead of being encountered by a prohibitive tariff at its boundaries, the state encounters the public policy of the United States, which is for Congress to express.

5)   **Comment.** This case illustrates the so-called geographic view of interstate commerce. This approach precluded congressional regulation over activity that begins and ends and at all times takes place within a single state. It was the first of many cases that frustrated attempts by Congress to deal with the social and economic problems created by the industrialization of America. The conflict between the legis-

lature and executive's broad view of congressional commerce power and the Court's narrow view of that power came to a peak during President Franklin Roosevelt's first term, when the Court struck down many of the programs of the New Deal.

3. **The Court's Threat to the New Deal.** Soon after President Roosevelt took office, a flood of new legislation was passed in an attempt to deal with the Depression, a national economic disaster. Much of this legislation was based on the Commerce Clause.

   a. **Relationship or nexus to interstate commerce.** In the first test of New Deal Commerce Clause legislation, the Supreme Court invalidated the Railroad Retirement Act of 1934. [*See* Railroad Retirement Board v. Alton Railroad Co., 295 U.S. 330 (1935)] The Act established a compulsory retirement and pension plan for all carriers subject to the Interstate Commerce Act. The argument was that such a plan was necessary to the morale of the workers, and that this morale affected efficiency, which in turn affected interstate commerce. The Court held that the relationship of such legislation to interstate commerce was too remote.

   b. **The "indirect effect" theory--A.L.A. Schechter Poultry Corp. v. United States,** 295 U.S. 495 (1935).

      1) **Facts.** Pursuant to the National Industrial Recovery Act of 1933, the federal government adopted a Live Poultry Code that imposed certain business standards on the live poultry industry in New York City. Among other things, the Code established a minimum wage and a 40-hour work week. The Schecters (Ds) operated a slaughterhouse in New York. Most of the poultry they purchased was shipped from other states to New York, but all of the Schecters' customers were local. Ds did not fully comply with the Code and were convicted. The court of appeals upheld the convictions and Ds appeal.

      2) **Issue.** May Congress regulate intrastate commerce that has only an indirect effect on interstate commerce?

      3) **Held.** No. Judgment reversed.

         a) The poultry that Ds purchased and slaughtered may have come from out of state, but Ds' own dealings with the poultry were entirely in New York. The poultry was no longer in a current or flow of interstate commerce; the flow had ceased once it arrived in New York and was held for local disposition and use. There is no basis for applying the Commerce Clause to products that are no longer in the flow of interstate commerce.

b) An alternative basis for regulation under the Commerce Clause is a finding that the transaction to be regulated "affects" interstate commerce. For this analysis, there must be a clear distinction between direct and indirect effects. To the extent that the Code sought to regulate the hours and wages of Ds' employees, who were engaged solely in local commerce, the violations could have no direct relation to interstate commerce. The fact that the Code could ultimately affect the prices involved in interstate commerce does not change the fact that such an effect would be indirect.

4) **Comment.** The Act was due to expire by its own terms about a month after this opinion was issued.

Carter v.
Carter Coal
Co.

c. **Regulation of employment conditions--Carter v. Carter Coal Co.,** 298 U.S. 238 (1936).

1) **Facts.** Carter (P) was president and a stockholder of Carter Coal Co. (D). P sued to enjoin D from paying a tax assessed against it under the Bituminous Coal Conservation Act, which sought to regulate hours and wages in coal mines and imposed a tax on the sales price or fair market value of all coal mined by any producer that did not comply with the regulations. The United States conceded that the tax was a penalty and that its validity depended on whether its regulatory aspects were within the federal commerce power. The district court held for D, and P appeals.

2) **Issue.** May Congress regulate the hours, wages, and other employment conditions of a national industry?

3) **Held.** No. Judgment reversed.

a) "Commerce" has been defined as "intercourse for the purposes of trade." The employment of men and the fixing of their wages, hours of labor, and working conditions constitute intercourse for purposes of production, not of trade. The local character of mining, manufacturing, or farming does not change merely because the products of those activities move into interstate commerce. The relations between employer and employee are local in nature and subject only to local regulation.

b) The production of every commodity intended for interstate sale and transportation has some effect upon interstate commerce. However, activities relating to production have only an indirect effect on commerce. The distinction between direct and indirect effects turns not upon the magnitude of either the cause or the effect, but entirely upon the manner in which the effect has been brought about. Congress can regulate only those things that have a direct effect on commerce. Mining is not one of them.

4) **Dissenting.** Mining, agriculture, and manufacture are not interstate commerce if considered by themselves, yet their relation to interstate commerce may be such that for the protection of the one there is need to regulate the other. This language of direct/indirect relation to commerce has not been literally applied in past cases. The proximity or remoteness of activities to commerce is a more logical way to approach the subject.

5) **Comment.** This case illustrates the Court's movement, just prior to 1936, away from a geographic approach towards the direct/indirect analysis. Under this analysis, an activity that takes place entirely within a single state may be regulated by Congress if it has a direct effect on interstate commerce. This approach faded after 1936 as the Court broadened its view of the congressional commerce power.

d. **The Court-packing plan.** President Roosevelt felt that the Court was judging the public policy of the New Deal, rather than its constitutionality. He proposed legislation to allow him to appoint an extra Justice for every Justice over age 70 who did not resign. The legislation never passed, but some observers believe that it prompted a change in the Court's analysis of New Deal legislation.

4. **Expansion of the Commerce Power After 1936.**

a. **The affectation doctrine.** Beginning in 1937, the Court abandoned the "geographical" and "direct vs. indirect" approaches to federal regulation under the Commerce Clause. The Court's position currently extends to Congress the power to regulate any activity, whether interstate or intrastate in nature, as long as it has any appreciable effect on interstate commerce. This approach is called the "affectation doctrine."

b. **Steel production--NLRB v. Jones & Laughlin Steel Corp.**, 301 U.S. 1 (1937).

1) **Facts.** The National Labor Relations Act provided for union-employer collective bargaining in all industries affecting interstate commerce. Jones & Laughlin Steel (D), a steel manufacturer, had discharged certain employees who were union activists. D was ordered by the National Labor Relations Board (P) to comply with the Act's provisions, but D claimed that Congress had no power to regulate its industry. P went to federal court to have its order enforced, but the court refused on the ground that federal power did not extend so far. During the hearings, the evidence showed that D was an integrated company that owned subsidiaries all over the

NLRB v.
Jones &
Laughlin
Steel Corp.

United States, that 75% of the product of the plant affected by P's order was shipped out of state, and that it received its raw materials from out of state. P appeals.

2) Issue. May Congress regulate a manufacturer if the manufacturer's activity significantly affects interstate commerce?

3) Held. Yes. Judgment reversed.

a) The term "affecting commerce" means burdening or obstructing commerce or the free flow of commerce, or having led or tending to lead to a labor dispute burdening or obstructing commerce or the free flow of commerce.

b) Labor strife at this plant could conceivably cripple the entire interstate operation of the company. Thus, interstate commerce was affected, and P may regulate D's activity.

Wickard   **c. Farming--Wickard v. Filburn,** 317 U.S. 111 (1942).
v. Filburn

1) Facts. Wickard (D), the Secretary of Agriculture, imposed a marketing penalty upon the portion of Filburn's (P's) crop grown in excess of his allotment under the Agricultural Adjustment Act of 1938. P sued to enjoin enforcement of the penalty, claiming that application of the marketing quota to him was beyond Congress's commerce power, because P used the wheat on his own farm. The trial court granted an injunction, and D appeals.

2) Issue. May Congress regulate individual home production of wheat and use of a major interstate commodity based on the substantial effect of the aggregate of such activity?

3) Held. Yes. Judgment affirmed.

a) The purpose of the Act is to restrict supply of wheat in order to maintain the price, and the power to regulate commerce includes the power to regulate the prices at which commodities are sold. Commerce among the states in wheat is large and important, so the subject is clearly within Congress's power.

b) P's activity involved small-scale, local production of wheat, partly for home consumption. But even if the activity is local and not regarded as commerce, it may be reached by Congress if it exerts a "substantial economic effect on interstate commerce, and this irrespective of whether such effect is what might at some earlier time have been defined as 'direct' or 'indirect'."

c) Home consumption of the wheat does not detract from the economic effect of the excess crop because it substitutes for purchases on the open market. That P's effect is trivial is irrelevant because, taken together with many others similarly situated, it is far from trivial.

    d)   Therefore, Congress may properly include wheat consumed on the farm in its scheme of regulation where it determines that such inclusion is essential to achievement of its policy purposes.

d.   **Manufacturing--United States v. Darby**, 312 U.S. 100 (1941).

    1)   **Facts.** The Fair Labor Standards Act of 1938 prescribed maximum and minimum wages for workers who manufactured goods for interstate commerce and prohibited interstate shipment of goods made by workers not employed in compliance with the Act. Darby (D), a lumber manufacturer, was charged with violating the Act. The district court quashed the indictment, finding the Act inapplicable to D's employees, who were involved in manufacturing, not interstate commerce. The United States (P) appeals.

    2)   **Issue.** May Congress establish and enforce wage and hour standards for manufacture of goods for interstate commerce?

    3)   **Held.** Yes. Judgment reversed.

        a)   The interstate shipment of manufactured goods is clearly subject to congressional regulation. Congress has in the past prohibited interstate shipment of various articles pursuant to public policy, and the Court has no control over legislative judgment of public policy. Prohibition of interstate shipment of goods covered by the Act is constitutional as long as the labor standards involved are properly within the scope of federal power.

        b)   Congress has adopted the policy of excluding from interstate commerce all goods produced for that commerce that do not conform to the specified labor standards, and Congress may choose appropriate means of accomplishing that policy. Federal power extends to intrastate activities directly affecting interstate commerce. The means here adopted so affect interstate commerce as to be within Congress's power to regulate.

        c)   The Act is directed at the suppression of "unfair" competition in interstate commerce, a valid purpose. Therefore, the Act is constitutional.

    4)   **Comment.** This opinion overruled *Hammer v. Dagenhart*. *Darby* involved manufacturing prior to interstate shipment; another case, *United States v. Sullivan*, 332 U.S. 689 (1948), upheld federal regulation extending to activity after interstate commerce had terminated. Sullivan, a druggist, had repackaged drugs he had received six months earlier from another state. He omitted certain directions and warnings required by federal law. The Court upheld Sullivan's conviction on the theory that the Commerce Clause allows Congress to regulate the branding of articles held for resale after being shipped interstate, and it did not matter that Sullivan repackaged them at the local level.

5.   **Use of Commerce Power to Fight Crime and Regulate Business.**

    a.   **Exclusion from commerce.** As discussed in the *Lottery Case, supra,* Congress may exclude from interstate commerce products and transactions that harm the health, morals, safety, or welfare of the nation. Congress has used this approach in regulating crime as well, prohibiting interstate transportation of certain stolen property and other contraband.

Perez v.
United States

    b.   **Regulation of local illegal activity--Perez v. United States,** 402 U.S. 146 (1971).

        1)   **Facts.** The Consumer Credit Protection Act contained a provision (Title II) that extended federal criminal jurisdiction to "extortionate credit transactions" (loan sharking). Perez (D) was convicted and sentenced under the Act. D appeals.

        2)   **Issue.** May Congress use the commerce power to define and regulate a class of activity that might include individual acts unconnected with interstate commerce?

        3)   **Held.** Yes. Judgment affirmed.

            a)   Congress may properly define a "class of activities" having an effect on interstate commerce, provided it appropriately considers the "total incidence" of the practice on such commerce. Even purely intrastate activities may affect interstate commerce.

            b)   Congress's definition of the class here is supported by adequate findings that loan sharking provides organized crime substantial revenue with which to affect interstate commerce in many forms.

            c)   Where the class of activities is regulated and that class is properly within the reach of federal power, the courts have no power to excise, as trivial, individual instances of the class, whether or not they occur solely within one state.

        4)   **Dissent.** There is no rational distinction between loan sharking and other crimes. The statute unconstitutionally infringes on the state power to define and prosecute local, intrastate crime.

c. **Regulation of local activity after interstate commerce ends.** Congress may regulate local business activity even after the interstate commerce ends, if the products traveled in interstate commerce. In *McDermott v. Wisconsin*, 228 U.S. 115 (1913), the Court held that Congress could require that labels meeting federal standards be attached to all "unsold" goods which travel interstate. This requirement facilitates inspection to enforce federal laws. In *United States v. Sullivan*, 332 U.S. 689 (1948), the Court reaffirmed *McDermott* and held that Congress could require a retailer to affix federal labels to the smaller containers into which he distributed the goods from a single large interstate container. The rationale for these decisions is that to enforce the Pure Food and Drug Act most effectively, Congress would have to authorize inspection and seizure when the goods are made available for final sale.

6. **Protection of Civil Rights Through the Commerce Clause.**

a. **Introduction.** The Court now recognizes few, if any, federalism constraints on congressional power to regulate commerce. The federal commerce power embraces almost every phase of the economy, national or local, that taken separately or in the aggregate affects interstate commerce. The major function of the Supreme Court in this area has become one of statutory construction; i.e., simply determining what Congress intends by its statutes that regulate commerce. Congress has elected to use this extensive power to protect civil rights within the sphere of commerce.

b. **Private motels--Heart of Atlanta Motel v. United States,** 379 U.S. 241 (1964).

Heart of Atlanta Motel v. United States

   1) **Facts.** The owner of the Heart of Atlanta Motel (P) refused to rent rooms to blacks. P sought a declaratory judgment that Title II of the Civil Rights Act of 1964 was unconstitutional. A three-judge federal court sustained the Act. P appeals.

   2) **Issue.** May Congress prohibit racial discrimination by private motels that accept out-of-state business?

   3) **Held.** Yes. Judgment affirmed.

      a) The legislative history of the Civil Rights Act contains numerous examples of how racial discrimination places burdens upon interstate commerce, which comprehends the movement of persons through more than one state.

      b) Even though the operation of the motel was local, if it is interstate commerce that feels the pinch, then it does not matter how local is the operation that applies the squeeze.

c. **Private restaurant--Katzenbach v. McClung**, 379 U.S. 294 (1964).

1) **Facts.** McClung (P), owner of a restaurant that excluded blacks from its dining accommodations, challenged Title II of the Civil Rights Act. The lower court granted an injunction against enforcement by Katzenbach (D), the assistant Attorney General, finding that P would lose a substantial amount of business if required to serve blacks.

2) **Issue.** May Congress use its commerce power to forbid racial discrimination by a restaurant on the sole ground that slightly under one-half of the food it serves originates from outside the state in which it operates?

3) **Held.** Yes. Judgment reversed.

a) Although the food originating out of state had "come to rest," the line of cases holding that interstate commerce ends when goods come to rest in the state of destination applies only with reference to state taxation or regulation, not to federal regulation of commerce.

b) The fact that discrimination in restaurants resulted in sales of fewer interstate goods and that interstate travel was obstructed directly by it shows sufficient connection between the discrimination and the movement of interstate commerce to allow federal intervention.

c) Once the court finds a rational basis for holding a chosen regulatory scheme necessary to the protection of interstate commerce, the only inquiry is whether the facts fit the scheme. Here the lower court found that P serves food, a substantial portion of which has moved in interstate commerce. Hence, P is covered by the regulation.

4) **Concurring** (Black, J.). Every possible speculative effect on commerce should not be accepted as an adequate constitutional ground to uproot and discard all our traditional distinctions between what is purely local, and therefore controlled by state laws, and what affects the national interest, and therefore is subject to control by federal laws. The one isolated local event, however, when added to many other similar events, could impose a burden on interstate commerce.

5) **Concurring** (Douglas, J.). This case is better decided under the fourteenth amendment, which gives Congress authority to act in this manner. The right of the people to be free of state action that discriminates against them because of race, like the right of persons to move freely from state to state, occupies a more protected position in our constitutional system than does the movement of cattle, fruit, steel, and coal across state lines. Deciding this case under the fourteenth amendment would put an end to strategies aimed at getting around the limitations inherent in using the Commerce Clause as a means of sustaining civil rights acts.

    d.   **Private recreation club.** In *Daniel v. Paul*, 395 U.S. 298 (1969), the Court upheld the application of Title II to a private recreation club on the ground that it offered to serve interstate travelers and served food made of ingredients that had traveled in interstate commerce.

7.   **State Immunity from Federal Regulation.**

    a.   **Introduction.** The Court's interpretation of the Commerce Clause has made congressional choices the primary determinant of the scope of national regulation. The first decision in 40 years to hold a federal law unconstitutional for exceeding the commerce power was *National League of Cities v. Usery*, below, and it has since been overruled. [*See* Garcia v. San Antonio Metropolitan Transit Authority, *infra*] The vitality of the state autonomy limitation on the commerce power may well turn on the composition of the Court, as decisions in this area are usually five to four votes. For the present, however, it seems that the Court's only function in Commerce Clause cases is statutory interpretation.

    b.   **Recognition of state autonomy--National League of Cities v. Usery,** 426 U.S. 833 (1976).

        1)   **Facts.** Congress passed amendments to the Fair Labor Standards Act that extended minimum wage and maximum hour provisions to almost all state and local government employees. National League of Cities (P) and other interested groups sought declaratory and injunctive relief against the amendments' application to them on grounds of state immunity from federal regulation under the tenth amendment. P's claim was dismissed. P appeals.

        2)   **Issue.** May Congress impose minimum wage and maximum hour regulations upon states in their role as employers?

        3)   **Held.** No. Judgment reversed.

            a)   Even though these amendments are within the scope of congressional power under the Commerce Clause, there are constitutional limits upon Congress's powers to override state sovereignty. The amendments would impose substantial costs, resulting in forced relinquishment of important state governmental activities. Additionally, they would displace state policies by which states structure delivery of those governmental services required by their citizens.

b)   If Congress may preempt the states' authority to make fundamental employment decisions essential to their systems of governance, there would be little left of the states' separate and independent existence, and their ability to function effectively within a federal system would be impaired. Thus, insofar as the challenged amendments operate to directly displace the states' freedom to structure integral operations in areas of traditional governmental functions, they are not within the authority granted to Congress by the Commerce Clause.

4)   **Concurring** (Blackmun, J.). The Court properly adopts a balancing approach to problems involving the relationship between the federal government and the states.

5)   **Dissenting** (Brennan, White, Marshall, JJ.). The only restraints on the federal commerce power lie in the political process, not the judicial process. These amendments are the proper result of the political process and should be upheld. There is no restraint based on state sovereignty requiring or permitting judicial enforcement anywhere expressed in the Constitution. The majority's opinion is merely a transparent cover for invalidating a congressional judgment with which they disagree.

6)   **Dissenting** (Stevens, J.). Federal regulation properly reaches a wide variety of employment-related activities of state and local public employees, and there is no specific limitation on the federal power to regulate wages, even of state employees.

7)   **Comment**. The opinion dealt only with exercise of the commerce power, leaving unaffected congressional authority to affect integral operations of state governments under other sections of the Constitution. The Court also noted that temporary federal emergency measures affecting state pay scales are proper.

8)   **Comment**. The Court summarized the test for governmental immunity in *Hodel v. Virginia Surface Mining & Reclamation Association*, 452 U.S. 264 (1981). Under this test, four conditions must exist for a state activity to merit immunity from federal regulation under the Commerce Clause:

a)   The federal statute must regulate the states as states;

b)   The statute must address matters that are indisputably attributes of state sovereignty;

c)   The state's compliance with the federal regulation must directly impair its ability to structure integral operations in areas of traditional governmental functions; and

d) The relation of state and federal interests must not be such that the nature of the federal interest justifies state submission.

c. ***National League of Cities*** **overruled--Garcia v. San Antonio Metropolitan Transit Authority,** 469 U.S. 528 (1985).

1) **Facts.** The San Antonio Metropolitan Transit Authority (D), a public mass-transit authority, received substantial federal financial assistance. In 1974 Congress extended the minimum-wage and overtime provisions of the Fair Labor Standards Act (FLSA) to mass-transit employees and virtually all state and local government employees. After *National League of Cities v. Usery* (*supra*), D told its employees that the FLSA no longer applied to them. In 1979, however, the United States Department of Labor determined that D's activity was not immune from FLSA. Garcia (P) sued D for overtime pay under FLSA. In a separate action, D sought a declaratory judgment that it was exempt from FLSA. The district court granted D's motion and denied P's cross-motion for partial summary judgment. P appeals.

2) **Issue.** May Congress enforce minimum-wage and overtime requirements against a local government's mass-transit authority?

3) **Held.** Yes. Judgment reversed.

a) If D is exempt from FLSA, it must be because of its status as a governmental agency, for if it were a private enterprise, Congress could clearly apply FLSA under the commerce power.

b) Under the four-part test of *Hodel* (*supra*), the third requirement—that the federal statute impair traditional governmental functions—is involved here. This requirement has produced confusion and a variety of interpretations, with no clear constitutional distinctions between what is and what is not a "traditional governmental function."

c) The problem with these standards is that they ignore the principle of federalism, which allows states to experiment with ways to solve problems. Thus, there are no "traditional," or "integral," or "necessary" government functions that should be more carefully protected than other government functions. Just as the "governmental/proprietary function" distinction used in cases involving state immunity from federal taxation eventually was discarded as unworkable, so the "traditional governmental function" analysis must be discarded.

d) The constitutional structure does impose limits on the commerce power. But the sovereignty of the states is limited by the Constitution itself, through the Supremacy Clause, the fourteenth amendment, and article I, section 10. The states have influence over Congress through equal representation in the Senate. State sovereign interests are more properly protected by procedural safeguards inherent in the structure of the federal system than by judicially created limitations on federal power. The limit on the commerce power is one of process, not result.

e) Nothing in the FLSA, as applied to D, destroys state sovereignty or violates any constitutional provision.

f) The states have been able to protect themselves. They receive significant federal aid. They are exempt from the operation of many federal statutes.

4) **Dissenting** (Powell, J., Burger, C.J., Rehnquist, O'Connor, JJ.).

a) The *National League of Cities* rationale has been followed in several cases. Departure from the doctrine of stare decisis requires special justification; the majority has undermined the stability of judicial decisions by so suddenly overruling *National League of Cities*.

b) Under the majority's opinion, the tenth amendment is nothing more than meaningless rhetoric when Congress exercises its commerce power. The Court cites no authority for its view that the role of the states in the federal system depends on the grace of elected federal officials rather than on the Constitution as interpreted by this Court.

c) *National League of Cities* adopted a familiar type of balancing test that requires weighing the respective interests of the states and federal government. Under the tenth amendment, the states' role is a matter of constitutional law, not of legislative grace. The Court holds that federal political officials, invoking the Commerce Clause, are the sole judges of the limits of their own power. Federal overreaching under the Commerce Clause undermines the constitutionally mandated balance of power between the states and the federal government.

d) The Court's view ignores the understanding of federalism that has long been accepted. Congress is not free under the Commerce Clause to assume a state's traditional sovereign power and to do so without judicial review. This relegates the states to precisely the trivial role feared by opponents of the Constitution.

5) **Dissenting** (O'Connor, Powell, Rehnquist, JJ.). The essence of federalism is that the states, as states, have legitimate interests which the national government is bound to respect even though its laws are supreme. It is not enough that the end be legitimate—the means to that end chosen by Congress must not contravene the

spirit of the Constitution. The proper resolution of this conflict is to weigh state autonomy as a factor in the balance when interpreting the means by which Congress can regulate the states as states. A state is different from a private citizen. Regardless of difficulty, the Court must reconcile these concerns.

      6)   **Dissenting** (Rehnquist, J.). The judgment should be affirmed under Justice Powell's approach, Justice Blackmun's concurrence in *National League of Cities*, or Justice O'Connor's approach. I am confident that the principle will, in time, command the support of a majority of this Court.

8.   **Protection of the Environment Through the Commerce Power**. Congress has exercised its commerce power to protect the environment by establishing national surface mining and reclamation standards. The Court upheld the law in *Hodel v. Virginia Surface Mining and Reclamation Association, supra*, based on congressional findings about the environmental and competitive effects of surface coal mining on interstate commerce. The plaintiff had argued that land as such is not subject to regulation under the Commerce Clause and that Congress could regulate land use only insofar as the Property Clause (article IV, section 3) grants it control over federal lands. The Court also upheld the restrictions on surface mining prime farmland, even though this portion of the statute applied to only 21,800 acres. [Hodel v. Indiana, 452 U.S. 314 (1981)]

C.   FOREIGN AFFAIRS POWER

1.   **Introduction**. The powers of the federal government concerning foreign or external affairs are different in origin and nature from those involving domestic or internal affairs. In external affairs, federal power is exclusive; the states may not conduct foreign affairs. There is no allocation of this power between the states and the federal government.

2.   **Treaties**. Article II, section 2 grants the President the power to make treaties with foreign nations, provided two-thirds of the Senators present concur. Such treaties become the supreme law of the land under the Supremacy Clause. The tenth amendment is not a limitation on the treaty power. Thus, pursuant to a treaty, Congress may legislate on matters over which it otherwise would have no power.

3.   **Principal Case--Missouri v. Holland**, 252 U.S. 416 (1920).

      a.   **Facts**. The Migratory Bird Treaty Act of 1918 implemented a treaty between the United States and Canada and prohibited killing or interference with migratory birds except as permitted by regulations made by the

Secretary of Agriculture. Missouri (P) brought suit in equity to enjoin Holland (D), a United States game warden, from enforcing the Act. P claims the Act unconstitutionally interferes with state rights and that an earlier similar act of Congress, not in pursuance to a treaty, was held invalid. The district court dismissed the action. P appeals.

b. **Issue.** May an act of Congress implementing a United States treaty create regulations that would be unconstitutional if the act stood alone?

c. **Held.** Yes. Judgment affirmed.

1) The tenth amendment is irrelevant since the power to make treaties is delegated expressly. Further, if the treaty is valid, the statute is equally so, being necessary and proper.

2) The important national interest here can be protected only by national action in concert with that of another nation. Such a joint effort is possible only through a treaty. Since there is no specific constitutional restriction and the national interest requires it, the treaty and its implementing statute are valid.

3) The state's interest, while sufficient to justify regulation in the absence of federal regulation, is too transitory to preempt specific national regulation, especially when the national action arises from exercise of the treaty power.

D.   NATIONAL TAXING AND SPENDING POWERS

1.   Regulation Through Taxing.

a.   Introduction. Article I, section 8 grants Congress power "to lay and collect taxes, duties, imposts and excises, to pay the debts and provide for the common defense and general welfare of the United States." Congress may exercise its taxing power as a means of promoting any objective that is within an enumerated power. If Congress has the power to regulate the activity taxed, the tax is valid even though clearly enacted for a regulatory, rather than a revenue-raising, purpose. If Congress has no power to regulate the activity taxed, the validity of the tax depends on its validity as a revenue-raising measure, although incidental regulatory effects are permissible. Congress generally does not now rely on the taxing power to regulate because of its extensive regulatory powers under other provisions, but this is still an important federal power.

b. **Child Labor Tax Case--Bailey v. Drexel Furniture Co.,** 259 U.S. 20 (1922).

1) **Facts.** A few months after the *Hammer v. Dagenhart* decision (*supra*), as a means to circumvent that decision, Congress imposed an excise tax of 10% on the yearly net profits of any employer knowingly using child labor in his business without regard to whether goods produced were shipped in interstate commerce. Drexel Furniture Co. (P) paid the tax and won a refund case in the lower courts. Bailey (D), the I.R.S. Commissioner, appeals.

2) **Issue.** May Congress use its taxing power to accomplish objectives that it cannot reach under any of its other powers?

3) **Held.** No. Judgment affirmed.

   a) The major purpose of a tax should be to raise revenue. However, many legitimate taxes also have incidental regulatory effects. Such taxes when imposed by Congress are still valid if their principal purpose is to raise revenue.

   b) Taxes that have a principal purpose of regulating are not authorized by the Constitution. The tax here was imposed only on those who knowingly do not comply with the child labor standards. This is a clear element of scienter. Scienter is used in penalties, not taxes. The tax is clearly a penalty and designed for regulation rather than to raise revenue. It is therefore invalid.

   c) If this tax were validated, then all Congress would have to do to take control of any one of a great number of areas of regulation reserved to the states would be to enact a detailed measure of complete regulation of the subject and enforce it by a so-called tax.

4) **Comment.** In *Bailey*, the Supreme Court indicated that the important factor is the motive of Congress. This means that the Court looks at the taxing statute to see its purpose, its intended effect, and its effect in normal operation (i.e., the Court examines the statute on its face). If the true purpose is to raise revenue, then the tax is valid. In *United States v. Kahriger*, 345 U.S. 22 (1953), the Court upheld a tax on wagering, despite its indirect effect of penalizing professional gamblers. The legislative history showed an intent to raise revenue, and the tax actually did raise funds, although the legislative history also showed an intent to suppress wagering. The penalty on wagering was considered as merely an indirect effect. Unless the penalty provisions are extraneous to the tax need, courts cannot limit the exercise of the taxing power. (As noted *supra*, after 1936 the Court ex-

panded its view of the commerce power, and it became less necessary for Congress to use its taxing power to regulate.)

2. Regulation Through Spending.

a. **Introduction.** The "general welfare" power of article I, section 8 is connected with the taxing and spending power. This clause can therefore be invoked only when there is an expenditure of money appropriated by Congress. Thus, Congress could not pass a law under the general welfare clause requiring seat belts in all cars. The rule is that Congress must tax for revenue and not merely regulatory purposes, and then it must spend for the general welfare. The spending must be for a national concern as opposed to a local one. However, the Supreme Court gives great deference to the determinations of Congress in deciding what is for the "common benefit."

United States
v. Butler

b. **Local vs. general welfare--United States v. Butler**, 297 U.S. 1 (1936).

1) **Facts**. The 1933 Agriculture Adjustment Act authorized the Secretary of Agriculture to extend benefit payments to farmers who agreed to reduce their planted acreage. Processors of the covered crops were to be taxed to provide a fund for the benefit payments. Butler (P) was receiver for a processor who had paid the tax. P brought suit to recover the tax paid on grounds that it was part of an unconstitutional program to control agricultural production. The court of appeals held the tax unconstitutional. The United States (D) appeals.

2) **Issue**. May Congress use its taxing and spending powers to operate a self-contained program regulating agricultural production?

3) **Held**. No. Judgment affirmed.

a) The power of Congress to authorize expenditures of public moneys for public purposes is not limited by the direct grants of legislative power found in the Constitution, but it does have limits. Appropriations cannot be made as a means to an unconstitutional end.

b) Regulation of agricultural production is not a power granted to Congress; therefore it is left to the states. Attainment of such a prohibited end may not be accomplished through the use of granted powers (here the taxing powers).

c) This scheme, purportedly voluntary, in reality involves purchasing, with federal funds, submission to federal regulation of a subject reserved to the states. Because the end is invalid, it may not be accomplished indirectly through the taxing and spending power.

    4)   **Dissenting** (Stone, Brandeis, Cardozo, JJ.). Courts are concerned only with the power to enact statutes, not the wisdom of the legislature. The depressed state of agriculture is nationwide; therefore, the Act does provide for the "general welfare." There is no coercion involved, since threat of loss, not hope of gain, which is involved here, is the essence of economic coercion. Conditioning the receipt of federal funds on certain activity does not infringe on state power.

    5)   **Comment.** *Butler* was one of the last of the series of cases striking down parts of the New Deal. Subsequent Commerce Clause cases indicate that the area involved in *Butler* would not now be held to be one of purely local concern.

c.   **Inducement of states permitted--Steward Machine Co. v. Davis,** 301 U.S. 548 (1937).

    1)   **Facts.** The Social Security Act taxed employers of eight or more persons a certain percentage of the salaries of their employees; the funds were to go to the United States Treasury. If an employer contributed to a state plan, he got a 90% credit toward the contribution of his federal responsibility. All state plans had to be approved by the Secretary of the Treasury, however. Steward Machine Co. (P) paid the tax and then sought a refund, claiming that the Act unconstitutionally sought to coerce the states to adopt state plans. P appeals lower court decisions upholding the Act.

    2)   **Issue.** May Congress reduce private employers' federal tax obligations by crediting payments made only to federally approved state plans?

    3)   **Held.** Yes. Judgment affirmed.

        a)   In the economic crisis of a depression, the spending here was clearly for the general welfare.

        b)   P claims the Act seeks to coerce the states. In reality, the Act merely provides for fairness by not permitting states with security plans to be penalized by the double taxation on their business that would result if there were no credit for payments to these state plans.

3.   **Spending for the General Welfare.** Congressional power to spend is limited by the General Welfare Clause. However, the determination of what is in the nation's general welfare is left to Congress, and the courts will defer to appropriate legislative findings. For example, the old age provisions of the Social Security Act were upheld, largely by ascribing wide latitude to congressional determination of the national interest. [*See* Helvering v. Davis, 301 U.S. 619 (1937)]

4. **Enforcement of the Reconstruction Amendments.**

    a. **Introduction.** Section 5 of the fourteenth amendment provides that "Congress shall have power to enforce, by appropriate legislation, the provisions of this article." Congress has enacted substantial legislation to enforce the Reconstruction amendments. The issues raised by this legislation include the question of whether Congress is limited to remedying what the Supreme Court finds unconstitutional, or whether Congress can remedy what Congress itself finds unconstitutional. In other words, does section 5 confer remedial or substantive powers?

    b. **Voting rights.** The right to vote for federal, state, and local officials is protected from both state and federal government infringement by the provisions of the fifteenth and nineteenth amendments, as well as from state infringement of this right by the fourteenth amendment. In 1965, Congress passed the Voting Rights Act, which essentially created a rebuttable presumption that literacy tests in certain states were used to perpetrate racial discrimination.

Katzenbach v. Morgan

    c. **Congressional control over state voting requirements--Katzenbach v. Morgan, 384 U.S. 641 (1966).**

       1) **Facts.** Morgan (P), a registered voter in the city of New York, challenged section 4(e) of the Voting Rights Act of 1965, which provides that any person who has successfully completed sixth grade in an accredited school in Puerto Rico cannot be denied the right to vote because of lack of English proficiency. P claims that the law pro tanto prohibits enforcement of New York election laws based on English proficiency. A three-judge district court granted P relief. Katzenbach (D), the United States Attorney General, appeals.

       2) **Issue.** May Congress prohibit enforcement of a state English-literacy voting requirement by legislating under section 5 of the fourteenth amendment, regardless of whether the judiciary would find such a requirement unconstitutional?

       3) **Held.** Yes. Judgment reversed.

         a) Congress need not wait for a judicial determination of unconstitutionality before prohibiting the enforcement of a state law. Congress may enact any legislation that is appropriate.

    b)   The test for appropriateness is whether (i) the end is legitimate, and (ii) the means are not prohibited by and are consistent with the letter and spirit of the Constitution.

    c)   Section 4(e) is plainly adapted to the legitimate end of assuring equal protection to all, including non-English-speaking citizens. P claims section 4(e) works an invidious discrimination in violation of the fifth amendment by failing to include persons attending schools not covered by the law. But section 4(e) extends the franchise and does not restrict or deny P. The fact that Congress went no further than it did does not constitute a constitutional violation.

4)   **Concurring** (Douglas, J.). The question of whether section 4(e) encompasses means not prohibited by but consistent with the Constitution should not be addressed until presented by a member of the class against which that particular discrimination is directed.

5)   **Dissenting** (Harlan, Stewart, JJ.). The Court has confused the issue of the extent of the section 5 enforcement power with the distinct issue of what questions are better resolved by the judiciary than by the legislature. Congress should not be permitted to enact remedial legislation where there is no constitutional infringement to be remedied, and the judiciary alone ultimately determines whether a practice or statute is unconstitutional. This Court has previously held that a state English-literacy test is permissible. Here, the Court grants Congress authority to override that judicial determination and define the substantive scope of the fourteenth amendment.

6)   **Comment.** The *Morgan* decision is a far-reaching decision that may exempt the fourteenth amendment from the principle of Court and Congress relationships set forth in *Marbury v. Madison*, i.e., that the judiciary is the final arbiter of the Constitution. This would allow Congress to act independently. Another view is that Congress was merely acting to strengthen the judicially declared right of equal access to government services.

IV. INTERSTATE COMMERCE

A. INTRODUCTION

The modern approach to the Commerce Clause gives Congress absolute power over interstate commerce. Congress may permit a state to exercise this power or may prohibit a state from so doing. Where Congress has in fact acted to prohibit state regulation, it has "preempted the field." Even when Congress has not acted, the very existence of the Commerce Clause forbids state regulation that places an unreasonable burden on interstate commerce. These areas have produced considerable litigation, partly because of the ambiguous nature of the standards involved and partly because of the large financial stakes affected. When Congress has not enacted legislation regarding the subject matter of commerce, the states may regulate local transactions even though they affect interstate commerce, subject to certain limitations. This principle applies to regulation of transportation as well.

1. Development of Principles.

a. Early approach. In *Gibbons v. Ogden, supra*, Chief Justice Marshall discussed the relationship between federal and state regulation. Ogden had argued that the commerce power was like the taxing power; since the taxing power is concurrent, the commerce power should be. Marshall noted that regulation of interstate commerce is an exclusively federal power. When a state regulates commerce with foreign nations or among the several states, it exercises the very power granted to Congress, and the analogy fails. The Constitution does recognize state power to inspect goods for health and safety, but such laws do not derive from a power to regulate commerce. Even though inspection laws may affect commerce, their existence does not imply that the states can directly regulate interstate commerce.

Cooley v.
Board of
Wardens

b. National vs. local issues--Cooley v. Board of Wardens, 53 U.S. (12 How.) 299 (1851).

1) Facts. Pennsylvania passed a statute requiring vessels entering or leaving the Port of Philadelphia to accept local pilots while in the Delaware River. The penalty for disobedience was one-half the pilotage fees. Cooley (D), consignee of two violating vessels, was sued by the Board of Wardens of the Port (P) for the penalty. P relied on a 1789 congressional statute that incorporated all then-existing state laws regulating pilots and that mandated conformity with subsequently enacted state regulation, such as the law in this case. D contended that Congress cannot delegate its powers in this manner. D appeals state court judgments for P.

2) **Issue.** May Congress permit the states to regulate aspects of commerce that are primarily local in nature?

3) **Held.** Yes. Judgment affirmed.

    a) Regulation of pilots is clearly a regulation of commerce. If Congress's power to regulate commerce is exclusive, the Act of 1789 could not confer upon the states the power to regulate pilots.

    b) The correct approach looks to the nature of the subjects of the power, rather than the nature of the power itself. Many subjects are national in nature, but some are local, like the one involved here. When a subject is national it is best governed by one uniform system and therefore requires exclusive legislation by Congress. But a local subject is best handled by the states, which can adapt regulation to the local peculiarities.

    c) The Act of 1789 manifests the understanding of Congress that the nature of this subject (pilotage of local ports) does not require its exclusive legislation. That understanding must be upheld, and the statute is constitutional.

4) **Comment.** The *Cooley* opinion was widely ignored at the time, although its approach was somewhat revived later on. After *Cooley*, the Court again applied the Marshall view that the states could not regulate interstate commerce. [*See, e.g.,* Paul v. Virginia, 75 U.S. (8 Wall.) 168 (1869)]

c. **Negative implications.** Congress may validate state laws regulating commerce that, in the absence of such consent, would violate the Commerce Clause.

1) **The Wilson Act.** In *Leisy v. Hardin*, 135 U.S. 100 (1890), the Court invalidated an Iowa law prohibiting the sale of liquors as applied to Illinois-brewed beer that was sold in the original package in Iowa. Later, however, after the passage of the federal Wilson Act, the Court held that a state may apply its prohibition laws to sales of intoxicating liquors in the original packages. In so ruling in *In re Rahrer*, 140 U.S. 545 (1891), the Court held that through the Wilson Act Congress had merely allowed certain designated subjects of interstate commerce to be divested of that character, so that the liquor, once imported, immediately fell within the local jurisdiction.

2) **Insurance business and the McCarran Act.** After passage of the McCarran Act of 1945, which deferred and limited the applicability of antitrust laws to the insurance business, the Court held that the Act validated state taxes that were discriminatory and invalid under Commerce Clause decisions. In *Prudential Insurance Co. v. Benjamin*, 328 U.S. 408 (1946), the plaintiff New Jersey company had objected to the continued collection of tax of 3% of the premiums received from business done in South Carolina, when South Carolina corporations were not similarly taxed.

2. **Traditional State Regulation of Transportation.** Where the subject matter is traditionally subject to local regulation, the Court is more likely to allow state regulation. Transportation has been one of the most highly regulated areas.

    a. **Basic principles.** Over time, the Court has developed an approach to transportation problems that is fairly principled. To be constitutional, state regulation must not violate these principles:

        1) **Uniform national regulation not required.** The subject matter must not inherently require uniform, national regulation. [*See* Wabash, St. Louis & Pacific Railway v. Illinois, 118 U.S. 557 (1886)]

        2) **No discrimination.** The state regulation must not discriminate against interstate commerce so as to "substantially impede" the free flow of commerce across state lines. [*See* Seaboard Air Line Railroad Co. v. Blackwell, 244 U.S. 310 (1917)]

        3) **Balance of interests favors the state.** The state interest underlying the regulation must not be outweighed by the burden on interstate commerce—i.e., the "balance of interests" favors the state as opposed to the national interest.

            a) **Public safety and welfare.** A state's interest in the public safety and welfare, where such is the predominant purpose of the state law, may justify obstruction of interstate commerce. For example, in *Bradley v. Public Utilities Commission*, 289 U.S. 92 (1933), the Court held that a state could restrict interstate truckers where the highway was already so badly congested by traffic that the proposed service would create excessive traffic hazards.

            b) **Controlling competition.** While state interests in protecting public health and welfare are given considerable weight, a state's interest in controlling competition is not. For example, in *Buck v. Kuykendall*, 267 U.S. 307 (1925), the Court held that a state could not deny an interstate carrier a permit to use its highways simply because the state determined that the territory was already adequately served.

B. PROTECTION AGAINST DISCRIMINATION

1. **Regulation of Trade.** Where Congress has not acted, the states have power to regulate any phase of local business (production, marketing, sales, etc.), even though such regulations may have some effect on interstate commerce, as long as they neither discriminate against, nor impose any unreasonable burden upon, interstate commerce.

   a. **Regulation of incoming commerce.** One way to develop a state's economy is to require businesses to operate within the state. The Commerce Clause prohibits such legislation if it burdens interstate commerce and is not necessary to promote a valid state purpose. Protecting local business against out-of-state competition is not a valid state purpose per se, but there may be valid reasons for excluding out-of-state products.

   b. **Protection of health and safety.**

      1) **Quarantine and inspection laws.** Quarantine and inspection laws enacted to protect public health are upheld as long as they do not discriminate against or unreasonably burden interstate commerce. [*See* Hannibal & St. Joseph Railroad v. Husen, 95 U.S. 465 (1877)]

         a) **Permissible regulation.** A local statute requiring that cattle or meat imported from other states be certified as free from disease by the state of origin has been upheld. The burden on interstate commerce caused by supplying such a certificate was outweighed by the public health objectives of the state law. [Mintz v. Baldwin, 289 U.S. 346 (1933)]

         b) **Impermissible regulation.** Although having a valid "public health" purpose, a state law requiring local inspection of slaughterhouses prior to slaughter of livestock destined for local consumption has been held unconstitutional because it discriminates against out-of-state slaughterhouses (i.e., it prevents importation of sound meats from animals slaughtered in other states). [Minnesota v. Barber, 136 U.S. 313 (1890)]

      2) **Protection of reputation.** State laws enacted to protect local, publicly owned natural resources are traditionally a proper exercise of the state's "police power," and will usually be upheld by the Court—i.e., the Court tends to "balance the interests" in favor of such regulations.

2. Environmental Protection and Conservation.

a. Introduction. Environmental problems are often difficult to solve, especially when the sources of pollution are out of state. States frequently impose environmental regulations, but the Court does not allow environmental concerns to override the Commerce Clause.

Philadelphia
v. New Jersey

b. Importation of wastes--Philadelphia v. New Jersey, 437 U.S. 617 (1978).

1) Facts. New Jersey (D) passed a law prohibiting importation into the state of solid or liquid wastes, in order to protect the public health, safety, and welfare from the consequences of excessive landfill developments. Philadelphia (P) and other cities, as well as New Jersey landfill operators, challenged the law under the Commerce Clause. The New Jersey Supreme Court upheld the law. P appeals.

2) Issue. May a state prohibit importation of environmentally destructive substances solely because of their source of origin?

3) Held. No. Judgment reversed.

a) D's reason for passing the law may be legitimate, but the evils of protectionism can reside in the legislative means used as well as legislative ends sought. D's ultimate purpose may not be achieved by discriminating against out-of-state items solely because of their origin. D has failed to show any other valid reason for its discrimination.

b) D's statute requires out-of-state commercial interests to carry the burden of conserving D's remaining landfill space in an attempt to isolate itself from a problem shared by all. Protection against such trade barriers serves the interest of all states, and may even work to the advantage of New Jersey in the future.

c) D claims that this statute resembles quarantine laws, which are exceptions to the general Commerce Clause rules. But quarantine laws merely prevent traffic in noxious articles, regardless of their origin. D claims no harm from the mere movement of waste into its borders and concedes that when the harm is felt (upon disposal), there is no basis to distinguish out-of-state wastes from domestic waste.

4) Dissent (Rehnquist, J., Burger, C.J.). Under the Court's decision, New Jersey must either prohibit all landfill operations or accept waste from every portion of the United States. The Commerce Clause should not present the state with this Hobson's choice. New Jersey may legally exclude such things as infected rags or diseased cattle from its borders while out of necessity disposing of such items that originate within New Jersey; the same rationale should apply to solid waste.

3. **Precision--Hunt v. Washington State Apple Advertising Commission,** 432 U.S. 333 (1977).

   a. **Facts.** A North Carolina statute required that all closed containers of apples sold, offered for sale, or shipped into the state bear "no grade other than the applicable United States grade or standard," and a related regulation required the USDA grade or none at all. The statute was intended to eliminate confusion resulting from a multiplicity of inconsistent state grades. The Washington State Apple Advertising Commission (P) brought an action against Hunt (D), a North Carolina official, challenging the statute as discriminating against interstate commerce. P had developed its own grades, widely recognized as superior to the USDA grades, and on which the reputation of its apples depended. The district court found for P. D appeals.

   b. **Issue.** Must a local statute which has a valid, good faith purpose but burdens interstate commerce actually achieve its stated purpose in order to be upheld against a Commerce Clause challenge?

   c. **Held.** Yes. Judgment affirmed.

      1) When discrimination against interstate commerce is shown, the burden falls on the state to justify its regulation both in terms of the local benefits flowing from the statute and the unavailability of nondiscriminatory alternative ways to accomplish the same objectives.

      2) This statute is clearly discriminatory as it covers only closed containers of apples, the very means by which apples are transported in commerce. The record also discloses that feasible, effective, and less discriminatory alternatives are available.

      3) D recognizes that the statute burdens the interstate sale of Washington apples but claims that the burden is outweighed by the local benefits of protection of the public from fraud and deception. In reality, the statute does little to further D's goal, at least with respect to P's apples. It permits marketing under no grades at all; it directs its primary efforts at wholesalers and brokers, rather than the consuming public; and since P's grades are in all cases equal or superior to USDA grades, they could only "deceive" or "confuse" a consumer to his

benefit. In light of the statute's ineffectiveness and the existence of reasonable regulatory alternatives, the statute is invalid.

4. The State as a Market Participant.

a. Introduction. The Court has recognized an exception to the normal Commerce Clause restrictions on state regulation when the state itself becomes a participant in the market. The proper scope of this exception has been the subject of much debate.

b. Purchases. In *Hughes v. Alexandria Scrap Corp.*, 426 U.S. 794 (1976), the Court permitted Maryland to impose more exacting documentation requirements on out-of-state junk-car processors than it imposed on in-state processors. The documentation was required to receive a "bounty" from the state of Maryland, which made the payments for each junk car registered in Maryland that was recycled. The purpose of the bounty was to improve the environment in the state. The Court reasoned that Maryland did not attempt to prohibit the flow of junk cars, but merely entered the market to bid up the value of Maryland junk cars. The state was a market participant, not a market regulator, so the Commerce Clause was not applicable.

South-Central Timber Development v. Wunnicke

c. Postsale obligations imposed by the state selling its resources--South-Central Timber Development v. Wunnicke, 467 U.S. 82 (1984).

1) **Facts.** The state of Alaska offered to sell its timber, but only with a contractual requirement that it be processed within the state before being exported. In return, the price for the timber was significantly reduced from what it otherwise would have been. South-Central Timber Development (P) normally sold unprocessed logs to Japan. P sought an injunction in federal court, claiming the requirement violated the negative implications of the Commerce Clause. The district court granted the injunction, but the court of appeals reversed, concluding that a similar federal policy for timber taken from federal land in Alaska constituted implicit congressional authorization of the state plan. The Supreme Court granted certiorari.

2) **Issue.** When it sells its own natural resources, may a state impose postsale obligations on the purchaser?

3) **Held.** No. Judgment reversed.

a) The Commerce Clause limits the power of the states to impose substantial burdens on interstate commerce, although Congress may authorize state regulation of such commerce. Here, there was no indication that Congress intended to give such power to Alaska. The existence of a federal program similar to the state's is insufficient evidence to support an inference that the state's action was authorized by Congress.

b)   This case involves three elements not present in the earlier case *Reeves, Inc. v. Stake,* 447 U.S. 429 (1980): foreign commerce is restrained, the state is selling a natural resource, and the state imposes restrictions on resale. Commerce Clause scrutiny must be more rigorous because of these factors.

c)   The fact that the state acted through a contract is not enough. The market-participant doctrine must be limited to allowing a state to impose burdens on commerce within the market in which it participates. Here, Alaska has gone too far by imposing conditions that have a substantial regulatory effect outside of the market it has entered. This program does not fall within the market-participant exception.

d)   The protectionist nature of Alaska's program results in interference with interstate and foreign commerce. Thus it violates the Commerce Clause.

4)   **Concurring in part** (Powell, J., Burger, C.J.). The case should be remanded to determine whether Alaska was acting as a market participant and whether the plan substantially burdens interstate commerce.

5)   **Dissenting** (Rehnquist, O'Connor, JJ.). The plurality's decision seems to draw on antitrust law. But antitrust laws apply to a state only when it is acting as a market participant. The plurality thus concludes that Alaska is acting as a market regulator by relying on cases that are relevant only if Alaska is a market participant. The state is merely paying timber purchasers to hire Alaska residents to process the timber, a result it could accomplish in a variety of ways. It is unduly formalistic to hold that this method violates the Commerce Clause.

5.   **Privileges and Immunities.**

     a.   **Introduction.** Article IV, section 2, the Privileges and Immunities Clause, states that the citizens of each state shall be entitled to all privileges and immunities of citizens in the several states. This prohibits discrimination by a state against noncitizens (or nonresidents) of the state with respect to "essential activities" or "basic rights," unless justified by a substantial reason. To justify an exception, the state must show that: (i) the nonresidents are a peculiar source of the evil sought to be avoided; and (ii) the discrimination bears a substantial relation to the problem.

b. **Protection of basic activities.** The clause protects activities such as pursuit of a livelihood, the transfer of property, access to the state's courts, etc. [Toomer v. Witsell, 334 U.S. 385 (1948)] The Court has held that sport hunting is not an essential activity, so that a state may discriminate against nonresidents in this area. [Baldwin v. Montana Fish & Game Commission, 436 U.S. 371 (1976)]

c. **Justification.** If the state's discriminatory scheme is overbroad, it will not withstand scrutiny under the Privileges and Immunities Clause. In *Hicklin v. Orbeck*, 437 U.S. 518 (1978), the Court determined that a state hiring preference for residents was an overbroad solution to the problem of unemployment, because the preference extended to highly skilled state residents who did not have the problem of unemployment.

United Building & Construction Trades Council v. Mayor of Camden

d. **Municipality's preference for its own residents on construction contracts--United Building & Construction Trades Council v. Mayor of Camden**, 456 U.S. 208 (1984).

1) **Facts.** The City of Camden (D) adopted an ordinance which required that at least 40% of the employees of contractors and subcontractors working on city construction projects be Camden residents. The United Building & Construction Trades Council of Camden County (P) challenged the ordinance as violating the Privileges and Immunities Clause. After the state treasurer approved the ordinance in administrative proceedings, the state supreme court upheld it, holding that the Privileges and Immunities Clause does not apply to discrimination on the basis of municipal residency. P appeals.

2) **Issue.** Does the Privileges and Immunities Clause apply to municipalities that require contractors to hire the municipality's own residents to work on the municipality's construction projects?

3) **Held.** Yes. Judgment reversed and remanded for further fact findings.

a) A municipality derives its authority from the state. If the state cannot discriminate in this manner, neither can a political subdivision of the state. Nor is the ordinance immune from attack because it discriminates against some in-state residents as well as out-of-state citizens. The former have the opportunity to directly change state law through the state legislature. The latter do not.

b) P must first show that the ordinance burdens a privilege or immunity protected by the clause. The opportunity to seek employment is a fundamental privilege protected by the clause.

    c)   The Privileges and Immunities Clause does not preclude discrimination against out-of-state residents if there is a substantial reason for the difference in treatment. Although D alleges several such reasons—including increasing unemployment in the city, declining population, and a depleted tax base—no trial has been held and no findings of fact have been made. The case must be remanded.

    4)   **Dissenting** (Blackmun, J.). With no historical or textual support, the Court has expanded the scope of the clause to prohibit laws that discriminate among state residents on the basis of municipal residence. This is substantially different from discrimination on the basis of state citizenship. The protection afforded by the disadvantaged state residents' power to change state law also protects the interests of nonresidents, so the political impotency of nonresidents which the clause was designed to cure does not exist here.

    5)   **Comment**. At some length the Court distinguished *White v. Massachusetts Council of Construction Employers, Inc.*, 460 U.S. 204 (1983), describing the different purposes of the Commerce Clause and the Privileges and Immunities Clause. The former acts as an implied restraint on state power to regulate interstate commerce, so when a state acts as a market participant, no Commerce Clause problem arises. The latter clause directly restrains state action so as to promote interstate harmony. Even if a state acts as a market participant, its actions must not violate the restraints of the Privileges and Immunities Clause. Hence the analysis applied to this case.

C. FACIALLY NEUTRAL STATUTES AFFECTING INTERSTATE COMMERCE

1.   **Introduction.** Where Congress has not enacted legislation regarding the subject matter of commerce, the states may regulate local transactions even though they affect interstate commerce, subject to certain limitations. To be constitutional, state regulation must satisfy these criteria:

    a.   **Uniform national regulation not required.** The subject matter must not be one that inherently requires uniform, national regulation.

b. **Nondiscriminatory.** The state regulation must not discriminate against interstate commerce so as to "substantially impede" the free flow of commerce across state lines.

c. **Balance of interests favors the state.** The state interest underlying the regulation must not be outweighed by the burden on interstate commerce; i.e., the "balance of interests" favors the state as opposed to the national interests.

Exxon Corp.
v. Governor
of Maryland

2. **Permissible State Barriers to Incoming Trade--Exxon Corp. v. Governor of Maryland,** 437 U.S. 117 (1978).

a. **Facts.** The state of Maryland (D) prohibited producers or refiners of petroleum products from operating retail service stations in the state, as a result of evidence that such retail stations had, in the past, received preferential treatment from suppliers. There were no producers or refiners within the state. Exxon Corp. (P) appeals lower court decisions upholding the statute.

b. **Issue.** May a state discriminate against a certain type of out-of-state business if there are no corresponding intrastate businesses?

c. **Held.** Yes. Judgment affirmed.

1) Since all the state's petroleum supplies come from outside the state, there was no discrimination against interstate goods.

2) Although the statute dealt with retail outlets, it did not discriminate against interstate retailers per se, but only against a certain type of interstate retailer for which there was no intrastate equivalent. Interstate retailers that were not also producers or refiners remain unaffected by the statute.

3) Although there may be some shifting of business among retailers, the Commerce Clause protects the interstate market, not particular interstate firms, from prohibitive or burdensome regulation.

Kassel v.
Consolidated
Freightways

3. **Modern Approach to Transportation Regulation--Kassel v. Consolidated Freightways,** 450 U.S. 662 (1981).

a. **Facts.** Consolidated Freightways (P) challenged an Iowa statute that, like Wisconsin's law in *Raymond Motor Transportations, Inc. v. Rice*, 434 U.S. 429 (1978), prohibited the use of 65-foot double trailers on Iowa highways, with certain exceptions. Kassel (D), an Iowa official, defended the law as a reasonable safety measure in light of the *Raymond* holding. The lower courts held the law unconstitutional as it seriously impeded interstate commerce while providing only slight, if any, safety. D appeals.

b. **Issue.** May the courts examine evidence to determine whether a state's purported interest in safety is real and substantial enough to justify applying its police power to burden interstate commerce?

c. **Held.** Yes. Judgment affirmed.

   1) A state cannot avoid a Commerce Clause attack merely by invoking public health or safety. The courts are required to balance the state's safety interest against the federal interest in free interstate commerce.

   2) Despite the "special deference" usually accorded to state highway safety regulations, and D's serious effort to support the safety rationale, the record here is no more favorable to D than was Wisconsin's evidence in *Raymond*. P has demonstrated that D's law substantially burdens interstate commerce. Therefore, D's law is unconstitutional.

d. **Concurring** (Brennan, Marshall, JJ.). D's law is unconstitutional under *Raymond* since it is protectionist. The plurality and the dissent insist on considering the legislative purposes advanced by D's lawyers. Separation of powers, however, requires that we defer to the elected lawmakers' judgment, not that we defer to the arguments of lawyers. D's statute exists because the governor of Iowa vetoed legislation that would have permitted 65-foot doubles, giving an essentially protectionist rationale for his action. This is an improper purpose. Safety became a purpose for the law only in retrospect, to defeat P's challenge.

e. **Dissenting** (Rehnquist, Stewart, JJ., Burger, C.J.). Both the plurality and concurring opinions have intruded upon the fundamental right of the states to pass laws to secure the safety of their citizens. D's law is rationally related to its safety objectives. We are essentially reweighing the state legislature's policy choice, and are forcing D to lower its safety standards merely because its sister states' standards are lower.

f. **Comment.** In *Raymond*, the Court also invalidated a prohibition against the use of double-trailer units on state highways because the state failed to show that the regulation contributed to highway safety, and because numerous exceptions to the regulation undercut the safety claims.

4. **Traditional State Regulation.** Where the subject matter is traditionally subject to local regulation, the Court is more likely to allow state regulation. In *South Carolina State Highway Department v. Barnwell Brothers*, 303 U.S. 177 (1938), the Court held

that where Congress had not acted, a state could impose highly restrictive width and weight limitations nondiscriminately on interstate carriers, which have the effect of seriously impeding interstate travel.

Southern Pacific Co. v. Arizona

5. **Promotion of a Valid State Interest--Southern Pacific Co. v. Arizona,** 325 U.S. 761 (1945).

a. **Facts.** The Arizona Train Limit Law imposed restrictions on the number of cars permitted on any train operating within the state; it allowed 14 passenger cars or 70 freight cars. Arizona (P) sued Southern Pacific Co. (D), an interstate carrier, for violation of the statute. D claimed that the statute unconstitutionally burdened interstate commerce. The trial court made extensive findings of facts and concluded that any possible safety benefits of the law were outweighed by increased hazards and that the law imposed unconstitutional burdens on interstate commerce. The Arizona Supreme Court accepted the legislature's findings and reversed, citing a lack of overriding federal legislation. D appeals.

b. **Issue.** In balancing the effect of a state regulation on interstate commerce against the state's safety and welfare interests, may a court consider the efficacy of the regulation in furthering the state's interest?

c. **Held.** Yes. Judgment reversed.

1) Although Congress has refused to pass national legislation regulating train lengths, the state law may violate the Commerce Clause if it unreasonably burdens interstate commerce without an offsetting state safety benefit. Additionally, state regulation is precluded in those phases of national commerce that, because of the need for national uniformity, demand that their regulation, if any, be prescribed by a single authority.

2) Constitutional doctrine mandates that the Court, and not the state legislature, is the final arbiter of competing state and national interests under the Commerce Clause.

3) The serious impediment of state car limitations on interstate commerce indicates the need for uniform national legislation on the subject. By taking no action, Congress must have intended not to restrict the number of train cars permitted.

4) Upon review of the record, it appears that the total effect of the law as a safety measure in reducing accidents and casualties is so slight or problematical as not to outweigh the national interest in keeping interstate commerce free from interference.

5)   The *Barnwell Brothers* case is distinguishable because it dealt with state highways, which are of more local concern than railroads, and because there the record supported the state's safety findings.

    d.   Dissenting (Black, J.). The Court in effect has found that the state legislature erroneously weighed the evidence before it as to train safety, and that regulation of train lengths would be unwise. The Court acts as a "super-legislature" instead of giving the traditional deference to legislative determinations.

    e.   Comment. A series of cases referred to as the *Full Crew Cases* upheld state laws dating from the early part of the century that required minimum crew sizes on trains. The Court recognized that conditions had changed, but held that since there remained a possible safety benefit, the determination of state policy belonged to the legislature and not the courts.

6.   Burden of Proof. When the challenged regulation significantly burdens interstate commerce, the state must meet a heavy burden of justification based on its interests. In *Bibb v. Navajo Freight Lines, Inc.*, 359 U.S. 520 (1959), the Court held that a state may not impose even nondiscriminatory safety regulations that conflict with the regulations of most other states where the asserted safety advantages are at best negligible. That case involved mudguards on trucks: 45 states permitted the conventional straight mudguards, but Illinois required the use of contour mudguards. The substantial burden on interstate commerce could not be justified by any compelling state safety consideration.

D.   FEDERAL PREEMPTION

1.   Introduction. As a general rule, federal law is interstitial; i.e., it rarely occupies a legal field completely. Rather, federal legislation is drafted on an ad hoc basis to accomplish limited objectives. It normally builds on legal relationships established by the states, altering or supplanting them only where necessary to accomplish a particular purpose. The Supreme Court has often stated that the question of preemption is primarily one of the intent of Congress.

2.   Significance of the State's Purpose for Regulating--Pacific Gas & Electric Co. v. State Energy Commission, 461 U.S. 190 (1983).

    a.   Facts. The California legislature prohibited certification of nuclear power plants until the State Energy Commission (D) made a finding that a demonstrated technology for permanent disposal of high-level nuclear waste had been approved by the federal government. Pacific Gas

& Electric Co. (P) brought suit for a declaratory judgment that the state law was invalid under the Supremacy Clause because the Nuclear Regulatory Commission (NRC) had federal authority to regulate use of nuclear energy. The district court found for P, but the court of appeals reversed. The Supreme Court granted certiorari.

b. **Issue.** May a state impose restrictions on an industry even when the federal government also regulates that industry, so long as the state acts for a purpose not preempted by Congress?

c. **Held.** Yes. Judgment affirmed.

1) The nuclear waste issue presents both safety and economic problems. So long as wastes are stored temporarily, a danger of leakage exists; until a permanent disposal technique is available, lack of storage space may force premature closings of power plants. The legislation in this case was motivated by both considerations.

2) The NRC has control over the safety aspects of nuclear energy generation, but no authority over the economic question of whether a particular plant should be built. Thus a state moratorium on nuclear power plants is preempted if based on safety concerns, but not if based on economic concerns. Because there was a valid economic rationale, not safety-related, for D's moratorium, the statute is not preempted.

3) Although the NRC has determined that it is safe to proceed with nuclear power plants despite the existing unavailability of permanent storage facilities, the NRC does not compel a utility to build a nuclear plant. Rather than enter this area, the state statute recognizes the federal responsibility to develop and license disposal technology.

4) The state law does not frustrate the purposes and objectives of Congress. Congress clearly intended to promote nuclear power plants, but it has allowed the states to determine, as a matter of economics, what types of power plants should be built. Congress, not the courts, must take action if a moratorium for economic reasons undercuts a federal objective.

d. **Concurring** (Blackmun, Stevens, JJ.). States should be allowed to prohibit nuclear power plants for safety reasons. Congress has occupied the narrow field of construction and operations standards, but not the broad field of "nuclear safety concerns." Even though the NRC has determined that nuclear plants are safe, nothing requires the states to decide such plants are safe. Nor would a safety-motivated state ban frustrate the federal purpose, because Congress has only intended to make nuclear power available as an option.

3.   **Other Cases.**

   a.   **Preemption only where conflict direct and unavoidable.** In *Kelly v. Washington*, 302 U.S. 1 (1937), the Court held that enforcement of a state law requiring safety inspections of tugs was not barred by enactment of the Federal Motor Boat Act of 1910. The Court indicated that state regulation would be superseded only where its conflict with federal law was direct and positive so that the two could not be reconciled.

   b.   **State safety regulations.** In *Maurer v. Hamilton*, 309 U.S. 598 (1940), the Court upheld the state's law prohibiting trucks carrying another vehicle above the cab of the carrier vehicle, citing the fact that the federal Motor Carrier Act contained no such provisions and no conflicting ones, and that preemption would not apply unless congressional intent was very clear, particularly in cases of state regulation involving public health and safety.

   c.   **Need for uniform national policy.** In *Hines v. Davidowitz*, 312 U.S. 52 (1941), the Court invalidated the Pennsylvania Alien Registration Act of 1939, holding that it was preempted by the federal Alien Registration Act of 1940 (although the two did not seem to conflict in any way). The Court cited the broad national power over aliens and the fact that the Constitution permitted only one uniform system (the federal one).

V. ALLOCATION OF NATIONAL POWERS

A. INTRODUCTION

The Constitution provides for separation of powers among the executive, legislative, and judicial branches, but there are grey areas in which responsibilities are shared to some extent. For example, the President may establish the national agenda and propose legislation, but only Congress can enact law. Yet the executive power also includes some legislative authority, such as the power to veto legislation under article I, section 7. Congress also may delegate essentially legislative power to administrative agencies operated under the executive branch.

B. EXECUTIVE AUTHORITY

1. **Introduction.** The Constitution, in article II, section 1, vests the whole executive power of the United States in the President. The Constitution also grants the President limited legislative powers.

   a. **Proposal of legislation.** Article II, section 3 grants the President power to report to Congress on the state of the union and to propose legislation he deems necessary and expedient.

   b. **Delegation by Congress.** Congress may delegate some of its legislative power to the President (as well as to other government agencies, such as the Securities and Exchange Commission, etc.) as long as the delegation is pursuant to reasonably definite standards.

   c. **The veto power.** Article I, section 7 gives the President the power to veto any act of Congress. However, Congress may override a presidential veto by a two-thirds vote of both houses.

Youngstown Sheet & Tube Co. v. Sawyer

2. **Emergency Lawmaking Power Denied to the President-- Youngstown Sheet & Tube Co. v. Sawyer (The Steel Seizure Case), 343 U.S. 579 (1952).**

   a. **Facts.** The steelworkers, after prolonged negotiations, went on a nationwide strike during the Korean War. Citing the serious national interest in steel production, President Truman ordered Sawyer (D), Commerce Secretary, to seize the steel mills and keep them running. Youngstown Sheet & Tube (P) challenged the seizure as unconstitutional and unauthorized by Congress. Congress had earlier passed the Taft-Hartley Act, giving the President authority to seek an injunction against such strikes, but had rejected an amendment to permit government seizures to avoid serious shutdowns. The district court issued a preliminary injunction against D, which was stayed by the court of appeals. The Supreme Court granted certiorari.

b.   **Issue**. May the President, acting under the aggregate of his constitutional powers, exercise a lawmaking power independent of Congress in order to protect serious national interests?

c.   **Held**. No. Judgment of the district court affirmed.

    1)   The President's power to issue the order must stem either from an act of Congress or from the Constitution itself. Congress clearly gave no such power. In fact, it specifically rejected the means used by D.

    2)   The President's authority as Commander-in-Chief does not warrant the seizure, as it is too far removed from the "theater of war." His general executive power is inapplicable since there is no relevant law to execute.

    3)   The order does not direct that a congressional policy be executed in a manner prescribed by Congress but that a presidential policy be executed in a manner prescribed by the President. Such presidential usurpation of the lawmaking power is unauthorized and invalid.

d.   **Concurring** (Frankfurter, J.). Congress specifically expressed its will on the subject, which is that the President ought not have the powers he has here attempted to exercise.

e.   **Concurring** (Clark, J.). The President must follow the procedures laid down by Congress, namely the Taft-Hartley Act.

f.   **Dissenting** (Vinson, Reed, Minton, JJ.). The President has a duty to execute the legislative programs of supporting the armed forces in Korea. The President's action was an effective means of performing his duty, and was clearly temporary and subject to congressional direction.

g.   **Comment**. Two of the majority Justices were willing to agree with the dissent that the President had inherent legislative powers to act in preserving the nation, but only when there was an absence of any provision passed by Congress purporting to deal with the situation. Here these Justices pointed to the fact that Congress had passed the National Labor Relations Act, which set forth specific provisions to be followed by the President in case of strikes that threatened the national security.

3.   **Authority to Enter Executive Agreements--Dames & Moore v. Regan, 453 U.S. 654 (1981).**

Dames &
Moore v.
Regan

a.   **Facts**. On November 4, 1979, American diplomatic personnel in Iran were captured and held hostage. On November 14,

President Carter declared a national emergency and froze all Iranian assets in the United States. The next day, the Treasury Department issued regulations requiring licensing of any judicial process against Iranian interests and specifying that any such licenses could be revoked at any time. Dames & Moore (P) sued Iranian defendants for $3.5 million and attached Iranian assets pending the outcome of the litigation. On January 19, 1981, the United States, through Algeria, agreed to terminate all legal proceedings in United States courts against Iran, to nullify all attachments and judgments obtained therein, and to terminate such claims through binding arbitration. This agreement was implemented through executive order. On January 27, P obtained a judgment against the Iranian defendants and attempted to execute the judgment on the attached property. The district court nullified the prejudgment attachments and stayed all further proceedings against the Iranian defendants in light of the executive order. P then sued Regan (D), the Treasury Secretary, for declaratory and injunctive relief against enforcement of the executive order and regulations on grounds that they were unconstitutional and that the President had exceeded his authority in implementing the agreement with Iran. The district court denied P's claim. P appeals.

b. **Issue.** May the President, in response to a national emergency, suspend outstanding claims in American courts?

c. **Held.** Yes. Judgment affirmed.

1) The questions presented by this case touch fundamentally upon the manner in which our republic is to be governed. Although little authority exists that is relevant to concrete problems of executive power, much relevant analysis is contained in *Youngstown Sheet & Tube Co. (supra)*. There the Court observed that exercise of executive power is closely related to congressional action; executive power is greatest when exercised pursuant to congressional authorization and weakest when exercised in contravention of the will of Congress.

2) The International Emergency Economic Powers Act (IEEPA), by its terms, permits the President to "regulate and nullify any acquisition of any right to any property in which any foreign country or a national thereof has any interest." In essence, IEEPA was intended to permit freezing of assets to serve as "bargaining chips." P's attachment and judgment were obtained after the President had acted pursuant to this specific statutory authority. We conclude that IEEPA authorized the nullification of the attachments.

3) IEEPA does not directly authorize the suspension of in personam lawsuits, which merely establish liability and fix damages and do not in themselves involve Iranian property. Neither does the Hostage Act of 1868 authorize such action.

However, the general tenor of these enactments, combined with the International Claims Settlement Act of 1949, which created the International Claims Commission, indicates congressional approval of, or at least acquiescence in, executive agreements settling the claims of United States nationals against foreign countries.

    4)   P can resort to the International Claims Commission as an alternative forum.

    5)   This holding is limited to the narrow facts at hand, where the settlement is a necessary element of a resolution of a major foreign policy dispute between our country and another and where Congress has acquiesced in the President's action.

d.   Concurring and dissenting (Powell, J.). The nullification of the attachment might constitute taking of property requiring compensation, separate from the question of whether suspension of the claims constitutes a taking. These "taking" arguments should be considered on a case-by-case basis.

4.   Domestic Affairs.

a.   Impoundment. Impoundment refers to the President's power to refuse to spend funds appropriated by Congress. Congress passed the Congressional Budget and Impoundment Control Act to limit the President's power to defer spending (he cannot do so if one house passes a resolution requiring him to spend the money) or to terminate a program or cut spending authorized by Congress. The statutory scheme contemplates a congressional response to a presidential proposal to defer or rescind a budget program. Both the President and Congress have generally followed the framework of this Act.

b.   Executive immunity.

    1)   **Introduction.** Executive officials are not given any express immunity in the Constitution. The case law seems to reject any implied immunity under the separation of powers doctrine.

    2)   **Immunity from civil damages.** In *Nixon v. Fitzgerald,* 457 U.S. 731 (1982), the Court held that absent explicit affirmative action by Congress, the President is absolutely, rather than qualifiedly, immune from civil liability for his official acts. In this action brought by a whistleblower who charged violation of his first amendment and statutory rights when he lost his job with the Department of Defense, the Court stated that absolute presidential immunity is a functionally mandated incident of the President's office that is rooted in the doctrine of separation of powers. Just as with judges

and prosecutors, who have absolute immunity, the President must make decisions on matters likely to arouse the most intense feelings. The public interest in his ability to deal fearlessly and impartially with these duties is a compelling one. The President's prominence would make him a target for numerous suits for civil damages. The President could not function if he were subject to inquiry about his motives and subject to trial on virtually every allegation of unlawful conduct. The proper protection against presidential misconduct is the constitutional remedy of impeachment. The dissenting Justices argued that this holding put the President above the law and that the better approach would make the scope of immunity depend on the function, not the office.

3) **Qualified immunity for presidential aides**. The Court held in *Harlow v. Fitzgerald*, 457 U.S. 800 (1982), that presidential aides are entitled to only qualified immunity. This is the normal type of immunity for executive officials, and it balances the interests of those citizens who suffer damages against the public need to protect officials who must exercise their discretion in an official capacity. Absolute immunity is available to such aides where the responsibilities of their offices include such a sensitive function that such immunity is required and the liability claim is based on performance of that protected function.

c. **Executive privilege**. Although not mentioned in the Constitution, a privilege has been recognized to protect against the disclosure of presidential communications made in the exercise of executive power. This privilege derives from both the doctrine of separation of powers and the inherent need to protect the confidentiality of high level communications.

d. **Military, diplomatic, or national security secrets**. Where the presidential communications relate to military, diplomatic, or sensitive national security secrets, the claim of privilege is given the utmost deference by the courts. However, other presidential communications are only presumptively privileged.

United States v. Nixon

e. **Evidence in a criminal trial--United States v. Nixon, 418 U.S. 683 (1974)**.

1) **Facts**. The special prosecutor, acting for the United States (P) in the Watergate investigation, sought and received a subpoena ordering President Nixon (D) to produce various tapes and other records relating to presidential conversations and meetings, despite D's motion to quash and motions to expunge and for protective orders. The Supreme Court granted certiorari.

2) **Issue**. Does executive immunity give the President an absolute, unqualified general privilege of immunity from judicial process under all circumstances?

3) **Held**. No. Judgment affirmed.

   a) D contends that the case is merely an intra-branch dispute between officers of the executive branch and thus lacks the requisite justiciability. However, the special prosecutor has been given special authority to pursue the criminal prosecution and has standing to bring this action in the courts.

   b) The doctrine of separation of powers does not preclude judicial review of a President's claim of privilege, because it is the duty of the courts to say what the law is with respect to that claim of privilege, even if the judicial interpretation varies from the President's.

   c) The President's need for and the public interest in the confidentiality of communications is accorded great deference. But absent a need to protect military, diplomatic, or sensitive national security interests, in camera inspection of presidential communications will not significantly diminish the interest in confidentiality. Legitimate judicial needs may therefore outweigh a blanket presidential privilege.

   d) Applying a balancing test to the interests involved supports the district court's order. P sought the subpoena to assure fair and complete presentation of evidence in a criminal proceeding, pursuant to the fundamental demands of due process. The generalized assertion of privilege must yield to the demonstrated, specific need for evidence in a pending criminal trial.

f. **Screening of presidential documents--Nixon v. Administrator of General Services**, 433 U.S. 425 (1977).

   1) **Facts**. Former President Nixon (P) challenged a law directing the Administrator of General Services (D) to take custody of P's papers and tapes and to (i) process and screen such records and to return to P those that are personal and private in nature and (ii) determine the scope of public access to those materials that are retained. The district court dismissed P's complaint. P appeals.

   2) **Issue**. May the ex-President prevent Congress from regulating the disposition and use of presidential documents by claiming executive immunity?

   3) **Held**. No. Judgment affirmed.

   a) The decision is limited to consideration of the facial validity of D's authority to take the materials into government custody subject to screening by government archivists.

Nixon v. Administrator of General Services

b)　The Act does not violate the separation of powers doctrine because the control over the materials remains in the executive branch, of which D is an officer. Although Congress wrote the law, both succeeding Presidents support it. The proper inquiry focuses on the extent to which the law prevents the executive branch from accomplishing its constitutionally assigned functions. Here there is no undue interference.

c)　Although executive privilege survives the individual President's tenure, the opinion of succeeding Presidents bears directly on the need to exercise the privilege. The screening process set up by D adequately assures protection of presidential confidentiality. The practice of establishing presidential libraries indicates that the expectation of confidentiality has always been limited and subject to erosion over time. The significant historical interest in such documents properly subjects them to congressional control.

5.　Foreign Affairs.

a.　Inherent powers in foreign affairs. The President has special powers in foreign affairs due to the need for decisive action and a uniform policy with regard to sensitive foreign relations. Congress, however, retains certain powers over foreign affairs, including the power to declare war, appropriate funds, and ratify treaties.

United States
v. Curtiss-
Wright Corp.

b.　Scope of federal power in foreign affairs--United States v. Curtiss-Wright Corp., 299 U.S. 304 (1936).

1)　**Facts.** Congress, by a joint resolution, provided that if the President found that a prohibition of the sale of arms from the United States to those countries involved in conflict in the Chaco would contribute to peace, then he could issue such a prohibition. Penalties for violation were prescribed. Curtiss-Wright (D) was indicted for conspiracy to violate the prescription; D appealed on the basis that the resolution was an invalid delegation of legislative power to the President. The lower court held the delegation unconstitutional. The government appeals.

2)　**Issue.** May Congress delegate legislative-type power to the President to conduct foreign affairs?

3)　**Held.** Yes. Judgment reversed.

a)　The power of the federal government in regard to external affairs is not delegated by the Constitution, but it is derived as a necessary concomitant of sovereignty. Thus, these powers are as broad as the powers held by any other nation.

b) Furthermore, federal power is exclusive in this realm. The states have no concurrent powers. Congress may delegate to the President much broader powers in this area than it could in internal affairs.

c. **Constitutional provisions.** Article II, section 2, provides that the President shall be the Commander-in-Chief to the Army and Navy and the state militias when they are called into the service of the United States.

1) **The use of armed forces.** Although the Constitution specifies that the President is the Commander-in-Chief of the Army and Navy, only Congress has the power to initiate or declare war. The interplay of these powers was not made clear in the Constitution. However, in the event of insurrection or invasion, the President may deploy our military forces against any enemy, foreign or domestic, without waiting for congressional declaration of war.

2) **Civil War approach--The Prize Cases,** 67 U.S. (2 Black) 635 (1863).

The Prize Cases

a) **Facts.** During a blockade of southern ports instituted by President Lincoln, Union ships seized vessels and cargoes of foreign neutrals, which were then condemned by federal court order. The ship and cargo owners appeal.

b) **Issue.** May the President, acting without a congressional declaration of war, institute a blockade of southern ports which neutrals are bound to respect?

c) **Held.** Yes. Decrees of condemnation affirmed.

(1) The law of nations requires that a war must exist de facto in order to legitimate the capture of a neutral vessel or property on the high seas. Congress had not declared a war, but had earlier authorized the President to call out the militia and use military force to resist invasion and suppress insurrection against the government of a state or of the United States. He need not wait for special legislative authority to respond to such challenges.

(2) The determination of the extent of an armed challenge to the United States rests with the President. His proclamation of blockade is, itself, adequate evidence to the court that a state of war existed which demanded the use of such force as the President deemed necessary.

(3) In this case, the legislature subsequently ratified the President's actions.

d) Dissent. Congress alone can determine whether war exists or should be declared, and until it has acted, there can be no penalty of confiscation for the acts of others with whom the owner had no concern. The congressional ratification of the seizures is invalid as an ex post facto law.

C. LEGISLATIVE AUTHORITY

1. **Introduction.** Congress has pursued two basic approaches to controlling executive power. One has been the enactment of quasi-constitutional statutes intended to set forth guidelines or a framework for interaction between the legislative and executive branches. An example of this is the Gramm-Rudman-Hollings Deficit Control Act, which attempts to control aspects of the budgeting process. Another example is the War Powers Resolution, discussed below. The other approach has been to preserve legislative authority in specific cases, such as through the legislative veto, discussed in *INS v. Chadha*, below.

2. **Domestic Affairs.**

a. **Legislative vetoes.**

1) **Introduction.** Congress has occasionally included provisions in legislation that leave it some power to override executive action taken pursuant to the legislation. This device, called the legislative veto, had been praised for bringing greater efficiency to the government, but it raised potential conflicts with the principle of separation of powers among the branches of government.

Immigration and Naturalization Service v. Chadha

2) **Rejection of legislative veto--Immigration and Naturalization Service v. Chadha,** 462 U.S. 919 (1983).

a) **Facts.** Chadha (P) was an East Indian who lawfully entered the United States on a non-immigrant student visa. After his visa expired, the Immigration and Naturalization Service (D) held a deportation hearing. The immigration judge suspended P's deportation and sent a report to Congress as required by section 244(c)(1) of the Immigration and Naturalization Act. Section 244(c)(2) provided that either House of Congress could veto a suspension of deportation. The House of Representatives adopted a unilateral resolution opposing P's permanent residence, and P was ordered deported. P sought review in the Ninth Circuit, which held section 244(c)(2) unconstitutional. The Supreme Court granted certiorari.

b) **Issue.** May Congress employ the legislative veto device to oversee delegation of its constitutional authority to the executive branch?

c) **Held.** No. Judgment affirmed.

   (1) Although this case has political ramifications, it is primarily a constitutional challenge which presents a bona fide controversy, properly subject to judicial action.

   (2) Article I of the Constitution vests all legislative powers in both Houses of Congress. Every bill or resolution must be passed by both Houses and approved by the President (or his veto overridden) before it takes effect. These provisions are intended to secure liberty through separation of powers. The bicameral nature of Congress similarly insures careful consideration of all legislation.

   (3) The action taken by the House in this case was essentially legislative in purpose and effect. The legislative veto replaced the constitutional procedure of enacting legislation requiring P's deportation (a private bill). Yet the Constitution enumerates only four instances in which either House may act alone—impeachment, trial after impeachment, ratification of treaties, and confirmation of presidential appointments. The legislative veto is not enumerated.

   (4) Although the legislative veto may be efficient, efficiency is not the overriding value behind the Constitution. Separation of powers, as set up by the Constitution, may not be eroded for convenience. Therefore, the legislative veto is unconstitutional. Once Congress delegates authority, it must abide by that delegation until it legislatively alters or revokes it.

d) **Concurring** (Powell, J.). There is no need to invalidate all legislative vetos. This one is an unconstitutional exercise of the judicial function by the House because it decided the specific rights of P.

e) **Dissenting** (White, J.). The legislative veto is a valid response to the dilemma of choosing between no delegation (and hence no lawmaking because of the vast amount of regulation necessary under our system) and abdication of the lawmaking function to the executive branch and administrative agencies. The legislative veto has been included in nearly 200 statutes and accepted by Presidents for 50 years. It allows resolution of major constitutional and policy differences between Congress and the President. Because the underlying legislation was properly enacted, and because the Constitution does not prohibit it, the legislative veto is constitutional.

f) **Dissenting (Rehnquist, White, JJ.).** Section 244(c)(2) is not severable from the rest of the Act, so the judgment below should be reversed.

b. **Appointments power.**

1) **Basic rule.** Article II, section 2, indicates that the President may appoint, with the consent of the Senate, ambassadors, consuls, Justices of the Supreme Court, and all other officers of the United States whose appointments are not otherwise provided for. In addition, Congress may vest the power to appoint "inferior officers" in the President alone.

Buckley
v. Valeo

2) **No appointment of officers by Congress alone--Buckley v. Valeo,** 424 U.S. 1 (1976).

a) **Facts.** Congress amended the Federal Election Campaign Act to create an eight-member commission, six of whom were voting members. Four of these voting members were to be appointed by Congress. The commission was to exercise broad executive as well as legislative powers. Buckley (P) challenged the amendments as violative of the Appointments Clause, granting the appointment power to the President. The court of appeals sustained the law based on the Necessary and Proper Clause. P appeals.

b) **Issue.** May Congress unilaterally appoint officers of the United States who will exercise executive powers?

c) **Held.** No. Judgment reversed.

(1) The constitutional separation of powers is a fundamental principle jealously safeguarded. The Appointments Clause is a substantive provision that must be adhered to. Clearly the members of the commission are officers and ought to be appointed as required by the Appointments Clause. This precludes congressional appointments.

(2) Congress may not ignore the Appointments Clause by claiming authority under the Necessary and Proper Clause, which, although granting broad powers, cannot justify constitutionally prohibited activity.

(3) Congress may properly appoint members of commissions whose powers are essentially investigative and informative. But where, as here, a commission's power includes enforcement and general administrative authority, the Constitution requires that its members be appointed by government officials outside the legislative branch.

c. **Delegation of spending power--Bowsher v. Synar,** 478 U.S. 714 (1986).

1) **Facts.** The Deficit Control Act of 1985 (Gramm-Rudman-Hollings Act) was enacted to reduce the federal budget deficit to zero over a period of years. Automatic reductions in federal spending were to take place in any fiscal year for which the deficit exceeded the statutory target. The reductions would take effect after the directors of the Office of Management and Budget and the Congressional Budget Office independently calculated the necessary budget reductions. These directors would then report their findings to the Comptroller General, who would make conclusions as to the necessary spending reductions. The President was then required to issue a "sequestration" order mandating the Comptroller General's conclusions. This order would become effective unless Congress reduced spending by legislation. An alternative procedure was also established in case the primary procedure was invalidated. The alternative procedure provided for an expedited congressional joint resolution which would become a sequestration order when the President signed it. Synar (P) and others challenged the statute. The district court held the reporting provisions unconstitutional. Comptroller General Bowsher (D) appeals.

2) **Issue.** May Congress assign to the Comptroller General the function of determining which accounts of the federal budget must be cut to meet deficit targets?

3) **Held.** No. Judgment affirmed.

a) Standing in this case lies in one plaintiff, an employees' union whose members would not receive a scheduled increase in benefits if the Act is sustained.

b) Although the Constitution gives Congress a role in appointment of executive officers, it does not give Congress an active role in supervising such officers. It has the power of removal only upon impeachment. Although Congress may limit the President's powers of removal, it cannot reserve for itself the removal power. Otherwise, Congress would have control over the execution of the laws in violation of the separation of powers.

c) Because Congress may not execute the laws, it cannot grant to an officer under its control the power to execute the laws. D argues that the Comptroller General performs his duties independently of Congress, but in fact Congress is the sole removal authority for the Comptroller General. Accordingly, the Comptroller General may not possess executive powers.

d) Under the Act, the Comptroller General prepares a report by exercising his independent judgment. This is more than a mechanical function; it requires interpretation of the Act and application of judgment concerning a set of facts. This constitutes execution of the law. In fact, the President is required to comply with the report in ordering the reductions.

e)   Because the reporting procedures are unconstitutional, the fallback provisions are effective.

4)   **Concurring** (Stevens, Marshall, JJ.). Labeling the Comptroller General's functions "executive powers" is uninformative. Under the fallback provisions, the congressional report based on the Comptroller General's report has the same legal consequences and could not be considered "executive." In fact, the infirmity of this Act is that Congress has delegated its exclusive power to make policy that will bind the nation to an individual agent of Congress, bypassing the constitutional processes.

5)   **Dissenting** (White, J.). Whether Congress or the Comptroller General determines the level of funding available to the President to carry out the Act's duties, the effect on the President is the same. The President has no authority to establish spending levels. Congress has not granted policy-making discretion; it has specified a detailed procedure based on specific criteria. The Act is an effective response to a serious national crisis and presents no real threat to separation of powers.

6)   **Dissenting** (Blackmun, J.). The better approach would be to invalidate the congressional removal statute, which in any case has never been invoked in its 65-year history.

Morrison
v. Olson

d.   **Creation of independent counsel--Morrison v. Olson,** 487 U.S. 654 (1988).

1)   **Facts.** The Ethics in Government Act of 1978, 28 U.S.C. sections 591 et seq., provides for the appointment of an "independent counsel" to investigate and prosecute specified government officials for violations of federal criminal law. Under the Act, the Attorney General conducts a preliminary investigation of possible violations, and then reports to the Special Division, a court created by the Act. If the Attorney General determines that there are reasonable grounds to believe further investigation or a prosecution is warranted, then he applies for appointment of independent counsel. The Special Division then appoints such counsel and defines the counsel's prosecutorial jurisdiction. The independent prosecutor is required to comply with Department of Justice policies to the extent possible. The Attorney General may remove an independent prosecutor for cause; otherwise, the counsel's tenure expires upon completion of the specified investigations or prosecutions. The counsel notifies the Attorney General of the completion; alternatively, the Special

Division may find the task completed. Certain congressional committees have oversight jurisdiction regarding the independent counsel's conduct. Pursuant to this Act, the Special Division appointed Morrison (D) to investigate allegations that Olson (P), an assistant attorney general, had lied in testimony to Congress. D obtained a grand jury subpoena against P. P moved to quash the subpoena, claiming that D had no authority to proceed because the Act was unconstitutional. The trial court upheld the Act, but the court of appeals reversed. D appeals.

2) **Issue.** May Congress provide for the judicial appointment of independent counsel for purposes of investigating and prosecuting federal criminal offenses?

3) **Held.** Yes. Judgment reversed.

   a) Under the Appointments Clause, there are two classes of officers: (i) principal officers, who are selected by the President with the advice and consent of the Senate; and (ii) inferior officers, whom Congress may allow to be appointed by the President alone, by the heads of departments, or by the Judiciary. Thus, if D is a principal officer, the Act violates the Constitution.

   b) The difference between principal and inferior officers is not always clear. It requires consideration of several factors.

      (1) D may be removed by a higher executive branch official, despite having independent powers.

      (2) D's authority is limited to performing specified, limited duties. D has no policymaking authority and must comply with Department of Justice policies.

      (3) D's office is limited in jurisdiction to the terms of the appointment. It is also limited in tenure; it does not extend beyond the completion of the specific task given.

      (4) Evaluation of these factors leads to the conclusion that an independent counsel is an inferior officer. However, P claims that Congress may not provide that an officer of one branch be appointed by officers of another branch.

   c) The Clause itself does not forbid interbranch appointments, but instead gives Congress discretion to determine the propriety of vesting the appointment of executive officials in the courts. The limitation on this power is where it implicates the separation of powers or impairs the constitutional functions assigned to one of the branches. The very reason for the Act was to remove the appointment power from the executive branch, and the judicial branch is the most logical alternative. By making members of the Special Division ineligible to participate in any matters relating to an independent counsel they have appointed, Congress has protected the separation of powers.

d) Article III limits the judicial power to cases and controversies. However, if the Appointments Clause gives Congress the power to authorize the courts to appoint officials such as an independent counsel, which it does, the appointment power is a source of authority independent of article III. The additional powers granted to the Special Division, such as defining the counsel's authority and tenure of office, are incidental to the exercise of the appointment power itself.

e) The Special Division also has power to terminate an independent counsel's office, which is an administrative power. This power must be narrowly construed to avoid constitutional problems. It is thus limited to removing an independent counsel who has served her purpose, but does not acknowledge that fact and remains on the payroll.

f) P also asserts a separation of powers problem because the Attorney General can remove an independent counsel only by showing "good cause." In *Bowsher* (*supra*), for example, Congress could not involve itself in the removal of an executive officer. Under the Act in this case, however, Congress did not acquire a removal power over executive officials beyond its power of impeachment and conviction.

g) The Attorney General retains the removal power, subject to the good cause requirement. But the Constitution does not give the President unbridled discretion to remove officials of independent agencies. Prior cases have distinguished purely executive officials from quasi-legislative and quasi-judicial officials, but this is an inappropriate distinction for analyzing removal powers. The proper question is whether the removal restrictions impede the President's ability to perform his constitutional duty. Because the independent counsel has a limited function, and because the Attorney General has removal authority for good cause, the good cause restriction does not unconstitutionally impede the President.

h) The second separation of powers issue is based on interference with the role of the executive branch. However, the Act does not permit either congressional or judicial usurpation of executive functions. It also leaves the executive branch with the ability to supervise the counsel's prosecutorial powers.

4) **Dissenting** (Scalia, J.). The power to conduct a criminal prosecution is a purely executive power, and the Act deprives the President of the exclusive control over the exercise of that power. It does not matter to what extent the Act reduces presidential control; the Act violates the separation of powers doctrine. In addi-

tion, D's appointment could only be constitutional if she is an "inferior" officer, but she is not inferior because she is not subordinate to another officer. The final infirmity of the Act is that it improperly imposes restrictions upon the removal of the independent counsel.

3.   **Foreign Affairs.**

   a.   **Constitutional provisions.** Under Article I, section 8, Congress has the power to declare war, to raise and support armies, to maintain a navy, to make rules for the regulation of the land and naval forces, and to provide for organizing, arming, disciplining, and calling forth the militia.

   b.   **War powers.** The Vietnam War called into question the whole matter of the relationship between Congress and the President in the conduct of war. Some commentators argued that the President had acquired more power in this area than was originally intended by the Constitution. Until President Theodore Roosevelt unilaterally sent troops into Panama in 1903, the Presidents did not initiate military action against foreign states without congressional approval. After World War II, troops were sent to several locations without congressional action, including Korea and Lebanon. The exact scope of executive and congressional powers in this area is not clearly defined by the Constitution. Consequently, each branch has been free to take initiatives to make national policy in this area. The basic issue is whether the President has the power to use armed forces against a foreign nation without the authorization of Congress.

   c.   **The War Powers Resolution.** In 1973, Congress adopted the joint War Powers Resolution [50 U.S.C. §§1541-48] which spells out the President's authority to use the armed forces. If the President uses the armed forces in foreign nations under specified conditions, without a congressional declaration of war, he must formally report to Congress. In the absence of any congressional action, the forces must (in most cases) be removed within 60 days. The constitutionality of the resolution has not been considered by the courts.

   d.   **The Boland Amendment.** In response to an alleged "secret war" carried on by the Administration against the government in Nicaragua, Congress added the "Boland Amendments" to appropriations bills. The Boland Amendments basically forbid any agency of the United States involved in intelligence activities from spending funds in support of military or paramilitary operations in Nicaragua. Despite these amendments, certain members of the Administration assisted in raising nongovernment funds to assist the Contra troops. There was a significant divergence of views regarding the constitutionality of the amendments to the extent that they interfered with the President's ability to conduct foreign affairs.

4. **Congressional Immunity Under the Speech or Debate Clause.**

    a.   **Introduction.** Article I, section 6 states that senators and representatives "shall not be questioned in any other place" for "any Speech or Debate in either House." This forbids criminal or civil proceedings against members of Congress for "legislative acts." In other words, neither acts that occur in the regular course of the legislative process nor the motivation for those acts may be used against a legislator in a judicial proceeding.

    b.   **Privilege extends to aides.** In *Gravel v. United States*, 408 U.S. 606 (1972), the Court held that the congressional privilege extends to the aides of senators and representatives on the theory that they act as agents of the congressmen. In that case, Senator Gravel had conducted a subcommittee meeting in which he read from the Pentagon Papers, dealing with the Vietnam War. He also allegedly arranged for private publication of the papers. A grand jury investigated the incident and subpoenaed Senator Gravel's assistant. The Court held that the aide could not be questioned as to the events at the subcommittee meeting, but that any arrangements for private publication were not protected because they were not part of the legislative process. The dissenting Justices argued that the legislative function includes an informing function, or a duty to inform the public, and that inquiry into the source of the Senator's information was an improper deterrent to acquisition of information for use by Congress.

    c.   **Privilege does not cover nonlegislative acts.** In *United States v. Brewster*, 408 U.S. 501 (1972), the Court held that the Speech or Debate Clause did not bar prosecution of a former senator for accepting a bribe relating to his actions on postage rate legislation. The clause does not protect all conduct relating to the legislative process. Political acts including communications with and services for constituents, and speeches and publications outside of Congress are not protected.

    d.   **News releases as legislative acts.** The Court has held that a news release is not a legislative act and therefore is not privileged. *Hutchinson v. Proxmire*, 443 U.S. 111 (1979), involved a news release and newsletter item by Senator Proxmire. The recipient of one of Proxmire's "Golden Fleece" awards, given for what Proxmire considered wasteful government spending, sued the Senator for defamation for the accusations made in the news release and newsletter. The Court held that the informing function of Congress extends to ways Congress informs itself, i.e., hearings, but not to ways Congress informs its constituents, such as the newsletter and news release. Therefore, Proxmire was subject to liability. His speech in the Senate on the same subject, however, was not a basis for liability.

VI. EQUAL PROTECTION

A. INTRODUCTION TO EQUAL PROTECTION ANALYSIS

1. **Basic Principles.** The fourteenth amendment provides that no state may deny to any person within its jurisdiction the equal protection of the laws. Although no comparable provision expressly limits acts by the federal government, the guarantee of equal protection is implicit in the concept of fifth amendment due process. Basically, "equal protection" is a limitation on the exercise of government power that means that government regulation cannot be "arbitrarily discriminatory." All laws are to some extent inherently unequal, because part of the purpose of legislation is to distinguish among citizens. For example, tax laws vary depending on the individual's sources and uses of income, and criminal sanctions apply only to those convicted of crimes. Thus, equal protection does not require that all persons be treated equally under the law at all times, but that whatever classifications are made in a statute must be reasonable.

2. **Standards of Review.**

   a. **Development of equal protection doctrine.**

      1) **Traditional approach.** At one time, courts used equal protection only to insure that the legislative means were reasonably related to the legislative purpose; i.e., that the regulation had a rational basis. This approach supported only minimal judicial intervention. This traditional approach is characterized by the following three requirements:

         a) The first requirement that must be established under the traditional equal protection test is that any statutory classification be "rational," or based on factors (economic, social, historic, geographic, etc.) that justify disparate treatment. This requirement is generally satisfied as long as the classifications are not patently arbitrary.

         b) The second requirement is that the classification (the disparate treatment) rationally promote a proper governmental purpose.

         c) Assuming that the classification drawn in the statute meets the first two requirements, it is also required that all persons affected by the classification be treated equally.

      2) **The Warren Court's "new" equal protection.** The Warren Court utilized the traditional equal protection analysis in most areas of economic and social

regulation. However, it also articulated a new, higher level of scrutiny applicable when legislation affected one of two areas: a "suspect classification" or a "fundamental right" or interest.

a) **Old standard.** In the absence of a suspect classification or fundamental right, equal protection requires that the legislative means must be "reasonably" related to "legitimate" state ends. This is also called the "rational basis" standard.

b) **New standard.** When a suspect classification such as race or a fundamental interest such as voting is involved, the legislative means must be "necessary" to achieve "compelling" state interests. This standard of review—also called "strict scrutiny"—has resulted in significant judicial intervention in assessing the constitutionality of legislation.

c) **Characteristics.** Common to most classifications that demand heightened scrutiny are the following characteristics: historical lack of political power; history of discrimination; immutableness of classification; irrelevance to performance; and obviousness (the basis for classification acts as a badge).

3) **The Burger and Rehnquist Courts.** The Burger and Rehnquist Courts have generally accepted the old and new standards of equal protection, although they have given greater effect to the old standard than the Warren Court did. The Court has also added a third, intermediate tier of scrutiny for certain classifications, including those based on sex, alienage, and illegitimacy. The new intermediate standard requires that the legislative means be "substantially related" to "important" governmental objectives. In actuality, the whole equal protection jurisprudence is confusing and at times inconsistent. The Court has never expressly adopted the "sliding scale" approach suggested by Justice Marshall, but clearly there are no rigid guidelines with which to decide every equal protection case.

3. **Types of Classifications.** If ☐ represents the evil being proscribed, ///// represent people that threaten the evil, and + + + + + represent people who do not threaten the evil, then the following types of classifications are possible:

a. [/////] The statute covers all of those that threaten the evil.

b. //// [   ] The statute covers none of those that threaten the evil.

c.   ///|///| The statute covers only a few. This is an under-inclusive classification.

d. |+ + +///| The statute covers the target population but also innocent persons. This is an over-inclusive classification.

e. |+ + +//|//   The statute is both under- and over-inclusive.

B.   THE CONSTITUTION AND RACE

1.   **Slavery.** Because the participation of the Southern states was critical to adoption of the Constitution, the terms of the Constitution tacitly recognized and even condoned slavery. The federal government was not empowered to regulate slavery, but the Constitution did not preclude emancipation. Article IV, section 2, clause 3 did require states to deliver up escaped slaves, however.

    a.   **State constitutional law--State v. Post,** 20 N.J.L. 368 (1845).   State v. Post

        1)   **Facts.** The constitution of New Jersey contained a clause that made "all men" "free and independent," having certain natural rights including those of life, liberty, the possession of property, and the pursuit of happiness. A demurrer to a lawsuit was based on the claim that slavery was illegal under the state constitution.

        2)   **Issue.** May slavery exist under a state constitution that makes all men free and independent?

        3)   **Held.** Yes.

            a)   The language of the constitution must be understood in the context of the society that adopted it. In reality, no man is absolutely free and independent; all are subject to the rights of others and the laws of the government. Each person yields a portion of his natural rights to the government in order to secure the remainder of those rights.

            b)   If the constitutional convention really meant to abolish slavery as it existed when the convention assembled, it would have clearly stated so in the constitution. This matter is too important to be resolved through construction of abstract political propositions. Even the Declaration of Independence declares that all men are created equal, yet the United States Constitution recognizes the existence of slavery.

Dred Scott
v. Sandford

b. **Status of slaves and former slaves under United States Constitution--Dred Scott v. Sandford,** 60 U.S. (19 How.) 393 (1857).

1) **Facts.** Dred Scott (P) was a slave whose owner took him from Missouri (a slave state) to Illinois, a non-slave state, and Minnesota, a part of the non-slave Louisiana Territory. P and his owner returned to Missouri, where P was sold to Sandford (D), a New York resident. Subsequently, P sued D for trespass. D claimed that P was not a citizen of Missouri, so there was no federal diversity of citizenship jurisdiction. D also claimed that P was not free.

2) **Issue.** May a former slave have all the rights of a citizen of the United States?

3) **Held.** No.

a) Under the Constitution, the citizens of the United States have the power to conduct the government through their representatives and are thus the sovereign people. This status was not accorded to persons imported as slaves, or their descendants, whether free or not. The federal government has exclusive authority to naturalize aliens; even if P was deemed a citizen of Missouri under state law, that status cannot confer federal citizenship. For this reason, P could not sue in federal court.

b) Even though Congress has declared that slavery is prohibited in the Louisiana Territory, Congress does not have power under the Constitution to deprive a citizen of his liberty or property merely because he brings the property into a particular Territory of the United States. The Constitution expressly upholds the right of property in a slave. Accordingly, the law that prohibits a slave owner from owning slaves in the Louisiana Territory is unconstitutional, and P was not made free by virtue of being taken to the territory by his owner.

c) Although P was taken to Illinois, a non-slave state, his current status is governed by Missouri law, not Illinois law. Under Missouri law, P is still a slave.

2. **Reconstruction.**

a. **Introduction.** The first eight amendments to the Constitution were originally intended to protect individual rights against the action of the federal government, which was perceived as the greatest threat to those rights. It was generally assumed that the states would protect individual liberty. By the end of the Civil War, however, it was obvious that the southern states would not protect the rights of the emancipated slaves. As a result, the Reconstruction Congress adopted three amendments to the Constitution.

   1) **Thirteenth Amendment.** The thirteenth amendment made the Emancipation Proclamation constitutional by prohibiting slavery throughout the United States. It also gave Congress power to enforce its provisions through appropriate legislation. However, it did not prohibit the states from discriminating against blacks, which many states did through enactment of so-called "Black Codes" that restricted the rights of blacks.

   2) **Fourteenth Amendment.** In response to the Black Codes, Congress enacted the Civil Rights Act of 1866, which made all persons born in the United States citizens, and gave citizens full civil rights. The constitutionality of the Act was disputed, however, so Congress adopted the fourteenth amendment to provide a constitutional basis for the Civil Rights Act, which was subsequently reenacted.

   3) **Fifteenth Amendment.** The final reconstruction amendment assured the right to vote to all persons.

   4) **Impact.** These amendments made an immediate impact, but the meaning they have today was developed only after many years of litigation. At first, the Court limited the application of the thirteenth and fourteenth amendments to the racial context. [*See* The Slaughter-House Cases, *infra*] Although the amendments were applied to protect the rights of blacks, they were not construed to apply to private discrimination in public accommodations. [*See* The Civil Rights Cases, *infra*] Early cases also recognized an exception to the equal protection requirement that permitted racial discrimination in public where separate but equal facilities were provided. The interpretation of these amendments over the years has given progressively expansive meaning and power to the amendments.

b. **Separate but equal doctrine--Plessy v. Ferguson, 163 U.S. 537 (1896).**

Plessy v. Ferguson

   1) **Facts.** Plessy (P), who was seven-eighths white and one-eighth black, refused to comply with a demand that he sit in the black railway carriage rather than the one for whites. P was convicted of violation of a state statute providing for separate railway carriages for the white and black races. P challenged the law but lost. P appeals.

2)   Issue. May a state require that separate railway carriages be provided for black citizens and white citizens?

3)   Held. Yes. Judgment affirmed.

    a)   The law does not imply the inferiority of one race or the other. The only proper restraint on the exercise of state police power is that it be reasonable and intended for the promotion of the general good. The state legislature may properly have concluded that the law would preserve the public peace and good order.

    b)   It certainly is no more obnoxious to the fourteenth amendment than laws requiring separate schools, which are universally accepted. Legislation cannot overcome social prejudices; the attempt to do so can only result in accentuating difficulties. The Constitution can act to equate civil and political rights of the two races, but cannot affect social standing.

4)   Dissenting (Harlan, J.). No legislature or court may properly regard the race of citizens where civil rights are involved. Every citizen, regardless of color, has a right to occupy the public transportation of his choice; governmental infringement of that right is unconstitutional. Our Constitution is color-blind, and neither knows nor tolerates classes among citizens. Any evils resulting from commingling of the races are less than those resulting from curtailment of civil rights upon the basis of race.

3.   School Desegregation and Repudiation of the Separate but Equal Doctrine. Even after the thirteenth amendment was ratified, several southern states adopted racially discriminatory statutes, referred to as the Black Codes. These were designed to keep blacks in an inferior position, socially, politically, and economically. The Civil Rights Act of 1866 and the fourteenth amendment were intended to counter this official discrimination, although apparently they were not originally supposed to insure full protection of civil rights for all races. For nearly 100 years, states followed a "separate but equal" doctrine, whereby state facilities, including public schools, could be racially segregated as long as they provided "equal" services. The doctrine was successfully challenged beginning in 1938 in cases involving state law schools. The most significant case, however, involved secondary and primary schools.

Brown v.
Board of
Education
(Brown I)

    a.   Application to secondary and primary schools--Brown v. Board of Education (Brown I), 347 U.S. 483 (1954).

        1)   Facts. Brown (P) and other black schoolchildren (the opinion consolidates appeals from four states) were denied admission to schools attended by white children under laws requiring or permitting segregation based on race. P challenged the law but was denied relief under the "separate but equal" doctrine. (In the Delaware case, the plaintiff was admitted solely because the white school was superior; i.e., separate was not equal.) P appealed.

2) **Issue.** May children be segregated in essentially "equal" public schools solely on the basis of race?

3) **Held.** No. Judgments vacated and reargument on the issue of appropriate relief ordered.

   a) The circumstances surrounding adoption of the fourteenth amendment are not determinative, especially here where public education, which barely existed then, is at issue. The effect of segregation on public education in its current setting is therefore determinative.

   b) Granted that black and white schools are substantially "equal" in tangible factors, there yet exists an invidious effect when black and white children are segregated. Namely, segregation creates a feeling of inferiority which may significantly affect a child's motivation to learn. Separate educational facilities are therefore inherently unequal, and their maintenance by government authority denies equal protection of the law.

b. **Implementation of desegregation.** The Court initially permitted gradual integration of public schools in recognition of the difficulties inherent in school desegregation. [Brown v. Board of Education (Brown II), 394 U.S. 294 (1955)] The opinion addressed solely the manner in which relief granted in *Brown I* was to be accorded:

1) The full implementation of the constitutional principles required solution of various local school problems, to be solved by school authorities and reviewed by courts to assure good faith compliance.

2) The cases were remanded to the lower courts, who were to be guided by equitable principles in fashioning decrees. The competing interests involved plaintiffs' rights to admission at the earliest date and the need for systematic, effective, and orderly removal of obstacles to full integration.

3) The Court emphasized its determination that all public schools be integrated by holding that threats of violence resulting from state actions against desegregation would not justify failure to integrate. [Cooper v. Aaron, 358 U.S. 1 (1958)] All nine Justices delivered the opinion to emphasize their unity.

4.   Remedying Segregation.

a.   **Introduction.** The significance of disproportionate impact has been articulated most fully in school desegregation cases. The Court has adopted a bifurcated approach to school desegregation problems. "De facto" segregation is nondeliberate segregation. If an official segregation policy existed as of 1954, there could not be de facto segregation in the school system. Thus, in the South, most school systems were characterized by "de jure" or deliberate segregation. The Court faced three alternatives in fashioning guidelines for remedying segregation:

1)   Prohibit only activity that results in segregation; i.e., require desegregation only (the emphasis is on process).

2)   Hold that any racially imbalanced school system is by itself a violation; i.e., require integration (the emphasis is on results).

3)   Hold that once de jure segregation is shown (process), integration is required (results). This is the approach the Court currently applies.

b.   **Early judicial remedies.** After the *Brown* case, *supra*, the Court decided several cases involving judicial responses to segregation.

1)   **Public schools.** In *Griffin v. Prince Edward County School Board*, 377 U.S. 218 (1964), the Court ordered the reopening of a public school system that the school board closed because of court-ordered integration. The record showed that the schools were closed to perpetuate segregation; the state and county were providing financial assistance to the remaining private schools, which were segregated.

2)   **Transfer plans.** In *Goss v. Board of Education*, 373 U.S. 683 (1963), a transfer plan (allowing a student in a school where he was in a racial minority to transfer to a school where he would be in the majority) was struck down. The Court also stated that what was deliberate speed in 1955 might not be deliberate speed in 1963.

3)   **Acceleration of desegregation.** In *Green v. New Kent County School Board*, 391 U.S. 430 (1968), the Court held that school boards had an affirmative duty to take immediate steps to desegregate schools.

Swann v.
Charlotte-
Mecklenburg
Board of
Education

c.   **Authority of district courts to order desegregation in southern metropolitan areas--Swann v. Charlotte-Mecklenburg Board of Education, 402 U.S. 1 (1971).**

1) **Facts.** The Board of Education (D) had a long history of maintaining a dual set of schools in a single system in order to perpetuate discrimination in spite of *Brown v. Board of Education, supra*. Swann (P) brought suit to force desegregation. The district court ordered D to establish a plan, which it did, but the court rejected it and instead adopted a plan created by a court-appointed master. The Supreme Court granted certiorari.

2) **Issue.** Are district courts justified in ordering compliance with their own desegregation plans when the local school authorities fail to desegregate voluntarily?

3) **Held.** Yes. Judgment affirmed.

   a) The objective of the federal courts from *Brown* to the present has been to eliminate all vestiges of state-imposed segregation in the public schools. Judicial authority to remedy violations expands when local authority defaults.

   b) The central problems here involve student assignment, and these are separated into four categories. The first is the extent to which racial quotas may be used to correct a segregation system. A remedial plan is judged by its effectiveness. Awareness of the racial composition of a school system is a useful starting point in shaping an effective remedy, and limited use of mathematical ratios is permissible. The guiding principle is that no pupil should be excluded from any school on account of race, but every school need not always reflect the racial composition of the school system as a whole.

   c) The remaining categories are elimination of one-race schools, remedial altering of attendance zones, and transportation of students in order to dismantle the dual school system. Demographic factors may result in virtually or completely one-race schools; these are not certain indications of imposed segregation. However, gerrymandering of school districts and attendance zones and provision for optional transfer of students to other schools is useful, and, to be effective, must grant free transportation and assurance of a place in the desired school.

d. **Judicial remedies for northern schools.**

1) **All minorities.** In determining whether a school is "segregated," the courts must consider the number of all minority groups (not just blacks) who have suffered unequal treatment in education.

2)   **Presumption.** A finding that school authorities intentionally segregated—or delayed integrating—any significant portion of the school district creates a presumption that the entire school district is being operated on a segregated basis. This is because of the "substantial reciprocal effect" that segregation of some schools may have on others.

   a)   This presumption is not rebutted or satisfactorily explained merely by showing that the board had adopted a "neighborhood school policy" (assigning students to the schools closest to their homes), even though such policy on its face appears to be racially neutral.

   b)   But the presumption may be rebutted by a showing that because of natural geographic boundaries, the school district is in fact divided into clearly unrelated areas, which require separate treatment. But the burden of proving this is on the school board.

Keyes v.
School District No. 1

3)   **Prima facie case--Keyes v. School District No. 1,** 413 U.S. 189 (1973).

   a)   **Facts.** Keyes (P) challenged certain actions taken by School District No. 1 of Denver (D) that allegedly were intended to create or maintain segregated schools. No law supported such segregation; the Colorado Constitution expressly prohibited it. The district court held that blacks and Hispanics must be counted separately for purposes of defining a "segregated" school. P appeals.

   b)   **Issue.** Must courts consider the number of all minority groups (not just blacks) who have suffered unequal treatment in education when determining whether a school is segregated?

   c)   **Held.** Yes. Judgment modified and remanded.

      (1)   When a school district does not have a history of legally imposed segregation, P must show intentional acts by school authorities intended to segregate schools and actual existence of currently segregated schools. If P shows that such acts were taken in one portion of a school system, he has made a prima facie case of unlawful segregation intent for all segregated schooling within the system.

      (2)   For purposes of determining whether a school is segregated, it is improper to separate minorities who are subject to similar disadvantages. The lower court erred in not combining proportions of blacks and Hispanic students for this purpose.

      (3)   When P has made a prima facie case, D must rebut by showing that no segregative intent even partially moti-

vated their actions. Alternatively, D could show that a lesser degree of segregation would not have resulted even if D had not acted as it did; i.e., D may rebut P's claim by showing that its past segregative acts did not create nor contribute to the current segregated condition of the core city schools.

d) **Concurring in part, dissenting in part** (Powell, J.). The ultimate goal is the best possible educational opportunity for all children. Busing programs must not so interfere with local sentiment as to negate achievement of this goal. *Brown* established a constitutional right to attend an integrated school. However, it is unprincipled that one little pocket of de jure segregation justifies widespread orders for integration; we should provide remedies regardless of de jure or de facto distinctions.

e) **Comment.** Permissible judicial remedies include designating the location of new schools and abandoning old schools so as not to perpetuate segregation; gerrymandering school districts and attendance zones, even if the result is that the new districts and zones are neither compact nor contiguous; and assigning students, faculty, and staff to schools in ratios substantially the same as in the community.

C. RATIONAL BASIS REVIEW

1. **Introduction.** As indicated *supra*, the equal protection doctrine is not limited to issues of race. The Court has adopted various standards of review for different types of classifications. Racial and other suspect classifications merit a stringent standard of review, while other classifications are upheld as long as they pass a rational basis review.

2. **Classification Based on Drug Usage--New York City Transit Authority v. Beazer,** 440 U.S. 568 (1979).

   a. **Facts.** The New York City Transit Authority (D) refused to hire persons who used narcotic drugs. Pursuant to its rule, D refused to hire Beazer (P) because he was using methadone. Methadone was used to treat heroin addiction. P brought a class action. The trial court found that many methadone users are as employable as non-methadone users and that D could use normal personnel-screening procedures to eliminate unqualified applicants. Accordingly, the court held that

New York
City Transit
Authority v.
Beazer

the methadone-use blanket exclusion policy was unconstitutional, but that D could impose limited restrictions for safety reasons. The court of appeals upheld the decision and the Supreme Court granted certiorari.

b. **Issue.** May a city refuse to employ all persons who use a particular substance because it is used for treatment of drug addiction?

c. **Held.** Yes. Judgment reversed.

1) Essentially, the district court held that D's rule was broader than it had to be to exclude those methadone users who are actually not qualified as employees. Even if this conclusion is correct, and D's policy is unwise, the personnel policy does not violate equal protection interests.

2) D's rule promotes D's objectives of safety and efficiency. The rule is not directed against any particular individual or category of persons, but instead is a policy choice. The classification is not based on an unpopular trait or affiliation, but has some rational basis. The courts are not authorized to interfere with the policy decision.

d. **Dissenting** (White, Marshall, JJ.). It is not rational to place successfully recovering drug addicts in the same category as those merely attempting to recover. P and members of his class should be included with the general population because they are no more likely to prove unsatisfactory employees than persons chosen from the general population. In addition, D has singled out this one group out of many groups that could be considered to be more likely to contain individuals not suitable as employees.

Cleburne v.
Cleburne
Living Center,
Inc.

3. **Mental Retardation--Cleburne v. Cleburne Living Center, Inc.,** 473 U.S. 432 (1985).

a. **Facts.** Under a city zoning ordinance, group homes for the mentally retarded may operate only with a special permit that requires the signatures of property owners within 200 feet of the property to be used. The applicants were unable to obtain the required signatures in a residential neighborhood. The lower courts held the ordinance unconstitutional. The Court granted certiorari.

b. **Issue.** Is mental retardation a suspect class for equal protection analysis?

c. **Held.** No. Judgment affirmed on other grounds.

1) Generally, under the Equal Protection Clause, legislation is presumed valid and will be upheld if the classification

drawn by the statute is rationally related to a legitimate state interest. Certain types of classifications are subject to strict scrutiny, others to heightened scrutiny.

2) The court of appeals held that mental retardation is a quasi-suspect classification. However, the legislature has a legitimate interest in providing for the various problems of the mentally retarded, and courts are ill-equipped to make substantive judgment about legislative decisions in this area. Legislatures have addressed the problems of the mentally retarded and need the flexibility of the rational basis test to be effective.

3) Under the rational basis test, however, the ordinance is defective. It does not apply to nursing homes for the aged or convalescents, apartment houses, sanitariums, or boarding houses. Nothing in the record explains how the permit requirement for only facilities for the mentally retarded is rationally related to any governmental purpose.

d. **Concurring** (Stevens, J., Burger, C.J.). The mentally retarded have historically been subject to unfair mistreatment. This ordinance reflects the irrational fears of neighboring property owners, not a concern for the welfare of the mentally retarded.

e. **Concurring and dissenting** (Marshall, Brennan, Blackmun, JJ.). The Court has created a "second order" rational basis review. Normally under the rational basis test, the legislature does not have to address all ills at once. Thus, zoning plans based on fears of proximity to a high school, location in a flood plain, and crowded living conditions or increased congestion are perfectly valid, even if applied one step at a time. However, the class of mentally retarded persons deserves heightened scrutiny, and the Court reaches the correct result.

4. **Extent of Deference Accorded--United States Railroad Retirement Board v. Fritz,** 449 U.S. 166 (1980).

United States Railroad Retirement Board v. Fritz

a. **Facts.** In 1974, Congress fundamentally altered the railroad retirement system that had been in effect since 1937. Essentially, Congress acted to place the system on a sound financial basis by eliminating future accruals of "windfall" benefits, resulting from concurrent qualification for railroad retirement and social security. The new system established several classes of employees whose benefits would be computed differently. Fritz (P) represented a class of employees who had between 10 and 25 years of railroad employment but who would be denied "windfall" benefits because they had no "current connection" with the railroad industry in 1974 or as of the date of retirement. P claimed the new system denied equal protection. The district court agreed, and the United States Railroad Retirement Board (D) appeals.

b. **Issue.** May legislation be upheld if there is a plausible reason for the classification made based on the plain language of the statute, regardless of the actual reason for which the statute was enacted?

c. **Held.** Yes. Judgment reversed.

1) The district court held that a differentiation based on whether an employee was "active" in the railroad business in 1974 was not "rationally related" to the congressional purposes of ensuring the solvency of the railroad retirement system and protecting vested benefits. However, in recent years we have refused to invalidate economic legislation on equal protection grounds just because it was unwise or inartfully drawn.

2) Congress could have eliminated "windfall" benefits entirely, so it is not improper for it to draw lines in order to phase out such benefits.

3) D has advanced plausible reasons for Congress's action. Thus, this Court's inquiry is at its end. It is constitutionally irrelevant whether this reasoning in fact underlay the legislative decision. We cannot say that Congress was unaware of what it accomplished or that it was misled by the groups that appeared before it.

d. **Concurring** (Stevens, J.).

1) The dissent correctly points out that a test using any "conceivable basis" reduces judicial review to a meaningless exercise. P represents a small class of persons deprived of vested rights while others in a substantially similar position have those rights enhanced. The proper inquiry should be whether there is a correlation between the classification and either the actual purpose or a purpose we may legitimately presume to have motivated an impartial legislature.

2) The determinative questions are whether Congress may deprive some persons of benefits while enhancing other persons' benefits, and whether it can classify persons based on how recent their employment was. Both questions must be answered affirmatively.

e. **Dissenting** (Brennan, Marshall, JJ.).

1) The Court's approach here virtually immunizes social and economic legislative classifications from judicial review. The rational basis standard is not "toothless." The test requires examination of both the purposes of the statute and the relationship of the classification to that purpose. The clas-

sification here is not only rationally unrelated to the congressional purpose; it is inimical to it.

2) The Court avoids serious analysis by, first, assuming purpose from result (Congress intended to do what it did do); second, by disregarding Congress's actual stated purpose for an unsupported justification that conflicts with the stated purpose; and third, by failing to ascertain whether the classification is rationally related to the identified purpose.

3) Equitable considerations of need, reasonable expectation and reliance, and contribution to the system show that P has as great a claim to earned dual benefits as those permitted to retain such benefits. The fortuity of one day of employment in a particular year is an irrational basis for classification.

4) Application of the Court's new analysis will mean that in future cases, we will defer not to the considered judgment of Congress, but to the arguments of skilled government litigators.

5. **Striking Workers--Lyng v. International Union, United Automobile, Aerospace and Agricultural Implement Workers, 485 U.S. 360 (1988).**

a. **Facts.** Section 109 of the Omnibus Budget Reconciliation Act of 1981 amended the Food Stamp Act to make ineligible for food stamps those households in which a member is on strike and to forbid any increase in allotment of food stamps per household due to loss of striker's income. The district court held section 109 unconstitutional.

b. **Issue.** Does section 109 violate the first amendment rights of expression and association?

c. **Held.** No. Judgment reversed.

1) "Rational basis" review is appropriate here since no fundamental right is burdened. The statute does not interfere with family living arrangements. Nor does it interfere with any right of association between individuals and unions. While a lack of food stamps may make it harder for strikers and families to maintain their standard of living, the Constitution does not require the government to subsidize this right. Similarly, there is no violation of the right of expression.

2) Section 109 is rationally related to the objectives of avoiding undue favoritism in labor disputes, cutting federal expenditures, and concentrating the use of food

Lyng v. International Union, United Automobile, Aerospace and Agricultural Implement Workers stamps where the need is greatest. Congress should be free to make economic policies, even though the statutes may provide only "rough justice." Congress is given great deference in deciding how to spend money for the general welfare.

d. **Dissent** (Marshall, Brennan, and Blackmun, JJ.). Section 109 does not pass review even under the rational basis test. There is no rational basis for the decision to eliminate strikers from the food stamp program in order to channel resources to the needy. Strikers are just as needy as others and are often willing to work. Section 109 is not neutral, since management employees qualify for food stamps.

D. HEIGHTENED SCRUTINY FOR CLASSIFICATIONS BASED ON RACE AND ETHNIC ANCESTRY

1. **Discrimination Against Racial and Ethnic Minorities.** Because racial discrimination prompted adoption of the fourteenth amendment, racial classifications are "suspect," meaning they invite the strictest judicial scrutiny. There are numerous types of discrimination based on race. The government may place unequal burdens on persons because of their race, or it may restrict interaction among people of different races, or it may gather and disseminate racial information. Discrimination may be expressly stated, or it may consist in discriminatory enforcement of an ostensibly neutral law. It may arise when the adoption of a neutral law is motivated by racial considerations. These situations present difficult issues for the courts.

a. **Use of fourteenth amendment.** In *Strauder v. West Virginia*, 100 U.S. 303 (1880), the Court used the fourteenth amendment to invalidate a state statute that permitted only white persons to serve on juries. The Court noted that the amendment was aimed against discrimination because of race or color.

Korematsu v. United States

b. **Proper distinction based on race--Korematsu v. United States,** 323 U.S. 214 (1944).

1) **Facts.** Korematsu (D) was convicted of remaining in a "military area" in violation of an Army command that all persons of Japanese ancestry be excluded from certain areas for national defense reasons. D was not accused of disloyalty. D appeals, claiming denial of equal protection.

2) **Issue.** May race be used as a criterion for curtailing civil rights in a time of grave threats to national security?

3) **Held.** Yes. Judgment affirmed.

a) Legal restrictions that curtail the civil rights of a single racial group are subject to the most rigid judicial scrutiny, but are not per se unconstitutional. Although never justified by racial antagonism, they may be permitted in times of pressing public necessity.

b) Here, military authorities determined that the existence of Japanese sympathizers was a threat. Espionage and sabotage must be deterred even at great cost. Under war emergency, nothing less than exclusion of the entire group would solve the problem of guarding against disloyalty. The power to protect must be commensurate with the threatened danger.

c) In light of the totality of the circumstances, the exclusion order cannot be held to be unjustified.

4) **Concurring** (Frankfurter, J.). The Court does not approve of the action, but defers to Congress and the Executive because the action is not prohibited by the Constitution.

5) **Dissenting** (Murphy, J.). The exclusion exceeds the brink of constitutional power. The exigencies were not so great as to preclude hearings for the persons involved, and there is no basis for the assumption that this racial group had distinct dangerous tendencies toward disloyalty.

6) **Dissenting** (Jackson, J.). The Court permits an inference of inheritable guilt, contrary to the fundamental assumption of our system. A civil court is not competent to determine whether a military command is reasonable, and should not attempt to justify one as the Court has done here.

7) **Comment.** *Korematsu* was the Court's last decision upholding overt racial discrimination.

2. **Classifications that Disadvantage Racial Minorities.**

   a. **Introduction.** A statute may create classifications that are not explicit based on race, but have disparate impacts on particular groups, including racial groups. Such statutes create difficult analysis problems.

   b. **Relevance of discriminatory impact in finding a discriminatory purpose.**

      1) **General rule.** Laws or other official actions that are racially neutral on their face and that rationally serve a permissible government end do not violate equal pro-

tection simply because they have a racially discriminatory impact (i.e., affect minorities more adversely than whites). A violation requires that the government action have a discriminatory purpose (intentional or deliberate discrimination).

2) **Qualification test--Washington v. Davis,** 426 U.S. 229 (1976).

    a)   **Facts.** Black applicants for positions on the police force (Ps) challenged the promotion policies and recruiting practices of the District of Columbia Police Department. Ps filed for partial summary judgment on the recruiting question, specifically challenging a qualification test that allegedly discriminated against blacks in violation of the fifth amendment Due Process Clause. The district court denied Ps' motions; the court of appeals reversed. Washington (D) appeals.

    b)   **Issue.** Does a qualification test that has not been established as a reliable measure of job performance and that fails a higher percentage of blacks than whites violate the fifth amendment Due Process Clause?

    c)   **Held.** No. Judgment reversed.

        (1)   A disproportionate impact on different races resulting from a general qualification test does not, by itself and independent of any discriminatory purpose, establish a constitutional violation. Government action is not unconstitutional solely because it has a racially disproportionate impact; there must be a racially discriminatory purpose to justify invalidation. The purpose need not be express, but it must exist, whether on the face of the statute or in its application.

        (2)   When a disproportionate racial impact is proven, the government must show that the law is neutral on its face and serves proper governmental ends, but the burden is not high. The test involved here has a reasonable relation to the need for competent police officers. Additionally, D has made affirmative efforts to recruit black officers, indicating a lack of intent to discriminate.

        (3)   Even though the test was not shown to relate directly to eventual job performance, it is closely related to the requirements of the training program for new recruits.

    d)   **Concurring** (Stevens, J.). The line between discriminatory purpose and impact is not bright and not determinative, since dramatic discriminatory impact is unacceptable.

c.   **De jure and de facto discrimination.**

1)   **Introduction.** "De jure" discrimination exists where the statute explicitly discriminates or where the law, although neutral on its face, is deliberately administered in a discriminatory way. "De facto" discrimination exists where an otherwise neutral law and administration results nevertheless in discrimination. Also, if the law was enacted with a discriminatory motive, it is de jure discrimination.

2)   **Discriminatory administration of law--Yick Wo v. Hopkins,** 118 U.S. 356 (1886).

Yick Wo v. Hopkins

a)   **Facts.** San Francisco passed an ordinance requiring that all laundries housed in wooden buildings be licensed before operating. Yick Wo (P), a Chinese citizen, was convicted and imprisoned for violation of the ordinance. P petitioned for a writ of habeas corpus, proving that his equipment was not a fire hazard and that, while he and 200 other Chinese laundrymen had been denied permits, virtually all non-Chinese who made application received permits. P's petition was denied by the state court; P appeals.

b)   **Issue.** Does discriminatory application of a statute that is fair and impartial on its face constitute denial of equal protection under the fourteenth amendment?

c)   **Held.** Yes. Judgment reversed and remanded, with directions to discharge P from imprisonment.

(1)   The fourteenth amendment equal protection provisions apply to all persons, whether or not citizens of the United States.

(2)   The statute appears fair and impartial on its face, but its administration makes illegal and unjust discriminations of a material character among people in similar circumstances. Discriminatory application such as this denies P equal protection of the law and cannot be sanctioned. P is therefore illegally imprisoned.

d.   **Other aspects of disparate impact.**

1)   **Standard procedures resulting in disproportionate impact--Village of Arlington Heights v. Metropolitan Housing Development Corp.,** 429 U.S. 252 (1977).

Village of Arlington Heights v. Metropolitan Housing Development Corp.

a)   **Facts.** Metropolitan Housing Development Corp. (P) applied to the village of Arlington Heights (D) for rezoning in order to build units for low-income tenants, many of whom would be racial minorities. When D denied the application, P sued, claiming the denial was racially discriminatory. The district court found for D, but the court of appeals reversed. D appeals.

b) **Issue.** Does the Constitution prohibit a denial of a zoning change request when the denial impacts disproportionately on certain racial groups but was made pursuant to standard procedures?

c) **Held.** No. Judgment reversed.

(1) The *Davis* case reaffirmed the requirement that governmental action having a racially disproportionate impact also have a discriminatory purpose in order to justify judicial invalidation. However, the challenged action need not rest solely on such a racially discriminatory purpose. It is enough to show that such a purpose was a motivating factor in the decision.

(2) Sensitive inquiry into relevant evidence concerning intent is necessary. Such inquiry here fails to reveal any such intent on D's part. D's zoning plan and policies existed long before P's application, and other proposals, not involving racial minorities, have been rejected in the same manner as P's. Without proof of improper intent, mere showing of disproportionate impact on a racial minority is inadequate to the constitutional question.

Personnel
Administrator
v. Feeney

2) **Disproportionate impact based on sex--Personnel Administrator v. Feeney,** 442 U.S. 256 (1979).

a) **Facts.** Feeney (P), a woman and nonveteran, challenged a Massachusetts statute that gave veterans an "absolute lifetime preference" for consideration for state civil service positions. Veterans with passing scores were automatically ranked above all other candidates. Ninety-eight percent of veterans were male. P claimed that this system discriminated against women and denied P equal protection. The federal court invalidated the law. The Personnel Administrator of Massachusetts (D) appeals.

b) **Issue.** Does a veteran's preference program which does not specifically favor males, but in reality benefits males almost exclusively, deny equal protection to women?

c) **Held.** No. Judgment reversed.

(1) Although a neutral law may have a disparate impact upon a group, the fourteenth amendment guarantees equal laws, not equal results. Thus, a two-part inquiry is needed. First, is the classification really neutral, i.e., not gender-based? If so, does the adverse effect on the group reflect invidious discrimination? If so, the law

is invalid, because purposeful discrimination is the condition that offends the Constitution.

(2) The statute is neutral on its face. Many men are non-veterans and are thus also excluded from preference. And some women are veterans. The distinction is clearly between veterans and nonveterans, not between men and women.

(3) Although the legislature was certainly aware that most veterans are male, "discriminatory purpose" implies more than intent as awareness of consequences. It implies action taken "because of," not merely "in spite of," its effect. Nothing indicates that the legislature acted in order to prevent women from getting these jobs. Instead, the record shows a valid interest in assisting veterans.

d) Concurring (Stevens, White, JJ.). The number of males disadvantaged is sufficiently large to refute P's claim.

e) Dissenting (Marshall, Brennan, JJ.). Because of the disproportionate impact, D should have the burden to affirmatively prove that sex-based considerations played no part in the adoption of this scheme.

3) Statistical evidence of disproportionate impact--McCleskey v. Kemp, 481 U.S. 279 (1987).

McCleskey
v. Kemp

a) Facts. McCleskey was sentenced to death after being convicted in Georgia state court of the murder of a white. McCleskey is black. He petitioned for habeas corpus, citing the Baldus study which, through statistical analysis, concluded that defendants who kill whites were 4.3 times more likely to receive the death penalty than defendants who killed blacks. The district court dismissed the petition. The court of appeals affirmed.

b) Issue. Does the Georgia capital punishment statute deny defendants who kill whites equal protection?

c) Held. No. Affirmed.

(1) The Baldus study alone is not enough to prove an equal protection violation. The Court cannot rely solely on statistics to prove discrimination in criminal sentencing, since capital sentencing is fundamentally different from jury selection or Title VII issues. The inferences drawn from the statistics are not as comparable, and, unlike venire selection and Title VII, the prosecutor has no opportunity to rebut the statistics.

(2) Defendant has not shown that the Georgia legislature maintains the capital punishment statute because of the

racially disproportionate impact suggested by the study. The discretion used in sentencing is critical to the criminal justice system. Lack of predictability does not warrant condemnation of discretion. The risk of racial bias is not significant due to safeguards already in place and the benefits of discretion to defendants. The legislature should determine the appropriate punishment for crimes.

> **d)** **Dissenting** (Brennan, Marshall, Blackmun, and Stevens, JJ.). Georgia has a long history of distinguishing between crimes committed by blacks and whites. Racial bias is antithetical to the justice system. Allowing criminal sentencing to be solely in the legislature's province would disrupt the separation of powers. The Constitution directs the judiciary to protect the voice of the minority, which may not be heard if left to majoritarian rule.

> **e)** **Dissenting** (Stevens, J.). Georgia should narrow the class of defendants eligible for the death penalty to crimes where the death penalty is consistently sought and imposed without regard to race.

3. Facially Neutral, Race-Based Classifications.

> **a.** **Introduction.** A statute may provide for racial classifications and yet not, on its face, disadvantage members of any particular classification. Such statutes have the potential to authorize or encourage actual discrimination, however.

> **b.** **Equal application to all races.** An early case, *Pace v. Alabama*, 106 U.S. 583 (1883), upheld a theory of "equal application," whereby a statute that created racial classes was upheld as long as it applied to all races equally.

Loving v.
Virginia

> **c.** **More than equal application required--Loving v. Virginia**, 388 U.S. 1 (1967).

> > **1)** **Facts.** Loving (D), a white man, married a black woman in violation of a Virginia (P) antimiscegenation statute. D was convicted. The state courts upheld the conviction. D appeals.

> > **2)** **Issue.** May a state prevent marriages between persons solely because they are of different races?

> > **3)** **Held.** No. Judgment reversed.

> > > **a)** The state claims that equal protection is afforded when any penalties due to interracial elements of an offense are applied equally to members of both

races. However, equal protection means more than mere "equal application."

b) Courts must consider whether statutory classifications constitute arbitrary and invidious discrimination. Racial classifications, especially in criminal statutes, are subject to the most rigid scrutiny and must be essential to the accomplishment of some permissible state objective to be permitted.

c) The state has failed to show any legitimate overriding purpose for the distinction between one-race and interracial marriages other than invidious racial discrimination, and the statute cannot be upheld.

4) **Concurring** (Stewart, J.). A state law that makes the criminality of an act depend on the race of the actor cannot be constitutional.

d. **Repeal of remedies for de facto segregation.** Significant public discontent with the various remedies for de facto segregation resulted in attempts to repeal such remedies.

1) **Restructuring the political process to eliminate busing--Washington v. Seattle School District No. 1, 458 U.S. 457 (1982).**

Washington v. Seattle School District No. 1

a) **Facts.** Seattle School District No. 1 (P) implemented several busing plans to eliminate segregation in the schools. In response, the voters of the state adopted Initiative 350, which precluded school boards from busing students farther than the geographically closest school to their places of residence. The initiative set forth several exceptions, but the only exception for racial purposes was in response to a court order. P sued the State of Washington (D) to have the initiative declared invalid. The courts held for P, and D appeals.

b) **Issue.** May a state redefine its governmental decision-making structure for racial purposes?

c) **Held.** No. Judgment affirmed.

(1) A law that structures political institutions according to neutral principles is not subject to equal protection attack even if it makes it more difficult for minorities to achieve favorable legislation because it applies equally to every group. But if the political structuring is based on racial considerations, it denies equal protection because it places a special burden on racial minorities.

(2) Although Initiative 350 is facially neutral, it clearly was aimed at racial busing. It restructures the political process by requiring those who seek

elimination of de facto school segregation to seek relief from the state legislature or the statewide electorate. Persons seeking busing for other reasons do not have such a high hurdle.

d) **Dissenting** (Powell, J., Burger, C.J., Rehnquist, O'Connor, JJ.). A school is not required to implement a busing program for racial integration when there is no constitutional violation. The majority holds that a local school district could adopt a neighborhood school policy, but that a state cannot. This theory of a vested constitutional right to local decision making is unprecedented. The effect of the majority's rule is that neither the legislature nor the people can alter the decision of a local school district, thus allowing the school district to forever preempt the state.

Crawford v.
Los Angeles
Board of
Education

2) **Constitutional amendment--Crawford v. Los Angeles Board of Education,** 458 U.S. 527 (1982).

a) **Facts.** The California Supreme Court held that the state constitution required state school boards to alleviate both de facto and de jure segregation. Three years later, the voters ratified Proposition 1, which amended the constitution to permit state courts to order busing only where federal courts could do so under the fourteenth amendment. The California courts rejected Crawford's (P's) challenge of the proposition, and the Supreme Court granted certiorari.

b) **Issue.** After a state grants its courts broader authority than is required by federal law to order busing to stop discrimination, may it then limit such power to the requirements of federal law?

c) **Held.** Yes. Judgment affirmed.

(1) California could not have violated the Equal Protection Clause by simply adopting it as its own. Besides, the school districts still have a duty to desegregate on their own, and they can adopt busing plans to do so.

(2) Proposition 1 does not use racial classifications; it is racially neutral. The fact that California at one time exceeded the federal requirement does not prevent it from returning to the generally prevailing standard. There is no reason to conclude that the voters acted for a discriminatory purpose.

d) **Concurring** (Blackmun, Brennan, JJ.). This case did not involve a distortion of the political process. The rights enforced by the courts originate elsewhere, as in state laws and constitutions. Repeal of a statute or a constitutional provision does not change the structure of the political process; it just repeals the rights to invoke a judicial busing remedy.

e)   **Dissenting** (Marshall, J.). This case is not different from an attempt to remove authority from local school boards.

4.   Affirmative Action.

a.   **Introduction.** Attempts to remedy adverse effects of past discrimination have resulted in various means such as affirmative action, quotas, and minority preferences which in effect discriminate in favor of minorities. Such means do not violate equal protection if they fall within certain constitutional parameters.

b.   **Special state school admissions program for minorities--Regents of the University of California v. Bakke,** 438 U.S. 265 (1978).

Regents of the University of California v. Bakke

1)   **Facts.** Bakke (P) was denied admission to the medical school of the University of California at Davis for two consecutive years. The Regents of the University of California (Ds) maintained both a regular admissions system and a special admissions program intended to assist disadvantaged minorities in getting admitted. P claimed that because he was white, he was denied consideration for the places reserved for minorities in the special program, denying him equal protection and violating Title VI of the 1964 Civil Rights Act. The California Supreme Court altered lower decisions and found that Ds' admissions program was illegal, that P must be admitted to the medical school, and that Ds may not accord any consideration to race in the admissions process. Ds appeal.

2)   **Issue.** May a state school use race as a factor in its admissions process?

3)   **Held.** Yes. Judgment affirmed in part and reversed in part.

a)   Title VI of the Civil Rights Act of 1964 must be held to proscribe only those racial classifications that would violate the Equal Protection Clause of the fifth amendment.

b)   Ds claim that since their procedure does not disadvantage minorities, it should not be subject to strict judicial review. However, Ds do disadvantage a specific race—whites. Equal protection requires that racial and ethnic distinctions of any sort be examined by the most exacting judicial scrutiny. It is incorrect to assert that the fourteenth amendment justifies "benign" preference for one race over another due to past discrimination, since its language is inconsistent with such an

interpretation, and the kind of variable sociological and political analysis necessary to produce and enforce such rank-
ings is beyond judicial competence. Such an interpretation
would be manifestly unjust. The Court has approved preferential classifications in some instances (school desegregation,
employment discrimination), but only after proof of constitutional or statutory violations, absent here, and only when the
remedy was closely related to the violation.

c)   The use of a suspect classification may be justified if the
state can show that its purpose or interest is both constitutionally permissible and substantial, and that its use of the
classification is necessary to the accomplishment of its purpose or the safeguarding of its interest. Ds' reasons for
using their special admissions process are inadequate under
this standard. Although Ds do have a valid interest in seeking diversity among the student body, their program, focusing
as it does solely on ethnic diversity, hinders rather than
promotes genuine diversity. An admissions process seeking
diversity may properly consider race as one of many characteristics of an applicant that are compared with those of all
other applicants to decide who is to be admitted, such as the
procedure used at Harvard. But reservation of a fixed number of seats to a minority group unnecessarily denies other
persons an equal chance to be considered, and is therefore
unconstitutional.

d)   The California court's judgment that Ds' special admission
program is unlawful and that P must be admitted is affirmed.
Its judgment that Ds be enjoined from any consideration of
race in their admissions process is reversed.

4)   **Concurring and dissenting** (Brennan, White, Marshall, Blackmun,
JJ.).

a)   The central meaning of the decision is that government may
take race into account when it acts not to demean or insult
any racial group but to remedy disadvantages caused by past
discrimination, when supported by appropriate findings.

b)   Ds' affirmative action program is constitutional. Congress
has enacted legislation under Title VI incorporating racial
quotas. Prior decisions of this Court suggest that remedial
use of race is permissible. Ds' goal of admitting minority
students disadvantaged by the effects of past discrimination
is sufficiently important to justify use of race-conscious
admissions criteria. Ds ought not be forced to abandon their
reasonable and effective procedure.

5)   **Concurring and dissenting** (Blackmun, J.). Ds' program is not so
different from Harvard's that it should be declared unconstitutional.

6) **Concurring and dissenting** (Stevens, Stewart, Rehnquist, JJ., Burger, C.J.). The California court judgment should be affirmed in its entirety based on the plain language of Title VI of the Civil Rights Act, which specifies that "No person . . . on the ground of race, color, or national origin, be excluded from participation in . . . any program . . . receiving federal assistance." There is no need to reach the constitutional issues.

c. **Public contracts--Fullilove v. Klutznick,** 448 U.S. 448 (1980).

Fullilove v. Klutznick

1) **Facts.** Congress enacted a statute that required that federal grants made by the Secretary of Commerce, Klutznick (D), to local governments for local public work projects be awarded only to applicants who assure that at least 10% of the grant will be spent for minority business enterprises. Fullilove (P), a nonminority contractor, alleged economic injury and sought injunctive relief. The district court denied relief, and the court of appeals affirmed, upholding the statute. P appeals.

2) **Issue.** May Congress affirmatively require a minimum minority participation as a condition of the expenditure of federal funds?

3) **Held.** Yes. Judgment affirmed.

    a) A program involving racial or ethnic criteria requires close examination, but Congress deserves appropriate deference, even where the legislation implicates fundamental constitutional rights.

    b) The objective of the legislation—to prohibit traditional procurement practices that perpetuate the effects of prior discrimination—is within the constitutional scope of congressional power. It primarily regulates state action in the use of federal funds.

    c) The means used, involving as they do racial criteria, must be narrowly tailored to achievement of the permissible objectives. Congress, of all parts of government, possesses the broadest remedial powers. This program is clearly remedial; its adverse effect on P is incidental. The administrative scheme, containing provisions for waiver, provides reasonable assurance that the application of racial criteria will be limited to accomplishing the proper objectives.

    d) Congressional legislation represents the culmination of the central purpose of our system—peaceful compromise of opposing viewpoints. Courts must hesitate before unraveling the results of this process, which would remove one of our defenses against domestic disorder and violence.

4) **Concurring** (Powell, J.). The statute uses a racial classification, which is unconstitutional unless necessary to advance a compelling governmental interest. Such an interest is present here, and the statute passes the *Bakke* test.

5) **Concurring** (Marshall, Brennan, Blackmun, JJ.). Racial classifications are prohibited if irrelevant; this statute is substantially related to achievement of important governmental objectives and is therefore constitutional. The question is not even close.

6) **Dissenting** (Stewart, Rehnquist, JJ.). The United States Constitution absolutely prohibits invidious discrimination by government. P is injured solely because of the color of his skin. The Court's decision is wrong for the same reason *Plessy v. Ferguson* was wrong. Congress is not a court of equity; even if it had remedial powers, it could only act to eradicate the actual effects of illegal race discrimination. Here, it clearly goes too far.

7) **Dissenting** (Stevens, J.). Grants of privileges based on characteristics acquired at birth cannot be justified by a government constrained to rule impartially. A classwide recovery for past wrong might be justified, but Congress here makes no attempt to correlate the classifications with the justification. Members of the class have suffered different wrongs. Additionally, the statute works to benefit those class members least in need of recovery. The statute perpetrates, even emphasizes, racial distinctions. The deference accorded the statute is unjustified by the perfunctory consideration of important issues on which Congress based its decisions.

City of Richmond v. J.A. Croson Co.

d. **Rejection of state and local set-aside programs absent evidence of direct discrimination--City of Richmond v. J.A. Croson Co.**, 488 U.S. 469 (1989).

1) **Facts.** Citing the authority of the *Fullilove* opinion, the City of Richmond (P) required prime contractors on city projects to set aside at least 30% of their subcontracts to minority business enterprises, using the *Fullilove* definition of minority group members. The program was adopted based on evidence that minority businesses had received a significantly lower percentage of contracts (.67%) than the percentage of minorities living in the city (50%). However, there was no evidence of racial discrimination on P's part or on the part of any of P's prime contractors. P brought suit against J.A. Croson Co. (D) to enforce the rule. The district court found for P. The court of appeals reversed. P appeals.

2) **Issue.** May a city adopt a set-aside program favoring minority-owned contractors on city projects when there is no evidence of direct discrimination on the part of the city or its prime contractors?

3)   Held. No. Judgment affirmed.

a)   P notes that under *Fullilove*, Congress was not required to make specific findings of discrimination to engage in race-conscious relief. P asserts that if the federal government could do this, a city such as P can as well. However, unlike the states and their subdivisions, such as P, Congress has a specific constitutional mandate to enforce the fourteenth amendment.

b)   To enable states to use racial classifications merely by reciting a benign or compensatory purpose would be to give them the full power of Congress under section 5 of the fourteenth amendment, and to insulate their actions from judicial scrutiny under section 1. However, the objective of the fourteenth amendment was to limit the states' use of race as a criterion for legislative action and to empower the federal courts to enforce those limitations.

c)   Under the Equal Protection Clause, a state or its subdivisions may eradicate the effects of private discrimination within its own legislative jurisdiction, but this requires that the discrimination be identified with the particularity required by the fourteenth amendment. P would have to show it had become a "passive participant" in a system of racial exclusion practiced by elements of the local construction industry, but it failed to do so.

d)   The Equal Protection Clause protects individual persons; P's plan denied certain citizens the opportunity to compete for a fixed percentage of public contracts based solely on their race, and thereby implicates the personal rights of the excluded persons. Such race-based regulations are subject to strict scrutiny, regardless of the race of those burdened or benefited by the classification. [Wygant v. Jackson Board of Education, 476 U.S. 267 (1986)]

e)   P's factual predicate for its plan consists of a generalized assertion that there has been past discrimination in the "construction industry," attributable to a series of racial as well as nonracial factors. P can do no more than speculate as to how many minority firms would exist absent past discrimination. It cannot show how many minority members are qualified to act as contractors, or how many minority members are eligible for membership in contractors' associations. All P can show is that minority businesses received less than 1% of prime contracts, even though its minority population is 50%, but statistical generalizations cannot substitute for evidence of discrimination. Permitting a racial classification on such generalizations would enable local governments to create a patchwork of racial preferences without ascertainable limit on size or duration.

f)   P's plan covers Spanish-speaking, Oriental, Indian, Eskimo and Aleut persons, against whom there is no evidence of discrimination in P's construction industry. This suggests that P's purpose was not to remedy past discrimination.

g)   A court cannot assess whether P's plan is narrowly tailored to remedy prior discrimination because it is not linked to identified discrimination. There is no indication that P considered race-neutral means to increase minority participation in the construction industry. The quota's only goal appears to be racial balancing. But unlike the plan upheld in *Fullilove*, P's plan does not provide for a waiver of the set-aside provision where the minority contractor's higher price was not attributable to the effects of past discrimination. P evaluates bids on a case-by-case basis, and can investigate the need for remedial action in particular cases as appropriate; P cannot use broad statistical requirements simply to minimize the administrative burdens of remedying specific prior discrimination.

4)   **Concurring** (Stevens, J.). Unlike the plan in *Wygant* that was intended to improve education by assuring an integrated faculty, P's plan has no objective to increase efficient performance of its construction contracts. P's plan was formulated by a legislative body, instead of a court which is better equipped to identify past wrongdoers and to fashion appropriate remedies. P's plan does not address the specific characteristics of the racial groups involved; it relies merely on a stereotypical analysis that cannot be condoned under the Equal Protection Clause.

5)   **Concurring** (Scalia, J.). There are no situations in which state and local governments may discriminate on the basis of race (except a social emergency, such as a prison race riot, or when necessary to undo the effects of their own unlawful racial classifications), because a solution to past discrimination that consists of aggravating present discrimination is no solution. The federal government is uniquely capable of dealing with past racial discrimination because racial discrimination finds more ready expression at the state and local levels than it does at the federal level. P's plan is an example of local racial classification; it directly benefits the dominant political group, which is also the dominant racial group. P is free to give a contracting preference to identified victims of discrimination, but this could apply to whites as well as blacks; it would be race-neutral. Remedies must address discrimination against individuals; a past injustice to a black man cannot be compensated for by discriminating against a white man.

6)   **Dissenting** (Marshall, Brennan, Blackmun, JJ.). P's plan was patterned after, and is indistinguishable from the *Fullilove* plan. The majority is unpersuaded by P's factual findings, but it should not second-guess the judgment of the former capital of the Confederacy, which found that its local construction industry did not devi-

ate from the national pattern Congress found as set forth in *Fullilove*. P has a compelling interest other than remedying past discrimination; it has an interest in preventing its own spending decision from furthering racial discrimination. P's plan is substantially related to these interests and is appropriately limited to five years in duration, has a waiver provision, and has a minimal impact on innocent third parties, since it only affects 3% of overall contracting in P's area. The majority also for the first time introduces strict scrutiny of race conscious remedial remedies as if racial discrimination and its vestiges have been eradicated in the United States. It also imposes a difficult factual standard of proof of a prima facie case of a constitutional or statutory violation before states and localities can act to remedy racial discrimination. This decision marks a full-scale retreat from the Court's longstanding solicitude to race-conscious remedial efforts.

7) **Comment.** The plurality, which stated that race-based regulations are subject to strict scrutiny in all cases, noted that while Justice Marshall's approach would apply a relaxed standard of review to race-conscious classifications designed to further remedial goals, in this case the majority of P's city council, and about half of P's population, were black. Under this view, if the level of scrutiny varied according to the ability of different groups to defend their interests in the representative process, the plurality argued that heightened scrutiny would be appropriate in this case, because the classification was to the advantage of the racial group that had a political majority. Justice Marshall noted that numerical inferiority is but one of several factors to be considered.

e. **Congressional authority to order remedial programs.** *Metro Broadcasting, Inc. v. Federal Communications Commission*, 110 S. Ct. 2997 (1990), involved FCC policies for granting broadcast licenses. Minority ownership both constituted a positive factor in deciding whether to grant an applicant a license, and qualified for an exception to the general rule against receiving an assignment of a license that is being challenged before the FCC. The policies were not justified as remedial compensation to victims of past discrimination, but merely reflected the fact that minorities were inadequately represented in broadcasting. The Court, in a 5 to 4 decision, upheld the policies as having been approved by Congress and having met the requirement of serving important governmental objectives and being substantially related to the achievement of those objectives. Congress could adopt a policy of minority ownership as a means of achieving greater programming diversity. The dissent argued that the government may not allocate benefits and burdens among individuals based on the assumption that race determines how they think, and that the majority wrongly departed from the traditional requirement that racial classifications may be used only if necessary and narrowly tailored to achieve a compelling result.

E. SEX CLASSIFICATIONS

1. **Introduction.** Although early decisions dealt with sex-based classifications under the traditional equal protection tests, more recent cases have judged sex-based classifications under a higher standard, but not so high a test as would apply to the inherently suspect classes. The Court declined to make sex a suspect classification in *Reed v. Reed*, 404 U.S. 71 (1971). However, it did hold that a state could not prefer men over women in appointing estate administrators simply to reduce the work load of probate courts. *Reed* was the first decision to hold that sex discrimination violated the Equal Protection Clause and was based on the arbitrary nature of the legislative choice favoring men.

2. **Development of the Intermediate Standard.** As late as 1961, the Court based a decision that generally excluded women from jury duty on the role of the woman as the center of home and family life. [Hoyt v. Florida, 368 U.S. 57 (1961)] After *Reed*, the Court began developing an intermediate standard of review for sex classifications.

Frontiero v. Richardson

    a. **Military benefits--Frontiero v. Richardson,** 411 U.S. 677 (1973).

        1) **Facts.** Frontiero (P), a woman officer in the Air Force, sought to claim her husband as a "dependent" in order to receive the additional benefits attached to such a claim. Male members of the armed forces could claim wives as dependents without any showing, but women in the service had to show that their spouses were actually dependent on them for over one-half of their support. P claimed that the distinctions violated the Due Process Clause. The district court upheld the statutes making the distinction. P appeals.

        2) **Issue.** May the military require that servicewomen but not servicemen make a showing that their spouses are actually dependent before claiming them as "dependents"?

        3) **Held.** No. Judgment reversed.

            a) Classifications based upon sex are included among those that are inherently suspect and therefore subject to close judicial scrutiny.

            b) This statute cannot withstand such scrutiny. Its sole justification lies in administrative convenience, which, though important in some circumstances, is hardly a significant governmental interest closely and reasonably related to the classification. The statutes involve arbitrary discrimination and deny due process.

4) **Concurring** (Powell, J., Burger, C.J., Blackmun, J.). The statutes are unconstitutional under *Reed*. There is no need to go further and characterize sex as a suspect classification. To do so unnecessarily preempts the prescribed constitutional processes of amending the Constitution, which at this time are being utilized on this very issue in the guise of the Equal Rights Amendment.

b. **Widows' tax benefits.** In *Kahn v. Shevin*, 416 U.S. 351 (1974), the Court upheld a property tax exemption for widows that did not apply to widowers. The law was reasonably designed to assist the sex for whom the loss of a spouse is a disproportionately heavy burden. The classification was not a mere administrative convenience as in *Frontiero*.

c. **Military career regulations.** The Court upheld a federal law that gave women more time to get promoted in the Navy because of the restricted sea and combat duty available to women. [Schlesinger v. Ballard, 419 U.S. 498 (1975)]

d. **Social security survivors' benefits.** The Court struck down a provision in the Social Security Act that granted "survivors' benefits" to widows, but not widowers, while they care for minor children of the deceased wage earner. The disqualification of widowers was held "irrational," since the purpose of the benefits was to enable the surviving parent to stay at home and care for the children. The classification thus discriminated against the children based on the gender of the surviving parent. [Weinberger v. Wiesenfeld, 420 U.S. 636 (1975)]

e. **Classifications favoring women--Craig v. Boren,** 429 U.S. 190 (1976).

Craig v.
Boren

1) **Facts.** Craig (P), a male, challenged an Oklahoma statute that denied beer sales to males under 21 and females under 18. The three-judge district court dismissed P's action. P appeals.

2) **Issue.** May a state properly impose gender-based differentials in regulating sales of alcoholic drinks?

3) **Held.** No. Judgment reversed.

a) To withstand constitutional challenge, classifications by gender must serve important governmental objectives and must be substantially related to the achievement of those objectives. The state objective here—enhancement of traffic safety—is clearly important. However, the relation between this objective and the challenged statute is based on statistical evidence fraught with shortcomings and is inadequate to show that sex represents a legitimate, accurate proxy for the regulation of drinking and driving.

   b) Failure to show a substantial relation between the gender-based classification and achievement of the state's objectives requires that the statute be invalidated as unconstitutional. The operation of the twenty-first amendment, limited as it is when applied outside Commerce Clause issues, does not alter application of the equal protection standards that govern here.

4) **Concurring** (Powell, J.). The Court has added confusion to the appropriate standard for equal protection analysis. The statistics do tend to support the state's view but are inadequate to support the classification.

5) **Concurring** (Stevens, J.). The classification here is not totally irrational, but it is unacceptable because it has little relation to traffic safety. It prohibits only sales of beer, not consumption, which is the real threat to traffic. The law punishes all males for the abuses of only 2% of their class.

6) **Dissenting** (Rehnquist, J.).

   a) Men challenging a gender-based statute unfavorable to themselves should not be able to invoke a more stringent standard of review than normally pertains to most other types of classifications, since men, as a group, have not suffered the type of prior discrimination that has always supported a standard of special scrutiny. Nor is the interest involved here—beer purchasing—"fundamental" in the constitutional sense of invoking strict scrutiny.

   b) The Court has added a new standard to the norm of "rational basis" and the "compelling state interest" required where a "suspect classification" is involved—that of the "important governmental objectives" and "substantial relation to achievement of those objectives." This new standard is unnecessary and invites judicial confusion and interference into the proper roles of the legislature.

   c) The correct standard here is the rational basis test, under which a classification is invalid only if it rests on grounds wholly irrelevant to the achievement of the state's objective. The state has provided sufficient evidence to show a rational basis, and the statute should be upheld.

3. **Real Differences vs. Generalizations.** Some sex-based classifications are based on generalizations derived from long-held percep-

tions about the respective roles of men and women. Others are based on the objective differences between men and women. The Court has distinguished between the two types of classifications.

a. **Statutory rape--Michael M. v. Superior Court,** 450 U.S. 464 (1981).

>   1) **Facts.** California's statutory rape law makes men alone criminally liable for the act of sexual intercourse with a female under age 18. Michael M. (D), age 17½, was prosecuted under the statute and challenged it as an unlawful discrimination on the basis of gender. The California Supreme Court upheld the law, and D appeals.

>   2) **Issue.** May a state's statutory rape law permit prosecution only against members of one sex?

>   3) **Held.** Yes. Judgment affirmed.

>>   a) A legislature may not make overbroad generalizations based on sex that are entirely unrelated to any differences between men and women or that demean the ability or social status of the affected class. However, legislation may realistically reflect the fact that the sexes are not similarly situated in certain circumstances.

>>   b) The asserted purpose of the statute is to prevent illegitimate pregnancy and its attendant social harms, a valid state purpose. The question is whether a state may attack the problem directly by prohibiting a male from having sexual intercourse with a minor female. We hold that such a statute is sufficiently related to the state's objectives to pass constitutional muster.

>>   c) D claims that the statute is underinclusive since a gender-neutral statute would serve the state's goal equally well. We do not sit to redraw constitutionally permissible lines, and even if we were so inclined we cannot say that a gender-neutral statute, attended by increased enforcement difficulties, would be equally effective.

>   4) **Dissenting** (Brennan, White, Marshall, JJ.). While the desirability of achieving the state's asserted statutory goal is unquestionable, this statute is not substantially related to success. California has failed to prove that its gender-based law is more successful than would be a gender-neutral law.

>   5) **Dissenting** (Stevens, J.). The validity of a total ban is not an adequate justification for a selective prohibition. A rule that authorizes punishment of only one of two equally guilty wrongdoers violates the essence of the constitutional requirement that the sovereign must govern impartially.

Rostker v.
Goldberg

b. **Draft registration--Rostker v. Goldberg, 453 U.S. 57 (1981).**

    1) **Facts.** The Military Selective Service Act permitted the registration and conscription only of men. A lawsuit initiated earlier by Goldberg (P), challenging the draft as improperly gender-based, was revived, and the district court held the Act unconstitutional.

    2) **Issue.** May Congress restrict draft registration to males?

    3) **Held.** Yes. Judgment reversed.

        a) Congress specifically considered the constitutionality of the Act and explicitly relied on its "broad constitutional power" to raise and regulate armies and navies. Thus, the courts must decide whether Congress has transgressed an explicit guarantee of individual rights which limits the specific authority relied on.

        b) Congress determined that the purpose of registration was to prepare for a draft of combat troops. Women are not eligible for combat. Thus, the exemption of women from registration is not only sufficiently but also closely related to Congress's purpose in authorizing registration. Because men and women are not similarly situated with respect to combat, the classification challenged does not violate the Constitution.

    4) **Dissenting** (White, Brennan, JJ.). There is no indication that Congress itself concluded that every position filled by an eventual draft must be filled with combat-ready men. While a gender-based classification might be permissible to fill all exclusively combat positions, it cannot be used to fill noncombat positions.

    5) **Dissenting** (Marshall, Brennan, JJ.). This statute excludes women from a fundamental civic obligation. It is not a conscription statute, as the majority seems to believe, but merely a registration statute. D has failed to carry its burden of showing that completely excluding women advances important governmental objectives.

4. **Discrimination Against Men.**

    a. **Proof of dependency requirement.** In *Califano v. Goldfarb*, 430 U.S. 199 (1977), the plurality held that *Wiesenfeld* applied to a requirement that a widower, but not a widow, must prove dependency on the deceased spouse in order to collect benefits. The differential treatment resulted not from a deliberate congressional intention to remedy the greater needs of widows, but rather from an intention to aid the dependent spouses of deceased wage earners, coupled with a presumption that wives are usually dependent. Such assumptions were not sufficient to justify the gender-based discrimination and so the requirement was struck down. The dissent distinguished *Wiesenfeld* on the grounds that the statute did not totally foreclose widowers and that favoring aged widows was not invidious discrimination. The only effect was to make it easier for widows to obtain benefits than it was for widowers, but this did not perpetuate the economic disadvantage that led the Court to apply heightened scrutiny to gender-based discrimination. The rule was actually overinclusive, not exclusive of a particular group.

b. **Calculation of Social Security benefits--Califano v. Webster**, 430 U.S. 313 (1977).

Califano v. Webster

1) Facts. Webster (P), an old-age Social Security insurance benefits recipient, challenged the statutory scheme for computing those benefits. The scheme effectively gave women fewer elapsed years from which to exclude lower earnings years in order to increase the average monthly wage. As a result, women generally were able to compute a higher average monthly wage than similarly situated men. A lower court held the scheme unconstitutionally discriminatory. Califano (D), Secretary of Health, Education, and Welfare, appeals.

2) Issue. May Congress discriminate between men and women in order to compensate women for adverse past discrimination?

3) Held. Yes. Judgment reversed.

a) Reduction of the disparity in economic condition between men and women caused by the long history of discrimination against women has been recognized as an important governmental objective.

b) This scheme is substantially related to achievement of that proper objective. The level of benefits is directly related to the level of past earnings. If women's past earnings were comparatively low because of discrimination, it is proper to correspondingly increase their benefits.

F. SPECIAL SCRUTINY FOR OTHER CLASSIFICATIONS

1. Introduction. Because racial discrimination prompted adoption of the fourteenth amendment, racial classifications are clearly "suspect," meaning that they invite the strictest judicial scrutiny. The fourteenth amendment was not phrased solely in terms of race, however. Other classifications may invite heightened scrutiny not reaching the strictest levels. Common to most of these classifications are the following characteristics: historical lack of political power; history of discrimination; immutability of the basis for classification; irrelevance to performance; and obviousness (the basis for classification acts as a badge).

2. **Alienage.**

   a. **Introduction.** Under the Constitution, Congress has plenary power over admission or exclusion of aliens, so the courts normally defer to federal law even when it draws distinctions based on alienage. State laws discriminating against aliens once admitted are inherently suspect, however. Most such laws are not upheld. The only significant exception permits such discrimination in situations involving state government functions. For example, a state may categorically exclude aliens from its police force [Foley v. Connelie, 435 U.S. 291 (1978)], but it cannot make citizenship a requirement for the practice of law [*In re* Griffiths, 413 U.S. 717 (1973)].

Sugarman
v. Dougall

   b. **General exclusion from state government--Sugarman v. Dougall,** 413 U.S. 634 (1973).

      1) **Facts.** The state of New York refused to accept aliens as civil servants, from menial labor jobs to policy-making positions. The exclusion did not extend to higher executive or elective positions, however. Sugarman (P) challenged the statute. The district court held the state statute unconstitutional. Dougall (D) appeals.

      2) **Issue.** May a state prohibit all aliens from all competitive state civil service positions?

      3) **Held.** No. Judgment affirmed.

         a) The issue in this case does not involve any particular alien or any particular basis for a refusal of employment; it is only a general question of a flat prohibition on all aliens. Aliens are clearly entitled to equal protection under the law.

         b) The State claims that its generic classification based on alienage is justified because of the identity between a government and its citizens, and the need for undivided loyalty in civil servants. The problem with this assertion is that the prohibition extends to jobs that have no relation to the state's interest in loyalty, yet does not cover high-level jobs where the state's interest is greatest. Equal protection requires greater precision than this.

c)　　When properly and carefully formulated, a state may adopt guidelines requiring citizenship as a condition of employment for certain positions, especially those that include direct participation in the creation, execution, or review of public policy. The statute challenged by P here is not sufficiently precise.

4)　　**Dissenting** (Rehnquist, J.). P and the other aliens could have become citizens if they wanted to, so there is no reason to apply strict scrutiny to the classification. Nor does anything in the Equal Protection Clause justify the treatment of alienage as a "suspect classification."

VII. IMPLIED FUNDAMENTAL RIGHTS

A. MEANING OF DUE PROCESS

The fourteenth amendment Due Process Clause prevents any state from depriving any person of life, liberty, or property without "due process" of law. The effect of this clause on economic regulation has been discussed *supra*. Today, however, the clause is probably most meaningful as a protection of individual rights. The scope of the clause in this area has changed greatly in recent years.

B. PRIVILEGES AND IMMUNITIES

1. Fourteenth Amendment Considerations.

a. Substantive due process under the fourteenth amendment. The concept of due process under the fifth amendment merely assured fair legal procedures. It applied only to the federal government. The fourteenth amendment Due Process Clause specifically prevents any state from depriving any person of life, liberty, or property without due process of law. Of course, the fourteenth amendment was adopted to prevent racial discrimination. However, the broad language used encouraged lawyers to try using it as a restriction on state regulation of business, not merely to attack the procedures used, but also to attack the substantive fairness of the regulations.

The
Slaughter-
House Cases

b. First look at the Civil War amendments--The Slaughter-House Cases, 83 U.S. (16 Wall.) 36 (1873).

1) **Facts.** The state of Louisiana granted a state corporation the exclusive right to operate facilities in New Orleans for the landing, keeping, and slaughter of livestock. The Butchers' Benevolent Association (Ps), a group of excluded butchers, sought an injunction against the monopoly on the grounds that they were prevented from practicing their trade unless they worked at the monopolist corporation and paid its fees. The state courts upheld the law. Ps appeal, based on four main grounds: (i) that the statute creates an involuntary servitude forbidden by the thirteenth amendment; (ii) that it abridges the privileges and immunities of citizens of the United States; (iii) that it denies Ps the equal protection of the laws; and (iv) that it deprives them of their property without due process of law, all under the fourteenth amendment.

2) **Issue.** Do the Civil War amendments grant United States citizens broad protection against the actions of state governments?

3) **Held.** No. Judgment affirmed.

    a) The proper interpretation of the Civil War amendments must reflect their historical setting. Thus, the meaning of "involuntary servitude" as used in the thirteenth amendment is restricted to personal servitude, not a servitude attached to property as Ps claim.

    b) The fourteenth amendment clearly distinguishes between citizenship of the states and citizenship of the United States. Only those privileges and immunities of United States citizens are protected by the fourteenth amendment. Privileges and immunities of state citizens upon which Ps rely here are unaffected, and rest for their security and protection in the power of the several states as recognized in article IV. The Constitution does not control the power of the state governments over the rights of their own citizens except to require that a state grant equal rights to its own citizens and citizens of other states within its jurisdiction. Therefore, Ps, as citizens of the United States, have no privilege or immunity that has been infringed by the state law.

    c) The Equal Protection Clause of the fourteenth amendment is intended primarily to prevent state discrimination against blacks, although Congress may extend its scope to other areas. But Ps have not claimed a denial of equal justice in the state courts and therefore have no reason to have a remedy under the Equal Protection Clause.

    d) The restraint imposed by Louisiana upon the exercise of Ps' trade simply cannot be held to be a deprivation of property within the meaning of the fourteenth amendment. That clause should not be construed to cover such state restraint upon trade.

4) **Dissenting** (Field, J., Chase, C.J., Swayne, Bradley, JJ.). These amendments were intended to protect the citizens of the United States against the deprivation of their common rights by state legislation. The majority holding as to the Privileges and Immunities Clause would add no more protection than existed prior to adoption of the amendment, making it meaningless. A distinguishing privilege of citizens of the United States is equality of right to the lawful pursuits of life throughout the whole country. To permit a state to interfere with such a basic privilege is to ignore the true purpose of the fourteenth amendment.

5) **Dissenting** (Bradley, J.). A state infringes personal liberty when it grants a monopoly to individuals or corporations. A law that

prohibits a large class of citizens from pursuing a lawful employment deprives them of liberty as well as property without due process of law. Their occupation is their property, their choice their liberty. The law also deprives them of equal protection.

6) Comment. This case, the first requiring interpretation of these amendments, rendered the Privileges and Immunities Clause ineffective in protecting individual rights against invasion by state governments. Instead, the Court looked to the Due Process and Equal Protection Clauses. Ps in this case were not attacking the procedure used, but the actual fairness of the state-approved monopoly. Although the Court rejected the notion of substantive due process in this case, the scope of the clause was unclear for many years. Gradually the Court began to examine the substantive reasonableness of state legislation.

C. INCORPORATION DOCTRINE

1. Introduction. Whether the Due Process Clause incorporates rights guaranteed at the federal level by the Bill of Rights is an important question. Some commentators and judges argued for total incorporation; i.e., the Bill of Rights should apply fully to state action. Others argued that "due process" includes only "fundamental" principles of liberty. The Supreme Court has consistently held that the fourteenth amendment only incorporates the Bill of Rights on a selective basis, although to date all provisions of the Bill of Rights have been incorporated except the second, third and seventh amendments and the Grand Jury Clause of the fifth amendment. The concept of due process is not limited to the protections in the Bill of Rights, however.

2. Philosophical Limits on Governmental Power. In *Calder v. Bull*, 3 U.S. (3 Dall.) 386 (1798), the Court refused to set aside state legislative action that overrode a judicial probate proceeding.

a. Justice Chase expressed the view that legislative action is limited by the social compact that gave the legislature its power; i.e., courts should be able to appeal to natural rights in making constitutional decisions.

b. Justice Iredell, on the other hand, argued that constitutional limitations were the only restraint on legislative action. There is no reason why the courts should be able to define and apply natural law better than the legislature.

c. The view expressed by Justice Chase is the approach generally taken today, partly by applying concepts of due process.

3. **Bill of Rights not Binding on States--Barron v. Mayor of Baltimore**, 32 U.S. (7 Pet.) 243 (1833).

Barron v.
Mayor of
Baltimore

a. **Facts.** Barron (P) sued the Mayor and City Council of Baltimore (Ds) for permitting street construction that had the effect of depositing silt in front of his wharf, making it inaccessible. P obtained a verdict for $45,000, which was reversed by the state court. P appeals on grounds that his property was not granted proper protection under the fifth amendment (i.e., there was a "taking" without compensation).

b. **Issue.** Does the Bill of Rights accord citizens of the United States protection from state government actions?

c. **Held.** No. Case dismissed.

1) The limitations on government power expressed in the federal Constitution are applicable only to the government created by that instrument. Had the framers intended them to limit the powers of the state governments, they would have expressed that intention.

2) Any limits on state powers can be found only in the respective state constitutions. For this reason the Court has no jurisdiction and must dismiss the case.

d. **Comment.** Although the Court readily presumed that the Bill of Rights did not apply to the states, it could have inferred otherwise from the fact that the language of all the rights is cast in general terms except the first, which specifically applies only to Congress.

4. **State Constitutional Law.** Most state constitutions contain a clause referring to "due process" or the "law of the land." Although these phrases originally were intended to establish a method of legal procedure, lawyers and state judges began to use them as a means of invalidating legislation. For example, in *Wynehamer v. People*, 13 N.Y. 378 (1856), the New York court held a state prohibition statute unconstitutional on due process grounds as applied to liquor already owned when the statute was enacted.

D. SUBSTANTIVE DUE PROCESS

1. **Increased Judicial Intervention in Economic Regulation.**

a. **Development of substantive due process.** As noted above, the state courts were the first to accept arguments in favor of some type of substantive due process. Then, in *Munn v. Illinois*, 94 U.S. (4 Otto) 113 (1876), the Court held that the Due Process Clause does protect private property, but a state may control such property if it is "affected with a public interest," so that a state could set maximum storage charges at central warehouses. Eventually, the Court began to scrutinize the substantive rights affected by legislation because there existed "fundamental rights" which were entitled to judicial protection. For example, in *Allgeyer v. Louisiana*, 165 U.S. 578 (1897), the Court invalidated a state law that prohibited the insuring of Louisiana property by any company not licensed to do business in Louisiana. Allgeyer had insured his property with a New York insurer in violation of the state law. The Court held that this statute deprived Allgeyer of his liberty to contract, without due process of law.

b. **Concept of substantive due process.** With the *Lochner* case that follows, the Court applied the following concepts of due process:

1) **Ends or purposes.** The Court examined the purposes of the legislation, asking whether the object was legitimate, appropriate, or necessary. Did the law promote in some way the health, safety, welfare, or morals of the people? These questions were answered from the language of the statute, the legislative record, and the history behind the passage of the statute. These were considered questions of law for the court.

2) **Means.** The Court also determined whether the means used to accomplish the legislation's purpose were reasonable and appropriate. That is, was there a real and substantial relationship between the means used and the legitimate end?

3) **Effect.** Finally, the Court inquired into the effect of the law on the liberty and property of the parties involved. If the effect was too drastic, then the law violated due process.

Lochner v. New York

c. **Pivotal case--Lochner v. New York,** 198 U.S. 45 (1905).

1) **Facts.** Lochner (D) was convicted of permitting an employee to work for him more than the statutory maximum of 60 hours per week. D appeals, claiming the law violated his freedom to contract under the fourteenth amendment Due Process Clause.

2) **Issue.** May a state generally prohibit private agreements to work more than a specified number of hours?

3) **Held.** No. Judgment reversed.

a) The general right to contract in business is clearly part of the individual liberty protected by the fourteenth amendment. However, both liberty and the right to hold property are subject to such reasonable conditions as may be imposed by a government pursuant to its police powers.

b) An earlier law restricting the work hours in certain dangerous occupations was upheld. The law here challenged, however, has no reference whatever to the health, safety, morals, or welfare of the public. The state claims an interest in the individual worker's health, but this goes too far; the individual's liberty must impose some restraint on the police power.

c) This is not a substitution of the Court's judgment for the legislature's but merely a determination of whether the attempted regulation is within the state's police power.

4) **Dissenting** (Harlan, White, Day, JJ.). There is room for debate about the validity of the state's interest in preventing more than 10 hours' work per day. Excessive work could impair the ability of workers to serve the state and provide for their dependents. The Court should not go further than to determine that such reasons for the law exist.

5) **Dissenting** (Holmes, J.). Many comparably restrictive uses of the police power have been upheld by the Court. The Constitution was not intended to embody a particular economic view but was framed to permit expression of dominant opinions, i.e., that the laws freely reflect the people's choices. The law is not clearly unrelated to public health and ought to be upheld.

6) **Comment.** In *Lochner*, the Court applied principles of general constitutional law which formerly had been applied only in diversity cases. The Court began to define the limits of the police power where it excessively imposed upon individual freedoms, the scope of which the Court in turn was broadening. The Court began inquiring as to the propriety and reasonableness of the objectives sought through exercise of the police power.

2. **Judicial Control over Legislative Policy.**

a. **Introduction.** After *Lochner*, the Court began substituting its judgment for legislative judgments in a variety of cases involving economic regulation. Most legislation held unconstitutional involved regulation of labor, prices, and entry into business.

b. **Maximum working hours.** The Court upheld a law fixing maximum work hours for women, distinguishing *Lochner* by the special state interest in healthy women. [*Muller v. Oregon*, 208 U.S. 412 (1908)] The Court later effectively overruled *Lochner* by upholding a general maximum work hour law in *Bunting v. Oregon*, 243 U.S. 426 (1917). In that case, the Court did not refer to *Lochner*, and substantive due process survived.

c. **"Yellow dog" contracts.** In *Coppage v. Kansas*, 236 U.S. 1 (1915), the Court held that a state law that prohibited employers from requiring employees to agree not to join a labor union ("yellow dog" contracts) violated due process because it interfered with the right to make contracts. *Adair v. United States*, 208 U.S. 161 (1908), invalidated a similar federal law.

d. **Minimum wages.** The Court invalidated a federal minimum wage law applicable only to the District of Columbia in *Adkins v. Children's Hospital*, 261 U.S. 525 (1923), again finding that interference with freedom to contract violated due process.

e. **Business entry and economic regulations.** In a series of decisions that have been undermined by subsequent developments, the Court invalidated restraints on competition that curtailed entry into a particular type of business. [*See* New State Ice Co. v. Liebmann, 285 U.S. 262 (1932)—manufacture of ice requiring a certificate of convenience and necessity; Adams v. Tanner, 244 U.S. 590 (1917)—employment agency fees collected from workers] In *Weaver v. Palmer Bros. Co.*, 270 U.S. 402 (1926), although the Court recognized the validity of the state interest in curtailing business practices that might defraud or endanger consumers, the Court invalidated an absolute ban on the use of shoddy (cut up or torn) fabrics for bedding. The Court held that the ban was purely arbitrary since other secondhand materials could be used if sterilized and labeled.

3. **Decline of Substantive Due Process.**

a. **Introduction.** Some time after *Lochner*, the Court changed its earlier view and began to apply less strict scrutiny to economic regulation. Instead it granted deference to legislative determinations of need and reasonableness.

Nebbia v.
New York

b. **Regulation of prices and wages--Nebbia v. New York,** 291 U.S. 502 (1934).

1) **Facts.** New York (P) passed a law establishing minimum and maximum retail prices for milk. The purpose was to aid the dairy industry, which was in a desperate situation because the prices received by farmers for milk were below the cost of production. Nebbia (D), a retail grocer, sold milk below the minimum price and was convicted for violating the statute. D challenges the statute as a violation of due process.

2) **Issue.** May a state strictly control retail prices, even where such control inhibits the use of private property and the making of contracts?

3) **Held.** Yes. Judgment affirmed.

    a) As long as the Court finds the law to have a reasonable relationship to a proper legislative purpose, to be not arbitrary or discriminatory, and to have means chosen that are reasonably related to the ends sought, due process is not offended.

    b) No area is outside the province of state regulation for police power purposes, including the direct regulation of prices.

4) **Comment.** In *West Coast Hotel Co. v. Parrish*, 300 U.S. 379 (1937), the Court overruled several prior decisions and held that a state could, consistent with due process, impose a minimum wage on employer-employee contracts.

5) **Comment.** In *United States v. Carolene Products Co.*, 304 U.S. 144 (1938), the Court held that Congress may prohibit the interstate shipment of food products that it deems injurious to the public health.

c. **Regulation of Labor.** In *Lincoln Federal Labor Union v. Northwestern Iron & Metal Co.*, 335 U.S. 525 (1949), the Court upheld a statute prohibiting employers from entering into "closed shop" contracts so as to exclude nonunion workers. It also upheld a law requiring employers to give employees paid time off for voting. [Day-Brite Lighting, Inc. v. Missouri, 342 U.S. 421 (1952)]

d. **Regulation of business entry.** The Court upheld a probably overly restrictive optician-optometrist regulation in *Williamson v. Lee Optical of Oklahoma*, 348 U.S. 483 (1955), restrictive regulation of the business of debt adjusting in *Ferguson v. Skrupa*, 372 U.S. 726 (1963), and a local-ownership legislative scheme in *North Dakota State Board v. Snyder's Drug Stores, Inc.*, 414 U.S. 156 (1973).

e. **Recent judicial abstention.** The Court's deference has reached virtual abstention from substantive due process attacks against economic regulation. In *Whalen v. Roe*, 429 U.S. 589 (1977), the Court held that the state could accumulate and computerize the names and addresses of patients for whom dangerous drugs are prescribed. In *Duke Power Co. v. Carolina Environmental Study Group, Inc.*, 438 U.S. 59 (1978), the Court upheld a statute limiting liability of private nuclear plants for nuclear accidents. The statute was intended to enable such plants to obtain financing by limiting liability to $560 million.

E.   FUNDAMENTAL INTERESTS

1.   **Introduction.** In addition to the suspect classifications that merit strict scrutiny, the Court has also applied heightened review when a classification impinges on a "fundamental" interest. Such fundamental interests include voting, access to the courts, and welfare.

2.   **Procreation--Skinner v. Oklahoma,** 316 U.S. 535 (1942).

   a.   **Facts.** Oklahoma provided for sterilization of habitual criminals, defined as people who, having been convicted two or more times in the United States for felonies involving moral turpitude, are then convicted in Oklahoma of such a felony and sentenced to an Oklahoma prison. The procedure requires a court or jury finding that the person is a habitual criminal and that sterilization would not harm his or her general health. However, the law does not apply to offenses arising out of the violation of the prohibitory laws, revenue acts, embezzlement, or political offenses. Skinner (D) was convicted of stealing chickens, then of armed robbery, and again of armed robbery. Williamson (P), the state attorney general, instituted the sterilization proceeding against D. The state courts rejected D's fourteenth amendment challenge. The Supreme Court granted certiorari.

   b.   **Issue.** May a state sterilize habitual criminals if it distinguishes among the types of crimes that satisfy the definition of "habitual criminal"?

   c.   **Held.** No. Judgment reversed.

      1)   There are several inequities in this act that render it invalid under the Equal Protection Clause. For example, a stranger who steals more than $20 from a cash register is subject to sterilization, but a clerk who takes the same amount is not, because embezzlement is not covered.

      2)   Because marriage and procreation are such fundamental interests, classifications made in a state's sterilization scheme are subject to strict judicial scrutiny. The classifications in P's scheme cannot withstand such scrutiny.

   d.   **Concurring** (Stone, C.J.). If the state knows habitual criminals transmit their tendencies genetically, it may also know that some classes of offenders have a greater propensity to transmit. Hence, equal protection analysis is inappropriate. Due process, however, requires that before such an invasion of personal liberty, the individual be given the opportunity to show that his case does not justify resort to so drastic a measure.

3.   **Voting.**

   a.   **The right to vote.** Several constitutional provisions relate to voting and elections. The fourteenth amendment Equal Protection Clause has been applied to the right to vote. The fifteenth amendment forbids denial or abridgment of the right to vote on account of race, color, or previous condition of servitude, and the nineteenth amendment granted the franchise to women. The twenty-fourth amendment abolished the poll tax for federal elections. The twenty-sixth amendment granted the right to vote in state and federal elections to 18-year-olds.

   b.   **Denial or qualification of the right to vote.**

      1)   **Impact of a poll tax--Harper v. Virginia State Board of Elections**, 383 U.S. 663 (1966).

         Harper v. Virginia State Board of Elections

         a)   **Facts.** Harper (P) and other Virginia residents brought suit to have Virginia's poll tax declared unconstitutional. The district court, under *Breedlove v. Suttles*, 302 U.S. 277 (1937), dismissed P's complaint. P appeals.

         b)   **Issue.** May a state exact a poll tax as a condition for exercise of the right to vote?

         c)   **Held.** No. Judgment reversed.

            (1)   Once the franchise is granted to the electorate, lines may not be drawn that are inconsistent with the Equal Protection Clause of the fourteenth amendment.

            (2)   Lines drawn by the affluence of the voter or by the payment of any fee violate equal protection. Undoubtedly, states may impose reasonable voter qualifications, but these must pass careful scrutiny because the franchise is preservative of other basic civil and political rights. Wealth or payment of a fee is an irrelevant factor in measuring a voter's qualifications.

            (3)   Notions of what constitutes equal treatment for purposes of the Equal Protection Clause do change, and *Breedlove* is overruled.

         d)   **Dissenting** (Black, J.). The Court has ignored the original meaning of the Constitution and has instead given the Equal Protection Clause a new meaning according to the Court's idea of a better governmental policy. Such changes are unjustifiable; they should be made only through the proper amendment procedure.

e) **Dissenting** (Harlan, Stewart, JJ.). The decision to abolish state poll taxes for state elections ought to be made by the states, not by the the United States Supreme Court.

Kramer v. Union Free School District No. 15

2) **Voter qualifications not based on wealth--Kramer v. Union Free School District No. 15**, 395 U.S. 621 (1969).

a) **Facts.** Kramer (P) challenged a state law that restricted eligibility to vote in certain school district elections to those who either own or lease taxable real property within the district, or who are parents (or have custody of) children enrolled in the local public schools. The lower courts upheld the law. P appeals.

b) **Issue.** May a state restrict the franchise for limited purpose elections merely on a showing of a rational basis for the restrictions?

c) **Held.** No. Judgment reversed.

(1) Statutes denying some residents the right to vote impinge on one of the most fundamental rights of a democratic society. Accordingly, such exclusions must be necessary to promote a compelling state interest.

(2) Even if the state interests here are substantial enough to justify limiting the exercise of the franchise to those "primarily interested" or "primarily affected" (which is not decided), this statute is not narrowly drawn to effectuate that purpose. It is both underinclusive and overinclusive. Therefore, it cannot stand.

d) **Dissenting** (Stewart, Black, Harlan, JJ.). If a state may impose valid restrictions based on residence, literacy, and age, it ought to be able to impose these requirements, which are rational. The Court should apply only the traditional equal protection standard.

3) **Additional restrictions on the franchise.**

a) **Special purpose elections.** In *Cipriano v. City of Houma*, 395 U.S. 701 (1969), a state law granted only property taxpayers the right to vote in elections to approve municipal utility bonds. The Court held the restriction invalid since all citizens have an interest in the quality of utility services and rates. In *City of Phoenix v. Kolodziejski*, 399 U.S. 204 (1970), the Court held that a statute limiting the vote for the issuance of general obligation bonds to real property owners was unconstitutional even though only property taxes would pay for the improvements, since all residents were said to have a substantial interest in the municipal improvements to be made. But in *Salyer Land Co. v. Tulare Lake Basin Water Storage District*, 410 U.S. 719 (1973), the Court upheld an election scheme in which only landowners could vote for the members of the district board, because costs were assessed against land benefited. The board had a special limited purpose, and its activities disproportionately affected landowners as a group. In *Ball v. James*, 451 U.S. 355 (1981), the Court applied *Salyer* to the Salt River District in Arizona, which delivers 40% of its water to urban users and is a major generator and supplier of hydroelectric power.

b)   **Durational residence requirements.** State residence requirements have been held to violate equal protection because they divide voters into two classes—old and new residents—and discriminate against the latter. The principal case was *Dunn v. Blumstein*, 405 U.S. 330 (1972), which used the burden on the right to travel, as well as the burden on the right to vote, to invalidate such state residence requirements. However, the Court has recognized the need for some registration requirements, and upheld a 50-day residency and registration requirement where necessary to prepare voters' lists, etc. [*See* Marston v. Lewis, 410 U.S. 679 (1973)] And in *Rosario v. Rockefeller*, 410 U.S. 752 (1973), the Court upheld a law requiring voters to enroll in the party of their choice at least 30 days before the November general election in order to vote in the next party primary. There was held to be no violation of equal protection—the lengthy time period was said to be connected with the important state goal of preventing "raiding," whereby one party's members register with another party to influence the result of the latter's primary. Distinguishing *Rosario*, the Court in *Kusper v. Pontikes*, 414 U.S. 51 (1973), invalidated an Illinois law restricting the voting in a primary by anyone who had voted in another party's primary in the preceding 23 months, because the provision restricted the voter's first amendment associational freedom to change political party affiliation.

c)   **Disenfranchisement of felons.** In *Richardson v. Ramirez*, 418 U.S. 24 (1974), the Court held that the states may disenfranchise convicted felons because section 2 of the fourteenth amendment specifically permits such a limitation on the right to vote.

d)   **Ballot access.** The Court has looked closely at attempts to impede ballot access by independent candidates and fringe political parties. Most of these are defended as attempts to maintain the integrity of the political process, and this is a legitimate state interest. But the states may not be unduly restrictive. In *Anderson v. Celebrezze*, 460 U.S. 780 (1983), the Court specifically relied on the first amendment instead of equal protection to invalidate an early filing deadline that applied to independents but not the nominees of political parties. The Court articulated a balancing test, comparing the restriction's injury to first amendment rights with the justifications asserted by the state.

Dilution through apportionment.

1) **Federal vs. state apportionment.** In early decisions, the Supreme Court consistently refused to review questions arising from a state's distribution of electoral strength among its political or geographical subdivisions. In *Baker v. Carr*, *infra*, the Court decided that federal courts had jurisdiction over challenges to apportionment plans. The modern approach to federal elections requires that representation must reflect the total population as precisely as possible. More flexibility is permitted in apportionment of state legislatures, but grossly disproportionate districts are not allowed. State apportionment may not be used to further discrimination, but numerical deviations resulting from political considerations may be allowed.

Reynolds v. Sims

2) **Constitutional standards--Reynolds v. Sims,** 377 U.S. 533 (1964).

a) **Facts.** Sims (P) and others challenged the apportionment of the Alabama legislature, which was based on the 1900 federal census and thus seriously discriminated against voters who lived in an area where the population had grown disproportionately in the intervening years. The district court ordered temporary reapportionment; Reynolds (D) and other state officials appeal.

b) **Issue.** Must a state apportion its legislative districts on the basis of population?

c) **Held.** Yes. Judgment affirmed.

(1) The right to vote is essential to a democratic society and is denied by abasement or dilution of a citizen's vote just as effectively as by wholly prohibiting the free exercise of the franchise. The fundamental principle of representative government is one of equal representation for equal numbers of people, regardless of race, sex, economic status, or place of residence within a state.

(2) The Equal Protection Clause guarantees the opportunity for equal participation by all voters in the election of state legislators. Therefore, votes cannot be weighed differently on the basis of where the voters happen to reside. This applies whether the state legislature is unicameral or bicameral.

(3) The federal Congress cannot be taken as a guide for state legislative district apportionment because it arose from unique historical circumstances and represents a union of sovereigns. Political subdi-

visions of states never have been sovereign entities in that sense.

(4) Each state district must contain as nearly an equal population as possible, although precision, being impossible, is not required. Substantial equality of population must be the overriding objective. States need not perpetually update their apportionment plans, but there must be a reasonable plan for periodic readjustment.

d) **Comment.** In one of the five companion cases to *Reynolds*, *Lucas v. Forty-Fourth General Assembly*, 377 U.S. 713 (1964), involving the Colorado apportionment scheme, the Court held that the fact that a scheme had been approved by the state's voters is without constitutional significance.

3) **Extent of deviation permitted--Karcher v. Daggett**, 462 U.S. 725 (1983).

a) **Facts.** The New Jersey legislature reapportioned the state's congressional districts. The districts were described as "bizarre" configurations that disregarded geographical compactness and county boundaries. Each district did not have the same population, but the largest district, with a population of 527,472, had only 3,674 people more than the smallest, which was less than a 1% deviation. The state legislature had available other plans with much smaller population deviations, one with a maximum population difference of only 2,375. Once the reapportionment plan was enacted, a group of congressmen and others (Ps) challenged it under article I, section 2 of the Constitution. The district court held the plan unconstitutional. Ds appeal.

b) **Issue.** Must a congressional apportionment plan represent a good-faith effort to achieve population equality in order to be upheld, even if the population of the largest district is less than 1% greater than the population of the smallest district?

c) **Held.** Yes. Judgment affirmed.

(1) The Constitution establishes a high standard of justice and common sense for apportionment of congressional districts. Exact mathematical equality may be impossible, but districts must be apportioned to achieve population equality as nearly as is practicable.

(2) Ps must prove that the population differences among districts could have been reduced or eliminated by a good-faith effort to equalize them. If Ps succeed, then the state must prove that each significant variance between districts was necessary to achieve some legitimate objective.

(3) Ds claim that because the population deviation is smaller than the predictable census errors, the existing plan should be regarded per se as the product of good-faith efforts to equalize population. However, the only standard that fulfills the Constitution's ideal of equal representation is total population equality. Equality must therefore be the standard in assessing congressional district apportionment plans.

(4) Because Ps have satisfied their burden of showing that the population differences could have been reduced, the state must justify the differences. There are several legislative policies that, if consistently applied, might justify some variance. These include making districts compact, respecting municipal boundaries, preserving the cores of prior districts, and avoiding contests between incumbents. Ds have not been able to justify the population deviations in their plan, however.

d) **Concurring** (Stevens, J.). Ps also claimed that the shapes of the districts demonstrated that the plan was the product of political gerrymandering, which is unconstitutional. The Equal Protection Clause requires every state to govern impartially, so that gerrymandering against any cognizable group of voters is unconstitutional. Inquiry into the process that led to the adoption of this plan reveals that the legislative majority selected it out of overt partisanship. The shapes of the districts should be a consideration as well as the mathematical equality of the populations residing therein.

e) **Dissenting** (White, J., Burger, C.J., Powell, Rehnquist, JJ.). The Court unreasonably insists on unattainable perfection in equalizing congressional districts. Under the Court's ruling, any variance between districts must be considered significant. It would be better to use the approach adopted for dealing with state legislative apportionment, whereby certain small deviations do not constitute a prima facie constitutional violation.

f) **Dissenting** (Powell, J.). Gerrymandering presents a greater threat to equal representation than does failure to attain equal populations based on inexact census figures. Constitutional challenges to partisan gerrymandering should be heard, but this issue was not addressed by the district court so we should not reach it here.

4) **Local government.**

a) The principles of *Reynolds v. Sims* were extended to legislators in local government [Avery v. Midland County, 390 U.S. 474 (1968)] but not to nonlegislative officers [Sailors v. Board of Education, 387 U.S. 105 (1967)]. The Supreme Court held that "general governmental powers over an entire geographical area need not be apportioned among single-member districts of substantially unequal population." [Dusch v. Davis, 387 U.S. 112 (1967)]

b) *Hadley v. Junior College District*, 397 U.S. 50 (1970), extended the "one man-one vote" rule to all instances where a state or local government decides to select persons by popular election to perform governmental functions. No distinctions are to be made for "legislative officers" versus "administrative officers." However, there might be some cases in which a state elects certain functionaries whose duties are so far removed from normal governmental activities and so disproportionately affect different groups that a popular election according to the one man-one vote principle might not be required.

5) **At-large system--City of Mobile v. Bolden,** 446 U.S. 55 (1980).

a) **Facts.** The city of Mobile (D) was governed by a three-member city commission, elected at large. Bolden (P), a black Mobile voter, challenged this system as unfairly diluting the black vote. The district court found for P and ordered D to institute a mayor-council system elected from single-member districts. The court of appeals affirmed. D appeals.

b) **Issue.** Does an at-large system of municipal elections not motivated by a discriminatory purpose violate the rights of a minority group constituting about one-third of the population?

c) **Held.** No. Judgment reversed.

   (1) D's system is a common one in our nation. State action that is neutral on its face, like D's, violates the fifteenth amendment only if motivated by a discriminatory purpose. There is no right to have black or other minority candidates elected. The amendment prohibits only the denial or abridgment of the freedom to vote, which P does not allege here.

   (2) At-large electoral schemes are subject to challenge under the fourteenth amendment Equal Protection Clause where they are intended to result in a lack of representation of racial or ethnic minorities. There must be proof of official discrimination. [*See* White v. Regester, 412 U.S. 755 (1973)] Failure to elect proportional numbers of minority representatives is not sufficient proof. Here, P has failed to show the fatal purpose. D's system is readily explained on grounds apart from race.

   (3) The dissent would find a substantive right of proportional representation, but no such right exists.

City of
Mobile v.
Bolden

d) **Concurring** (Blackmun, J.). The relief accorded was excessive; the case should be remanded for reconsideration of an appropriate remedy.

e) **Concurring** (Stevens, J.). There is a distinction between state action that inhibits the right to vote, which is subject to strict scrutiny, and action affecting group political strength, which is judged by a standard that allows effective functioning of the political process. The proper test is the objective results of the state action, not the subjective motivation behind it. Under that test, D's plan is permissible.

f) **Dissenting** (Brennan, J.). Proof of discretionary impact is sufficient. Even if it were not, P has adequately proven discriminatory purpose.

g) **Dissenting** (White, J.). Invidious discriminatory purpose can be inferred from objective factors. The lower courts' findings were based on such a reasonable inference and should not be discarded.

h) **Dissenting** (Marshall, J.). The plurality concludes that, absent proof of intentional state discrimination, the right to vote is meaningless for the politically impotent. There is a substantive constitutional right to equal participation in the electoral process that D denies P. There is no right to proportional representation per se, but the Court must affirmatively protect minorities such as P from vote dilution.

Davis v. Bandemer

6) **Political party's equal protection challenge to apportionment--Davis v. Bandemer,** 478 U.S. 109 (1986).

a) **Facts.** The Indiana State House of Representatives consisted of 100 members serving two-year terms. Members were elected from single-member and multi-member districts. The 1981 reapportionment plan, adopted by the majority Republican party, provided for 7 triple-member, 9 double-member, and 61 single-member districts. The multi-member districts were primarily in metropolitan areas. Davis and other Democrats (Ps) sued, claiming the plan was intended to disadvantage Democrats, violating their equal protection rights. Before the case went to trial, an election was held and 43 Democrats were elected to the house. Statewide, Democratic candidates received almost 52% of the vote. In specific multi-member districts, Democratic candidates won 46.6% of the vote, but only 3 of 21 seats. The district court declared the reapportionment unconstitutional and ordered the legislature to prepare a new plan. Bandemer (D) appeals.

b) **Issue.** Is a claim by a political party that a legislative apportionment plan violates the party's equal protection rights a justiciable claim?

c) **Held.** Yes. Judgment reversed on the merits.

(1)   Equal protection claims about legislative districting have been justiciable insofar as they involve population inequalities between districts ever since *Baker v. Carr*, which established the one-person, one-vote principle. Racial gerrymandering claims are also justiciable regardless of population equality, as are challenges against multi-member districts that diminish the effectiveness of the votes of racial minorities. Such holdings support an inference that purely political challenges are also justiciable.

(2)   Ps' claim is based on the proposition that each political group in a state should have the same chance to elect representatives of its choice as any other political group. It is not significant for justiciability purposes that the characteristics of Ps' group are not immutable or that Ps' group has not historically been subject to stigma. Nor does it matter that claims such as Ps' may present practical problems, for these are present in the racial cases as well. Accordingly, Ps' claim is justiciable.

(3)   On the merits, Ps have the burden to prove both intentional discrimination against an identifiable political group and an actual discriminatory effect on that group. The intention requirement was satisfied by the district court's findings, and at any rate is virtually inherent in the legislative process of redistricting.

(4)   However, the district court's findings that the plan had such an adverse effect on Ps as to constitute a violation of the Equal Protection Clause is not sustainable. The Constitution does not require proportional representation, nor does it require a plan that draws lines as near as possible to allocating seats to the contending parties in proportion to what their anticipated statewide vote will be.

(5)   Winner-take-all district-based elections inherently present the potential for disproportionate party representation as compared with the popular vote. Challenges to multi-member districts require a showing much greater than mere lack of proportional representation. One consideration is the responsiveness of elected officials to the concerns of the groups involved, because even defeated parties have influence on the winning candidate. The test is whether the electoral system is arranged so as to consistently degrade a voter's or a group's influence on the political process as a whole. In other words, has a group been unconstitutionally denied its chance to effectively influence the political process?

(6)   The district court relied primarily on the results of the 1982 election. One election is not enough to prove unconstitutional discrimination. There was no finding that the plan would render the Democrats a minority party throughout the 1980s.

(7)   Justice Powell's approach focuses on various factors, including the deliberate distortion of voting district boundaries to achieve arbitrary ends. This approach would permit a finding of constitutional violation even when the only proven effect on a political

party's electoral power was disproportionate results in one election. The better approach is to require proof that the challenged plan will consistently degrade the party's influence on the political process as a whole.

    d)   **Concurring** (O'Connor, J., Burger, C.J., Rehnquist, J.). Partisan gerrymandering claims by major political parties are nonjusticiable political questions that should be left to the legislative branch. The Equal Protection Clause should not be used to make fundamental policy choices. Even foreseeable, disproportionate long-term election results do not constitute a constitutional violation; this approach leads to a proportionality requirement. It also raises significant problems of implementation, such as how to account for independents who vote for one party or another in a particular election.

    e)   **Dissenting** (Powell, Stevens, JJ.). Once a discriminatory purpose is shown, it is not enough to rely on the one-person, one-vote principle to uphold a clearly discriminatory redistricting plan. Courts should consider other factors as well, including whether the boundaries of the voting districts have been distorted deliberately and arbitrarily to achieve illegitimate ends.

  d.   **Ballot access.** The Court has looked closely at attempts to impede ballot access by independent candidates and fringe political parties. Most of these are defended as attempts to maintain the integrity of the political process, and this is a legitimate state interest. But the states may not be unduly restrictive.

    1)   In *Williams v. Rhodes*, 393 U.S. 23 (1968), the Court invalidated a scheme under which major political parties had to receive just 10% of the vote to maintain ballot position in the next election, while new parties had to petition for ballot access with signatures totaling 15% of the ballots cast in the prior election, and also had to meet state organizational standards and hold a primary.

    2)   In *Jenness v. Fortson*, 403 U.S. 431 (1971), the Court upheld a less restrictive ballot access scheme which permitted access by independent candidates who filed petitions with signatures of only 5% of those eligible for the previous election.

    3)   In *Storer v. Brown*, 415 U.S. 724 (1974), the Court applied strict scrutiny but upheld a California law prohibiting a person from running as an independent if she had registered as a party member within a year prior to the primary election immediately preceding the election in which she was running.

    4)   The Court invalidated an Illinois system requiring new political parties and independent candidates to gather more voter signatures to appear on the Chicago city ballot than on the statewide ballot. [Illinois Elections Board v. Socialist Workers Party, 440 U.S. 173 (1979)] Justice Marshall emphasized the less drastic means available to the state in screening out frivolous candidates and the overbroad restriction on ballot access of the provision.

4. **Access to Courts.**

a. **Administration of criminal justice.** The Court has shown sensitivity to burdens placed on the access of litigants, especially criminal defendants, to the courts. Both procedural due process and equal protection have been invoked for analysis.

1) **Right to a record on appeal.** In *Griffin v. Illinois*, 351 U.S. 12 (1956), the Supreme Court relied on equal protection to hold that in a state prosecution where no appeal was possible without a transcript from the trial court, the state must provide indigent defendants a free transcript in all felony criminal cases. The rationale is that in criminal prosecutions (where the defendant is involuntarily involved), matters of "justice" are charged with too much social interest to be decided on the basis of some defendants being poor and others being rich. The dissent argued that due process did not require this result, since there is no constitutional right to an appeal, and equal protection was not applicable because the state was treating everyone the same.

2) **Right to counsel on appeal--Douglas v. California,** 372 U.S. 353 (1963).

a) **Facts.** California (P) permitted one appeal as of right. Douglas (D), an indigent who had been convicted, sought appointed counsel to represent him in his appeal. The appellate court, after reviewing the transcript and determining that it would assist neither D nor the court to have counsel appointed, denied D's request. The Supreme Court granted certiorari.

b) **Issue.** Must a state provide counsel for indigent criminal defendants to pursue an initial appeal?

c) **Held.** Yes. Judgment reversed.

(1) Denial of counsel in this situation is the same kind of invidious discrimination against indigents as was involved in *Griffin*.

(2) While absolute equality between rich and poor may not be required, the merits of the one and only appeal a person is entitled to are too important to allow decision without ben-

efit of counsel just because the appellant is indigent.

d) **Dissenting** (Harlan, Stewart, JJ.). Equal protection does not impose on the states an affirmative duty to lift the handicaps flowing from differences in economic circumstances. The only relevant constitutional provision is due process, and the state's rules are not so arbitrary or unreasonable that they deny due process.

e) **Comment.** In *Ross v. Moffit*, 417 U.S. 600 (1974), the Court refused to extend the *Douglas* approach to discretionary appeals. In *Fuller v. Oregon*, 417 U.S. 40 (1974), the Court sustained a recoupment law through which the state sought recoupment of legal expenses from convicted defendants and conditioned probation on reimbursement of expenses incurred when a now-solvent defendant was indigent. In so ruling, the Court rejected the argument that the obligation to repay might indirectly chill a defendant's right to counsel.

b. **Civil litigation.** In many of the cases dealing with civil litigation there is disagreement whether due process or equal protection should apply.

1) **Divorce fee.** In *Boddie v. Connecticut*, 401 U.S. 371 (1971), the Court used the Due Process Clause to hold that states may not require indigents to pay court fees as a condition for judicial dissolution of marriage. The Court limited the scope of the decision by noting (i) the basic position of the "marriage relationship" in society and (ii) the "state monopolization of the means for legally dissolving this relationship." It reasoned that due process requires that "absent a countervailing state interest of overriding significance, persons forced to settle their claims . . . through the judicial process must be given a meaningful opportunity to be heard."

2) **Bankruptcy.** The Court has given *Boddie* a narrow construction in other contexts. In *United States v. Kras*, 409 U.S. 434 (1973), the Court held that the Bankruptcy Act filing fee requirement as a condition for discharge is "rational" and does not violate equal protection as applied to indigent persons who seek voluntary bankruptcy. The right to bankruptcy is not a "fundamental" interest but is in the "area of economics and social welfare."

5. **The Right to Travel.**

a. **Interstate mobility.** A citizen has a constitutional right to travel freely from state to state. State durational residence requirements that would impair this right must be justified by a "compelling" state interest, at least where they affect the citizen's right to receive some vital government benefit or service. However, states may apply a requirement of residency at the time of (and during) receipt of governmental benefits, subject only to the "traditional" test. For example, *McCarthy v. Philadelphia Civil Service Commission*, 424 U.S. 645 (1976), held that requiring personal residence at the place of governmental employment does not violate the right to travel.

b. **State welfare--Shapiro v. Thompson,** 394 U.S. 618 (1969).

Shapiro v. Thompson

1) **Facts.** The Thompsons (Ps) were denied welfare benefits solely because they had not been residents of Connecticut for a full year prior to their applications. Two similar cases were joined before the Supreme Court. In all three instances, the district courts found that the state's denial of benefits to otherwise eligible residents of less than a year constituted an invidious discrimination denying Ps equal protection of the laws. Shapiro (D), representing Connecticut, appeals.

2) **Issue.** May a state create a one-year residency requirement as a condition for receiving state welfare assistance?

3) **Held.** No. Judgment affirmed.

   a) D argues that the statute preserves the fiscal integrity of state public assistance programs, which it clearly does, but only by discouraging the influx of poor families needing assistance. However, a state purpose of inhibiting immigration by needy persons is constitutionally impermissible as a burden on the right to travel. Any law whose sole purpose is the chilling of the exercise of constitutional rights is invalid. D's argument that the statute intends to discourage immigration of needy people seeking solely to obtain larger benefits does not save it from this constitutional defect, since in such circumstances it still infringes on those persons' right to travel.

   b) States may not withhold welfare benefits from short-term residents who have contributed through taxes any more than they may withhold state services such as fire and police protection from short-term residents.

   c) Because the classification here touches on a fundamental constitutional right, it must be judged under the strict standard of whether it promotes a compelling state interest. D's assertion that other administrative objectives are served by the one-year requirement falls short of satisfying this standard. D claims that the statutes are approved by federal legislation. Even if true, it is the state statutes, by themselves, that must be examined for constitutional defects. Congress cannot authorize the states to deny equal protection.

    d)   The state statutes violate the Equal Protection Clause and are therefore invalid.

4)   **Concurring** (Stewart, J.). The Court has simply recognized and protected an established constitutional right.

5)   **Dissenting** (Warren, C.J., Black, J.). Congress has the power both to impose minimal nationwide residence requirements and to authorize the states to do so. Since the states here acted pursuant to congressional authorization, the statutes should be upheld.

6)   **Dissenting** (Harlan, J.). The compelling interest doctrine should be applied only to racial classifications and not to the enlarged list of suspect criteria that includes classifications based upon recent interstate movement and perhaps the exercise of any constitutional right. In addition, when a statute affects only matters not mentioned in the Constitution and is not arbitrary or irrational, then the Court should not characterize these matters as affecting fundamental rights, thereby giving them the added protection of an unusually stringent equal protection test. Applying the rationality standard, a welfare residence requirement has valid governmental objectives and has advantages not shared by other methods.

6.   **Limit of Fundamental Rights.**

    a.   **Introduction.** The Court has limited the fundamental rights approach by refusing to extend it to certain areas. Certain opinions written by the Warren Court indicated that classifications based on wealth might be suspect, and hence that there may be a fundamental right to economic benefits. Since then the Court has held that there is no constitutional right to receive public welfare. Welfare classifications are subject only to the traditional equal protection test, unless they affect a "fundamental" right other than mere receipt of public assistance.

Dandridge
v. Williams

    b.   **Family size and public assistance--Dandridge v. Williams,** 397 U.S. 471 (1970).

        1)   **Facts.** Maryland imposed an upper limit of $250 per month per family for federal aid to families with dependent children (AFDC). Williams (P) challenged the statute as denying equal protection since large families received less aid per child than small families. The lower court held the statute invalid. Dandridge (D) appeals.

2) **Issue.** Does imposition of a ceiling on welfare benefits deny equal protection to large families, which receive less assistance per family member than do smaller families?

3) **Held.** No. Judgment reversed.

   a) No fundamental right is at stake here. In areas of economics and social welfare, a state does not deny equal protection merely because the classifications made by its laws are unequal.

   b) The fourteenth amendment does not grant federal courts power to set economic or social policy on the states. It is enough that the state's action be rationally based and free from invidious discrimination. This statute, intended to encourage gainful employment, meets that test.

4) **Dissenting** (Marshall, Brennan, JJ.). A state may not, in the provision of important services or the distribution of governmental payments, supply benefits to some individuals while denying them to others who are similarly situated. This case illustrates the impropriety of the abstract dichotomy between the "traditional test" and the "strict scrutiny test." The Court equates the interest of these needy children with the interests of utilities and other corporations by classifying their interests as "economic."

c. **Housing.** The right to housing is not guaranteed by the Constitution. State classifications in housing laws are subject only to the traditional test of reasonableness. Thus, a state may permit landlords to bring summary actions to evict tenants from rented premises but cannot require posting of a bond for twice the amount of rent in order to appeal. [Lindsey v. Normet, 405 U.S. 56 (1972)]

d. **Education.** Because there is no constitutional right to education, regulation of education is judged only by the traditional (rational basis) test.

   1) **State spending for education--San Antonio Independent School District v. Rodriguez**, 411 U.S. 1 (1973).

San Antonio Independent School District v. Rodriguez

   a) **Facts.** Rodriguez (P), a Mexican-American, challenged the Texas system of financing public education. The system involved a combination of state, local, and federal funding, and was operated so that state and local expenditures per pupil varied according to the market value of taxable property per pupil within the various districts. P claimed that the system denied equal protection by invidiously discriminating against the poor. The district court found the system unconstitutional. The San Antonio Independent School District (D) appeals.

b) **Issue.** Is a state system of financing public education that closely correlates spending per pupil and the value of local taxable property subject to strict judicial scrutiny?

c) **Held.** No. Judgment reversed.

    (1)   D's system might be regarded as discriminating against functionally indigent persons, against persons relatively poorer than others, or against all who, regardless of their personal incomes, happen to reside in relatively poorer school districts. However, there is no evidence to support a finding that any persons in the first two groups are discriminated against, and the third group clearly cannot fit the traditional definition of a suspect class.

    (2)   Although the system does not operate to the peculiar disadvantage of any suspect class, strict review is still required where the state's action impermissibly interferes with the exercise of a "fundamental" right, which P claims includes education. Although education is an important state service, that importance is not determinative of equal protection examination. Only those rights explicitly or implicitly guaranteed by the Constitution are "fundamental" for purposes of equal protection.

    (3)   Education is neither explicitly nor implicitly guaranteed. Additionally, D's system was implemented to extend public education, not to interfere with any rights. Finally, courts ought not interfere with state fiscal policies if not necessary. Therefore, D's system is not subject to strict judicial scrutiny.

d) **Dissenting** (White, Douglas, Brennan, JJ.). The Court merely requires D to establish that unequal treatment is in furtherance of a permissible goal, but it should also require D to show that the means chosen to effectuate that goal are rationally related to its achievement.

e) **Dissenting** (Marshall, Douglas, JJ.). The Court appears to find only two standards of equal protection review--strict scrutiny or mere rationality. In reality, there is a wide spectrum of review, depending on the constitutional and societal importance of the interest adversely affected and the recognized invidiousness of the classification. The amount of review accorded to nonconstitutional rights or interests varies according to the nexus between those rights and specific constitutional guarantees. Discrimination on the basis of group wealth in this case calls for careful judicial scrutiny.

Plyler v. Doe   **2)**   **Education of children of illegal aliens--Plyler v. Doe,** 457 U.S. 202 (1982).

a) **Facts.** Texas enacted a statute that withheld state funds for the education of illegal alien children and that allowed local school districts to deny enrollment to such children. Doe (P) challenged the constitutionality of the statute. The lower courts found the law unconstitutional. Plyler (D) appeals.

b) **Issue.** May a state deny to undocumented school-age children the free public education that it provides to citizens and legally admitted aliens?

c) **Held.** No. Judgment affirmed.

(1) The fourteenth amendment guarantees equal protection and due process to "any person within [a state's] jurisdiction." Even illegal aliens are entitled to this protection.

(2) Equal protection analysis does not require that illegal aliens be treated as a suspect class just because their illegal presence is not a constitutional irrelevancy. Education is not a fundamental right, although it is more than a mere government benefit. However, this case presents another consideration. The statute imposes a lifetime stigma on children who are not accountable for their disabling status. Therefore, the discrimination cannot be allowed unless it fulfills a substantial state purpose.

(3) Although national policy does not support unrestricted immigration, no policy exists that would deny these children an elementary education. The state interests—protection against excessive illegal immigration, avoidance of the special burden of educating such children, and the likelihood that the children will not remain in the state—are not furthered by the means chosen, even assuming that the policies are legitimate. Because no showing of furthering a state interest was made, the statutory discrimination is unconstitutional.

d) **Concurring** (Marshall, J.). An individual's interest in education is fundamental. This case is further proof that a rigid approach to equal protection is impractical.

e) **Concurring** (Blackmun, J.). Because of the political disadvantage incurred by uneducated persons, denial of an education is the analogue of denial of the right to vote. To uphold a discriminatory denial of education, the state must give more than a rational basis for the classification.

f) **Concurring** (Powell, J.). The children discriminated against here are innocent with respect to their status. The legislative classification threatens the creation of an underclass of future residents. Therefore, the state must show a fair and substantial relation to substantial interests. This D has failed to do.

g) **Dissenting** (Burger, C.J., White, Rehnquist, O'Connor, JJ.). Although it is foolish and wrong to create an illiterate segment of society in the manner at issue here, the courts were never intended to set policy. The only issue here is whether Texas has a legitimate reason to distinguish between legal and illegal residents. The state purpose of preserving its limited resources for school financing is rationally related to the legislative classification. The majority admits that traditional equal protection analysis does not require a different result. Instead, the majority decided what the best result should be and then created an analysis to reach that result.

F. PRIVACY AND FAMILY

1. **Introduction.** Although substantive due process no longer imposes any serious restraints on economic regulations, the Court has revived the notion as a means of protecting certain fundamental personal rights not specifically enumerated in the Constitution, including the right of privacy. Early cases began to recognize privileges recognized at common law but not specifically mentioned in the Constitution.

   a. **Family.** In *Meyer v. Nebraska*, 262 U.S. 390 (1923), the Court recognized the rights to marry, raise children, and acquire useful knowledge as essential to the liberty protected by due process.

   b. **Education.** In *Pierce v. Society of Sisters*, 268 U.S. 510 (1925), the Court invalidated a state law requiring attendance at public school as violative of parents' liberty to direct the education of their children.

2. **Fundamental Privacy Rights.** The right of privacy is nowhere mentioned in the Constitution. However, the fourth and fifth amendments protect against invasion of privacy by search and seizure. The right of personal choice in matters of marriage and the bearing and raising of children is so fundamental to society that it is afforded protection. Some consider this right to be protected by the ninth amendment, others by the "penumbra" of the Bill of Rights.

Griswold v.
Connecticut

   a. **Marital privacy within the Bill of Rights--Griswold v. Connecticut,** 381 U.S. 479 (1965).

      1) **Facts.** Griswold (D), the Executive Director of Planned Parenthood in Connecticut, and the organization's Medical Director for New Haven, gave information, instruction, and medical advice about contraception to married persons. Ds were convicted as accessories to the crime of using contraceptives in violation of a Connecticut (P) stat-

ute prohibiting all such use. The conviction was upheld in all the state courts. D appeals.

2) **Issue.** Does a constitutional right of privacy exist that prohibits states from making use of contraceptives by a married couple a crime?

3) **Held.** Yes. Conviction reversed.

   a) The specific guarantees in the Bill of Rights have penumbras, or peripheral rights, that make the specific rights more secure. A right of educational choice has been noted in earlier cases, such as *Pierce* and *Meyer, supra,* even though it is not mentioned in the Constitution, because it is a peripheral right without which the specific first amendment rights would be less secure.

   b) Various guarantees in the Bill of Rights create zones of privacy. The first amendment protects the right of association with the related privacy. The third amendment protects the privacy of the home against quartering of soldiers. The fourth and fifth amendments protect other facets of privacy, including the sanctity of the home. The ninth amendment protects rights retained by the people.

   c) This case involves a relationship lying within the zone of privacy created by several fundamental constitutional guarantees. The law at issue has a maximum destructive impact on that relationship. The privacy of marriage is older than the Bill of Rights. The association of marriage is for as noble a purpose as any involved in prior decisions protecting the right of association.

4) **Concurring** (Goldberg, Brennan, JJ., Warren, C.J.). The ninth amendment expressly recognized fundamental personal rights not specifically mentioned in the United States Constitution. In determining which rights are fundamental, judges must look to the traditions and collective conscience of the people. Privacy in the marital relation is clearly one of these basic personal rights "retained by the people." The Court's holding does not interfere with a state's proper regulation of sexual promiscuity or misconduct, such as adultery and fornication.

5) **Concurring** (Harlan, J.). The fourteenth amendment's Due Process Clause independently requires rejection of the Connecticut statute without reference to the Bill of Rights. The incorporation doctrine should not be used to restrict the reach of the Due Process Clause. (Dissenting in *Poe v. Ullman,* 367 U.S. 497 (1961), Justice Harlan argued that if the Due Process Clause were merely a procedural safeguard, it would be no protection against legislation that could destroy the enjoyment of life, liberty, and property, even through the fairest procedures. He argued that the meaning of due process is based on a balance between the demands of

organized society and respect for individual liberty, guided by tradition, good judgment, and restraint.)

6) **Concurring** (White, J.). Application of the law to married couples deprives them of "liberty" without due process of law.

7) **Dissenting** (Black, Stewart, JJ.). While the law is offensive, it is not prohibited by any specific constitutional provision and therefore must be upheld. Constitutional amendments, not judge-made alterations, are the correct means of modernizing the Constitution.

8) **Dissenting** (Stewart, Black, JJ.). The law is silly since it is obviously unenforceable, but there is no general right of privacy found in the Constitution, so we cannot hold that it violates the Constitution.

9) **Comment.** More recently, the Court has simply held that the right of personal privacy is implicit in the concept of "liberty" within the protection of the fourteenth amendment Due Process Clause—i.e., it is one of those basic human rights which are of "fundamental" importance in our society. [Roe v. Wade, *infra*]

b. **Further development of substantive due process.** Regardless of its source, the right of privacy is regarded as a fundamental right for due process purposes, which means that regulation in these areas can only be justified by a compelling state interest. The right of privacy protects the individual interest in avoiding disclosure of personal matters and the interest in independently making certain kinds of important decisions.

c. **Contraceptives.** In *Eisenstadt v. Baird*, 405 U.S. 438 (1972), the Court held that the decision whether to use contraceptives was one of individual privacy; thus, the right belongs to single as well as married persons. In *Carey v. Population Services International*, 431 U.S. 678 (1977), the Court held that a state could not prohibit distribution of nonmedical contraceptives to adults except through licensed pharmacists, nor prohibit sales of such contraceptives to persons under 16 who did not have approval of a licensed physician.

3. **The Abortion Problem.**

a. **Introduction.** It is currently held that a woman's decision to terminate her pregnancy is within her constitutionally protected right of privacy, and cannot be made conditional on parental or spousal consent. However, at some point during pregnancy, the state's interest in protecting the mother's life and in protecting prenatal life become sufficiently "compelling" to justify state regulation of abortion.

b. Basic constitutional rule on abortion--Roe v. Wade, 410 U.S. 113 (1973).

1) **Facts.** Roe (P), unmarried and pregnant, sought declaratory and injunctive relief against Wade (D), a county district attorney, to prevent enforcement of Texas criminal abortion statutes. The district court invalidated the statutes but declined to grant injunctive relief. P appeals.

2) **Issue.** May a state constitutionally make it a crime to procure an abortion except to save the mother's life?

3) **Held.** No. Judgment affirmed.

   a) P claims a constitutional right to terminate her pregnancy, based on the fourteenth amendment concept of personal "liberty," the Bill of Rights penumbras, and the ninth amendment. D claims a state interest in regulating medical procedures to insure patient safety and in protecting prenatal life.

   b) The right of privacy generally relates to marriage, procreation, and contraception, and includes the abortion decision, but is not without restraint based on the state's compelling interests. The state's interest in prenatal life cannot be based on the fetus's right to life, for a fetus cannot be considered a "person" in the constitutional sense. Unborn children have never been recognized in any area of the law as persons in the whole sense. However, the pregnant woman cannot be isolated in her privacy. The state may decide that at some point in time another interest, that of health of the mother or that of potential human life, becomes significantly involved. The woman's right of privacy must be measured accordingly.

   c) The state's interest in the health of the mother becomes "compelling" at approximately the end of the first trimester, prior to which mortality in abortion is less than mortality in normal childbirth. Only from this point forward may the state regulate the abortion procedure as needed to preserve and protect maternal health.

   d) The state's interest in potential life becomes "compelling" at viability. A state interested in protecting fetal life after viability may proscribe abortion except when necessary to preserve the life or health of the mother.

   e) The Texas statute challenged here is overbroad and cannot be upheld.

4) **Concurring** (Stewart, J.). The Court has generally recognized freedom of personal choice in matters of marriage and family

life as a liberty protected by the fourteenth amendment. The Texas statute directly infringes on that right and is correctly invalidated.

5) **Concurring** (Burger, C.J.). The Texas statute was overbroad in not permitting legal exceptions for rape and incest.

6) **Dissenting** (Rehnquist, White, JJ.). An abortion is not "private" in the ordinary use of this word. The Court seems to define "privacy" as a claim of liberty from unwanted state regulation of consensual transactions, protected by the fourteenth amendment. But that liberty is not guaranteed absolutely against deprivation, only against deprivation without due process of law. The traditional test is whether the law has a rational relation to a valid state objective, but this test could not justify the Court's outcome. Instead, the Court adopts the "compelling state interest test," which is more appropriate to a legislative judgment than to a judicial one. The Court's conclusions are more like judicial legislation than determination of the intent of the drafters of the fourteenth amendment. Further, the fact that most states have had restrictions on abortion for over a century indicates that the asserted right to an abortion is not so universally accepted as P claims.

7) **Comment.** The Court has held that a state law may require notice be given to an unemancipated minor's parents prior to her undergoing an abortion. A compelling state interest is present when the minor is a dependent, there is no emergency, and notifying the parents is in the child's best interest. [H.L. v. Matheson, 450 U.S. 398 (1981)]

c. **Government refusal to pay for abortions.** Despite its strict scrutiny of regulation of abortion, the Court has held that the government may choose not to fund abortions.

1) **1977 cases.** *Maher v. Roe*, 432 U.S. 464 (1977), was the first major case in this area. The state had excluded nontherapeutic abortions from its Medicaid-funded program, although it did cover childbirth. The Court applied a rationality standard of review instead of strict scrutiny. The Court held that *Roe v. Wade* did not preclude the states from favoring childbirth over abortion, as long as they did not unduly interfere with the woman's freedom to choose an abortion. The dissent argued that the exclusion effectively forced indigent women to bear children instead of procuring a desired abortion. *Beal v. Doe*, 432 U.S. 438 (1977), and *Poelker v. Doe*, 432 U.S. 519 (1977), applied the same rationale to other programs.

Harris
v. McRae

2) **Public funding of medically necessary abortions--Harris v. McRae**, 448 U.S. 297 (1980).

a)   **Facts.** The Medicaid Act, which mandates compliance with all its
requirements by all states that elect to participate in its reimbursement program, was amended annually by various Hyde amendments, which denied public funding for certain medically necessary
abortions. McRae (P), a Medicaid recipient in the first trimester
of pregnancy who sought an abortion, sued for an injunction
against enforcement of the restriction. The district court found
all versions of the Hyde amendment unconstitutional. Harris (D),
Secretary of HEW, appeals.

b)   **Issue.** May Congress, consistent with the Due Process Clause,
deny public funding for certain medically necessary abortions while
funding substantially all other medical costs, including costs of
carrying pregnancy to term?

c)   **Held.** Yes. Judgment reversed.

   (1)   A law is presumptively unconstitutional if it impinges on a
         recognized constitutional right. P asserts that *Roe v. Wade*
         recognized a constitutional right to the liberty to choose
         whether to terminate a pregnancy. However, a legitimate
         state interest in protecting potential human life was also
         recognized. That case placed limits on the state's ability to
         interfere with that choice.

   (2)   Here, P contests a completely different form of activity—
         state encouragement of an alternative activity consonant with
         legislative policy. *Wade* recognized no constitutional entitle-
         ment to the financial resources needed to pursue the pro-
         tected choice, and no such entitlement exists.

   (3)   P contends that the Hyde amendments tend to establish cer-
         tain religious doctrines, in violation of the Establishment
         Clause. However, the fact that a statute coincides with a
         religious tenet does not, by itself, show an establishment of
         any religion.

   (4)   A classification is unconstitutional if based on "suspect"
         criteria or if not rationally related to a legitimate govern-
         ment objective. Earlier cases such as *Maher v. Roe* (*supra*)
         have held that poverty, standing alone, is not a suspect
         classification. The amendments clearly bear a rational rela-
         tionship to the legitimate interest in protecting the potential
         life of the fetus. Therefore, there is no denial of equal
         protection.

d)   **Concurring** (White, J.). *Roe v. Wade* recognized the right to
choose to undergo an abortion without coercive interference by
the government. There is no such official interference here.

e)   **Dissenting** (Brennan, Marshall, Blackmun, JJ.). The amendments
intrude upon the constitutionally protected decision of abortion by,

in reality, coercing indigent pregnant women to bear children they would otherwise choose not to have.

    f)   **Dissenting** (Marshall, J.). The amendments deny the constitutional right of choice to poor women at the cost of serious and long-lasting health damage.

    g)   **Dissenting** (Stevens, J.). The government rules with partiality when it denies otherwise available medical benefits to a woman solely to further an interest in potential life, at the risk of that woman's health.

Akron
v. Akron
Center for
Reproductive
Health

    d.   **Strict review of regulation of abortions and Justice O'Connor's dissent--Akron v. Akron Center for Reproductive Health,** 462 U.S. 416 (1983).

    1)   **Facts.** The city council of Akron (D) adopted an ordinance to regulate abortion, including the following five provisions: (i) that all abortions performed after the first trimester of pregnancy be performed in a hospital; (ii) that parents be notified and give consent before abortions may be performed on unmarried minors; (iii) that the attending physician make certain specified statements to the patient to insure that the consent given is truly informed consent; (iv) that the woman wait 24 hours after signing the consent form before the abortion can be performed; and (v) that the fetal remains be disposed of in a humane and sanitary manner. The Akron Center for Reproductive Health (P) challenged the validity of the ordinance. The lower courts held the restrictions unconstitutional, and D appeals.

    2)   **Issue.** Must state regulation of abortion comply with prevailing medical practice and not diminish the availability of abortions without promoting important health benefits?

    3)   **Held.** Yes. Judgment affirmed.

    a)   The first requirement that an abortion after the first trimester be performed in a hospital is unconstitutional because it introduces a significant obstacle for those seeking abortions but does not reasonably promote health benefits. While at the time of *Roe v. Wade* the accepted medical view favored hospitalization for second-trimester abortions, the increased safety of later abortions has resulted in a change in medical views. Now abortions performed between 12 and 16 weeks may be safer than childbirth, and may be performed on an outpatient basis in nonhospital facilities. Hence the line drawn by the ordinance unreasonably infringes on the right to an abortion.

    b)   The second requirement for written consent of a parent, or approval by a court, is constitutionally insufficient because it does not provide for an alternative procedure whereby a pregnant minor may demonstrate that she is sufficiently mature to make the abortion decision herself, or that, despite her immaturity, an abortion would be in her best interests.

c) The third requirement is unconstitutional because it removes from the physician the responsibility to appropriately counsel the patient, in favor of a rigid list of state-mandated information. It also specifies that the "attending physician" inform the woman, instead of recognizing that other qualified individuals may provide the necessary information and counseling. Although the state may require that a woman give informed consent to an abortion, these requirements are unreasonable obstacles.

d) The fourth requirement that a woman wait 24 hours is arbitrary and does not reasonably serve any legitimate state concern that the woman's decision be informed. The fifth requirement is too vague to support a criminal conviction and is therefore unconstitutional.

4) **Dissenting** (O'Connor, White, Rehnquist, JJ.).

a) The trimester approach of *Roe v. Wade* cannot be defended as a basis for constitutional interpretation when the stages, and their concomitant standards of review, vary with the changing medical technologies. Instead, a regulation imposed on a lawful abortion should not be held unconstitutional unless it unduly burdens the right to seek an abortion, and this standard should apply throughout the entire pregnancy without reference to the particular stage of pregnancy involved.

b) The fallacy of the trimester approach is apparent because improvements in medical technology both move forward the point at which the state may regulate abortion for reasons of maternal health and move backwards the point of viability at which the state may proscribe abortions except when necessary to preserve the life and health of the mother. The *Roe* framework is on a collision course with itself. Stare decisis is insufficient justification for continuing to follow such an unworkable framework for analysis.

c) The state has two important interests in regulating abortion—the health and safety of the mother and protecting the potentiality of human life. These interests are present throughout the pregnancy. Because potential life is just as potential before as after viability, the state's interest in protecting human life should exist during the entire pregnancy.

d) The constitutional right to an abortion is not unqualified. The best approach would require that state interference heavily burden the right before heightened scrutiny be applied, as in other fundamental-rights cases. In abortion cases, a heavy burden would be an absolute obstacle or a severe limitation on the abortion decision, such as was involved in *Roe* itself. The requirement that a second-trimester abortion be performed in a hospital does not constitute a significant obstacle. Because it is rationally related to a valid state objective, it should be upheld.

5) **Comment.** The Court upheld a requirement that a second physician attend a postviability abortion and a requirement that a pathologist examine all tissue surgically removed in hospitals. [Planned Parenthood Association v. Ashcroft, 462 U.S. 476 (1983)] The Court also upheld a state law that required that second-trimester abortions be performed in licensed hospitals, because the statutory definition included licensed outpatient surgical clinics. [Simopoulos v. Virginia, 462 U.S. 506 (1983)]

4. **Family Living Arrangements, Parental Rights, and the Right to Marry.**

a. **Basic rule.** As discussed *supra*, the privacy of family life is a fundamental right. Numerous cases have raised questions about the scope of this aspect of privacy. The Court has continued to apply strict scrutiny to governmental interference with personal privacy in these areas.

Moore v. City of East Cleveland

b. **Housing--Moore v. City of East Cleveland,** 431 U.S. 494 (1977).

1) **Facts.** Moore (D) lived with her son and two grandsons, who were cousins. The City of East Cleveland (P) filed a criminal charge against D for her violation of a city ordinance restricting occupancy of a dwelling unit to members of a single family, defined by certain categories, none of which included D's arrangement. D moved to dismiss, but her motion was overruled, and she was convicted. The state courts upheld the conviction. D appeals.

2) **Issue.** May a local ordinance restrict occupation of dwelling units to certain specified categories of related individuals?

3) **Held.** No. Judgment reversed.

a) The state courts based their decision on *Village of Belle Terre v. Boraas*, 416 U.S. 1 (1974). That case involved restrictions only on unrelated individuals.

b) When the government intrudes on choices of family living arrangements, the legitimacy of the governmental interests and the effectiveness of the regulations must be carefully examined. This statute cannot stand such scrutiny since it only marginally, if at all, works to reduce overcrowding and traffic problems.

    c)   P contends that a constitutional right to live together extends only to the nuclear family. Such legislative classifications are appropriate limits on substantive due process only if they reflect respect for and recognition of the basic values that underlie our society. The extended family has a strong tradition in our history, and the United States Constitution prohibits P from forcing all its people to live in certain narrowly defined family patterns.

    4)   **Dissenting** (Stewart, Rehnquist, JJ.). The constitutionally protected freedom of association relates to promotion of speech, assembly, the press, or religion, not to an interest in the gratification, convenience, and economy of sharing the same residence. D's interest in sharing the dwelling cannot be equated with the fundamental decisions to marry and to bear and raise children, as the majority has done. P's line-drawing is no more onerous than other lines that have been upheld in earlier cases.

    5)   **Dissenting** (White, J.). The Court ought not expand the substantive content of the Due Process Clause in order to strike down what it considers unfavorable legislation. The issue is whether there is actual deprivation of life, liberty, or property. The Due Process Clause should not be used to protect any right or privilege that the Court deems deeply rooted in the country's tradition from all but the most important state regulatory interests.

5.   **The Right to Marry--Zablocki v. Redhail,** 434 U.S. 374 (1978).

    Zablocki
    v. Redhail

    a.   **Facts.** Redhail (P), a Wisconsin resident, was denied a marriage license for failure to comply with a Wisconsin statute requiring that an applicant who has a support obligation for a child not in his custody prove that the child is not a public charge and that he has complied with the support obligation. P challenged the statute and obtained declaratory and injunctive relief. Zablocki (D), the county clerk, appeals.

    b.   **Issue.** May a state protect the welfare of out-of-custody children by denying a marriage license to persons not fulfilling their support obligations to such children?

    c.   **Held.** No. Judgment affirmed.

    1)   Marriage is a fundamental right, and significant interference with its exercise cannot be upheld unless closely tailored to effectuate sufficiently important state interests. Assuming that the state's interests of protecting out-of-custody children and motivating applicants to fulfill prior support obligations are valid, the means used by the state unnecessarily impinge on the right to marry.

2) The state's procedure relies on a collection device rationale that is inappropriate. The state has numerous other effective means for exacting compliance with support obligations that do not restrict the right to marry. In addition, the statute tends to impair an applicant's ability to improve his financial situation and thus improve his ability to meet prior support obligations.

d. **Concurring** (Stewart, J.). The problem here is not discriminatory classifications but unwarranted encroachment on liberty protected by the Due Process Clause. The equal protection doctrine as applied here is no more than substantive due process by another name.

e. **Concurring** (Powell, J.). The Court's rationale intrudes too broadly into the state's traditional power to regulate the marriage relation. This statute is improper only because it fails to provide for those without means to comply with child-support obligations.

Bowers v. Hardwick

6. **The Limits of Privacy—No Constitutional Right to Commit Consensual Sodomy--Bowers v. Hardwick, 478 U.S. 186 (1986).**

a. **Facts.** Hardwick (P) was charged with committing sodomy with another adult male in P's bedroom in violation of a state law forbidding sodomy by any person. The district attorney decided not to pursue the case, but P sued, challenging the constitutionality of the statute as applied to consensual sodomy. The district court dismissed the suit, but the court of appeals reversed. The Supreme Court granted certiorari.

b. **Issue.** Does a person have a fundamental constitutional right to engage in consensual homosexual sodomy?

c. **Held.** No. Judgment reversed.

1) Prior cases have recognized a right of privacy in matters of child-rearing and education, family relationships, procreation, contraception, and abortion. None of those rights bears any resemblance to the right P claims to engage in homosexual sodomy. The precedent does not recognize a constitutional right to engage in any kind of private sexual conduct between consenting adults.

2) Rights that qualify for heightened judicial protection are those fundamental liberties implicit in the concept of ordered liberty, such that neither liberty nor justice would exist without them, and those that are deeply rooted in the country's history and tradition. A right to homosexual sodomy falls within neither category. Sodomy is a common law offense that is still forbidden by 24 states. The Court must be prudent in expanding the substantive reach of the Due Process Clause.

3) The fact that an offense takes place in the home does not make it immune from criminal sanction. Adultery, incest, and other sexual crimes may be punishable even when they are committed in a home. *Stanley v. Georgia* involved first amendment freedoms and is distinguishable from this case.

d. **Concurring** (Burger, C.J.). There is no such thing as a fundamental right to commit homosexual sodomy. The act has long been denounced as immoral. The states have legislative authority to forbid such conduct.

e. **Concurring** (Powell, J.). P may have had an eighth amendment issue, since the statute permits a punishment of up to 20 years imprisonment for a single act of private, consensual sodomy. That issue is not raised, however.

f. **Dissenting** (Blackmun, Brennan, Marshall, Stevens, JJ.). P's claim that the statute impinges on his privacy and right of intimate association does not depend on his sexual orientation, because the statute does not apply only to homosexuals. The right of privacy extends to personal decisions such as how a person may define himself through sexual intimacy. There may be many "right" ways of conducting intimate sexual relationships and much of the richness of a relationship may come from the freedom an individual has to choose the form and nature of the intensely personal bond. Additionally, the right of an individual to conduct intimate relationships in the intimacy of his or her own home is the heart of the Constitution's protection of privacy.

g. **Dissenting** (Stevens, Brennan, Marshall, JJ.). The law applies as well to married persons, thereby affecting intimate decisions clearly protected by the Due Process Clause. Thus the statute is overbroad at least. The state cannot justify selectively applying the law to homosexuals.

7. **The Right to Die--Cruzan v. Director, Missouri Department of Health**, 110 S. Ct. 2841 (1990).

a. **Facts.** Cruzan (P) was injured in an automobile accident and entered a persistent vegetative state, her body kept functioning by artificial nutrition and hydration procedures. P's parents asked that the medical procedures be terminated, which would cause P's death. When the hospital employees refused to do so without a court order, P's parents sued the Director, Missouri Department of Health (D) on P's behalf. At the trial, one of P's friends testified that P had said, prior to her accident, that she would not want to live if she became a vegetable. Based on this evidence, the trial court granted P relief. The Missouri Supreme Court reversed on the ground that the evidence was insufficient to constitute clear and convincing proof of P's desire to have hydration and nutrition withdrawn. The Supreme Court granted certiorari.

b. **Issue.** May a state require proof by clear and convincing evidence of an incompetent patient's wishes as to the withdrawal of life-sustaining medical treatment?

c. **Held.** Yes. Judgment affirmed.

1) The common-law doctrine of informed consent to medical procedures, developed out of the law of battery, includes the right of a competent individual to refuse medical treatment. This right is a constitutionally protected liberty interest, and it may be assumed that a competent person has a constitutionally protected right to refuse lifesaving hydration and nutrition, but this right must be balanced against the relevant state interests.

2) P asserts that an incompetent person should have the same right as a competent person to refuse lifesaving medical procedures. However, the incompetent person cannot by definition exercise this right; it must be exercised on her behalf by someone else. Missouri has determined that a surrogate may act on behalf of an incompetent patient such as P, but only if there is clear and convincing evidence of the incompetent's wishes as to the withdrawal of the treatment.

3) Missouri has an important interest in the protection and preservation of human life. In this case, the choice between life and death is a deeply personal decision, and the state may safeguard the personal element by requiring a high standard of proof. The state has placed the increased risk of an erroneous decision on those seeking to terminate the incompetent patient's life, and this does not violate the Constitution.

4) Nor is the state required by the Constitution to defer to the "substituted judgment" of P's parents, even though in other cases the Court has permitted state schemes in which parents make decisions for minors.

d. **Concurring** (O'Connor, J.). The Constitution may require a state to give effect to the decisions of a surrogate decision-maker, but that issue is not decided in this case.

e. **Concurring** (Scalia, J.). The States, not the Constitution or the Supreme Court, have the power to prevent suicide, and the citizens of Missouri must decide whether to honor the wishes of a patient who wants life-sustaining medical procedures to be withdrawn. The Due Process Clause only protects against deprivation of liberty without due process of law. The Constitution says nothing about P's alleged desire to die. The limits that ought not to be exceeded in requiring an individual to preserve her own life are not set forth in the Due Process Clause, but are to be determined by the democratic majority. The Equal Protection Clause, which requires the majority to accept for themselves what they impose on others, assures that the appropriate limits are not exceeded, whatever those limits are.

f. **Dissenting** (Brennan, Marshall, Blackmun, JJ.). The liberty interest in being free of unwanted medical treatment is fundamental, and no State interest can outweigh the rights of a person in P's position. Missouri does have a general interest in preserving life, but this does not outweigh an individual's choice to avoid medical treatment. Missouri, as parens patriae for the incompetent P, also has an interest in safeguarding the accuracy of the determination of P's wishes. But by imposing a heightened evidentiary standard, Missouri has excluded relevant evidence and moved away from an accurate determination. Instead of protecting life, Missouri has defined life as the biological persistence of P's bodily functions. There is no reasonable ground to believe that P has any personal interest in the perpetuation of what Missouri has decided is her life. In cases such as this, the best interests of all related third parties should prevail over Missouri's general state policy that ignores those interests.

G. PROCEDURAL DUE PROCESS

1. Due Process and Entitlements.

a. **Introduction.** Both the fifth and fourteenth amendments protect against the deprivation of "life, liberty, or property" without due process of law. Although due process was traditionally used most often to provide procedural safeguards for criminal defendants, it also protects a range of liberty and property interests outside the criminal context. The liberty and property interests of which persons cannot be deprived without due process do not turn upon whether the interest involved is a "right" rather than a "privilege." Such a definitional approach has been rejected by the Court. The scope of liberty and property rights protected by due process, however, has not always been easy to describe.

1) **Liberty.** It is clear that "liberty" connotes more than freedom from the bodily restraints imposed by the criminal process. It includes at least the right to contract, to engage in gainful employment, and "generally to enjoy those privileges long recognized at common law as essential to the orderly pursuit of happiness by free men."

2) **Property.** Similarly, "property" includes more than just actual ownership of realty, chattels, or money. It includes "interests already acquired in specific benefits." However, there must be more than a mere abstract need or desire for, or unilateral expectation of, the benefit. The Constitution does not create property interests; there must be a legitimate claim to an existing interest already derived from state or federal law. Thus there is a property interest in public education when school attendance is required [Goss v. Lopez, 419 U.S. 565 (1975)], in retention of a driver's license under prevailing statutory standards [Bell v. Burson, 402 U.S. 535 (1971)], and in having continued utility service where state law permits a municipal utility company to terminate service only "for cause" [Memphis Light, Gas & Water Division v. Craft, 436 U.S. 1 (1978)].

b. **Procedural due process requirements.** Procedural safeguards against invasion of private liberty and property rights have gained increased attention in recent years. The Court applies a two-pronged test. The first question is whether the implicated right is a constitutionally protected interest in life, liberty, or property. If so, the courts must examine the procedural safeguards to determine their constitutional adequacy.

c. **Welfare benefits.** In *Goldberg v. Kelly*, 397 U.S. 254 (1970), the Court held that welfare benefits are an entitlement. By definition, a person entitled to receive welfare needs the assistance for essentials such as food, clothing, housing, and medical care. Termination of benefits despite a controversy over eligibility may deprive an eligible recipient of the necessities of life. The same governmental interests behind the welfare program also support its continuation to eligible recipients. These interests are not outweighed by the need to conserve governmental fiscal and administrative resources; the latter interests are not overriding in the welfare context. Thus, welfare benefits may not be terminated without due process.

d. **Public employment.** Whether there is a "property" interest in continued public employment is determined by state (or federal) law. A statute (or ordinance), the employment contract, or some clear practice or understanding must provide that the employee can be terminated only for "cause." [Arnett v. Kennedy, 416 U.S. 134 (1974)] There is no "property" interest if the position is held "at the will of " the public employer. [Bishop v. Wood, 426 U.S. 341 (1976).

e.   **Applicability of due process protections--Board of Regents v. Roth,** 408 U.S. 564 (1972).

1)   **Facts.** Roth (P) was hired as a teacher in a public university for a fixed term of one academic year. He was not rehired and was given no reason for the decision. State law allows tenure only after four years' employment and leaves hiring decisions for nontenured teachers to the discretion of university officials. P sued the Board of Regents (D), claiming that he was deprived of liberty and property without a constitutionally required hearing. The lower courts held for P. D appeals.

2)   **Issue.** Does a government employee have a constitutional right to a statement of reasons and a hearing on his employer's decision not to rehire him?

3)   **Held.** No. Judgment reversed.

a)   Liberty and property interests protected by the fourteenth amendment are broadly construed, but not infinite. Certain boundaries must be respected to give the words meaning. P simply was not rehired, and D did nothing to interfere with or restrict his freedom to seek another job. The concept of "liberty" does not extend to an otherwise nonexistent right to be employed by a certain employer.

b)   Property interests are not created by the Constitution but by independent sources, such as state law, that also define their dimensions. P here was given no specific contractual interest in being rehired, nor did state law recognize any such property interest. P has only an abstract concern in being rehired, which cannot be considered a property interest to be protected by the fourteenth amendment. Therefore the Constitution does not require that P be given a hearing before not being rehired.

4)   **Dissenting** (Marshall, J.). Every citizen is entitled to every government job he applies for unless the government can establish a reason for denying employment. This is a property right protected by the fourteenth amendment. It is also liberty to work, which is likewise protected.

5)   **Comment.** In *Perry v. Sindermann*, 408 U.S. 593 (1972), a companion case to *Roth*, the Court held that if the state has a program of de facto tenure (i.e., teachers are assured that they have the equivalent of tenure), even a nontenured teacher is entitled to a hearing and the opportunity to rebut the charges that led to his termination.

6)   **Comment.** A plaintiff can establish a prima facie case by showing that the government had an improper purpose that

was a motivating factor in its decision not to rehire, which the government can rebut only by showing it would have made the same decision even were the improper purpose not present.

Cleveland Board of Education v. Loudermill

f. **Property interest in public job--Cleveland Board of Education v. Loudermill,** 470 U.S. 532 (1985).

1) **Facts.** Loudermill (P) was hired as a security guard by the Cleveland Board of Education (D). He had indicated on his application that he had never been convicted of a felony, but 11 months later D discovered that he had been convicted of grand larceny. D fired P by letter, citing his dishonesty. Under state law, P could only be fired for cause. P claimed the manner of his dismissal violated his due process rights. The lower courts agreed, and the Supreme Court granted certiorari.

2) **Issue.** Is a public employee who may only be terminated for cause entitled to a hearing before being terminated?

3) **Held.** Yes. Judgment affirmed.

   a) Property interests are protected by, but not created by, the Constitution. P clearly had a property interest here because under state law he could not be dismissed except for cause.

   b) D claims that because state law created the property interest, P's property right is conditioned on the legislature's choice of procedure for the termination of the right. While this notion once was accepted by the Court in *Arnett v. Kennedy*, 416 U.S. 134 (1974), it is no longer the law. Instead, under the Due Process Clause, once a property right exists, it cannot be taken away except pursuant to constitutionally adequate procedures.

4) **Dissenting** (Rehnquist, J.). The state created a limited right in employment, a type of tenure, and set forth the procedure for termination of the tenure. The majority is disregarding this limitation on P's property interest.

g. **Liberty.** In *Paul v. Davis*, 424 U.S. 693 (1976), the Court held that the plaintiff suffered no deprivation of liberty as a result of his identification as an active shoplifter in a flyer produced by the local police and distributed to local merchants. Defamation resulting only in damage to one's reputation was held not to be a denial of protected "liberty." As a result, the definition of liberty was assumed to depend on state determinations.

Vitek v. Jones

h. **Prisoner transfer--Vitek v. Jones,** 445 U.S. 480 (1980).

1) **Facts.** Jones (P), a convicted felon, was transferred involuntarily from state prison to a mental hospital under a Nebraska statute that permitted such transfers upon certain findings made by a designated physician or psychologist. P intervened in a suit brought by other prisoners against Vitek (D), the Director of Correctional Services, challenging the statutory procedures on procedural due process grounds. The district court held that the transfer, without adequate notice and an opportunity for a hearing, deprived P of liberty without due process, contrary to the fourteenth amendment. D appeals.

2) **Issue.** Does an incarcerated prisoner have a liberty interest that requires notice and hearing before he can be transferred to a mental hospital?

3) **Held.** Yes. Judgment affirmed.

   a) A criminal conviction and sentence of imprisonment extinguish an individual's right to freedom from confinement for the term of his sentence. However, states may create liberty interests such as parole, probation, or good-time credits that, once granted, cannot be revoked without satisfying the procedural protections of the Due Process Clause.

   b) The state statute challenged here created an "objective expectation" that a prisoner would not be transferred unless certain mental conditions existed. This constitutes a liberty interest entitling P to the benefits of appropriate procedures.

   c) Even without the statute, P's interest in not being transferred to a mental hospital constituted a liberty interest because of the social stigma and increased restriction on freedom he would face in the mental institution.

4) **Dissenting** (Burger, C.J., Blackmun, Rehnquist, Stewart, JJ.). The case is moot.

5) **Comment.** Only four Justices felt that a prisoner has a right to counsel in such a proceeding, so no such right exists.

i. **Use of rational basis standard.** In an unusual set of concurring opinions, the majority of the Court held that a state scheme that permitted a hearing on an employment discrimination complaint only if processed within 120 days violated equal protection because the limitation was not rationally related to any legitimate governmental objective. [Logan v. Zimmerman Brush Co., 455 U.S. 422 (1982)]

2. **Determination of What Process Is Due.**

a. **Introduction.** In recent years the courts have given increased attention to the actual procedural safeguards against invasion of private liberty and property rights. Once the existence of a constitutionally protected interest in life, liberty, or property is established, the courts must examine the adequacy of the procedures afforded. The courts must weigh the following factors to determine the extent of the procedures required:

1) The importance of the individual interest involved;

2) The value of specific procedural safeguards to that interest; and

3) The governmental interest in fiscal and administrative efficiency.

Goldberg
v. Kelly

b. **Minimum procedural rights--Goldberg v. Kelly,** 397 U.S. 254 (1970).

1) **Facts.** Kelly (P) was a recipient of public assistance payments in New York. P's benefits were terminated after an informal review by government officials but without giving P an opportunity for a hearing until after the termination. P challenged the procedure, claiming it was a deprivation of due process. The lower courts held that only a pretermination evidentiary hearing would satisfy the constitutional requirements. Goldberg (D), a government official, appeals.

2) **Issue.** Must the government provide an opportunity for an evidentiary hearing before it terminates public assistance to a recipient?

3) **Held.** Yes. Judgment affirmed.

a) Welfare benefits are a statutory entitlement to those qualified to receive them. Termination of such benefits is state action. The extent of the process due to such recipients depends on the balance between the recipient's interest in avoiding the loss and the government's interest in summary adjudication.

b) By definition, a person entitled to receive welfare needs the assistance for essentials such as food, clothing, housing, and medical care. Termination of benefits despite a controversy over eligibility may deprive an eligible recipient of the necessities of life. The same governmental interests behind the welfare program also support its continuation to eligible recipients. D would outweigh these interests by the need to conserve governmental fiscal and administrative resources, but the latter interests are not overriding in the welfare context. Thus, welfare benefits may not be terminated without due process.

c) A full judicial or quasi-judicial trial is not necessary to satisfy the requirements of due process. A fair hearing need only have the following attributes:

(1) Notice of the reasons for a proposed termination and a hearing at a meaningful time and in a meaningful manner;

(2) The right to confront and cross-examine adverse witnesses;

(3) The right to counsel, although the state need not furnish counsel in all cases;

(4) A decision resting on the legal rules and evidence adduced at the hearing, shown by a statement of the reasons for the decision and the evidence relied on; and

(5) An impartial decision-maker.

4) **Dissenting.** The government's promise of charity to an individual is not property when the government denies that the individual is entitled to receive the payment. This decision is not based on the language of the Constitution, but only on what the majority feel would be a fair and humane procedure in this case. This is a matter for legislatures, not courts.

c. **Weighing test--Mathews v. Eldridge,** 424 U.S. 319 (1976).

Mathews v. Eldridge

1) **Facts.** Eldridge (P) was awarded Social Security disability insurance benefits in 1968. About four years later the state agency that administered the benefits determined, based on medical reports, that P's disability terminated. The agency so notified P by letter, and after receiving a written rebuttal from P, terminated P's benefits. Rather than seek reconsideration, P sued, seeking an immediate reinstatement of benefits pending a hearing on the issue of his disability. The lower courts, relying on *Goldberg*, upheld P's claim. Mathews (D) appeals.

2) **Issue.** Is a recipient of disability insurance benefits entitled to an evidentiary hearing prior to the initial termination of benefits?

3) **Held.** No. Judgment reversed.

a) The requirements of due process vary depending on the particular circumstances involved. In setting forth the constitutional requirements, courts must balance the private interest affected, together with the risk of an erroneous deprivation and the added value of additional procedural safeguards, against the government's interest.

        b)   P's sole interest is in continuing payments, because if upon reconsideration he prevails, he will receive full retroactive relief. Unlike in *Goldberg*, a disabled person has other sources of income; disability payments are not based on financial need. Welfare benefits are available if the termination of disability places P below the subsistence level. Thus, P's interest is significant, but less than was at issue in *Goldberg*.

        c)   The administrative pretermination procedures are less likely to err in disability cases as opposed to welfare cases because in the former, only medical records are involved. Welfare cases require consideration of a variety of factors. P was notified and given a chance to respond before benefits were terminated. An oral evidentiary hearing would add little.

        d)   Finally, the government's interest in conserving resources must be considered, even though financial cost is not the controlling factor. Weight must be given to the good-faith judgments of those who administer the disability programs.

    4)   **Dissenting** (Brennan, Marshall, JJ.). The legislative decision to provide disability benefits assumes a financial need the majority ignores. In fact, after his benefits were terminated, P's home and furniture were repossessed; P and his entire family had to sleep in one bed.

    5)   **Comment.** In summary, to determine whether a prior hearing is required, and the extent of procedural requirements, the court must weigh (i) the importance of the individual interest involved, (ii) the value of the specific procedural safeguards to that interest, and (iii) the governmental interest in fiscal and administrative efficiency.

  d.   **Commitment of children to mental hospitals.** In *Parham v. J.R.*, 442 U.S. 584 (1979), the Court held that formal adversary hearings are not required when parents commit their children to state mental hospitals, because children's rights are circumscribed by parental interests and responsibilities.

  e.   **Termination of parental rights.** The Court has held that counsel need not be appointed when the state seeks to terminate an indigent's parental rights, except in particular circumstances. [*See* Lassiter v. Department of Social Services, 452 U.S. 18 (1981)]

  f.   **Irrebuttable presumptions.** The use of irrebuttable presumptions as to membership in a class may deny equal protection to individuals who meet the class qualifications but whose particular situations are divergent from the legislative purpose for the classification. Such persons have a right to a hearing to rebut the presumption of class membership.

VIII. FREE EXPRESSION

A. INTRODUCTION

1. **Constitutional Provision.** The first amendment provides that "Congress shall make no law . . . abridging the freedom of speech, or of the press; or the right of the people peaceably to assemble, and to petition the Government for a redress of grievances."

2. **Balancing Interests.** The right to freedom of expression is not an absolute right to say or do anything that one desires. Rather, the interests of the government in regulating such expression must be balanced against the very strong interests on which this right is based.

   a. **Rationale.** The rationale behind freedom of speech is that such freedom will lead to the discovery of truth and better ideas through the competition of differing viewpoints. Such speech and action is a necessity for a free society that is to be governed by democratic principles. It allows the people to bring about changes through nonviolent expression.

   b. **Presumption of validity.** Legislation is normally presumed valid. This rule also applies for restrictions on expression, although freedom of speech is an important interest which cannot be restricted unless the government has a clearly overriding interest. A statute may be invalid on its face, which means that it is unconstitutional in all of its applications. More commonly, however, a statute is held unconstitutional only as applied to the particular fact situation presented by the case.

   c. **Special scrutiny.** There is a general consensus that first amendment rights are special. The issue in most cases involves the proper balance between the free speech interest and the countervailing government interest that is being asserted. In some areas involving expression, the law is clear. In other areas, the law remains unsettled.

B. RESTRICTIONS ON DANGEROUS IDEAS AND INFORMATION

1. **Advocacy of Illegal Action.**

   a. **Development of basic principles.** Certain types of expression may be punished as criminal acts. For example, a riot may constitute an expression of dissent, but damaging property is a criminal act. Speech which is likely to produce illegal activity may itself be illegal. World War I prompted a series of cases in which the Court dealt with advocacy of illegal action.

1) **Incitement--Masses Publishing Co. v. Patten,** 244 F. 535 (S.D.N.Y. 1917).

    a) **Facts.** Patten (D), the New York postmaster, refused to accept for mailing a magazine published by Masses Publishing (P). D claimed the publication violates the Espionage Act. P seeks an injunction.

    b) **Issue.** May the government refuse to permit use of the mails by private magazines that criticize public policy?

    c) **Held.** No. Injunction granted.

        (1) The Act prohibits false statements that interfere with the military or aid its enemies. P has not made such false rumors but has published political arguments.

        (2) The Act forbids anyone from willfully causing disloyalty among the military. Although anyone who adopts P's views would be more prone to insubordination than one having faith in the existing policies, such an interpretation of causation would prohibit any expression of views counter to those currently prevailing, an impermissible restriction in a democratic society. Of course, one may not counsel or advise violation of the law as it now stands, but everyone is free to advocate changing the law.

        (3) The Act also forbids willful obstruction of the enlistment service. But here only direct advocacy of resistance, or actual incitement, is prohibited. P has not done such an incitement.

    d) **Comment.** The decision by Judge Learned Hand was reversed on appeal. The circuit court did not agree with the incitement test and deferred to the Postmaster General's discretion.

2) **Clear and present danger test--Schenck v. United States,** 249 U.S. 47 (1919).

    a) **Facts.** The Espionage Act of 1917 made it a crime to cause or attempt to cause insubordination in the military forces or to obstruct recruitment. Schenck (D) published a pamphlet that attacked the Conscription Act and encouraged disobedience to it. D distributed the pamphlet directly to draftees. D was convicted of attempting to cause insubordination. D appeals.

    b) **Issue.** May Congress outlaw speech that presents a clear and present danger to an important government interest?

    c) **Held.** Yes. Judgment affirmed.

(1) The right of free expression is not absolute but varies with the circumstances; e.g., a man is not free to falsely yell "fire" in a crowded theater.

(2) The first question is whether Congress is pursuing a proper end or purpose in the legislation. Here it is. Congress has the right to prohibit the evils at which this statute is aimed, especially in time of war.

(3) The next question is to what extent Congress can go in seeking to effectuate its purposes; i.e., how far can it go before it violates the first amendment? Congress cannot make speech a crime unless there is a "clear and present danger" of action resulting from the accused's words that would lead to the legitimately proscribed evil.

(4) The evidence in this case supports the conviction.

d) **Comment.** The Court in *Schenck* also seemed to set up some sort of a scale concerning types of speech. At one end, receiving a low degree of judicial protection, is highly emotional speech, commands which do not appeal to reason or logic but which have the effect of force and advocacy of action ("Strike!"). At the other end, receiving a high degree of protection, is speech that has a high degree of ideological content (political ideas, debate, etc.).

3) **Public speech--Debs v. United States,** 249 U.S. 211 (1919).

Debs v.
United
States

a) **Facts.** Debs (D) made two public speeches promoting socialism and denouncing capitalism and the war. He was convicted under the Espionage Act and appeals.

b) **Issue.** May a political speech denouncing public policy and advocating an alternative be made a criminal act?

c) **Held.** Yes. Judgment affirmed.

(1) D addressed potential draftees, encouraging them to resist the recruiting services as a way to oppose the war. His speech created a clear and present danger that his listeners would actually resist the draft, which is an illegal activity.

4) **Intent.** In *Abrams v. United States*, 250 U.S. 616 (1919), the Court upheld the conviction of Abrams and others under amendments to the Espionage Act that prohibited conspiracy to incite resistance to the United States and conspiracy to urge curtailment of war material production with the intent to hinder the United States in the prosecution of the war. The defendants had anonymously printed and distributed leaflets calling for a general strike to protest the American intrusion into eastern Russia during the first world war. Their sentences ranged from three to twenty years. Justice Holmes dissented, however. He felt that Congress could limit expression only where there was the present danger of immediate evil or an intent to bring it about. He felt that both were lacking in this case because the defendants intended to stop American intervention in Russia, not to hinder the war efforts. He also felt that the first amendment did not leave the common law in force as to seditious libel, and implied that the majority believed that it did. The adoption of the clear and present danger test is generally attributed to this dissent.

b. **State sedition laws.** After World War I, several states enacted what became known as sedition laws.

Gitlow v.
New York

1) **Legislative facts--Gitlow v. New York,** 268 U.S. 652 (1925).

    a) **Facts.** Gitlow (D) was convicted and imprisoned for violating a New York law that prohibited language advocating, advising, or teaching the overthrow of organized government by unlawful means. D appeals. There was no evidence of any effect resulting from D's actions.

    b) **Issue.** May states prohibit advocacy of criminal anarchy when there is no concrete result, or likelihood of such a result, flowing from such advocacy?

    c) **Held.** Yes. Judgment affirmed.

        (1) The state has penalized not doctrinal exposition or academic discussion, but language urging criminal action to overthrow the government. D's expressions clearly fit the statutory prohibition; his words were the language of direct incitement.

        (2) The state has determined that such activity is so inimical to the general welfare that it must be controlled through use of the police power and suppressed in its incipiency. Because the statute is not arbitrary or unreasonable, it must be upheld.

        (3) If the statute itself is constitutional and D's use of language falls within its reach, absence of actual results is irrelevant. The state's determination that these utterances involve sufficient likelihood of causing harm is not clearly erroneous.

    d) **Dissenting** (Holmes, Brandeis, JJ.). D's words did not constitute a present danger of an actual attempt to overthrow the government; they were too indefinite and ineffective. To say D's words were an incitement proves nothing, for every idea is an incitement, and may move the recipient to action depending on outside circumstances.

weapons were present and a speech was made. There was no threat of imminent lawless action. The state courts upheld the conviction. D appeals.

2) **Issue.** May a state law prohibit advocacy of civil disruption without distinguishing between mere advocacy and incitement to imminent lawless action?

3) **Held.** No. Judgment reversed.

a) The constitutional guarantees of free speech and free press do not permit a state to forbid advocacy of the use of force or of lawlessness except where such advocacy (i) is directed to inciting or producing imminent lawless action and (ii) is likely to incite or produce such action.

b) Ohio's law fails to make the required distinction and cannot be upheld.

4) **Concurring** (Black, J.). The Court cites the *Dennis* case (*supra*) but properly does not agree with the *Dennis* "clear and present danger" doctrine.

5) **Concurring** (Douglas, J.). The line between permissible and impermissible acts is the line between ideas and overt acts. The "clear and present danger" test has no place under the Constitution.

6) **Comment.** Applying the *Brandenburg* incitement standard, the Court reversed a disorderly conduct conviction in *Hess v. Indiana*, 414 U.S. 105 (1973), a case involving a campus antiwar demonstration. The Court held that since appellant's statement could be interpreted in various ways, there was no rational inference from the language that the words were intended to produce imminent disorder. The Court stated that words that only had a tendency to lead to violence could not be punished by the state.

2. **Criticism of the Judicial Process--Bridges v. California,** 314 U.S. 252 (1941).

Bridges v. California

a. **Facts.** Two rival labor unions were involved in litigation. The trial judge ruled against the union headed by Bridges (D), and D published a statement criticizing the judge's ruling as "outrageous" and threatening a strike if the ruling was not overturned. At about the same time, the *Los Angeles Times* published an editorial encouraging the judge to sentence two convicted union members to prison. Both D and the *Times's* publisher were convicted of contempt. They appeal.

b. **Issue.** May comments made about the judicial process during the pendency of the case involved be punished as contempt of court?

c. **Held.** No. Judgment reversed.

1) Under the *Schenck* clear and present danger rule, utterances may be punished only when the substantive evil is extremely serious and the degree of imminence extremely high. Another consideration is the practical impact of a restriction on speech.

2) In this case, the restriction on speech is significant because public interest is at its peak when the case is pending; using the contempt power to suppress this speech has a large impact on freedom of speech.

3) The first substantive evil allegedly resulting from the speech is disrespect for the judiciary, but such respect cannot be won or preserved by suppressing speech. The second evil is disorderly and unfair administration of justice. While this interest may be affected by publications that interfere with pending litigation, the actual speech in this case could not have that effect. The *Los Angeles Times* expresses a consistent opinion in these matters, and its editorial was to be expected. It could not reasonably be considered to influence the judge. D's speech was nothing more than an explicit statement of what the judge must have been aware was a possibility anyway.

d. **Dissenting.** The speech used in this case was clearly intended to intimidate the judge involved. The *Los Angeles Times* has a powerful influence on public opinion, and its views would likely be a factor when the judge comes up for reelection. D's strike threat was an obvious attempt to secure a favorable ruling. The right to free speech does not override the right to the impartial disposition of lawsuits.

3. **Provoking a Hostile Response.**

a. **Basic rule.** Free speech does not include the right to disrupt the community. Fighting words are not protected, but an unfavorable response by the audience is not necessarily enough to render the speech unprotected. In *Terminiello v. Chicago*, 337 U.S. 1 (1949), the Court held unconstitutional a breach of the peace statute that included a restriction on speech that stirs the public to anger, invites dispute, or causes unrest. One of the functions of free speech is the invitation to dispute; free speech is often provocative and challenging.

b. **Breach of the peace--Cantwell v. Connecticut,** 310 U.S. 296 (1940).

    1) **Facts.** Cantwell (D) played a religious phonograph record on a public street. The record attacked generally all organized religious systems and was offensive to some, who threatened D with harm. D peacefully moved up the street. D was later convicted of breaching the peace. D appeals.

    2) **Issue.** May public expression, offensive to some but not personally abusive, which does not result in a clear and present danger to a substantial state interest, be punished as a breach of the peace?

    3) **Held.** No. Judgment reversed.

        a) Although breach of the peace embraces a variety of conduct dangerous to public order and tranquility, including fighting words, it cannot extend to undue suppression of free communication of views, religious or otherwise. No complaints indicated that the sound of D's phonograph disturbed the public.

        b) Although D's activity aroused animosity, it was not the personal abuse that is unprotected by the first amendment, but instead an attempt to persuade others of D's apparently unpopular views. D avoided actual confrontation. Therefore, he did not breach the peace.

c. **Protective suppression--Feiner v. New York,** 340 U.S. 315 (1951).

    1) **Facts.** Feiner (D) was addressing a street meeting and attracted a crowd, but there was no disorder. One man told the police officers that if they did not stop D, he would. The police asked D to stop speaking and arrested him when D refused to obey. He was convicted of disorderly conduct and appeals.

    2) **Issue.** May police act to suppress speech that in their judgment is causing a breach of the peace?

    3) **Held.** Yes. Judgment affirmed.

        a) D was accorded a full, fair trial, the result of which was a determination that D was arrested and convicted not for his speech but for the reaction it caused. The police were justified in acting to preserve peace and order.

    4) **Dissenting** (Black, J.). The police had a duty to protect D's right to talk, even to the extent of arresting the man who threatened to interfere.

5) Dissenting (Douglas, Minton, JJ.). The police improperly sided with the person who sought to deny D's right to speak, and in effect became censors.

6) Comment. The problems of freedom of expression in public places really have two aspects—one is the idea of the content of the speech. For example, political dialogue or comment is clearly going to receive greater protection than is business advertising. The second element is that of the conduct involved. As in *Feiner*, when there is a clear and present danger that the conduct involved will lead to harmful results, greater restrictions on the speech are permitted.

d. Fighting words.

1) Categorization approach. In *Chaplinsky v. New Hampshire*, 315 U.S. 568 (1942), the Court held that a state may forbid the use in a public place of words that would be likely to cause an addressee to fight—so-called fighting words. Chaplinsky had called the city marshall a "damned Fascist" and a "God damned racketeer." The Court held that fighting words are one of the "well-defined and narrowly limited classes of speech" not protected by the Constitution. Other classes included bribery, perjury, and criminal solicitation.

2) Balancing approach. Because categorization presents such a high risk of being over—inclusive, the Court has adopted a balancing approach to most content-based restrictions on speech. Balancing presents the danger of being susceptible to manipulation by those who apply the law.

3) Current status of fighting words analysis. The *Chaplinsky* approach appears to retain validity as long as the statute involved is narrowly construed. In *Gooding v. Wilson*, 405 U.S. 518 (1972), the Court reversed a conviction for using provocative words because the statute was overbroad. The Court apparently would uphold a statute applicable only to words that "have a direct tendency to cause acts of violence by the person to whom, individually, the remark is addressed."

4. Disclosure of Confidential Information.

a. Protection against prior restraint. There is a strong policy against prior restraints of media reporting of criminal proceedings. Such reporting is a means of ensuring a fair trial for the accused. On the other hand, there is a risk that media coverage could taint a trial by giving jurors evidence not properly admitted at trial or by creating an atmosphere that makes a fair trial impossible. Before an injunction against media reporting can be granted, the court must find that (i) there is a clear and present danger that pretrial publicity would (not merely could) threaten a fair trial, (ii) alternative measures are inadequate, and (iii) an injunction would effectively protect the accused.

b.   **Reasonable protections.** In *Sheppard v. Maxwell*, 384 U.S. 333 (1966), the Court agreed with the lower court's finding that the media had exceeded reasonable bounds in covering the accused's murder trial. The jurors, witnesses, and counsel were photographed as they came and went, and publicity contained information not presented at trial. The jury was sequestered only for deliberations. The Court, despite its reluctance to limit the media's freedom to report the public proceedings, set forth several means for trial judges to use to reasonably protect defendants, including sequestration of the jury at an early stage, transfer of the trial to another court, and a continuance.

c.   **Restriction on pretrial reporting--Nebraska Press Association v. Stuart,** 427 U.S. 539 (1976).

1)   **Facts.** Stuart (D), a state district judge, presided over the criminal trial involving a shocking multiple murder that had occurred in a small Nebraska town. To avoid the dangers that pretrial publicity would present to the fairness of the accused's trial, D entered a restrictive order that prohibited Nebraska Press Association (P) and others from reporting certain subjects relating to the trial. The order applied only until the jury was impaneled. On appeal, the Nebraska Supreme Court modified D's order to prohibit reporting only of any confessions made by the accused (except to members of the press) and other facts "strongly implicative" of the accused. P appeals.

2)   **Issue.** Is a prior restraint on pretrial publicity, intended to ensure the fairness of a criminal defendant's trial, subject to a lesser standard of review than prior restraints generally?

3)   **Held.** No. Judgment reversed.

a)   Generally, pretrial publicity does not threaten the right to a trial by an impartial jury because of the trial judge's control over proceedings (e.g., change of venue, continuance, and sequestration of jury). However, in certain "sensational" cases, like the one here, the possibility arises that these normal means of preserving fairness are inadequate. Accordingly, resort is sometimes made to a restrictive order such as that used by D.

b)   Prior restraints on speech and publication pose the most serious and least tolerable infringements on first amendment rights. The barriers to prior restraint may not be relaxed even where there is a possible conflict with an equally important constitutional right. The barrier may be breached only where "the gravity of the 'evil,' discounted by its improbability, justifies such invasion of free speech as is necessary to avoid the danger."

    c)   The "evil" of an unfair trial is clearly great. However, the evidence here is insufficient to show that, except for the prior restraint imposed by D, the accused would certainly have had an unfair trial. Before any prior restraint is permissible, a court must find a clear and present danger that pretrial publicity would (not merely could) threaten a fair trial, that alternative measures would be inadequate, and that the prior restraint would actually protect the accused.

    4)   **Concurring** (Brennan, Stewart, Marshall, JJ.). Resort to prior restraints on the freedom of the press is a constitutionally impermissible means of enforcing the right to a fair trial. Judges have less drastic means of ensuring fundamental fairness. There can be no prohibition on the publication by the press of any information pertaining to pending judicial proceedings or the operation of the criminal justice system, no matter how the information is obtained. There is no need to subordinate first or sixth amendment rights to one or the other.

New York Times Co. v. United States

d.   **Prevention of publication of sensitive government documents--New York Times Co. v. United States** (The Pentagon Papers Case), 403 U.S. 713 (1971).

    1)   **Facts.** The United States (P) sought to enjoin publication by the New York Times (D) and Washington Post of a classified study known as the Pentagon Papers. All federal courts involved except the court of appeals in the New York Times case held that P had not met its heavy burden of justification. D appeals the judgment of the court of appeals in its case.

    2)   **Issue.** May the executive branch prevent publication of items that it considers to threaten grave and irreparable injury to the public interest?

    3)   **Held.** No. Judgment affirmed.

        a)   The United States has failed to meet its heavy burden of showing justification for the enforcement of such a prior restraint.

    4)   **Concurring** (Black, Douglas, JJ.). The injunctions should have been vacated and the cases dismissed without oral argument because it would be impossible to find that the President has "inherent power" to halt the publication of news by resorting to the courts.

5) **Concurring** (Douglas, J.). The only possible power possessed by the government to restrict publication by the press of sensitive material arises from its inherent power to wage war successfully. Congress has not declared war, so the government cannot exercise this power.

6) **Concurring** (Brennan, J.). Courts cannot issue temporary stays and restraining orders to accommodate the government's desire to suppress freedom of the press without adequate proof of a direct, inevitable, and immediate serious adverse effect.

7) **Concurring** (Stewart, White, JJ.). The executive branch has the duty to protect necessary confidentiality through executive regulations. The courts are limited to construing specific regulations and applying specific laws. Since the courts were asked to do neither here, they cannot act.

8) **Concurring** (White, Stewart, JJ.). Some circumstances might justify an injunction as requested, but not these. Congress has relied on criminal sanctions and their deterrent effect to prevent unauthorized disclosures, and the courts should not go beyond the congressional determinations.

9) **Concurring** (Marshall, J.). The Court would violate the concept of separation of powers by using its power to prevent behavior that Congress has specifically declined to prohibit.

10) **Dissenting** (Burger, C.J.). The Court has not had sufficient time to gather and analyze the facts.

11) **Dissenting** (Harlan, J., Burger, C.J., Blackmun, J.). Judicial review of executive action in foreign affairs is narrow. The Court should inquire only whether the subject matter is within the President's foreign relations power and whether the head of the department concerned has personally made the determination that disclosure would irreparably impair national security.

e. **Injunction permitted.** Distinguishing the Pentagon Papers case, a federal district court enjoined a magazine from publishing technical material on hydrogen bomb design, which was available in public documents. In exercising the first instance of prior restraint against a publication, the court cited the government's showing of the likelihood of injury to the nation and the fact that the suppression of the technical portions of the article would not impede the publication in its goal of stimulating public knowledge of nuclear armament and enlightened debate on national policy. [United States v. Progressive, Inc., 467 F. Supp. 990 (W.D. Wis. 1979)] An appeal in that case was dismissed after the government dropped its prosecution.

C.   MANNER OF RESTRICTION

1.   **Introduction.** The fact that particular speech may be constitutionally regulated does not constitute a license for any
type of regulation. The courts have adopted three doctrines
to control the means used to regulate speech regardless of
the type of speech involved.

2.   **Overbreadth.** Legislation that restricts or regulates speech is
tested under the first amendment on the basis of its potential applications. This approach is much broader than the
normal test used in judicial review; i.e., the application of
the statute to the particular facts of the case. The overbreadth doctrine permits consideration of potential applications not before the court. In effect, this is an exception to
the standing requirements because it allows litigation of the
interests of persons, or even hypothetical situations, not
involved in the actual facts of the case. The rationale is
that persons whose expression is constitutionally protected
might refrain from that expression for fear of criminal sanctions if the statute could reach their expression. There is
no requirement that such persons subject themselves to sanctions to have their first amendment rights vindicated.

3.   **Vagueness.** A statute may not be overbroad, yet it may be
impermissible because it is too vague. Any law that forces
persons of common intelligence to necessarily guess at its
meaning and differ as to its application is considered void
for vagueness. This principle applies to all statutes, but in
first amendment cases, courts frequently require a heightened
degree of specificity.

Gooding v.
Wilson

4.   **Application of Overbreadth Doctrine--Gooding v. Wilson,** 405
U.S. 518 (1972).

a.   **Facts.** Georgia law defined as a misdemeanor the use of
"opprobrious words or abusive language, tending to
cause a breach of the peace." Gooding (P) called a
police officer who was responding to an antiwar demonstration a "son of a bitch" and threatened the officer
with bodily harm. P was convicted under the Georgia
statute and petitioned for federal habeas corpus relief.
The court of appeals granted relief and Wilson (D)
appeals.

b.   **Issue.** May a state forbid the use of "opprobrious words
or abusive language" that tends to cause a breach of
the peace?

c.   **Held.** No. Judgment affirmed.

1)   Because the Georgia statute applies only to spoken
words, it can be upheld if it cannot be applied to

protected speech. But the states may not punish the use of words not within narrowly limited classes of speech.

2) D claims that the Georgia statute is narrowly drawn because it applies only to fighting words, a category of speech that is not protected under *Chaplinsky*. However, the words of the statute encompass much more than fighting words, and the Georgia courts have not limited the application of the statute to fighting words. In fact, the statute has been applied to punish harsh, insulting language that would not tend to incite an immediate breach of the peace. Thus the statute is overbroad.

d. **Dissenting.** P's conduct was not protected by the first amendment. The words of the statute are sufficiently clear to constitute adequate notice.

5. **Prior Restraint.**

a. **Early cases.** Government normally cannot regulate in advance what expressions may or may not be uttered or published, even to guard against speech or ideas that, once published, would be constitutionally unprotected and subject to state punishment, such as defamatory speech. Individual as well as public rights are deemed sufficiently protected by the deterrent effect of such punishment. The further step of prior restraint would make the government a censor, thereby undermining the core of the first amendment. The early cases in this area involved attempts at prior restraint through licensing requirements and court injunctions.

b. **Licensing.**

1) **Introduction.** A state cannot condition the right of a person to express her views publicly on obtaining a permit to do so from local authorities where such permits are given on a purely discretionary basis. There must be some reasonable standard established on which to decide who gets a permit, when, and why.

2) **Permit to distribute circulars--Lovell v. Griffin,** 303 U.S. 444 (1938).

    a) **Facts.** The city of Griffin (P) enacted an ordinance requiring written permission from the city manager for the distribution of literature of any kind at any time, at any place, and in any manner. Lovell (D) was convicted of violating the statute by distributing religious literature without a per-

Lovell v. Griffin

mit. D appeals, claiming the ordinance violates both freedom of the press and of religion.

b) **Issue.** May government prohibit all distribution of all literature without prior approval of a government agent?

c) **Held.** No. Judgment reversed.

(1) The ordinance is invalid on its face. Freedom of the press includes a right to publish without a license.

(2) The ordinance is overbroad because it prohibits distribution that does not in any way interfere with proper government functions.

Near v.
Minnesota

c. **Injunctions--Near v. Minnesota,** 283 U.S. 697 (1931).

1) **Facts.** Minnesota (P) enacted a statute that provided for the abatement, as a public nuisance, of any "malicious, scandalous and defamatory" publication. Near (D) published a periodical that criticized law enforcement officers. P brought an action seeking to suppress D's publication. The state courts granted P's request. D appeals.

2) **Issue.** May a state grant an injunction against publication of allegedly defamatory material?

3) **Held.** No. Judgment reversed.

a) Permitting public authorities to suppress publication of scandalous matter relating to charges of official dereliction, restrained only by the publisher's ability to satisfy the judge that the charges are true, is the essence of censorship. Liberty of the press under the Constitution has meant, principally although not exclusively, immunity from previous restraints or censorship.

b) The only permissible restraint is the deterrent effect of actions against defamatory publications arising after publication.

4) **Dissent** (Butler, Van Devanter, McReynolds, Sutherland, JJ.). The previous restraints precluded by the first amendment refer to subjection of the press to the arbitrary will of an administrative officer. There is no similarity between such impermissible previous restraint and the decree authorized by this statute to prevent further publication of defamatory articles, and the statute should be upheld.

D. RESTRICTIONS ON "LOW VALUE" SPEECH

1. **False Statements of Fact (Libel).** Libelous speech is in somewhat the same category as obscenity—it receives little constitutional protection. However, the same difficult questions exist here as with obscenity; i.e., what constitutes libel and what tests should be used to distinguish protected from unprotected speech?

   a. **Public officials and seditious libel.**

      1) **Introduction.** The first amendment clearly protects disclosure and debate on matters of public interest. On the other hand, society must protect personal reputations against injurious falsehoods. The conflict between these interests has produced some close decisions, but the Court has balanced the interests by creating a constitutional privilege for certain kinds of defamation. Thus, criticism of public officials relating to their official conduct cannot result in either criminal or civil liability for libel unless made with "actual malice." Society's interest in this type of expression is great, and public officials can normally refute false charges because they have access to the media.

      2) **Public officials--New York Times Co. v. Sullivan,** 376 U.S. 254 (1964).

         a) **Facts.** Sullivan (P) was a commissioner of the city of Montgomery, Alabama, and supervised the police department. The New York Times Co. (D) carried a full-page advertisement that included several false statements about repressive police conduct in Montgomery. Although P's name was not mentioned, the accusation of the ad could be read as referring to him. P sued for damages on grounds that D libeled him. The trial court awarded damages of $500,000, which were upheld in the state courts. The controlling state rule of law dealt with libel per se, established here by merely showing that D's statement reflected upon the agency that P supervised. Once libel per se is demonstrated, the only defense is the truth. D appeals.

         b) **Issue.** May a state allow a public official to recover damages for a defamatory falsehood relating to his official conduct without proof of actual malice?

         c) **Held.** No. Judgment reversed.

New York
Times Co.
v. Sullivan

(1) The Constitution expresses a profound commitment to uninhibited debate on public issues. This protection does not turn on the truth of the ideas or beliefs expressed, nor does concern for official reputation remove defamatory statements from the constitutional shield.

(2) The deterrent effect of damage awards—without the need for any proof of actual pecuniary loss—is so great as to severely chill public criticism, which should be openly permitted under the first amendment.

(3) Despite first amendment considerations, a public official may recover damages for a defamatory falsehood relating to his official conduct if he proves the statement was made with actual malice (knowledge of falsity or reckless disregard of truth). P's proof falls short.

d) **Concurring** (Black, Douglas, JJ.). D has an absolute, unconditional privilege to criticize official conduct despite the harm which may flow from excesses and abuses.

e) **Comment.** The Supreme Court has held that the same privilege to make statements about "public officials" exists for statements made about "public figures." In *Curtis Publishing Co. v. Butts*, 388 U.S. 130 (1967), Wally Butts, the former director of athletics at the University of Georgia, was reported to have thrown a football game while at the University. In *Associated Press v. Walker* (decided with *Butts*), the Court held that General Walker, a retired Army general, was a public figure. The *New York Times* rule was extended to private plaintiffs involved in matters of public concern in *Rosenbloom v. Metromedia, Inc.*, 403 U.S. 29 (1971). Although *Gertz v. Robert Welch, Inc.*, below, rejected that distinction, it was resurrected to a certain extent in *Dun & Bradstreet, Inc. v. Greenmoss Builders, Inc.*, 472 U.S. 749 (1985). In that case, a majority of the Court rejected the media-nonmedia distinction suggested by *Gertz*, and ruled that the *Gertz* requirements for private plaintiffs only apply to "matters of public concern."

b. **Private individuals and public figures.**

1) **General rule.** The *New York Times* rule applies to suits by public figures as well as by public officials. A person may become a public figure by achieving general fame or notoriety in a given community, either generally or as to particular issues. Where the defamed person is neither a public figure nor a public official (or candidate for public office), "free

speech" considerations are not as strong. Private individuals are more susceptible to injury because they do not usually have media access to counteract false statements published about them. Consequently, under the rules established by *Gertz*, the states may impose whatever standard of defamation liability they choose, except that, for matters of public concern:

a)   The factual misstatement must be such as would warn a reasonably prudent editor or broadcaster of its defamatory potential;

b)   There must be a finding (by the trier of fact or the appellate court) that the publisher or broadcaster was at least negligent in publishing the misstatement (i.e., liability without fault cannot be imposed); and

c)   Damages must be limited to "actual injury" (which includes any out-of-pocket loss plus impairment of reputation, personal humiliation, and mental anguish). An award of "presumed" or punitive damages is permissible only if the publication was made with knowledge of its falsity or in reckless disregard for the truth (i.e., actual malice).

2)   **Application--Gertz v. Robert Welch, Inc.,** 418 U.S. 323 (1974).

Gertz v. Robert Welch, Inc.

a)   **Facts.** Gertz (P), an attorney, represented the family of a homicide victim in the family's civil suit against the police officer who had murdered him. Robert Welch (D), publisher of *American Opinion*, printed an article, concededly untrue, that discredited P's reputation and motives. P sued D for libel. After a jury awarded damages to P, the trial court reconsidered and decided that D was protected by application of the *New York Times* rule, holding that discussion of any public issue is protected, regardless of the status of the person defamed. Because P was unable to prove that D acted with "actual malice," the court entered a judgment n.o.v. for D. The court of appeals affirmed. P appeals.

b)   **Issue.** May a member of the press who published defamatory falsehoods about a person who is neither a public official nor a public figure, but who is involved in a public issue, claim a constitutional privilege against liability for injuries?

c)   **Held.** No. Judgment reversed.

(1)   The need to avoid self-censorship by the news media must be balanced against the legitimate interest in permitting compensation for harm resulting from defamatory falsehoods. Defamation plaintiffs are not all in the same class, however. Public officials and public figures have more access to the media in order to counteract falsehoods than do private individuals such as P. Private individuals are also more deserving of recovery because their public exposure is not voluntary. There-

fore, the rationale behind the *New York Times* rule does not extend to private individuals.

    (2)   Involvement in a public issue, by itself, does not bring a private individual within the class covered by the *New York Times* rule. D was not a public official or public figure. To protect defamations whenever a "public issue" was involved would introduce new uncertainties and broadly expand the scope of the *New York Times* rule.

    (3)   States may define their own standards of liability for defamation by a publisher or broadcaster, but may not impose liability without fault. However, states may not permit recovery of presumed or punitive damages in the absence of proof of "actual malice" (knowledge of falsity or reckless disregard for the truth). The only permissible recovery for a private defamation plaintiff who establishes liability under any standard less demanding than the *New York Times* test is compensation for actual injury.

  d)   **Dissenting** (Brennan, J.). The *New York Times* rule should apply to discussions of public issues.

  e)   **Dissenting** (White, J.). The states should be free to impose strict liability in cases such as this.

  3)   **Determination of public figure status.** As discussed *supra*, a person may be a public figure for all purposes and in all contexts by gaining general fame or notoriety, or may become a public figure for special issues by becoming involved in the controversy. The critical element is the voluntariness of the public standing. A person is not a public figure simply because she is extremely wealthy and engaged in divorce proceedings of interest to the reading public. The fact that she files for divorce (and even holds press conferences during the proceedings) does not mean that she voluntarily chooses to publicize her married life, because going to court is the only way she can legally dissolve her marriage. [Time, Inc. v. Firestone, 424 U.S. 448 (1976)] Nor does a person become a public figure by being charged with a crime. [Wolston v. Reader's Digest Association, 443 U.S. 157 (1979)]

Beauharnais   **2.**   **Group Libel--Beauharnais v. Illinois,** 343 U.S. 250 (1952).
v. Illinois

    a.   **Facts.** Beauharnais (D) published a leaflet calling on Chicago officials to halt the encroachment of Negroes on white people's property and neighborhoods. D asserted that if the need to prevent the Negroes from mongrelizing the white race was not enough to unite whites, then the rapes, robberies, knives, guns, and marijuana of the Negro would be enough. D was convicted under a state statute that prohibited exhibition of any publication that portrayed a class of citizens of any race, color, or creed in a derogatory manner so as to expose them to derision or be productive of a breach of the peace. D appeals.

b. **Issue.** May group libel be made per se illegal, even without a showing of a clear and present danger?

c. **Held.** Yes. Judgment affirmed.

   1) Every American jurisdiction punishes libels aimed at individuals. Libel is treated much like lewd and obscene speech; punishment of these types of expression does not violate the first amendment. Such speech is not communication of information or opinion protected by the Constitution.

   2) Because the fourteenth amendment does not prevent the states from enforcing libel laws to protect individuals, it should not prevent laws against group libel unless they are unrelated to a legitimate government purpose. Illinois has a history of tense race relations. The legislature could certainly conclude that group libel tends to exacerbate these problems. It could also have found that group libel directly affects individuals in the group by impugning their reputations.

   3) There is no requirement for a showing of clear and present danger because libel is not within the protection of the Constitution.

d. **Dissenting** (Black, Douglas, JJ.). Restrictions of first amendment freedoms should not be judged by the rational basis standard. Criminal libel has always been intended to protect individuals, not large groups. Additionally, the words used by D were part of a petition to the government, and part of his argument on a question of wide public importance and interest.

e. **Dissenting** (Reed, Douglas, JJ.). The statute is unconstitutionally vague. It forbids portrayal of a lack of "virtue" on the part of a class of citizens which leads to "derision." The meaning of these terms is too uncertain to describe a criminal offense.

f. **Dissenting** (Douglas, J.). This type of speech could constitutionally be punished only with a showing that it provides a clear and present danger of causing disaster.

3. **Newsworthiness of Disclosures of Private Information--Cox Broadcasting Corp. v. Cohn,** 420 U.S. 469 (1975).

    a. **Facts.** Cohn's (P's) daughter was the victim of a murder-
rape. A reporter for Cox Broadcasting Corp. (D) obtained
the name of the victim from official public court records and
made the identification in a broadcast. A Georgia statute
prohibited the publication or broadcast of a rape victim's
identity. P sued D for invasion of privacy. D appeals state
court judgments in favor of P.

    b. **Issue.** May a state protect individual privacy by forbidding
the publication or broadcast of sensitive personal information
which is officially available to the public?

    c. **Held.** No. Judgment reversed.

       1) The right of privacy has acquired increasing importance
in recent years, and the information disseminated by D,
although true, would clearly be offensive to a person of
ordinary sensibilities. However, the law of invasion of
privacy recognizes that those interests fade when the
information involved appears on the public record.

       2) A rule making public records available to the media but
forbidding their publication would seriously impinge on
the public's right to know and would clearly violate the
first and fourteenth amendments.

    d. **Concurring.** The first amendment prohibits the use of state
law to impose damages for the discussion of public issues.

4. **Commercial Speech.**

    a. **Introduction.** Commercial speech is entitled to some degree
of protection under the first amendment, although subject to
more stringent regulation than would be permissible with
respect to noncommercial speech. In determining the degree
of protection, the free speech interest in the contents of the
speech must be weighed against the public interest served by
the governmental regulation. [*See* Bigelow v. Virginia, 421
U.S. 809 (1975)—that commercial speech merits some protec-
tion]

Virginia State
Board of
Pharmacy v.
Virginia Citi-
zens Con-
sumer Council

    b. **Scope of protection--Virginia State Board of Pharmacy v.
Virginia Citizens Consumer Council,** 425 U.S. 748 (1976).

       1) **Facts.** The Virginia State Board of Pharmacy (D) pro-
hibited advertisement of the retail prices of prescription
drugs by pharmacists. The Virginia Citizens Consumer
Council (P), for itself and on behalf of users of prescription drugs, sought an injunction against the en-

forcement of D's rule. The three-judge district court granted the injunction. D appeals.

2) **Issue.** Is purely commercial speech wholly outside first amendment protection?

3) **Held.** No. Judgment affirmed.

   a) First amendment protection extends to the communication, to its source, and to its recipients. P, as a potential recipient of the advertising, has standing to bring this action.

   b) The speech in question, commercial advertising, is not disqualified from protection merely because the speaker's interest is purely economic. The particular consumer has a vital interest in the free flow of commercial information, possibly a greater interest than in current political debates, which are clearly protected.

   c) Society in general has a strong interest in the free flow of commercial information. Actually, such a free flow is essential to the proper functioning of our economic system. It is likely that no line can properly be drawn between "important," and hence protected, advertising and the opposite kind.

   d) D claims an interest in protecting the public from unscrupulous pharmacists who would use advertising to their own advantage and the public's detriment. But the choice between the dangers of suppressing information and the dangers of its misuse if it is freely available has been made by the first amendment. Therefore, D cannot prohibit commercial advertising of the type involved here.

   e) Although commercial speech is protected, it remains subject to proper restrictions; e.g., time, place, and manner restrictions, false and misleading advertising prohibitions, and prohibitions against advertising illegal transactions.

4) **Dissenting** (Rehnquist, J.). The Court expands the standing requirements and extends first amendment protection beyond what is necessary. This ruling prevents the states from protecting the public against dangers resulting from excessive promotion of drugs that should be used only with professional guidance.

5) **Comment.** The Court emphasized the importance of a free flow of information by invalidating an ordinance that prohibited the posting of "for sale" signs on real estate. The township had justified the ordinance as a means of preventing "white flight" from racially integrated neighborhoods, but this justification was inadequate. [*See* Linmark Associates, Inc. v. Township of Willingboro, 431 U.S. 85 (1977)]

Ohralik v.
Ohio State
Bar Asso-
ciation

c. **Attorney advertising--Ohralik v. Ohio State Bar Association,** 436 U.S. 447 (1978).

    1) **Facts.** Ohralik (P) solicited two clients in person after discovering they had been injured. When the clients later sought other counsel, P sued for breach of contract. The Ohio State Bar Association (D) suspended P indefinitely. P challenged the suspension, but the lower courts upheld D's action. P appeals.

    2) **Issue.** May a state prohibit attorneys from soliciting clients in person for pecuniary gain?

    3) **Held.** Yes. Judgment affirmed.

        a) Commercial speech is protected under the first amendment, although the protection is limited as compared with noncommercial speech. A course of conduct may be prohibited even if it is carried out by means of language.

        b) P's solicitation was a business transaction. The state has a significant interest in regulating lawyers because of the role they play in society. Solicitation of clients has several evils, including stirring up litigation, possible misrepresentation, etc., which provide grounds for regulation. In-person solicitation is even more likely to pressure potential clients than mere advertising, which was permitted in *Bates v. State Bar*, 433 U.S. 350 (1977).

        c) Even though P claims no harm was done in this case, the state does not need to prove actual injury. The only witnesses to such solicitation are normally the attorney and the solicitee. The difficulty of proving what actually occurred should not immunize attorneys against improper solicitation.

Central
Hudson Gas
& Electric
Co. v. Public
Service
Commission

d. **Four-part analysis of commercial speech--Central Hudson Gas & Electric Co. v. Public Service Commission,** 447 U.S. 557 (1980).

    1) **Facts.** The Public Service Commission (D), in response to an energy shortage, temporarily banned all advertising by electric utilities that "promote the use of electricity." Over the objections of Central Hudson Gas & Electric Co. (P), D extended the ban and distinguished between promotional advertising, which was totally prohibited, and institutional and informational advertising, which D permitted. The state courts upheld D's order. P appeals.

    2) **Issue.** Does a public service commission's prohibition of promotional advertising by an electric utility violate the utility's first amendment rights?

3) **Held.** Yes. Judgment reversed.

   a) Although D's regulation applies only to commercial speech, such speech is protected by the first amendment because of its informational functions. Thus, a four-part analysis has developed regarding commercial speech.

   b) First, is the expression protected? If it concerns lawful activity and is not misleading, it generally is; P's speech is protected.

   c) Second, is the asserted governmental interest in regulation substantial? D based its regulation on the need for energy conservation, clearly a substantial interest.

   d) Third, does the regulation directly advance the governmental interest? If demand for electricity were unaffected by advertising, P would not have brought this suit. Therefore D's regulation does advance the governmental interest.

   e) Fourth, is the regulation more extensive than necessary? Here D's regulation fails, because it would prohibit information about electric devices or services that would not increase net energy use, although they might increase electric use; e.g., use of electricity as a backup to solar heating. D's rule is overbroad, and in the absence of a showing that a more limited rule could not serve D's interest, it cannot be upheld.

4) **Concurring** (Blackmun, Brennan, JJ.). The four-part test is inadequate in that it permits deprivation of information needed by the public to make a choice. D attempts to manipulate choices of private persons by withholding information rather than by persuasion or direct regulation. Such covert attempts are illegal regardless of their "necessity."

5) **Concurring** (Stevens, Brennan, JJ.). The issue is whether D has banned nothing but commercial speech. D's ban covers more than purely commercial speech and is therefore invalid, regardless of the four-part analysis.

6) **Dissenting** (Rehnquist, J.). D here is placing an essentially economic regulation on a heavily regulated state-created monopoly. Economic regulation traditionally merits virtually complete deference by the Court; D's regulation should also.

7) **Comment.** The majority of the Court would uphold a restriction on commercial billboards to further the aesthetic and traffic safety interests of a city. [Metromedia, Inc. v. San Diego, 453 U.S. 490 (1981)] In *Bolger v. Youngs Drug Products Corp.*, 463 U.S. 60 (1983), the Court held that informational pamphlets about contraceptives were commercial speech, even though they contained discussion of important public issues, because they promoted the sponsor's products. Still, the Court invalidated a federal statute

prohibiting the unsolicited mailing of the brochures, under the *Central Hudson* test.

e. **Application of *Central Hudson* test--Posadas de Puerto Rico Associates v. Tourism Co. of Puerto Rico,** 478 U.S. 328 (1986).

1) **Facts.** Puerto Rico legalized casino gambling, but prohibited advertising of such gambling to the public of Puerto Rico. Posadas de Puerto Rico Associates (P), a hotel and casino operator, printed the word "casino" on its stationery and on other objects used in its business. This violated the interpretation of the advertising statute adopted by the Tourism Co. of Puerto Rico (D). D fined P for the violations. P then unsuccessfully sought a declaratory injunction against D's regulations on the ground that they violated P's commercial speech rights. The Supreme Court of Puerto Rico dismissed P's appeal, and P appeals.

2) **Issue.** May a ban on a particular type of advertising of legal activities satisfy the *Central Hudson* test?

3) **Held.** Yes. Judgment affirmed.

a) The *Central Hudson* test applies because the speech involved was purely commercial. Because P's advertising concerns a lawful activity and is not misleading or fraudulent, it is entitled to a limited form of First Amendment protection. Thus the three remaining *Central Hudson* tests must be applied.

b) The second test involves the strength of the governmental interest in restricting the speech. The government interest here is the reduction of demand for casino gambling by Puerto Rico residents. This is the same concern that most states cite in prohibiting casino gambling altogether, and is a substantial government interest.

c) The third test is whether the challenged restrictions directly advance the government interest. In this case, it clearly does. The very purpose of advertising is to increase patronage.

d) The final test is whether the restrictions are not more extensive than necessary to serve the government's interest. P claims that the first amendment requires D to promulgate speech that discourages gambling, not by prohibiting speech that encourages gambling. However, this is a choice wisely left to the legislature. Thus, the restrictions are permissible.

e) Unlike the *Carey* and *Bigelow* cases, this case does not involve advertising of constitutionally protected activity. D could have banned casinos altogether. This legalization does not mean that that the government must now permit advertising. Instead, by permitting the activity but prohibiting its advertisement, the government has taken the less intrusive step.

4) **Dissenting** (Brennan, Marshall, Blackmun, JJ.). D has not shown any serious harmful effects that would result from Puerto Rico residents participating in the casinos. D permits such activity anyway. Even if the advertising ban would reduce patronage by residents, it is not clear how the ban addresses the serious harmful effects of casino gambling. Finally, there was no showing that D considered less intrusive steps to protect against the harmful effects.

5. **Obscenity.**

a. **Introduction.** Obscene publications are not protected by the constitutional guarantee of freedom of speech and press. Both federal and state governments may restrict such expression. The difficulty is in defining such speech. Freedom of expression is not an end in itself. To be protected, the speech must have some content of value to society. Obscene speech has no societal value, so it is unprotected, but speech that does not descend to the level of "obscene" remains protected.

b. **Difficulty of defining obscenity--Roth v. United States, Alberts v. California,** 354 U.S. 476 (1957).

Roth v. United States, Alberts v. California

1) **Facts.** Roth (D) was convicted of mailing obscene materials in violation of a federal obscenity statute. Alberts (D) was convicted of a similar state offense. Ds appeal their convictions.

2) **Issue.** Is obscenity presumptively without redeeming social value and therefore unprotected by the first amendment?

3) **Held.** Yes. Judgment affirmed.

a) The unconditional phrasing of the first amendment was not intended to protect every utterance; e.g., libel is unprotected. Obscenity is utterly without redeeming social importance. Therefore, obscenity cannot claim constitutional protection.

b) Ds claim that their material does not create a clear and present danger to society, but merely incites impure sexual thoughts. It is true that mere portrayal of sex does not deny the material constitutional protection. But obscenity is not synonymous with sex. Obscenity deals with sex in a manner appealing to prurient interest. As such, it is unprotected.

   c)   The test for obscenity is: whether, to the average person applying contemporary community standards, the dominant theme of the material taken as a whole appeals to the prurient interest.

4)   Concurring and dissenting (Harlan, J.). We deal with different statutes. The states may properly regulate in this area, but federal regulation must be more narrow, since Congress has no substantive power over sexual morality. Also, each challenged item must be examined individually to determine whether it is suppressible.

5)   Dissent (Douglas, Black, JJ.). The first amendment protects all speech and precludes the courts from weighing the values of speech against silence.

6)   Comment. After *Roth*, the Court was unable to make a majority statement on the proper standard for evaluating pornography until *Miller, infra*, in 1973. In the meantime, however, the Court decided obscenity cases with plurality opinions. For example, in *Kingsley International Pictures Corp. v. Regents*, 360 U.S. 684 (1959), the Court invalidated a New York motion picture licensing law that banned films portraying acts of sexual immorality or presenting such acts as proper behavioral patterns. The Court held that the concept of sexual immorality differed from the concepts of obscenity or pornography, and that the state law prevented the advocacy of an idea protected by the basic guarantee of the first amendment.

c.   **Inability to define obscenity.** In *Memoirs v. Massachusetts*, 383 U.S. 413 (1966), the state had ruled that the book *Memoirs of a Woman of Pleasure* was obscene under Massachusetts law. The Court reversed in a plurality opinion. The Court stated that under *Roth*, material is protected unless it meets three criteria: (i) the dominant theme of the material taken as a whole appeals to a prurient interest in sex; (ii) the material is patently offensive because it affronts contemporary community standards relating to the description or representation of sexual matters; and (iii) the material is utterly without redeeming social value. The Court stated that a book could have redeeming social value even if the other two parts of the test are met. An indication of the social value of the material is the manner in which it is sold. If the seller's sole emphasis is on the sexually provocative aspects of the material, a court could accept his evaluation at its face value.

d.   **Approach to obscenity cases.** In one opinion, Justice Stewart, writing about obscenity, stated "I cannot define it, but I know it when I see it." The Court seemed to follow this approach between 1967 and 1971 when it overturned obscenity findings in 31 cases. During this period, the Court never upheld obscenity findings when the material was textual, or when film or pictures showed only nudity. When film or pictures showed explicit sexual activity, however, it upheld obscenity findings.

e. **Modern standard for defining obscene materials--Miller v. California,** 413 U.S. 15 (1973).

1) **Facts.** Miller (D) was convicted under a California statute of knowingly distributing obscene matter to unwilling recipients. The statute incorporated the *Memoirs* test of obscenity. D appeals the conviction.

2) **Issue.** Is the *Memoirs* test the appropriate measure of obscene expressions?

3) **Held.** No. Judgment vacated and remanded.

   a) Obscenity is not within the area of constitutionally protected speech or press. *Roth* presumed obscenity to be "utterly without redeeming social value," but the *Memoirs* case transformed that presumption into a necessary element of proof. *Memoirs* thus requires the prosecution to prove a negative, and that test cannot be upheld.

   b) Regulation of obscene material is restricted to works that depict or describe sexual conduct, and must specifically define that conduct. The basic guidelines for the trier of fact must be:

      (1) Whether the average person, applying contemporary community standards, would find that the work, taken as a whole, appeals to the prurient interest;

      (2) Whether the work depicts or describes, in a patently offensive way, sexual conduct specifically defined by the applicable state law; and

      (3) Whether the work, taken as a whole, lacks serious literary, artistic, political, or scientific value.

   c) Under this test, material can be regulated without a showing that it is "utterly without redeeming social value."

4) **Dissenting** (Brennan, Stewart, Marshall, JJ.). The difficulty in defining obscenity means that laws prohibiting it are necessarily vague. The Court has been able to resolve cases between parties but has not provided useful guidance to legislatures and other courts. Experience teaches that it is impossible to reconcile the first amendment concerns in this area with the state's interest in regulating obscenity. The best solution is to permit government to regulate the manner

of distribution of sexually oriented material to protect juveniles and unconsenting adults, but not to wholly suppress such materials.

f. **Rationale for regulating obscenity.**

1) **Possession and distribution of obscene materials.** The Court reversed a conviction for possession of obscene materials found in appellant's home in *Stanley v. Georgia*, 394 U.S. 557 (1969). In so ruling, the Court held that the first amendment grants the right to receive information and ideas and that there is a fundamental right to be free from unwanted governmental intrusion in one's home. However, in *United States v. Reidel*, 402 U.S. 351 (1971), the Court reversed the lower court's dismissal of an indictment under the federal law prohibiting the mailing of obscene materials. The Court rejected the lower court's contention, based upon the ruling in *Stanley*, that if a person has a right to possess obscene material, then a person also has a right to deliver it. The Court held that the indictment was not an infringement of the right to freedom of mind and thought or of the right to privacy in one's home.

Paris Adult Theatre I v. Slaton

2) **State regulation of obscene films--Paris Adult Theatre I v. Slaton,** 413 U.S. 49 (1973).

    a) **Facts.** Slaton (P), a state district attorney, filed civil complaints against Paris Adult Theatre I (D), seeking to enjoin exhibition of films claimed to be obscene. The films were available only to "consenting adults." The trial judge dismissed the complaint, but the Georgia Supreme Court reversed, holding that the films were without first amendment protection. D appeals.

    b) **Issue.** May a state prohibit commercial exhibition of "obscene" films to consenting adults?

    c) **Held.** Yes. Judgment vacated and remanded.

        (1) The state afforded D the best possible notice, as no restraint on exhibition was imposed until after a full judicial proceeding determined that the films were obscene and therefore subject to regulation.

        (2) Obscene, pornographic films do not acquire constitutional immunity from state regulation merely because they are shown to consenting adults only. The states have power to make a morally neutral judgment that public exhibition of obscene material, or commerce in such material, has a tendency to injure the community as a whole, even if actual exposure is limited to a few consenting adults.

(3) While the right of privacy may preclude regulation of the use of obscene materials within the home, commercial ventures such as D's are not private for the purpose of civil rights litigation. Commerce in obscene material is unprotected by any constitutional doctrine of privacy.

(4) Incidental effects on human "utterances" or "thoughts" do not prevent state action to protect legitimate state interests where the communication is not protected by the first amendment and where the right of privacy is not infringed. Such state action is permitted as long as it conforms to the standards of *Miller*.

d) **Dissenting** (Brennan, Stewart, Marshall, JJ.). The Court's attempts to define obscenity have clearly failed. Government cannot constitutionally bar the distribution even of unprotected material to consenting adults.

g. **Child pornography--New York v. Ferber, 458 U.S. 747 (1982).**

New York
v. Ferber

1) **Facts.** New York (P) enacted a statute that outlawed production and promotion (including distribution) of child pornography, regardless of whether the material was legally obscene. "Child pornography" consisted of any performance that includes sexual conduct by a child under 16 years old. Ferber (D) was convicted of selling two films of young boys masturbating. The New York Court of Appeals reversed the conviction, holding that the statute violated the first amendment. The Supreme Court granted certiorari.

2) **Issue.** May a state prohibit distribution of all child pornography, even without requiring that it be legally obscene?

3) **Held.** Yes. Judgment reversed.

a) Obscenity is not protected by the Constitution. States have even greater leeway in dealing with child pornography than with obscenity because of the compelling state interest in safeguarding their children's physical and psychological well-being.

b) Distribution of child pornography is intrinsically related to sexual abuse of children because the distribution aggravates the harm to the child and because, without a market, the pornography would not be produced. Prohibiting distribution of obscene materials would not adequately promote the state's interest because the harm of abuse is unrelated to any possible literary, artistic, political, or social value of the material.

c) Production of child pornography, of which distribution is an integral part, is illegal; the first amendment does not protect against commission of a crime. There is no cognizable value in permitting production of child pornography.

    d)   The definition used in the statute is sufficiently clear and precise. The statute is not overbroad. Even if it could conceivably extend to medical or educational material, such applications of the statute would be a tiny fraction of the materials prohibited. The cure in such instances is a case-by-case analysis of the circumstances.

h.   Feminism and pornography. In *American Booksellers Association v. Hudnut*, 598 F. Supp. 1316 (S.D. Ind. 1984), *aff'd*, 771 F.2d 323 (7th Cir. 1985), *aff'd mem.*, 475 U.S. 1001 (1986), a federal district court held that a city may not enact an ordinance prohibiting pornography on the theory that it discriminates against women. The interest in preventing sex discrimination does not outweigh the free speech interest. The court concluded that acceptance of the civil rights approach could lead to prohibition of any speech the legislature finds unfair to a particular group.

6.   Offensive Speech and Content Regulation. While the government may regulate the content of broadcasts when necessary to protect the public interest, including prohibitions against inappropriate content, such as indecent but not obscene speech [*see* FCC v. Pacifica Foundation, *infra*], the government may not prohibit discussion of public issues that lie at the heart of the first amendment protections.

Cohen v. California

    a.   Offensive words--Cohen v. California, 403 U.S. 15 (1971).

        1)   Facts. Cohen (D) wore a jacket bearing the words "Fuck the Draft" in a Los Angeles courthouse corridor. He was convicted of violating a state statute that prohibited disturbing the peace by offensive conduct. He appeals after the state courts upheld his conviction.

        2)   Issue. May a state prohibit as "offensive conduct" public use of an offensive word?

        3)   Held. No. Judgment reversed.

            a)   Government has special power to regulate speech that is obscene, that constitutes "fighting words," or that intrudes on substantial privacy interests in an essentially intolerable manner.

            b)   D's expression falls within none of these categories. D's jacket could not be considered erotic. Neither would D's jacket violently provoke the common citizen in the manner of fighting words.

Persons present in the courthouse were not unwilling captives of the offensive expression; they could simply have averted their eyes. Thus there was no intrusion on privacy interests.

c) The state's regulatory attempt must fail because it would permit the state to outlaw whatever words officials might deem improper, thus running a substantial risk of suppressing ideas. Such power would permit official censorship as a means of banning the expression of unpopular views.

4) **Dissenting** (Blackmun, J., Burger, C.J., Black, J.). D's antic was mainly conduct and involved little speech. As such, it could be regulated.

b. **Protecting unwilling audiences--Erznoznik v. Jacksonville,** 422 U.S. 205 (1975).

1) **Facts.** Erznoznik (D), manager of a drive-in theater, exhibited a movie containing nudity in violation of a Jacksonville (P) ordinance prohibiting such exhibitions if visible from a public street or place. The lower courts upheld the ordinance. D appeals.

2) **Issue.** May a city prohibit exhibition of all films containing nudity by drive-in theaters whose screens are visible from a public street or place?

3) **Held.** No. Judgment reversed.

a) By extending beyond the permissible restraints on obscenity, the ordinance applies to films protected by the first amendment. P claims that any movie containing nudity may be suppressed as a nuisance if it is visible from a public place. However, selective restrictions based on content have been upheld only where the privacy of the home is invaded, or where the unwilling viewer cannot avoid exposure. The limited privacy interest of persons on public streets cannot justify this censorship of otherwise protected speech on the basis of its content.

b) The ordinance is too broad to be justified as an exercise of the police power to protect children, because all nudity cannot be deemed obscene even as to minors. Neither can it be upheld as a traffic regulation, since other types of scenes might be equally distracting. The ordinance lacks the precision of drafting and clarity of purpose that are essential when first amendment freedoms are at stake.

4) **Dissenting** (Burger, C.J., Rehnquist, J.). The Court has never established such inexorable limitations upon state power in this area.

c. **Indecent speech--FCC v. Pacifica Foundation,** 438 U.S. 726 (1978).

1) **Facts.** A New York radio station owned by Pacifica Foundation (D) broadcast a monologue by George Carlin that contained several indecent words. A listener complained to the FCC (P), which issued a declaratory order finding the monologue indecent as broadcast and therefore subject to regulation. The district court reversed D's determination. P appeals.

2) **Issue.** Does the federal government (FCC) have power to regulate a radio broadcast that is indecent but not obscene?

3) **Held.** Yes. Judgment reversed.

a) The statute upon which D based its power to regulate P's broadcast (18 U.S.C. section 1464) forbids the use of any "obscene, indecent, or profane" language. Because the disjunctive is used, each word has a separate meaning, and language need not be obscene to be indecent. D's words were admittedly not obscene, but P could still properly find them indecent.

b) Broadcasting, of all forms of communication, has the most limited first amendment protection because of its unique ability to penetrate privacy and its accessibility to children.

c) The first amendment does not prohibit all governmental regulation that depends on the content of speech. Neither is P's action invalidated by its possible deterrent effect on similar broadcasts.

4) **Concurring** (Powell, Blackmun, JJ.). While P's finding does not violate the first amendment, the Court should not decide on the basis of content which speech is less "valuable" and hence less deserving of protection.

5) **Dissenting** (Brennan, Marshall, JJ.). The word "indecent" must be construed to prohibit only obscene speech. Since the broadcast was concededly not obscene, and since it does not fit within the other categories of speech that are totally without first amendment protection, it should not be subject to government control. The government does not have a duty to protect its citizens from certain broadcasts merely because some citizens, even if a majority, object to the broadcast.

6) **Dissenting** (Stewart, Brennan, White, Marshall, JJ.). Since "indecent" properly means no more than "obscene," P had no authority to ban D's broadcast.

d. **Land-use restrictions on theatres showing "adult" movies--Young v. American Mini Theatres, Inc.,** 427 U.S. 50 (1976).

1) **Facts.** The city of Detroit (represented by Young (D)) adopted amendments to an Anti-Skid Row Ordinance that regulated the locations of theaters showing sexually explicit "adult" movies. American Mini Theatres, Inc. (P) was denied use of its theaters because they violated D's location regulations. P sought declaratory and injunctive relief. The court of appeals held for P. D appeals.

2) **Issue.** May a city use exhibition of sexually explicit "adult" movies as a basis for statutory classification of theaters?

3) **Held.** Yes. Judgment reversed.

   a) The location regulations clearly are within D's police power and do not, by themselves, violate the first amendment.

   b) The question whether speech is, or is not, protected by the first amendment often depends on the content of the speech. Society's interest in protecting expression of erotic materials is wholly different, and lesser, than its interest in protecting political or philosophical discussion. Although the first amendment does not permit total suppression of erotic material, it does permit the states to use content as a basis for classification.

   c) The line drawn by D's regulation is reasonable in light of D's valid objectives.

4) **Concurring** (Powell, J.). This is a case of an innovative land-use regulation, only incidentally affecting first amendment rights. The regulation is not aimed at expression but at the quality of life in the city, and it does not offend the first amendment.

5) **Dissenting** (Stewart, Brennan, Marshall, Blackmun, JJ.). The Court's holding drastically departs from precedent in allowing D to use a system of prior restraints and criminal sanctions to enforce content-based restrictions on expression. The first amendment prohibits selective interference with protected speech, even if distasteful.

e. **Zoning ordinances applied to adult movie theaters--City of Renton v. Playtime Theatres, Inc.,** 475 U.S. 41 (1986).

1) **Facts.** The City of Renton (D) adopted a zoning ordinance that prohibited adult motion picture theaters within 1,000 feet of any residential zone, single- or multiple-family dwelling, church, park, or within one mile of a school. Subsequently, Playtime Theatres, Inc. (P) purchased two theaters within D's jurisdiction and within the prohibited areas. Desiring to use the theaters for adult films, P sought declaratory and injunctive relief against the ordinance. In the meantime, P added a statement of reasons for the ordinance and reduced the one-mile distance to 1,000 feet from a school. The district court granted summary judgment for D. The court of appeals reversed. The Supreme Court granted certiorari.

2) **Issue.** May a city prohibit the operation of adult movie theaters within 1,000 feet of residences, churches, parks, and schools?

3) **Held.** Yes. Judgment reversed.

   a) An ordinance similar to D's was approved in *Young v. American Mini Theatres, Inc. (supra)*. D's ordinance is not a total ban; it is a time, place, and manner regulation. It is neither explicitly content-based nor content-neutral. The ordinance is aimed at the secondary effects of such theaters; D's predominate concern was with protecting and preserving the quality of life in neighborhoods and commercial districts, not with suppressing unpopular views.

   b) Because D's ordinance is not content-based and is aimed at undesirable secondary effects, it must be reviewed under the standards applicable to content-neutral time, place, and manner regulations. As long as the ordinance is designed to serve a substantial governmental interest and allows for reasonable alternative avenues of communication, it is permissible.

   c) D relied on the experiences of the city of Seattle in determining the substantial governmental interest justifying its ordinance, and there is no requirement that a city produce new evidence when the experience of other cities is relevant. Nor does it matter that Seattle chose a different type of zoning.

   d) D's ordinance leaves open over 5% of the city's land area, or 520 acres, for P's use. It does not matter that there are no readily available adult theater sites in the 520 acres; there is no first amendment protection against competition in the real estate market. D has not denied P a reasonable opportunity to open and operate an adult theater within the city.

4) **Dissenting** (Brennan, Marshall, JJ.). The ordinance is clearly content-based. It is designed to suppress constitutionally protected expression. D has not shown that P's theaters will necessarily result in undesirable secondary effects that could not be effectively addressed by less intrusive restrictions. Nor does it leave open

reasonable alternative avenues of communication, because the 520 acres is largely occupied or unsuited for movie theaters.

E. CONTENT-NEUTRAL RESTRICTIONS

1. **Introduction.** The first amendment forbids governments from regulating speech so as to favor some viewpoints at the expense of others. A viewpoint-neutral regulation may be upheld as long as:

    a. It is within the constitutional power of the government;

    b. It furthers an important or substantial governmental interest;

    c. The governmental interest is unrelated to the suppression of free expression; and

    d. The incidental restriction on alleged first amendment freedoms is no greater than is essential to the furtherance of that interest.

2. **The Public Forum.**

    a. **Streets and parks.** Public streets and parks have traditionally been available for those who seek to express opinions or distribute literature. Such government property is considered a public forum for dissemination of information by citizens. However, use of such a forum is subject to reasonable restrictions.

        1) **Distribution of literature.** An ordinance which bans the unlicensed communication of any views or the advocacy of any cause from door to door, and subjects public canvassing to the power of a police officer to determine, as a censor, what literature may be distributed from house to house and who may distribute it, has been held invalid. The claimed interest of the community in the prevention of littering the streets could be achieved by a statute specifically directed at that practice. [*See* Schneider v. State, 308 U.S. 147 (1939)]

        2) **Parades--Cox v. New Hampshire,** 312 U.S. 569 (1941).   Cox v. New Hampshire

            a) **Facts.** A New Hampshire law prohibited public parades or processions without first obtaining a local license. Cox (D) and others participated in a religious-oriented, single-file procession along city sidewalks without obtaining a permit. D was convicted of violating the statute. D appeals.

> **b)** **Issue.** May government prohibit public parades or processions conducted without prior governmental permission?
>
> **c)** **Held.** Yes. Judgment affirmed.
>
> > **(1)** States clearly have the right, even duty, to prevent unscheduled parades for traffic and safety purposes.
> >
> > **(2)** The state supreme court interpreted the statute to be nondiscriminatory in application. Local licensing boards are not vested with arbitrary power but must permit marches that do not unduly interfere with public use of the streets and that avoid disturbance. Under this interpretation, the statute is permissible.

Adderley
v. Florida

b. **Jails--Adderley v. Florida,** 385 U.S. 39 (1966).

> **1)** **Facts.** Adderley and others (Ds) were convicted for trespassing upon the premises of a county jail. Ds had entered the premises to protest the arrest of fellow students and had refused to leave after being notified that they would be arrested for trespass. Ds appeal, claiming that their convictions violated their constitutional right of assembly.
>
> **2)** **Issue.** May a state use a trespass action to prohibit peaceful assembly on a special purpose public property?
>
> **3)** **Held.** Yes. Judgment affirmed.
>
> > **a)** The record reveals that the sheriff objected not to Ds' ideas or protests but only to their presence on that part of the jail grounds reserved for jail uses. The area occupied by Ds was not open to the general public but was reserved for those having specific jail duties. The state has power to preserve its property for the use to which it is lawfully dedicated, and the sheriff did not discriminate against these particular Ds.
> >
> > **b)** Ds presume that people who want to propagandize protests or views have a constitutional right to do so whenever, however, and wherever they please, but this Court has previously rejected such a concept.
>
> **4)** **Dissenting** (Douglas, J., Warren, C.J., Brennan, Fortas, JJ.). A prison is a seat of government and an obvious center for protest against unjust confinement. We do violence to the first amendment by permitting this "petition for redress of grievances" to be turned into a trespass action.
>
> **5)** **Comment on public schools.** The Court has upheld an ordinance prohibiting demonstrations near schools, during school

hours, which materially disrupt classwork. Although school property (or adjacent property) cannot be declared "off limits" for expressive activity, such activity cannot be permitted to invade the right of students to an education. [*See* Grayned v. City of Rockford, 408 U.S. 104 (1972)]

c. **Military installations--Greer v. Spock,** 424 U.S. 828 (1976).

1) **Facts.** Fort Dix, an Army post, banned demonstrations, political speeches, etc., on the post and prohibited distribution or posting of any publication without prior permission. Spock (P) and others challenged the regulations, and the court of appeals held them invalid. Greer (D) appeals.

2) **Issue.** May a military base prohibit all outward political expression within its boundaries?

3) **Held.** Yes. Judgment reversed.

   a) Not all government property is a public forum under the first amendment, even if members of the public are permitted to visit the place. The military has a special constitutional function, and its facilities are intended to further that purpose, not to provide a public forum.

   b) The regulations are not invalid on their face, nor are they enforced unfairly. The policy of prohibiting partisan political campaigns on the post is consistent with the tradition of a politically neutral military establishment under civilian control.

4) **Dissenting** (Brennan, Marshall, JJ.). Government property does not have to be a public forum before expression thereon is protected. Ps here distinguish between the base as a whole and the portions of the base that are open to the public. They only wish to express themselves in the latter locations.

d. **State fair--Heffron v. International Society for Krishna Consciousness, Inc.,** 452 U.S. 640 (1981).

1) **Facts.** The Minnesota Agricultural Society is authorized by state law to operate a state fair, and thereby promulgated a fair rule that forbids sale or distribution of any merchandise, including literature, except from a duly licensed fixed location. Such locations are rented to all comers on a first—come, first-serve basis. International Society for Krishna Consciousness, Inc. (P) challenged the rule as a suppression of its religious ritual of distributing or selling religious literature and soliciting donations. The Minnesota Supreme Court held the rule unconstitutional. Heffron (D) appeals.

2) **Issue.** May a state restrict the sale of literature and solicitation of funds at a state fair to a fixed booth?

3) **Held.** Yes. Judgment reversed.

    a) The first amendment does not guarantee the right to communicate one's views at all times and places or in any manner that might be desired. D's rule is a proper time, place, and manner restriction because it is not based on content and serves the significant governmental interest in protecting the "safety and convenience" of persons using a public forum. Also, the rule does not foreclose all means of expression, because P is not restricted outside the fair and has equal access to booths within the fair.

    b) The Minnesota Supreme Court held the rule invalid by weighing the state's interest in avoiding whatever disorder might result from granting P an exception to the rule. This is too narrow a view of the state's interest. An exception for P would require exceptions for other groups and would eventually swallow the rule.

4) **Concurring and dissenting** (Brennan, Marshall, Stevens, JJ.). Restricting the sale of literature and solicitation of funds is permissible, but restricting free distribution of the literature is not.

e. **Letter boxes--Postal Service v. Council of Greenburgh Civic Associations,** 453 U.S. 114 (1981).

1) **Facts.** A local postmaster informed the Council of Greenburgh Civic Associations (P) that its practice of depositing unstamped "mailable matter" in a letter box approved by the United States Postal Service (D) violated 18 U.S.C. section 1725. P sued D for declaratory and injunctive relief, claiming that enforcement of section 1725 denied P freedom of speech. The district court found that the curtailment of P's speech outweighed D's interests, and held the statute unconstitutional. D appeals.

2) **Issue.** Does the first amendment guarantee a civic association the right to deposit literature, without payment of postage, in mail depositories authorized by the Postal Service?

3) **Held.** No. Judgment reversed.

    a) A postal customer, although he pays for the depository, agrees to abide by D's regulations in exchange for D's handling his mail. D's authorization of such depositories does not make them a "public forum." Property owned or controlled by the government which is not a public forum may be subject to a prohibition of speech, picketing, etc., without violating the first amendment.

    b) To adopt P's argument would lead to a constitutional ban on locked letter boxes typically found in apartment

Postal Service v. Council of Greenburgh Civic Association

buildings. D's interest in efficient mail service justifies the restriction on what can be placed in letter boxes, and the restriction is sufficiently related to the interest.

4) **Concurring** (Brennan, J.). A letter box is a public forum, but section 1725 is a reasonable time, place, and manner restriction.

5) **Concurring** (White, J.). Section 1725 is justified by D's interest in defraying its operating expenses. A letter box is a public forum for all who pay the fee.

6) **Dissenting** (Marshall, J.). Section 1725 burdens free speech and is not necessary to advance a substantial and legitimate interest.

7) **Dissenting** (Stevens, J.). A letter box is private property, and should remain open unless the owner places a "no trespassing" sign on it.

8) **Comment.** The Court has held that a school district may restrict access to its mail system, consisting of teachers' mailboxes and an interschool mail delivery system, to an exclusive labor bargaining representative. The reason is that such public property was not by tradition or designation a public forum, and the comprehensive restriction was necessary to preserve its use for its primary function—school communications. [Perry Education Association v. Perry Local Educators' Association, 460 U.S. 37 (1983)]

f. **Utility poles--Los Angeles City Council v. Taxpayers for Vincent,** 466 U.S. 789 (1984).

Los Angeles City Council v. Taxpayers for Vincent

1) **Facts.** Taxpayers for Vincent (P) attached political signs to utility poles in the City of Los Angeles (D). D had an ordinance that prohibited the posting of signs on public property, and D's employees routinely removed all posters attached to utility poles, including P's posters. P brought suit in federal court for an injunction against enforcement of the ordinance. The trial court granted D's motion for summary judgment, holding that the ordinance was constitutional. The court of appeals held that D did not justify its total ban on posting signs. D appeals.

2) **Issue.** May a city prohibit the posting of all signs on public property?

3) **Held.** Yes. Judgment reversed and remanded.

a) D has constitutional power to enhance its appearance, and this interest is basically unrelated to the suppression of ideas. Thus D's ordinance furthers a significant governmental interest.

        b)   D's ordinance is not overbroad; it eliminates the precise source of the evil, which is the signs themselves that have an adverse impact on the appearance of the city. The incidental restriction on first amendment freedoms is not greater than is essential to accomplish the purpose.

        c)   Even though the ban does not extend to private property, D could properly conclude that the private owners' interest in controlling their own land justifies different treatment. Private owners will likely keep clutter on their property under control.

    4)   **Dissenting** (Brennan, Marshall, Blackmun, JJ.). The Court's permissive approach toward restriction of speech for aesthetic purposes undermines the protection of the first amendment. Aesthetics are too subjective to allow meaningful judicial review. The Court should scrutinize the validity of D's bare declaration of an aesthetic objective. D should be required to pursue its objective comprehensively if it is to impose a total ban on a particularly valuable method of communication.

3.   **Symbolic Conduct.** The protection afforded unpopular words extends to symbolic conduct that can be considered expression, i.e., conduct undertaken to communicate an idea. Not all such conduct is protected, however. If regulation of the conduct has only an incidental restriction on expression, the regulation may be permitted.

United States
v. O'Brien

    a.   **Draft card burning--United States v. O'Brien,** 391 U.S. 367 (1968).

        1)   **Facts.** O'Brien and others (Ds) publicly burned their draft cards, in violation of federal law. Ds claim their action was intended to influence others to adopt their antiwar beliefs. Ds were convicted, but the court of appeals held that the statute was an unconstitutional abridgment of freedom of speech. The Supreme Court granted review.

        2)   **Issue.** When conduct contains both "speech" and "nonspeech" elements, may an important governmental interest in regulating the nonspeech element justify incidental limitations on first amendment freedoms?

        3)   **Held.** Yes. Judgment reversed.

            a)   The statute on its face does not abridge free speech, but deals with conduct having no connection with speech, i.e., destruction of draft cards. It is similar to a motor vehicle law prohibiting destruction of drivers' licenses.

b)   Although freedom of expression includes certain symbolic speech, it does not include any and all conduct intended to express an idea. Even conduct that contains a protected communicative element is not absolutely immune from government regulation. A sufficiently important governmental interest in regulating the nonspeech element of conduct can justify incidental limitations on the speech element.

c)   A government regulation is justified if: (i) it is within constitutional authority; (ii) it furthers an important governmental interest; (iii) the interest is unrelated to the suppression of free expression; and (iv) the incidental restriction on first amendment freedoms is no greater than is essential to the furtherance of that interest.

d)   The draft card laws meet this test. Therefore, D may properly be prosecuted for his illegal activity.

b.   **Improper use of the flag--Spence v. Washington,** 418 U.S. 405 (1974).

1)   **Facts.** Spence (D) hung an American flag, on which he had attached a peace symbol made of tape, upside down from his apartment. He was arrested and convicted of violating a Washington "improper use" statute. Claiming that the statute violates his right of free expression, D appeals his conviction.

2)   **Issue.** May a state prohibit the peaceful, nondestructive use of the national flag as a means of communication?

3)   **Held.** No. Judgment reversed.

a)   Flags have long been used as a means of symbolic expression. The context in which the symbol is used may also give meaning to the symbol. Here, D's display, occurring as it did within days of the Cambodia invasion and Kent State killings, had a clear meaning, both intended by D and likely to be understood by viewers. Therefore, it was an expression protected by the first amendment.

b)   Since D acted peacefully and did not destroy or desecrate the flag, P's only purpose in regulating D's display was to preserve the national flag as an unalloyed symbol of our country. Assuming this purpose is valid, the statute was still unconstitutional as applied to D because his act did no harm to any valid state interest.

4)   **Dissenting** (Burger, C.J.). Each state should be able to decide how the flag should be protected.

5) **Dissenting** (Rehnquist, White, JJ., Burger, C.J.). The state merely withdraws a unique national symbol from use as a background for communication. The Constitution does not require that D be permitted to use the flag however he pleases, just as long as he is being expressive.

4. Money and Free Expression.

a. **Campaign expenditures.** Although Congress has constitutional power to regulate federal elections, it may not unreasonably interfere with first amendment freedoms when it regulates such elections. The Court attempted to strike a balance between these competing interests when it considered the 1974 amendments to the Federal Election Campaign Act of 1971 and the Internal Revenue Code of 1954. The opinion, *Buckley v. Valeo*, below, consumed nearly 300 pages in the U.S. Reports. Basically, it held that Congress can limit the amounts individuals may contribute to federal political campaigns, but it may not limit expenditures by candidates.

Buckley
v. Valeo

b. **Balancing approach to regulation of campaign financing--Buckley v. Valeo, 424 U.S. 1 (1976).**

1) **Facts.** Buckley (P) and other candidates and groups brought suit against Valeo (D) and other federal officials, seeking a declaration that the reporting and disclosure requirements of the Federal Election Campaign Act were unconstitutional. The requirements applied to all political committees and candidates and involved detailed reporting of contributors and amounts contributed. Ps also challenged the contribution and expenditure limitations, which included the following restrictions:

(i) $1,000 limit on individual and group contributions to a candidate or authorized campaign committee per election;

(ii) $1,000 limit on expenditures relative to a clearly identified candidate;

(iii) Annual ceiling on a candidate's expenditures from personal or family resources; and

(iv) Public financing of presidential campaigns.

The court of appeals upheld the Act in its entirety. Ps appeal.

2) **Issues.**

a)   May Congress impose contribution limitations on federal elections?

b)   May Congress impose expenditure limitations on federal elections?

c)   May Congress impose detailed reporting and disclosure requirements on political contribution activity?

d)   May Congress permit public financing of presidential campaigns?

3)   **Held.** Judgment affirmed in part and reversed in part.

a)   Yes.

(1)   The financial limitations imposed on political campaigns cannot be considered as regulation of conduct alone, since exercise of free speech depends largely on the ability to finance that speech. This is especially true when the electorate depends on the mass media for so much of its information.

(2)   The $1,000 limit on campaign contributions has minimal effect on freedom of association or on the extent of political discussion. On the other hand, it deals directly with the sources of political corruption, or the appearances thereof, which are the objective of the statute. It does not violate the first amendment.

b)   No.

(1)   Even though the expenditure limitations are content-neutral, they impose severe restrictions on freedom of political expression. Equalizing the relative ability of individuals and groups to influence elections is not a sufficient rationale to justify the infringement of first amendment rights.

(2)   The interest in avoiding the danger of candidate dependence on large contributions, which is asserted as a reason for limiting expenditures, is served by the contribution limits and disclosure requirements. It is not within the government's power to determine that spending to promote one's political views is wasteful, excessive, or unwise.

c)   Yes.

(1)   The government interest in assuring the free functioning of our national institutions is served by the disclosure requirement. The electorate is provided with relevant information, thereby deterring corruption and facilitating enforcement of contribution limitations.

(2) P claims the requirements are overbroad as applied to minor parties and independent candidates, but P has failed to show any actual harm to these groups. If such harm actually occurs, courts will be available to provide appropriate remedies, but a blanket exemption is unnecessary.

d) Yes. Public financing of presidential campaigns does not constitute invidious discrimination against minor and new parties in violation of the fifth amendment. Even though the scheme provides full funding only for major parties, it assists minor parties and does not limit the ability of minor party candidates to raise funds up to the applicable spending limit.

4) **Dissenting in part** (Burger, C.J.). It is an improper intrusion on the first amendment to limit contributions. It is inappropriate to subsidize presidential campaigns.

5) **Dissenting in part** (Blackmun, J.). It is illogical to restrict contributions but permit unlimited expenditures.

First National
Bank of
Boston v.
Bellotti

c. **Political expenditures by corporations--First National Bank of Boston v. Bellotti,** 435 U.S. 765 (1978).

1) **Facts.** A Massachusetts criminal statute prohibited certain expenditures by banks and business corporations for the purpose of influencing the vote on referendum proposals, unless the proposals materially affected any of the property, business, or assets of the corporation. The First National Bank of Boston (P) wanted to publicize its views in opposition to a state constitutional amendment authorizing a graduated personal income tax and sought declaratory relief after Bellotti (D), the Attorney General of Massachusetts, indicated that he would enforce the statute against P. The state courts upheld the statute. P appeals.

2) **Issue.** May a state limit a corporation's right of free speech to expression about issues materially affecting the corporation's property, business, or assets?

3) **Held.** No. Judgment reversed.

a) P's proposed speech, an expression of views on an issue of public importance, is at the heart of the first amendment's protection. Although earlier cases extended first amendment rights to corporations involved in the business of communications, the right was extended not because of its relation to that business but because of the amendment's protection of public discussion.

b) D's interest in promoting individual citizen participation in the electoral process and preventing erosion of confidence in government has not been shown to be adversely affected by P's proposed speech. Nor is there a risk of corruption here.

      c)   D asserts an interest in protecting the rights of shareholders whose views differ from those expressed by P, but the statute is not carefully drawn to deal with this concern. Additionally, it is not certain that such an interest is sufficiently compelling to override the first amendment rights of P.

    4)   **Dissenting** (White, Brennan, Marshall, JJ.). The statute represents a permissible state protection of shareholder interests. The first amendment does not prohibit such regulation.

    5)   **Dissenting** (Rehnquist, J.). Business corporations have no constitutional right to engage in political activity not materially related to their business.

  d.   **Impermissible financing limitations.** The Court has held that a city may not limit contributions to committees formed to advocate positions on ballot measures, in part because it restrained association (there were no limits on individuals acting alone), and in part because it involved ballot measures and so did not present the dangers of influencing candidates. [*See* Citizens Against Rent Control v. City of Berkeley, 454 U.S. 290 (1981)]

5.   **Freedom of Association.**

  a.   **Introduction.** The first amendment right to associate has been developed fairly recently in the Court's opinions. The first cases involved political associations, but in *Roberts v. United States Jaycees, infra*, the Court suggested a liberty interest in associating itself, protected by the Due Process Clause.

  b.   **Associations for obtaining legal services.** Several types of associations have been created to improve members' access to legal services. The activities of these associations have conflicted with bar rules on solicitation by attorneys and other attorney conduct. Due to the first amendment implications, the Court has generally protected these associations against regulation.

    1)   **Attorneys paid by organization instead of by clients-- NAACP v. Button,** 371 U.S. 415 (1963).

      a)   **Facts.** The NAACP (P) followed a policy of having its lawyers represent persons in cases involving

NAACP
v. Button

racial discrimination. The staff lawyers received compensation only from P on a per day basis. P encouraged the bringing of such suits. The State of Virginia passed a law that forbade "any agent for an individual or organization to retain a lawyer in connection with an action to which it was not a party and in which it had no pecuniary right or liability." P challenged the constitutionality of the law because it would have prevented P from compensating the staff lawyers for their work on individuals' cases. The state courts upheld the law and P appeals.

b)   Issue. May states restrict the right of minority groups to associate in order to obtain better legal service?

c)   Held. No. Judgment reversed.

(1)   Although "solicitation" has generally been frowned upon in the legal profession, and Virginia has a legitimate interest in regulating it, the regulation in this case impinges on P's constitutional rights. The state was applying a mere label to P's conduct in order to suppress its right to institute litigation on behalf of members of an unpopular minority group.

d)   Dissent. Virginia's regulation was reasonable. Under P's scheme, attorneys may be unable to maintain undivided allegiance to their true clients when P is paying their fees.

2)   Union referral program. In *Brotherhood of Railroad Trainmen v. Virginia*, 377 U.S. 1 (1964), the Court held that the state could not interfere with a union's program by which it set up a system for referring union members to certain attorneys for representation in union-related matters. The Court stated that the rights of freedom of expression and association would not permit the state to regulate the conduct of the attorneys in this situation.

3)   Assistance by union's attorneys. In *United Mine Workers v. Illinois Bar Association*, 389 U.S. 217 (1967), the Court struck down a state ban against a union's employment of a salaried attorney to assist with workers' compensation claims, on the grounds that the ban impaired the associational rights of the union members and was not a necessary protection of the state's interest in the high standards of legal ethics. Later, in *United Transportation Union v. State Bar*, 401 U.S. 576 (1971), after emphasizing that collective activity to obtain meaningful access to the courts is a fundamental first amendment right, the Court also invalidated a state injunction against a union's plan to protect members from excessive fees of incompetent attorneys in FELA actions.

c. **Protection of right to associate based on type of association--**
    Roberts v. United States Jaycees, 468 U.S. 609 (1984).

1) **Facts.** The United States Jaycees (P), an organization dedicated to developing young men for activity in civic affairs, excluded men over 35 years of age and all women from participation as regular members. These groups could participate as nonvoting, nonofficeholding associate members, however. Two local chapters of P, located in Minnesota, violated P's national bylaws and admitted women as regular members. P's national president announced an intent to revoke the local charters involved, and the local chapters filed charges of discrimination with the Minnesota Department of Human Rights. P sued Roberts and other state officials (Ds) for declaratory and injunctive relief. The district court found for Ds, but the court of appeals reversed. Ds appeal.

2) **Issue.** May a large organization which is basically unselective about membership exclude applicants solely on the basis of sex?

3) **Held.** No. Judgment reversed.

    a) "Freedom of association" comprehends two distinct types of association. There are certain intimate human relationships which the state cannot interfere with as a principle of fundamental personal liberty. There are also associations for the purpose of engaging in activities protected by the first amendment, such as speech and religion. The degree of protection given to an association varies depending on the type of liberty involved.

    b) Personal affiliations, such as family relationships, demand the fullest possible protection. They are characterized by small numbers, a high degree of selectivity, and seclusion from others in critical aspects of the relationship. On the other hand, large business enterprises, while in a sense associations, do not involve the concerns underlying the first amendment protection.

    c) P in this case consists of local chapters of large and basically unselective groups. The evidence indicated that members were actively recruited and applicants were never denied membership, except on the basis of sex. Women were allowed to participate in P's functions even though they were denied membership.

    d) The state statute prohibiting sex discrimination may infringe in some hypothetical way on P's freedom of expressive association, because women now are unable to vote or hold office. This interference with the internal organization, however, is justified by the state's compelling interest in eradicating discrimination against its female citizens. Besides, the impact is likely to be minimal because the state law does not change P's objective of promoting the interests of young men. The impact on P's protected speech is no greater than that necessary to accomplish the state's legitimate purpose.

4) **Concurring** (O'Connor, J.). The Court's analysis is both overprotective of activities undeserving of constitutional shelter and underprotective of important first amendment concerns. An association engaged exclusively in protected expression should be protected in its choice of members. On the other hand, there should be only minimal constitutional protection of the freedom of commercial association; regulation of commercial enterprises must meet only the rational basis test. P is a commercial association. The amount of expression it engages in is not enough to preclude state regulation of its commercial activities, including the commercial opportunity presented by regular membership.

F. OTHER PROBLEMS

1. Equal Access and Free Expression.

a. **Introduction.** If a restriction on speech relies on the content of the speech, the Court will scrutinize it much more carefully than if the restriction is content-neutral. This analysis underlies many of the Court's recent cases.

Chicago Police Department v. Mosley

b. **Ban on labor picketing--Chicago Police Department v. Mosley,** 408 U.S. 92 (1972).

1) **Facts.** The city of Chicago passed an ordinance which prohibited picketing, except for peaceful labor picketing, near public schools at certain times. Mosley (P), who had picketed a certain school over several months, sought declaratory and injunctive relief in order to continue his picketing. The Chicago Police Department (D) appeals a judgment in favor of P.

2) **Issue.** May a government entity regulate picketing solely on the basis of subject matter?

3) **Held.** No. Judgment affirmed.

a) Although picketing is protected by the first amendment, reasonable "time, place, and manner" regulations are permitted to further significant governmental interests.

b) D's ordinance, however, invalidates certain picketing solely in terms of subject matter, while permitting other picketing of the same time, place, and manner. This cannot be permitted in the absence of a showing that the regulation is narrowly tailored to a legitimate objective.

c. **Government regulation and captive audiences.**

1) **Special radio station in public transportation vehicles.** In *Public Utilities Commission v. Pollak*, 343 U.S. 451 (1952), the Court upheld a practice by a District of Columbia transit company of broadcasting special programs (mostly music, but some news and commercial advertising) in its buses and streetcars. The Court noted that the programs were not challenged as objectionable propaganda. It also stated that the individual's right to be left alone is not as great in public transit as it is in his or her own home.

2) **Advertising space in public transportation--Lehman v. Shaker Heights, 418 U.S. 298 (1974).**

Lehman
v. Shaker
Heights

a) **Facts.** Lehman (P), a candidate for public office, sought advertising space on the cars of the rapid transit system of Shaker Heights (D). The advertising was managed by a private firm under contract with D. One provision of the contract prohibited any political advertising. P sued, claiming that public transportation is a public forum protected by the first amendment. P appeals a state court decision in favor of D.

b) **Issue.** Is a city's transit system advertising space a public forum that cannot be foreclosed to political advertising?

c) **Held.** No. Judgment affirmed.

(1) The nature of a forum and the conflicting interests involved are important in determining the degree of first amendment protection to be afforded.

(2) Although owned by the city, the advertising venture is essentially commercial in nature and has never been used for any political or public issue advertising.

(3) The existence of state action requires that rules relating to advertising access not be arbitrary, capricious, or invidious. D's rules are not. They advance reasonable legislative objectives of mini-

mizing chances of abuse, the appearance of favoritism, and the risk of imposing upon a captive audience.

    d)   **Concurring** (Douglas, J.). In asking us to force the system to accept his message as a vindication of his constitutional rights, P overlooks the constitutional rights of the commuters. Commuters have a right to be free from forced intrusion on their privacy.

    e)   **Dissenting** (Brennan, Stewart, Marshall, Powell, JJ.). Having opened this forum for communication, D is barred by the first amendment from discriminating among forum users solely on the basis of message content.

Board of Education v. Pico

    d.   **Government control over school library material--Board of Education v. Pico,** 457 U.S. 853 (1982).

    1)   **Facts.** The Board of Education (D) obtained a list of "objectionable" books and removed them from the high school library for review by board members. D appointed a committee to recommend whether the books should be retained in the library, then rejected the recommendations and returned only one of the removed books. D based its decision on the claim that the books were anti-American and that they presented moral danger to the students. Pico (P) challenged the decision in federal court. The district court granted summary judgment for D, but the court of appeals reversed and remanded for trial. D appeals.

    2)   **Issue.** Does the first amendment impose limitations on a local school board's discretionary removal of books from a high school library?

    3)   **Held.** Yes. Judgment affirmed.

        a)   This case does not involve the use of books in the classroom, but merely optional library books. Nor does it involve acquisition of books. Because of the procedural posture of the case, the judgment must be affirmed if there is any question of fact.

        b)   Local school boards have discretion in managing school affairs. However, this discretion is subject to the first amendment rights of the students. These rights may be impinged by the removal of books from a school library. D's discretion may not be exercised so as to deny students access to ideas with which the board members disagree, although they could remove books that were pervasively vulgar or educationally unsuitable.

        c)   The evidence as to D's motive in removing the books is unclear. There is evidence that D acted out of disagreement with the ideas contained in the books. By disregarding the committee's recommendations, the board acted in an ad hoc manner. The case must be remanded for necessary fact findings.

4) **Concurring** (Blackmun, J.). The state may not suppress exposure to ideas without a sufficiently compelling reason. And it may not deny access to an idea simply because state officials disapprove of or disagree with the idea. However, there is no right to receive ideas on the part of students. The determinative question is the motive of the school officials.

5) **Dissenting** (Burger, C.J., Powell, Rehnquist, O'Connor, JJ.). School boards, not judges and students, are charged with administering schools. Such boards are responsive to the voters and therefore reflect the views of the community. The values of morality, good taste, and relevance to education may properly be considered by elected officials in performing their duty.

6) **Dissenting** (Powell, J.). The majority removes from school boards the responsibility of determining the educational policy of the public schools. Local citizens are thereby further removed from the operation of a fundamental institution of a free people.

7) **Dissenting** (Rehnquist, J., Burger, C.J., Powell, J.). D did not deprive the public generally of the ideas in the books. Education, especially short of the university level, is necessarily selective, and those charged with providing the education must be free to determine what is necessary and what is not. The first amendment right to receive information does not apply to an institution that is necessarily selective in the ideas it may impart.

8) **Dissenting** (O'Connor, J.). D has been deprived of one of the fundamental elements necessary to properly operate a school. It is D's responsibility, not ours, to decide what books to have in the library.

e. **Subsidies and tax expenditures--Regan v. Taxation with Representation of Washington**, 461 U.S. 540 (1983).

Regan v. Taxation with Representation of Washington

1) **Facts.** The Internal Revenue Code grants a tax exempt status to various nonprofit organizations, including veterans' organizations and charitable organizations. Individual contributions to veterans' organizations and charitable organizations that do not participate in political lobbying are deductible from the contributor's taxable income, but contributions to charitable organizations that do lobby, such as Taxation with Representation of Washington (P), are not deductible. P challenged the deductibility provisions as a violation of its

first amendment rights. The court of appeals upheld P's claim. Regan (D), Secretary of the Treasury, appeals.

2) **Issue.** May Congress use tax expenditures to permit some types of organizations, but not others, to lobby at taxpayer expense?

3) **Held.** Yes. Judgment reversed.

a) Both tax exemptions and tax deductibility are government subsidies. The effect of the IRS provisions is to subsidize lobbying less than other activities undertaken by charitable organizations. Failure of Congress to subsidize P's first amendment activities does not constitute a violation of those rights, even when veterans' organizations do receive a subsidy for lobbying. The tax code does not involve a suspect classification, nor does strict scrutiny apply whenever Congress subsidizes some, but not all, speech.

b) A legislature's decision not to subsidize the exercise of a fundamental right does not infringe that right, so it is not subject to strict scrutiny. Although government may not place obstacles in the path of P's freedom of speech, it is not required to remove those not of its own creation.

c) It is rational for Congress to decide to subsidize lobbying by veterans' organizations even when other groups do not receive such a subsidy. Veterans have made special contributions to the nation and can be compensated in a variety of ways.

2. **Restricted Environments**.

a. **Military.** In *Parker v. Levy*, 417 U.S. 733 (1974), the Court upheld the court-martial conviction for "conduct unbecoming an officer and gentleman" of an Army officer who had publicly told enlisted personnel that the Vietnam war was wrong and that they should not fight in it. The Court noted that the military is a specialized society separate from civilian society, with its own laws and traditions. Because it is not a deliberative body, and because obedience and command are critical, first amendment freedoms must yield to the need for disclipline. However, the Court noted that first amendment freedoms continue to apply to soldiers to the extent possible.

Tinker v. Des Moines School District

b. **Schools--Tinker v. Des Moines School District**, 393 U.S. 503 (1969).

1) **Facts.** Tinker and other students (Ps) wore black armbands to school to protest the Vietnam war, in spite of a school policy against such action. Ps were suspended

and sought an injunction against the Des Moines School District (D) to prevent D from disciplining them. The lower courts upheld D's action as reasonable to maintain school discipline. Ps appeal.

2) **Issue.** May school officials ban a silent, peaceful expression of opinion such as wearing an armband, and punish offenders?

3) **Held.** No. Judgment reversed.

    a) Wearing an armband is a symbolic act worthy of first amendment protection. Constitutional rights are not abandoned at the schoolhouse gate. Yet school authorities may properly prescribe and control conduct in the schools.

    b) P's expression was silent and passive, unaccompanied by disorder or interference with the school's work. Prohibition of a particular expression of opinion is only justified by a showing that the expression would materially interfere with the school's discipline, which D has failed to show. Avoidance of the controversy attending unpopular opinion is an inadequate reason to ban expression of such opinions.

3. **Public Employment.** Free speech and free association issues may be raised by statutes or rules that limit a government employee's right to engage in political activities. Although such restrictions would be clearly improper if imposed against employees in private industry, the strong public interest in freeing government from graft and political favoritism justifies reasonable restrictions on the political activities of those employed by government.

    a. **Federal employees--United States Civil Service Commission v. National Association of Letter Carriers,** 431 U.S. 548 (1973).

        1) **Facts.** The National Association of Letter Carriers (P) and other interested parties challenged 5 U.S.C. section 7324(a)(2), also known as section 9(a) of the Hatch Act, which prohibits federal employees from taking "an active part in political management or in political campaigns." The district court held the statute invalid as unconstitutionally vague and fatally overbroad. The United States Civil Service Commission (D) appeals.

        2) **Issue.** May Congress prevent federal employees from participating in certain forms of partisan political conduct?

        3) **Held.** Yes. Judgment reversed.

United States Civil Service Commission v. National Association of Letter Carriers

a)   Neither the right to associate nor the right to partici-pate in political activity is absolute, and the conduct of political campaigns is manifestly subject to governmental regulation.

b)   Congress has balanced the interest of federal employees as citizens against the interest in promoting the effi-ciency of public services, and no constitutional provision requires that their determination be invalidated.

b.   **Criticizing government policy--Pickering v. Board of Education, 391 U.S. 563 (1968).**

1)   **Facts.** Pickering (P), a school teacher, sent a letter to a local newspaper criticizing the Board of Education (D). P was fired after D determined that the publication of the letter was detrimental to the operation and administration of the schools. The lower courts upheld the dismissal. P ap-peals.

2)   **Issue.** May a school teacher be fired for criticizing the policies of the school board when the teacher has no peculiar or special knowledge of the matters involved?

3)   **Held.** No. Judgment reversed.

a)   Public employment may not be subjected to unreasonable conditions. While the government may have a signifi-cantly different interest in regulating the speech of its employees than it does in regulating speech of the gen-eral public, the government employees retain an interest in commenting on matters of public concern.

b)   P in this case criticized D's allocation of funds between educational and athletic programs. The letter was not directed at any of P's coworkers or immediate super-visors. There was no personal loyalty between P and D at stake. D has no authority to dismiss teachers for their comments on matters of public concern.

c)   P did make some false statements in the letter, but everyone except D was unaffected by the letter and did not believe it. D could have exposed the errors by publishing the true figures. Essentially, P made errone-ous public statements on matters of public concern, but there is no proof that this conduct impaired P's perfor-mance of his duties or interfered with the operation of the schools. Absent that, D had no greater interest in regulating P's speech than in regulating the speech of any other member of the general public. Thus the *New York Times v. Sullivan* standard applies, and D failed to meet the burden of proof required by that case to jus-tify the dismissal.

c. **Political patronage--Branti v. Finkel,** 445 U.S. 507 (1980).

1) **Facts.** Finkel (P), a Republican assistant public defender, was terminated and replaced upon the election of Branti (D), a Democrat, to the position of County Public Defender. P claimed that his dismissal violated his first and fourteenth amendment rights. The district court found that P was discharged solely for his political beliefs and that, since P was not a policymaking, confidential employee under *Elrod v. Burns*, 427 U.S. 347 (1976), the discharge was improper. The court of appeals affirmed, and D appeals.

2) **Issue.** May an elected public defender discharge his assistants solely on political partisan grounds?

3) **Held.** No. Judgment affirmed.

a) *Elrod v. Burns* prohibited dismissals from public employment based solely on belief and associations as violative of those rights as well as imposing an unconstitutional burden on receipt of a public benefit. D claims this rule should apply only where the employee was first requested to change his beliefs, but such a holding would ignore the basis for the *Elrod* holding.

b) *Elrod* exempted positions of policymaking or confidentiality in which party affiliation and beliefs would significantly affect the effectiveness and efficiency of government. P's position did not fall within this exception. An assistant public defender's duty is to represent individual citizens, not his superior, and party affiliation is irrelevant to the performance of that duty.

4) **Dissenting** (Stewart, J.). P here is not a "nonconfidential" employee. D's office closely resembles a private law firm, and thus requires the type of mutual confidence and trust which can be affected by partisan politics.

5) **Dissenting** (Powell, Rehnquist, Stewart, JJ.). The Court undertakes unjustified lawmaking in broadly expanding *Elrod* in defiance of our nation's political history. The governmental interests at stake in this case surely justify the tangential burden on P's rights. The decision will promote further party decay to the detriment of our system based on party loyalty and compromise. It also ignores the role of non-policymaking employees in implementing political programs.

d. **Loyalty oaths to prevent subversive advocacy and association.**

1) **Oaths covering protected activities.** The Court has recognized that a governmental employer—just as any private employer—should have the power to inquire of its employees or potential employees about any matters that may prove rele-

vant to their fitness for public employment. [Garner v. Board of Public Works, 341 U.S. 716 (1951)] At the same time, however, such power cannot be exercised so as to impinge on freedom of speech. Neither the federal nor the state government may condition employment on an oath that the employee has not engaged, or will not engage, in protected speech activities. Protected activities include supporting political candidates, criticizing institutions of government, and engaging in mere discussions of political doctrines that approve overthrow of certain forms of government. [*See* Cole v. Richardson, 405 U.S. 676 (1972)]

2) **Oaths to support the Constitution.** Oaths to support the federal and/or state constitutions are proper requirements, there being an obvious relationship between a commitment of such support and one's fitness for public office or employment. [Connell v. Higginbotham, 403 U.S. 207 (1971)]

    a) **To oppose overthrow.** An oath to "oppose the overthrow" of government by illegal means has been upheld on the same reasoning. The Court refused to interpret this as requiring anything more than the basic duty to defend government; it is the same as the "support" oath. [Cole v. Richardson, *supra*]

    b) **Discharge for refusal to take oath.** The government may refuse to hire any person, or may discharge summarily (without a hearing) an existing public employee, who refuses to take an oath to "support" the Constitution. [Cole v. Richardson, *supra*]

Elfbrandt v. Russell

3) **Knowing but guiltless association--Elfbrandt v. Russell,** 384 U.S. 11 (1966).

    a) **Facts.** Elfbrandt (P), a teacher, refused to take an allegiance oath required of state employees by Arizona law. The state legislature had made membership in the Communist party a per se violation of the oath. P sought declaratory relief, and appealed state court decisions upholding the oath.

    b) **Issue.** May a state require its employees to make an oath and specify that membership in certain organizations is a per se violation of the oath?

    c) **Held.** No. Judgment reversed.

       (1) The Arizona law applies to membership without the "specific intent" to further the illegal aims of the organization. Those who join an organization but do not share its unlawful purposes and who do not participate in its unlawful activities do not pose the threat sought to be avoided by the legislature.

       (2) The oath and accompanying statutes rest on the doctrine of guilt by association and cannot stand.

d) **Dissenting** (White, Clark, Harlan, Stewart, JJ.). A number of prior cases uphold the state's privilege to condition public employment on abstention from knowing membership in the Communist party and similar organizations. Possibly the criminal action made possible by the statute is invalid, but the basic state purpose is valid, and the state need not retain such members as employees.

e. **Confidential information.** In *Snepp v. United States*, 444 U.S. 507 (1980), the Court held that the government could obtain a constructive trust on the profits from a book written by a former CIA employee which was published without CIA clearance. The employee had signed an agreement to this effect, and the Court held that the agreement was a reasonable way to protect the government's substantial interest in its information.

4. **Right to Refrain from Speaking.** The first amendment incorporates the concept of individual freedom of mind. Thus it protects the right not to speak as well as the right to speak.

a. **State-mandated speech.** In *Wooley v. Maynard*, 430 U.S. 705 (1977), the Court struck down a state law requiring display of auto license plates carrying the state motto, "Live Free or Die." The motto represented an ideological point of view that the challengers, members of Jehovah's Witnesses, found unacceptable. The Court failed to find any state interest sufficient to justify the infringement on the first amendment right to refrain from speaking.

b. **State-permitted speech on private property--PruneYard Shopping Center v. Robins**, 447 U.S. 74 (1980).

PruneYard Shopping Center v. Robins

1) **Facts.** Robins (P) set up a table inside the PruneYard Shopping Center (D) for the purpose of distributing pamphlets and seeking signatures. D had a policy to forbid such activity if not directly related to D's commercial purposes. P was asked to leave and did so. P then sued D to enjoin it from denying P access. The California Supreme Court held that the California Constitution protected P's reasonable speech, even in privately owned shopping centers. D appeals.

2) **Issue.** Does a state constitution that permits free speech on privately owned, publicly available shopping centers deny the owner's fifth amendment property rights or his first amendment freedom of speech?

3) **Held.** No. Judgment affirmed.

a) Although the United States Constitution does not grant P the right granted by the California Constitution, states may recognize more expansive rights than those existing under federal law. The limit on those rights is the extent to which they would impinge on another person's federal rights.

    b)   The fifth amendment Taking Clause is violated where a state forces some people alone to bear public burdens that, in all fairness and justice, should be borne by the public as a whole. Here, D has realized no economic injury and retains power to establish reasonable time, place, and manner restrictions to minimize interference with its commercial function. Hence, there is no taking.

    c)   D claims a right not to be forced by the state to use his property as a public forum. However, D has chosen to open his property to the public. P's message is not dictated by the state. D is free to disclaim association with P. Therefore, D's free speech rights are not impinged.

    4)   **Concurring** (Powell, White, JJ.). This type of state action could raise serious first amendment issues if the opinions expressed required rebuttal by the owner to remove mistaken impressions, which would impinge the owner's right to choose not to speak, or if the speakers used the owner's premises to propagate views morally repugnant to the owner.

    5.   **Compelled Disclosure.** In addition to its interference with privacy interests, compelling disclosure of organizational memberships may constitute an effective restraint on the group's freedom of expression and association. Such forced disclosure is permitted only when the government can demonstrate a legitimate public interest that outweighs the deterrent effect on first amendment rights.

NAACP v.
Alabama

    a.   **Private association's membership lists--NAACP v. Alabama,** 357 U.S. 449 (1958).

    1)   **Facts.** The Attorney General of Alabama (P) sued the NAACP (D) to enjoin D's activities in the state. P sought large amounts of D's records, including membership lists. D refused to provide the lists and was fined by the court for contempt. D appeals.

    2)   **Issue.** May a state force production of a private association's membership lists?

    3)   **Held.** No. Judgment reversed.

    a)   P's production order clearly entails the likelihood of a substantial restraint on D's members' right to freedom of association. D's immunity from state scrutiny of its membership lists, being closely related to its members' right of association, is protected by the fourteenth amendment.

    b)   P has shown no controlling justification for its attempt to curb D's members' rights, and the fine levied against D must fail.

4)   **Comment.** Registration requirements for the Communist Party and its members, prescribed by the Subversive Activities Control Act, were upheld because they became operative only after a finding that the organization was dangerous to the government. [*See* Communist Party v. Subversive Activities Control Board, 367 U.S. 1 (1961)]

b.   **Bar admission.** The government may not impose membership disclosure requirements as a condition for the obtaining of licenses or other benefits from the government unless it has a legitimate need to know the membership information sought.

    1)   **Impermissible inferences.** In *Konigsberg v. State Bar*, 353 U.S. 252 (1957), Konigsberg was refused admission to the state bar because of his alleged failure to show good moral character and nonsubversive beliefs. He had refused to answer questions as to his political beliefs and associations. The Court held that the bar examiners could not infer bad moral character merely because of this refusal.

    2)   **Past membership in the Communist Party.** A state cannot refuse to permit a law graduate to take the bar examination on the ground that he had previously been a member of the Communist Party. [Schware v. Board of Bar Examiners, 353 U.S. 232 (1957)] The reasons used to exclude a person from the practice of law must have a rational connection with the fitness or capacity for law practice. But in *Konigsberg v. State Bar*, 366 U.S. 36 (1961), which followed Konigsberg's second refusal to answer questions about his membership in the Communist Party, the Court held that the state's interest in seeing that its lawyers believed in orderly change outweighed the inhibition on the freedom of association and allowed the state to exclude Konigsberg from the practice of law.

    3)   **Knowing membership.** State bar examiners may properly require applicants to disclose any membership in organizations advocating violent overthrow of the government, and if so, whether they had the specific intent to further such goals. The state may deny admission to those who refuse to answer these questions. [*See* Law Students Civil Rights Research Council v. Wadmond, 401 U.S. 154 (1971)] However, if the inquiry is not confined to knowing membership, the applicant may not be excluded for his refusal to answer. Mere membership or beliefs cannot be sufficient grounds for imposing criminal punishment. [*See* Baird v. State Bar, 401 U.S. 1 (1971)] Thus, the Court has overturned a state bar denial of admission to an applicant who refused to list all the organizations to which he had belonged at any time since age sixteen, or since registering as a law student. [*See In re* Stolar, 401 U.S. 23 (1971)]

c.   **Legislative investigations.** The power of Congress or a state legislature to conduct investigations in aid of proposed legislation is deemed inherent in its legislative functions, and for Congress is implied under the Necessary and Proper Clause. Thus, a legislative body may compel the attendance of witnesses, order that they answer the questions put to them, and punish as contempt any refusal by a witness to appear or testify.

1)   **Constraints on legislative investigations.** The congressional power of investigation is limited to areas in which Congress may potentially legislate or appropriate. When the first amendment is invoked to prevent government interrogation, the courts may have to balance the competing private and public interests at stake. In addition, a legislative committee must show a substantial relation between the information sought and the state interest.

Barenblatt v.
United States

2)   **Scope of investigation--Barenblatt v. United States,** 360 U.S. 109 (1959).

a)   **Facts.** Barenblatt (D), a teacher, refused to answer questions relating to his involvement with the Communist Party that were posed by a congressional subcommittee during a congressional investigation of Communist infiltration into the field of education. D based his refusal on first amendment grounds, expressly disclaiming reliance on the fifth amendment. D was convicted of contempt, fined, and imprisoned. D appeals.

b)   **Issue.** Is inquiry by a congressional committee into a person's involvement with the Communist Party precluded by the first amendment?

c)   **Held.** No. Judgment affirmed.

(1)   The congressional power of investigation is limited to areas in which Congress may potentially legislate or appropriate and the Bill of Rights. Congress is not precluded from interrogating a teacher merely because of the constitutional protections accorded to education.

(2)   When the first amendment is invoked to bar governmental interrogation, the courts must balance the competing private and public interests at stake.

(3)   The dominant purpose of this investigation was to ascertain the extent of Communist infiltration furthering the alleged ultimate purpose of over-

throw of the government, which is a valid subject of congressional inquiry. Identification of a witness's Communist involvement properly falls within the scope of such investigation. The Court cannot intervene on the basis of the motives behind the valid exercise of the investigative power.

(4) No other factors are present to raise D's personal interest above the important governmental interests here at stake. Based on a fair balancing, D's first amendment rights have not been offended.

d) **Dissenting** (Black, J., Warren, C.J., Douglas, J.). Abridgment of the first amendment freedoms may not be justified by a balancing process. Congress here has impermissibly inquired into beliefs, not actions. The real purpose of the investigation is to try witnesses and punish them by humiliation and public shame, solely for what Congress considers to be their political "mistakes."

e) **Dissenting** (Brennan, J.). The government's sole purpose is exposure for the sake of exposure. Such a purpose cannot outweigh D's first amendment rights.

f) **Comment.** *Uphaus v. Wyman*, 360 U.S. 72 (1959), decided the same day as *Barenblatt*, dealt with a one-man investigation in New Hampshire. The director of the World Fellowship group was found in contempt for failing to produce the list of guests at a summer camp. The Court stated that there was sufficient reason to believe that subversive persons were involved in the camp, and the state interest was important enough to infringe on the Fellowship's right of privacy. The Court also held unconstitutional a state disclosure requirement as applied to the Socialist Workers Party, which had historically been subject to official and private harassment. [*See* Brown v. Socialist Workers, 459 U.S. 87 (1982)]

3) **Nexus requirement.** In *Gibson v. Florida Legislative Investigation Committee*, 372 U.S. 530 (1963), the Court held that a legislative committee could not force disclosure of the membership records and contributors lists of a concededly legitimate, non-subversive organization because the committee could not show a compelling interest. There was an insufficient nexus between the information sought and the state interest.

4) **Timeliness.** In *DeGregory v. New Hampshire Attorney General*, 383 U.S. 825 (1966), the appellant stated he had not been a member of the Communist Party for many years, but the Attorney General still wanted information of his activities while a member. The Court ruled that the staleness of the reason for investigating and the subject matter rendered the state's interest insufficient to outweigh the individual's privacy. Historical information is not compelling unless there is a present danger.

6.   Freedom of the Press.

a.   **Introduction.** Although the first amendment separately mentions freedom of the press, the Court has not recognized any special right for the press additional to the general freedom of speech. Yet the institutional press often faces problems different from those faced by citizens in general, which has prompted some claims that special protection is appropriate.

b.   **No special status.** In considering the exact constitutional protection of the press in *First National Bank of Boston v. Bellotti*, 435 U.S. 765 (1978), an election expenditure case, the Court stated that the Press Clause did not confer a special status or institutional privilege on a limited group, and that there was no difference in the first amendment freedom to disseminate ideas through the newspaper or through those who gave lectures that encourage publication and wide dissemination.

Minneapolis Star & Tribune v. Minnesota Commissioner of Revenue

c.   **Special tax treatment for the press--Minneapolis Star & Tribune v. Minnesota Commissioner of Revenue,** 460 U.S. 575 (1983).

1)   **Facts.** Minnesota imposed a general sales tax and a related use tax for items on which no sales tax had been paid. Publications were exempt from these taxes until 1971, when the state imposed a use tax on the cost of paper and ink products consumed in producing a publication. Three years later, the state exempted the first $100,000 of paper and ink used. As a result, the Minneapolis Star (P), one of eleven newspapers (out of 388 in the state) that had to pay a use tax, paid nearly two-thirds of all the use tax collected. P sued the Minnesota Commissioner of Revenue (D) for a refund. The state courts upheld the tax, and P appeals.

2)   **Issue.** May the states single out the press for special tax treatment?

3)   **Held.** No. Judgment reversed.

a)   Other than the structure of the tax itself, there is no indication that the state imposed the tax with an impermissible or censorial motive. This case therefore differs from *Grosjean v. American Press Co.*, 297 U.S. 233 (1936), in which a publishing tax was held invalid because of improper government motive.

b)   Differential taxation of the press, unrelated to any special characteristic that requires such treatment, is unconstitutional. Such treatment suggests suppression of expression, a presumptively unconstitutional goal. In the absence of a compelling counterbalancing interest, differential taxation may not be allowed.

    c)   D has no adequate justification for the tax. Even though the tax burden may be lighter than it would be under general application of the regular sales tax, differential treatment of any kind opens the door for more burdensome treatment.

    d)   The tax also targets a small group of large newspapers, presenting an impermissible potential for abuse.

4)   **Concurring in part** (White, J.). The Court need not reach beyond the unconstitutional targeting of the tax to hold it unconstitutional.

5)   **Dissenting** (Rehnquist, J.). This tax favors newspapers. It does not abridge the freedom of the press. D's scheme is rational because the large volume of inexpensive items involved (newspapers) makes the regular sales tax impractical.

7.   **Regulation Intended to Improve the Idea Marketplace.**

    a.   **Access to the mass media.** The mass media presents difficult first amendment problems because of its pervasiveness and the barriers to entry. There are a limited number of frequencies to be used by radio and television, and the government allocates these frequencies according to established procedures. Those who are permitted to broadcast have a special privilege. Government therefore also imposes a special responsibility to provide a range of programs that are in the public interest. Newspapers, which are also part of the mass media, do not of course operate on allocable frequencies. Yet some argue that the expense of establishing a significant newspaper is such that government should also regulate to some extent the content of newspapers, or at least assist the general public in gaining access to newspapers.

    1)   **Access by statute.** In response to the problems of access to the media, some states and Congress itself have provided rights of access by statute. In assessing such statutes, the Court looks to the nature of the media involved. In this context, the first amendment acts as a protection against government interference.

    2)   **Access to newspapers--Miami Herald Publishing Co. v. Tornillo,** 418 U.S. 241 (1974).

        a)   **Facts.** Tornillo (P) was a candidate for the Florida state legislature. The Miami Herald Publishing Co. (D), a newspaper publisher, printed editorials

Miami Herald Publishing Co. v. Tornillo

critical of P's candidacy. P sued to force D to publish P's response under a Florida "right of reply" statute. The state supreme court reversed the lower court and held the statute constitutional. D appealed.

b) **Issue.** May the state require a newspaper to publish a candidate's reply to criticism made by the newspaper?

c) **Held.** No. Judgment reversed.

(1) P demonstrates the consolidation of control over the public media, and argues that an enforceable right of access is a necessary remedy to assure open public debate. However, such a right requires some mechanism, either governmental or consensual. If governmental, as here, the first amendment protections are invoked.

(2) Although a responsible press is desirable, it is not mandated by the Constitution and, like many other virtues, cannot be legislated. P would use governmental coercion to compel D to publish material that D deems improper for publication. Such interference with editorial decisionmaking exceeds constitutional bounds.

(3) To uphold the state law would encourage editors to avoid controversial subjects, to the detriment of public discussion.

d) **Concurring** (Brennan, J.). This case is not a consideration of "retraction" statutes that require publication of a retraction of defamatory falsehoods.

b. **Access to the electronic media.** The Court has indicated that a greater scope of regulation may be permissible as to radio and television broadcasting than as to the print media. For example, the Court has upheld orders by the Federal Communications Commission under a statutory "fairness doctrine" that requires broadcasters to provide broadcast time for discussion of public issues as well as fair coverage for each side of issues presented. In *Red Lion Broadcasting Co. v. FCC*, 395 U.S. 367 (1969), the Court upheld FCC orders that required a radio station to offer free broadcasting time to opponents of political candidates or views endorsed by the station, and to any person who has been personally attacked in the course of a broadcast, for reply to the attack. A broadcasting licensee has no right to monopolize a frequency to the exclusion of fellow citizens. The right of viewers and listeners is paramount to the right of the broadcaster. Broadcasters may be treated as proxies for the entire community, obligated to give suitable time and attention to matters of great public concern, including time to respond to personal attacks or political endorsements.

Columbia
Broadcasting
System, Inc.
v. Democratic
National
Committee

c. **Access by constitutional right--Columbia Broadcasting System, Inc. v. Democratic National Committee, 412 U.S. 94 (1973).**

1) **Facts.** Radio station WTOP, owned by the Columbia Broadcasting System, Inc. (D), followed a policy of refusing to sell air time for spot announcements to individuals and groups who wished to express their views on controversial issues. The Democratic National Committee (P) sought a declaratory ruling that a broadcaster such as D could not as a general policy refuse to sell time to responsible parties for comment on public issues. The FCC rejected P's request, but the court of appeals reversed. D appeals.

2) **Issue.** May a government-regulated broadcaster refuse, as a general policy, to sell broadcast time to responsible parties for comment on public issues?

3) **Held.** Yes. Judgment reversed.

a) The broadcast media are a unique vehicle of expression because physical limitations require allocation of frequencies among applicants. Such allocation is performed by the government, which accordingly seeks assurance that licensees operate in the public interest. In broadcasting, the rights of the viewers and listeners, not those of the broadcasters, are paramount. The scheme of broadcast regulation evinces an intent to preserve the widest journalistic freedom consistent with the public obligation. The fairness doctrine makes broadcasters responsible for providing the public with access to a balanced presentation of information on issues of public importance.

b) The first amendment restrains governmental, not private, action. Congress was careful to preserve the fullest journalistic independence possible for broadcast licenses. D's challenged policy was not mandated by the government but resulted from independent editorial decision. Thus, although government does regulate the broadcast media in various respects, D's policy is sufficiently removed from government interference as to fall beyond the first amendment mandate.

c) The system of broadcast regulation requires that licensees meet a "public interest" standard in their operation. This standard does not require licensees to accept editorial advertisements, nor, assuming governmental action, would the first amendment. The FCC, charged with executing the statute, determined that such a requirement would undermine the public interest by favoring the ideas of those with access to greater wealth. The alternative would be heavier government involvement in the licensee's editorial decisionmaking, which would infringe the first amendment.

4) **Concurring** (Stewart, J.). The first amendment could require government control over private broadcasters only if the latter were government. Such a holding would violate the rights of those broadcasters.

5) **Concurring** (White, J.). Conduct of broadcasters may well be government action, but even if so, D's action would be consistent with the first amendment.

6) **Concurring** (Blackmun, Powell, JJ.). Because the first amendment would not compel the result reached by the court of appeals, the governmental action issue should not be reached.

7) **Concurring** (Douglas, J.). The broadcast media are as protected by the first amendment as are newspapers and magazines. The latter are in actuality as unavailable to the public as are the broadcast media. Although government properly regulates technical aspects of broadcasting, P has no place in editorial aspects; the fairness doctrine itself is excessive government interference.

8) **Dissenting** (Brennan, Marshall, JJ.). The fairness doctrine, standing alone, is insufficient to provide the kind of broad interchange of ideas to which the public is entitled. The Court permits exclusions from a public forum based on content alone, contrary to our prior cases.

8. Right of Access to Gather News.

a. **Introduction.** While reporters generally have the same right of access to sources of information as the public, they do not have any special newsgathering privilege. Hence, they may not refuse to answer relevant and material questions asked during a good faith grand jury investigation.

Branzburg
v. Hayes

b. **Reporter's testimonial privilege--Branzburg v. Hayes,** 408 U.S. 665 (1972).

1) **Facts.** Branzburg (D), a reporter, observed illegal drug transactions that he used in a news article. D was subpoenaed to appear before a grand jury. D sought prohibition and mandamus to avoid having to reveal his confidential information, but the state courts denied his petition. D appeals. (Two other cases involving two similarly situated reporters were consolidated with this appeal).

2) **Issue.** Does the first amendment grant a special testimonial privilege to reporters, protecting them from being forced to divulge confidential information to a grand jury's investigation?

3) **Held.** No. Judgment affirmed.

    a) D claims that forcing reporters to reveal confidences to a grand jury will deter other confidential sources of information, thus curtailing the free flow of information protected by the first amendment. However, journalists have no constitutional right of access to several types of events (grand jury proceedings, meetings of private organizations and of official bodies gathered in executive sessions, etc.). Although these exclusions tend to hamper news gathering, they are not unconstitutional.

    b) All citizens have an obligation to respond to a grand jury subpoena and to answer questions relevant to crime investigation. The only testimonial privilege for unofficial witnesses is the fifth amendment; there is no necessity to create a special privilege for journalists based on the first amendment.

    c) The public interest in pursuing and prosecuting those crimes reported to the press by informants and thus deterring future commission of those crimes is not outweighed by the public interest in possible future news about crime from undisclosed, unverified sources.

    d) A judicially created journalist's privilege would necessarily involve significant practical and conceptual problems in its administration. However, Congress and the state legislatures are not precluded from fashioning whatever standards and rules they might deem proper if they choose to create a statutory journalist's privilege.

4) **Concurring** (Powell, J.). Journalists are not without remedy in the face of a bad faith investigation. Motions to quash and appropriate protective orders are available where the requested testimony is not within the legitimate hold of law enforcement.

5) **Dissent** (Stewart, Brennan, Marshall, JJ.). The Court undermines the independence of the press by inviting authorities to annex the journalistic provision as an investigative arm of government. Exercise of the power to compel disclosure will lead to "self-censorship" and, as a consequence, significantly impair the free flow of information to the public. To force disclosure, the government must show:

    a) Probable cause that the journalist has information clearly relevant to a specific probable violation of law,

    b) Absence of less obtrusive means of obtaining the information, and

    c) A compelling and overriding interest in the information.

c.   **Jails.** Prison inmates can be prohibited from being interviewed by news media as long as alternative means of communication are available, such as mail and visitors. There is no freedom of the press to interview prisoners. [Pell v. Procunier, 417 U.S. 817 (1974)] However, if the government voluntarily grants such access, the public and the press must be treated equally. Where limitations that might be reasonable as to individual members of the public would impede effective reporting (e.g., prohibition on cameras), such limitations may not, consistent with reasonable prison rules, be used to hamper effective media presentation of what is seen by individual visitors. [*See* Houchins v. KQED, Inc., 438 U.S. 1 (1978)]

Richmond
Newspapers,
Inc. v.
Virginia

d.   **Right of access to courtroom proceedings--Richmond Newspapers, Inc. v. Virginia,** 448 U.S. 555 (1980).

1)   **Facts.** Early in the fourth criminal trial of the same defendant, the trial judge granted an uncontested closure motion made by the defendant. Later, reporters for Richmond Newspapers (P) sought a hearing on a motion to vacate the closure order; the hearing was granted, but the public was excluded from the hearing. At the hearing, the court denied the motion, considering the defendant's interest paramount. The defendant was acquitted in the closed trial. P appealed from the trial court's closure order, but the state courts affirmed. P appeals.

2)   **Issue.** Is the right of the public and press to attend criminal trials guaranteed by the Constitution?

3)   **Held.** Yes. Judgment reversed.

a)   In *Gannett Co. v. DePasquale*, 433 U.S. 368 (1979), this Court held that neither the public nor the press has an enforceable right of access to a pretrial suppression hearing.

b)   Throughout the evolution of the trial procedure, the trial has been open to all who cared to observe. However, the Constitution contains no explicit provisions protecting the public from exclusion.

c)   The first amendment protects freedom of speech and press, including expression regarding events at trials. These guaranteed rights would be meaningless if access to the trial could be foreclosed arbitrarily. Other constitutional rights, not explicitly established, have been recognized as implied. Clearly, the public interest in judicial functions and in freedom of speech requires open trials.

d)   In some circumstances, where an overriding interest is articulated in findings, a criminal trial may be closed to the public, but only where the common alternatives are insufficient (e.g., jury sequestration, witness sequestration, etc.).

4) **Concurring** (Brennan, Marshall, JJ.). Publicity is an important means of assuring the right to a fair trial. What happens in a courtroom is public property. The first amendment requires open access, and agreement between the judge and the parties cannot override the first amendment.

5) **Concurring** (Stewart, J.). The first and fourteenth amendments give the press and the public a right of access to civil and criminal trials. A courtroom is a public place, even more so than city streets and parks. The right is not absolute, but in this case the judge gave no recognition to the right of the press and the public to be present.

6) **Concurring** (Blackmun, J.). The Court does not apparently accept a sixth amendment right to a public trial, but at least it recognizes some protection for public access under the first amendment.

7) **Concurring** (Stevens, J.). This is the first time the Court has held that the acquisition of newsworthy matter has constitutional protection.

8) **Dissenting** (Rehnquist, J.). There are no provisions in the Constitution that prohibit a state from denying public access to a trial when both the prosecution and the defense consent to the closure order.

IX. RELIGION

The first amendment provides that "Congress shall make no law respecting an establishment of religion, or prohibiting the free exercise thereof." These two clauses, the Establishment Clause and the Free Exercise Clause, have provided considerable grounds for litigation. One other reference to religion is found in the Constitution. Article VI provides that "no religious test shall ever be required as a qualification to any office or public trust under the United States."

A. ESTABLISHMENT CLAUSE

1. **Introduction.** The central purpose of the Establishment Clause is to ensure governmental neutrality in matters of religion. "When government activities touch on the religious sphere, they must be secular in purpose, evenhanded in operation, and neutral in primary impact." [Gillette v. United States, 401 U.S. 437 (1971)] Many cases arising under the Establishment Clause have involved schools. As applied to schools, the clause prevents governments from enacting laws that further the religious training or doctrine of any sect.

2. **Alternative Approaches to Establishment Clause Problems.**

   a. **No-aid theory.** This view requires the government to do nothing that involves governmental support of religion, or that is favorable to the cultivation of religious interests. It leaves open the problem of the constitutionality of legislation having incidental impact on religion.

   b. **Neutrality theory.** This view requires the government to be neutral with respect to religious matters, doing nothing to either favor or hinder religion. This combines the no-aid test with a no-hinder test.

   c. **Balancing test.** This view assumes that it is impossible for the government to preclude all aid to religion, or to observe absolute neutrality. Governmental action must take into account the free exercise guarantee. In some situations, the government must, and in others, may, accommodate its policies and laws to further religious freedom. This is the most prevalent view.

Everson v. Board of Education

   d. **Application: transportation to parochial schools--Everson v. Board of Education,** 330 U.S. 1 (1947).

      1) **Facts.** A local New Jersey board of education (D) authorized reimbursement to parents of the costs of using the public transportation system to send their children to school, whether public or parochial. Everson (P) challenged the scheme as an unconstitutional exercise of state power to support church schools. P appeals adverse lower court decisions.

2) **Issue.** May a state use public funds to assist student transportation to parochial, as well as public, schools?

3) **Held.** Yes. Judgment affirmed.

   a) The Establishment Clause was intended to erect a wall between church and state. It does not prohibit a state from extending its general benefits to all its citizens without regard to their religious belief.

   b) Reimbursement of transportation is intended solely to help children arrive safely at school, regardless of their religion. It does not support any schools, parochial or public. To invalidate D's system would handicap religion, which is no more permissible than favoring religion.

4) **Dissenting** (Jackson, Frankfurter, JJ.). The Court's rationale contradicts its conclusion.

5) **Dissenting** (Rutledge, Frankfurter, Jackson, Burton, JJ.). The Court should be as strict to prohibit use of public funds to aid religious schools as P is to prevent introduction of religious education into public schools.

3. **Official Acknowledgment of Religion.**

   a. **State-employed chaplains.** In *Marsh v. Chambers*, 463 U.S. 783 (1983), the Court upheld the practice of the Nebraska legislature of opening each day with a prayer by a chaplain paid by the state. The Court noted that the colonies, federal courts, and the Continental Congress itself followed such a practice. As deeply imbedded in history and tradition as such prayer is, it cannot be held to violate the first amendment. The dissenting Justices noted that the practice does not pass any of the *Lemon* tests (*infra*).

   b. **Government sponsorship of Christmas display--Lynch v. Donnelly,** 465 U.S. 668 (1984). Lynch v. Donnelly

   1) **Facts.** The city of Pawtucket, Rhode Island, annually erects a Christmas display that includes Santa Claus and related figures, colored lights, and a creche, or nativity scene, containing the infant Jesus, Mary, Joseph, and other traditional figures. Donnelly (P) and other citizens brought suit in federal court against Lynch (D) and other city officials to have the creche removed. The district court enjoined Ds from including the creche in the display, and the court of appeals affirmed. The Supreme Court granted certiorari.

   2) **Issue.** May a city include a nativity scene in its annual Christmas display?

3) Held. Yes. Judgment reversed.

    a)   The first amendment is intended to prevent the intrusion of either the church or the state upon the other, but total separation is not possible. Some relationship between the two must exist. The Constitution requires accommodation of all religions.

    b)   The same week that Congress approved the Establishment Clause as part of the Bill of Rights, it provided for itself paid chaplains. The role of religion in American life has been officially acknowledged in numerous ways. For example, the government subsidizes holidays with religious significance, such as Christmas and Thanksgiving, by giving its employees paid time off.

    c)   Under *Lemon*, the display of the creche has a valid secular purpose—to celebrate the holiday and depict its origins. Its inclusion in Ds' display has less effect on advancing religion than do other types of government accommodation of religion, including providing textbooks to religion-sponsored schools and tax exemptions for church properties. Nor does the minimal cost cause excessive entanglement between religion and government.

4) Concurring (O'Connor, J.). The Establishment Clause prohibits government from making adherence to a religion relevant to a person's standing in the political community. Excessive entanglement with religious institutions and government endorsement or disapproval of religion violates this principle. Ds' creche display falls within neither category of government activity.

5) Dissenting (Brennan, Marshall, Blackmun, Stevens, JJ.). Ds' display constitutes an impermissible governmental endorsement of a particular faith. The display does not satisfy the *Lemon* test. It excludes non-Christians on religious grounds. Christmas has both secular and religious aspects, and the government should not emphasize the religious aspects.

4.   Regulation in Aid of Religion.

    a.   **Sunday closing laws.** In *McGowan v. Maryland*, 366 U.S. 420 (1961), the Court upheld a state law which required most retail stores to close on Sundays. It found that such laws do not involve the "establishment" of religion in that they do not directly aid or inhibit any religion, but merely set aside a uniform day of rest, which is a proper exercise of the police power to promote the public welfare. This is true even though the laws also incidentally accomplish another purpose (aiding church attendance), which by itself would be improper.

b. **Restrictions on teaching particular subjects.** While the state undoubtedly has the right to prescribe curriculum for the public schools, it does not have the right to forbid the teaching of any scientific theory, doctrine, or other subject, merely because it may be contrary to some religious doctrine. The Court held that an Arkansas statute which forbade the teaching of evolution in public schools violated freedom of religion under the first and fourteenth amendments. The statute was not "religiously neutral"; it was aimed at one doctrine (evolution) that was offensive to certain fundamentalist religions. [*See* Epperson v. Arkansas, 393 U.S. 97 (1968)] More recently, Louisiana enacted a law requiring "balanced treatment" of the theories of creation and evolution if the subject of the origin of man, life, the Earth, or the universe is dealt with in public schools. The lower courts, including a sharply divided Fifth Circuit, held that the law was unconstitutional because the theory of creation is a religious belief. The Supreme Court affirmed, holding that the law was motivated primarily by religious purposes. [Edwards v. Aguillard, 482 U.S. 578 (1987)]

5. **Financial Aid to Religion.**

a. **Basic test.** The Court has promulgated three guidelines for determining the validity of state statutes granting financial aid to church-related schools. To be valid, the statute must: (i) reflect a clearly secular purpose; (ii) have a primary effect that neither advances nor inhibits religion; and (iii) avoid "excessive government entanglement" with religion. [*See* Lemon v. Kurtzman, *infra*] The wall of separation between church and state works both ways. It prevents religion from seeping into the functions of government, and it also prevents government from encroaching on matters of religion.

b. **Use of state university's facilities.** The three-part test of *Lemon* was successfully used to invalidate a state university's ban against religious groups using its buildings. The university opened its facilities to student groups in general, except for religious groups. The Court held that this violated the first amendment rights of the religious groups; a fully open-forum policy would satisfy the three-part test because it would have a secular purpose, would avoid entanglement, and would not have a primary effect of advancing religion. [Widmar v. Vincent, 454 U.S. 263 (1981)]

c. **Tax deduction for tuition--Mueller v. Allen,** 463 U.S. 388 (1983).

Mueller
v. Allen

1) **Facts.** Minnesota allowed citizens paying state income tax to deduct the cost of their children's tuition, physical education clothing, supplies, and other items. The deduction applied whether the school was public or private. Most private schools in the state were sectarian. Allen (P) challenged the statute under the Establishment Clause. The state courts upheld the deduction. The Supreme Court granted certiorari.

2) **Issue.** May a state permit parents to deduct from their income tax the cost of their children's education, including tuition paid to private sectarian schools?

3) **Held.** Yes. Judgment affirmed.

   a) The deduction is limited to actual expenses incurred for the tuition, textbooks, and transportation of dependents attending elementary or secondary schools. The validity of the deduction depends on application of the three-part *Lemon* test.

   b) The tax deduction has a secular purpose because it promotes education in all types of schools. The statute does not have the primary effect of advancing the sectarian aims of non-public schools because it is part of a broader scheme of tax deductions, it is available to all parents, and whatever aid it provides to parochial schools is available only through the decisions of individual parents. Thus there is no imprimatur of state approval.

   c) The statute does not excessively entangle the state in religion, because the only state involvement is the determination as to which textbooks qualify for a deduction (the cost of religious books is not deductible).

4) **Dissenting** (Marshall, Brennan, Blackmun, Stevens, JJ.). The Establishment Clause prohibits state subsidies to sectarian schools, including deductions for tuition payments. Aid to sectarian schools must be restricted so it is not used to further the religious mission of those schools. This tax education scheme is not so restricted, so it is unconstitutional.

5) **Comment—excessive entanglement.** In *Aguilar v. Felton*, 473 U.S. 373 (1985), the Court struck down a federal plan for educationally deprived children from low-income families which permitted payment of federal funds to public school employees for remedial and guidance services provided in parochial school classrooms. The plan included a system for monitoring the religious content of the services. The Court held that this supervisory surveillance resulted in excessive entanglement of church and state.

B. FREE EXERCISE CLAUSE

The Free Exercise Clause is designed to protect against governmental compulsion in regard to religious matters. It bars governmental acts that would regulate religious beliefs as such or interfere with the dissemination thereof, impede the observance of religious practices, or discriminate in favor of one religion over another, where such acts are not otherwise justifiable in terms of valid governmental aims.

1. Conflict with State Regulation.

a. Introduction. Although the Free Exercise Clause prohibits any infringement of the freedom to believe, it does not constitute an absolute protection of all activity undertaken pursuant to religious beliefs. Such activity may be regulated or prohibited by government if there is an important or compelling state interest that prevails when balanced against the infringement on religious freedoms.

b. Development of belief-action distinction. The belief-action distinction arose in *Reynolds v. United States*, 98 U.S. 145 (1879), which upheld a law against bigamy aimed at stopping the practice of polygamy by Mormons. The Mormons practiced polygamy as a religious belief. The Court held that because polygamy was traditionally condemned, the practice could be outlawed. In *Cantwell v. Connecticut*, 310 U.S. 296 (1940), an action involving fund solicitation by a Jehovah's Witness, the Court abandoned the *Reynolds* ruling that conduct was outside the protection of the first amendment. The Court found that the freedom to act under the Free Exercise Clause, although not absolute like the freedom to believe, could only be regulated without undue infringement of the freedom to believe.

c. Flag cases. In *Board of Education v. Barnette*, 319 U.S. 624 (1943), the Court overruled its previous decision in *Minersville School District v. Gobitis*, 310 U.S. 586 (1940), which had sustained another flag salute public school regulation that had been challenged on religious grounds by Jehovah's Witnesses. Characterizing *Barnette* as a freedom of expression, rather than free exercise, action, the Court held that there is no power to make a salute a legal duty, that such a compulsory rite infringes an individual's constitutional liberty, and that under the Bill of Rights, orthodoxy in politics cannot be prescribed.

d. Day of worship.

    1) Introduction. Sunday closing laws have been upheld against attack by Sabbatarians (e.g., Orthodox

Jews). Such laws do not promote or discourage any religious beliefs, but simply make the practice of certain beliefs more expensive. [*See* Braunfeld v. Brown, 366 U.S. 599 (1961)] However, the state may not punish a person for worshipping on a day other than Sunday. [*See* Sherbert v. Verner, *below*] On the other hand, a state may not establish an obligation to give a day off to the employees choosing to worship. [*See* Estate of Thornton v. Caldor, 472 U.S. 703 (1985)]

Sherbert
v. Verner

2) **Application--Sherbert v. Verner, 374 U.S. 398 (1963).**

a) **Facts.** South Carolina (through Verner (D)) denied unemployment compensation benefits to workers who failed to accept offered employment without good cause. Sherbert (P) was denied benefits because she failed to accept a job that required Saturday work. Her basis for refusal was her membership in the Seventh Day Adventist Church, which recognized Saturday as the Sabbath day. The state courts upheld the denial of benefits. P appeals.

b) **Issue.** May a state deny benefits to otherwise eligible recipients whose failure to meet all the requirements is based on a religious belief?

c) **Held.** No. Judgment reversed.

(1) Conditioning the availability of benefits upon P's willingness to violate a cardinal principle of her religious faith effectively penalizes the free exercise of her constitutional liberties, and can only be justified by a compelling state interest.

(2) The only state interest lies in discouraging spurious claims, but D has failed to show that this possibility is significant or that no alternative, less damaging regulation exists.

(3) The result here reflects merely the governmental obligation of neutrality in the face of religious differences and does not promote or favor one religion over the other.

d) **Concurring** (Stewart, J.). The Establishment Clause as previously construed by this Court requires denial of P's claim. Otherwise the government would be establishing P's religion by granting her benefits because of her beliefs, while others, not of P's faith, are denied benefits. The decision proves that the Court has incorrectly construed that clause in prior cases. *Braunfeld* (*supra*) should be specifically overruled.

e) **Dissenting** (Harlan, White, JJ.). The Court actually overrules *Braunfeld*, since the secular purpose of the statute here is even clearer than the one in that case. The Court goes too far in holding that a state must furnish unemployment benefits to one who is unavailable for work whenever the unavailability arises from the exercise of religious convictions.

e. **Compulsory education--Wisconsin v. Yoder,** 406 U.S. 205 (1972).

1) **Facts.** Yoder (D) and other Amish parents refused to send their children to school beyond the eighth grade despite a Wisconsin (P) law requiring attendance until age 16. Ds claimed that further education would violate their religious beliefs because the values taught in public high schools contrasted with the Amish values and way of life. Ds were convicted, but the conviction was reversed by the Wisconsin Supreme Court. P appeals.

2) **Issue.** Must a state make provision in its compulsory education laws for students whose religious beliefs prevent them from attending secondary schools?

3) **Held.** Yes. Judgment affirmed.

a) The values of parental direction of the religious upbringing and education of their children in their formative years have a high place in our society. Only essential state interests not otherwise served can prevail over legitimate claims to the free exercise of religion.

b) The Amish way of life is an essential part of their religious beliefs and practices. Elementary education, given locally, did not subject Ds' children to adverse influences, and is not challenged. Ds have adequately shown, however, that secondary education would tend to severely infringe on Ds' religious beliefs.

c) P's interest in assuring education is substantially achieved in the elementary grades. Ds' children continue their education through parent-supervised agricultural vocational training. The children are thus fully prepared for responsibility. Because the state's interest in requiring the one or two extra years of education is minimal compared with Ds' religious interests, Ds' interests must prevail.

4) **Concurring** (Stewart, Brennan, JJ.). The case does not involve the right of Amish children to attend public high schools if they so desire.

5) **Concurring** (White, Brennan, Stewart, JJ.). The balancing of these important but conflicting interests favors D.

6) **Dissenting in part** (Douglas, J.). We ought to reverse the judgment as to the parents of those students who have not affirmatively indicated a desire not to attend public high school.

f.   Other cases.

1)   **Social Security payments.** An employer may be required to pay Social Security on his employees' wages despite objections based on religious belief. [United States v. Lee, 455 U.S. 252 (1982)]

2)   **Conscientious objection.** The Selective Service Act permitted exemption from the draft for those who, by reasons of religious belief, are conscientiously opposed to war in any form. This has been construed to apply only to persons opposed to all wars, not just to particular wars in which the United States is involved, such as the Vietnam war. [Gillette v. United States, 401 U.S. 437 (1971)]

3)   **Tax-exempt status.** The IRS may deny tax-exempt status to religious schools that practice racial discrimination. [Bob Jones University v. United States, 461 U.S. 574 (1983)]

4)   **Veterans' preferences.** The Court has upheld a federal law that grants educational benefits to veterans while denying the same benefits to conscientious objectors, even though the conscientious objectors performed the alternate civilian service required by the draft laws. The distinction was considered at most an incidental burden of the free exercise of religion and was justified by the need to raise and support armies. [Johnson v. Robison, 415 U.S. 361 (1974)]

5)   **Exclusion of clergy from public office.** In *McDaniel v. Paty*, 435 U.S. 618 (1978), the Court overturned a state constitutional provision that prohibited ministers from serving as state legislators. The Court noted that experience had shown that ministers were not less faithful to their oaths of civil office than unordained legislators, and that, applying a balancing test, the restriction violated the Free Exercise Clause.

Employment Division, Department of Human Resources v. Smith

g.   **Limitation on required accommodation--Employment Division, Department of Human Resources v. Smith,** 110 S. Ct. 1595 (1990).

1)   **Facts.** The State of Oregon made it a crime to use peyote. Smith (P) was dismissed from his job for using peyote as part of his religious ritual as a member of the Native American Church. P was denied unemployment benefits because his dismissal was due to misconduct. P sued the Employment Division, Department of Human Resources (D), claiming that his use of peyote was inspired by religion and therefore was protected under the Free Exercise Clause of the first amendment. The Oregon Supreme Court reversed, holding that the criminal sanction was unconstitutional as applied to the religious use of peyote, and ruled that P was entitled to unemployment benefits. The Supreme Court granted certiorari.

2)   **Issue.** May a state make criminal certain conduct that is part of a religious organization's ritual?

3) **Held.** Yes. Judgment reversed.

    a)   P relies on *Sherbert*, which held that a State could not condition the availability of unemployment insurance on an applicant's willingness to forgo conduct required by his religion. In that case, however, the conduct was not prohibited by law; in this case, peyote use was prohibited by law.

    b)   The States cannot ban acts or abstentions only when they are engaged in for religious reasons, or only because of the religious belief they display, because this would constitute a prohibition on the free exercise of religion. This does not mean that a religious motivation for illegal conduct exempts the actor from the law. If prohibiting the exercise of religion is merely an incidental effect of a generally applicable and otherwise valid law, the first amendment is not implicated.

    c)   In some cases, such as *Wisconsin v. Yoder*, the first amendment may prevent application of a neutral, generally applicable law to religiously motivated action, but these cases involve the Free Exercise Clause in connection with other constitutional protections, such as parents' right to direct the education of their children.

    d)   P argues that the *Sherbert* test should be applied, but this test has never invalidated governmental action except the denial of unemployment compensation, and should not be extended beyond that field to require exemptions from a generally applicable criminal law. In the unemployment cases, the test is applied to prevent a state from refusing to extend religious hardship cases to a system of individual exemptions.

    e)   If the compelling interest requirement were applied to religion cases such as this, many laws would not satisfy the test, and the result would approach anarchy, particularly in a society such as ours that contains a diversity of religious beliefs. This alternative would raise a presumption of invalidity, as applied to the religious objector, of every regulation of conduct that does not protect an interest of the highest order. The states are free, as many have, to exempt from their drug laws the use of peyote in sacramental services, but the states are not constitutionally required to do so.

4) **Concurring in part.** A law that prohibits religiously motivated conduct implicates first amendment concerns, even if it is generally applicable. The first amendment does not distinguish between laws that are generally applicable and laws that target particular religious practices; it applies to generally applicable laws that have the effect of significantly burdening a religious practice. The balance between the first amendment and the government's legitimate interest in regulating conduct is struck by applying the compelling interest test. To be sustained, a law that burdens the free exercise of religion must either be essential to accomplish an overriding governmental interest or represent the least restrictive means of achieving some compelling state interest. In this case, the prohibition on use of peyote does satisfy the compelling state interest test.

5) **Dissenting.** The State's broad interest in fighting the war on drugs is not the interest involved in this case; the interest is the State's refusal to make an exception for the religious, ceremonial use of peyote. There is no evidence that the religious use of peyote ever harmed anyone, and 23 other states have adopted exemptions for the religious use of peyote. The assertion that requiring the state to make an exemption in this case would open the government to anarchy is speculative; such a danger is addressed through the compelling interest test.

Corporation of Presiding Bishop of the Church of Jesus Christ of Latter-Day Saints v. Amos

2. **Permissible Accommodation--Corporation of Presiding Bishop of the Church of Jesus Christ of Latter-Day Saints v. Amos,** 483 U.S. 327 (1987).

a. **Facts.** The Corporation of Presiding Bishop of the Church of Jesus Christ of Latter-Day Saints (D) operated the nonprofit Deseret Gymnasium. Amos (P) was a janitor at the gym. P did not qualify for a temple recommend, which required observance of D's standards including church attendance, tithing, and abstinence from coffee, tea, alcohol, and tobacco. P was fired. Section 702 of the Civil Rights Act of 1964 [42 U.S.C. §2000e-1] exempts religious organizations such as D from the general prohibition against employment discrimination on the basis of religion. P sued, claiming the exemption should not apply to secular nonprofit activities of religious organizations. The district court and court of appeals upheld P's claim. D appeals.

b. **Issue.** May Congress accommodate religious practices by permitting religious organizations to discriminate in employment on the basis of religion even in secular nonprofit activities?

c. **Held.** Yes. Judgment reversed.

1) Governmental accommodation of religious practices does not necessarily violate the Establishment Clause. Such benevolent neutrality permits free exercise of religion without either sponsorship or interference.

2) The three-part *Lemon* analysis of religion cases may be applied to accommodation cases. The first requirement, that the challenged law serve a secular legislative purpose, is intended to prevent Congress from abandoning neutrality and acting to promote a particular point of

view in religious matters. A legislative purpose to alleviate significant governmental interference with a religious group's ability to exercise its religion is a permissible purpose.

3) Congress amended the Civil Rights Act to extend the exemption to secular nonprofit activities of religious organizations because the exemption previously applied only to religious activities. The exemption acted to minimize governmental interference with the decisionmaking process in religious groups, which is a permitted purpose.

4) The second *Lemon* requirement is that the law have a principal effect that neither advances nor inhibits religion. A law may permit churches to advance religion; the prohibition is only against governmental advancement, through its own activities and influence, of religion. Any advancement of religion that D might achieve through its gymnasium cannot be fairly attributed to the government, as opposed to D.

5) The third requirement is that Congress must have chosen a rational classification to further a legitimate end. Section 702 is rationally related to the legitimate purpose of alleviating significant governmental interference with the ability of religious organizations to define and carry out their religious missions.

d. **Concurring** (Brennan, Marshall, JJ.). The exemption from Title VII's prohibition of religious discrimination burdens the religious liberty of employees such as P. However, religious organizations such as D have an interest in autonomy in ordering their internal affairs, including defining the religious community. While individual interests in religious freedom would only permit an exemption for religious activities, a case-by-case determination of what nonprofit activities are religious and what are not would involve unacceptable entanglement with religion and a chill on religious expression, and the balance between these interests must fall in favor of the broader exception relied on by D.

e. **Concurring** (O'Connor, J.). Judicial deference to all legislation that purports to facilitate the free exercise of religion would vitiate the Establishment Clause. The Court suggests that the "effects" prong of the *Lemon* test is not implicated if the government action merely "allows" religious organizations to advance religion. A better approach is to recognize that by exempting religious organizations from a generally applicable regulatory burden, the government does advance religion; it only remains to be determined whether the benefit accommodates free exercise or unjustifiably awards assistance to religion. The probability that a nonprofit activity is involved in the organization's religious mission is sufficient to justify a conclusion that the government action exempting such activities is an accommodation, not a government endorsement, of religion.

f. **Comment.** In *Texas Monthly v. Bullock*, 489 U.S.1 (1989), the

Court held that a statute exempting religious publications from a state sales tax was unconstitutional. The exemption had insufficient breadth of coverage; it did not apply to nonreligious publications that contributed to the community's cultural, intellectual, and moral betterment. Hence, it constituted an unjustifiable award of assistance to religious organizations and conveyed a message of endorsement. The dissent argued that breadth of coverage was not relevant unless the state asserted purely secular grounds for the exemption. When religion was singled out, particularly for an exemption from a tax that could be construed as an unconstitutional burden on religion, the exemption should be construed as an accommodation.

3. **Unusual Religious Beliefs and Practices.** The definition of "religion" for purposes of the first amendment has not yet been definitively determined. The Court has set forth certain parameters, however.

   a. **Inquiry into truth of religious precepts forbidden.** In *United States v. Ballard*, 322 U.S. 78 (1944), the Court articulated its position that, under the first amendment, submission to a jury of the truth of a party's religious beliefs is barred because of the subjective nature of such proof. "Men may believe what they cannot prove," so the truth or reasonableness of a belief cannot be questioned by a court.

   b. **Belief in God.** Belief in God may not be used as an essential qualification for office. When Maryland denied a commission as a notary public to an otherwise qualified appointee because he refused to declare his belief in the existence of God (as required by the Maryland Constitution for those who seek to qualify for "any office or profit or trust"), the Court held that such a "religious test for public office" imposed a burden on the applicant's freedom of belief and religion. [Torcaso v. Watkins, 367 U.S. 488 (1961)]

   c. **Draft-exemption definition.** In a draft case turning on whether a person was exempt as a conscientious objector by virtue of his "religious training and belief" (a requirement of the Selective Service Act, not a constitutional issue), the Court held:

      1) "Religious" belief is something more than essentially sociological, philosophical, economic, or political views.

      2) It does not require belief in any particular dogma, or in any supernatural force or Supreme Being.

      3) It must, however, be sincere and meaningful and occupy a place in the life of its possessor parallel to that filled by the orthodox belief in God of those who are customarily regarded as "religious" persons. [United States v. Seeger, 380 U.S. 163 (1965)]

X. ECONOMIC LIBERTIES

A. THE CONTRACT CLAUSE

1. **Introduction.** Article I, section 10 provides that "no state shall pass any law impairing the obligation of contracts." Note that the clause applies only to the states; there is no mention in the Constitution of a similar prohibition against the federal government. However, the Court has held that the Due Process Clause of the fifth amendment is broad enough to extend a similar prohibition to federal action. [Lynch v. United States, 292 U.S. 571 (1934)] The term "impairs" includes a substantial invalidation, release, or extinguishment of the obligation of a contract. "Obligation" includes the existing legal rules as well as the terms of the contract itself. This does not mean that the law can never change, but legitimate expectations of the parties cannot be impaired.

2. **Development of Contract Clause Doctrine.** The Contract Clause was a major restraint on state economic regulation in the nineteenth century. It applied to both private and public contracts. More recently, the Court has applied a balancing test. Not all substantial impairments of contracts are unconstitutional. Private parties may not claim immunity from state regulation through private contractual arrangements. Rights and duties may be modified by legislation necessary to an important and legitimate public interest as long as the impairment of the contract is reasonable.

3. **Basic Requirements for a Valid Impairment--Home Building & Loan Association v. Blaisdell,** 290 U.S. 398 (1934).

   a. **Facts.** Minnesota passed a law that permitted extensions of the period of redemption from a foreclosure and sale of real property under a mortgage. The Blaisdells (Ds) obtained such an extension. Home Building & Loan (P) challenged the extension as improper state interference in a private contract. The state defended the law as needed emergency legislation to deal with the Depression. The state courts upheld the law, and P appeals.

   b. **Issue.** May a state alter existing contractual obligations in order to respond to emergency conditions?

   c. **Held.** Yes. Judgment affirmed.

      1) An emergency does not create power, but it may justify the exercise of existing power. As maintenance of government is essential to having enforceable contracts, circumstances may arise when exercise of the police power to alter contracts is justified in order to maintain effective government.

Home Building & Loan Association v. Blaisdell

2) Legislation impairing contracts may be upheld when:

    a) The state legislature declares that an emergency exists;

    b) The state law is enacted to protect a basic societal interest, not a favored group;

    c) The relief is appropriately tailored to the declared emergency;

    d) The imposed conditions are reasonable; and

    e) The legislation is limited to the duration of the emergency.

3) The statute at issue here meets all five of the requirements and is therefore constitutional.

4. **State Obligations--United States Trust Co. v. New Jersey,** 431 U.S. 1 (1977).

    a. **Facts.** New York and New Jersey (Ds) formed the New York and New Jersey Port Authority by interstate compact. In 1962, both states passed statutes prohibiting financing of passenger railroad facilities with revenues pledged to pay the authority's bonds, unless the facility was self-supporting. In 1974, the states retroactively repealed the 1962 covenant in order to permit greater subsidizing of mass transit. United States Trust Co. (P), trustee and holder of Authority bonds, challenged the 1974 law on Contract Clause grounds. The state courts upheld the 1974 law. P appeals.

    b. **Issue.** May a state impair the obligation of its own contracts, based on its own determination of reasonableness and necessity?

    c. **Held.** No. Judgment reversed.

      1) The Contract Clause does not require state adherence to a contract that surrenders an essential attribute of its sovereignty. However, this contract is purely financial and does not compromise the state's sovereignty. Impairment of D's duties is constitutional only if it is reasonable and necessary.

      2) Allowing a state to reduce its financial obligations whenever it wanted to spend the money for what it regarded as an important public purpose would negate all Contract Clause protection. For this reason, complete deference to legislative assessments of reasonableness and necessity is inappropriate. After independently examining the existence of less drastic alternatives, we

hold that D's repealing acts are excessively harmful to P's contractual interests.

d. **Dissenting** (Brennan, White, Marshall, JJ.). Elevation of the Contract Clause to the status of regulation of the municipal bond market, at the heavy price of frustration of sound legislative policymaking, is unwise and unnecessary. P's realistic economic interests are adequately protected by the political processes and the bond marketplace itself. The Court ought not restrict the legislature's responsiveness to changing public needs by preventing adoption of measures not plainly unreasonable and arbitrary. D's proper legislative decision ought to be upheld.

5. **Private Obligations--Allied Structural Steel Co. v. Spannaus**, 438 U.S. 234 (1978).

Allied Structural Steel Co. v. Spannaus

a. **Facts.** Allied Structural Steel Co. (P) established a pension plan, pursuant to IRS regulations, which provided that qualifying employees would acquire pension rights but which gave no assurance that any employee would not be dismissed at any time. P had an office in Minnesota which it began to close. A few months previously, Minnesota had passed a law that subjected employers to a "pension funding charge" upon termination of a pension plan or closing of a Minnesota office. The law had the effect of making several of P's otherwise unqualified employees pension obligees, resulting in a charge to P of $185,000. P sued Spannaus (D), a Minnesota official, for injunctive and declaratory relief. The federal district court held the act valid. P appeals, claiming the law violates the Contract Clause.

b. **Issue.** Does the Contract Clause preclude state legislation that significantly expands duties created by private contract?

c. **Held.** Yes. Judgment reversed.

    1) The Contract Clause is not an absolute prohibition against any impairment of contracts. It does not operate to obliterate state police power, but it does limit a state's ability to abridge existing contractual relationships.

    2) The first query is whether the state law has substantially impaired a contractual relationship. The challenged law nullifies express terms of P's contractual obligations and imposes a completely unexpected liability in potentially disabling amounts. Such severe impairment may be condoned only if justified by the need for the law.

    3) Unlike the law challenged in *Blaisdell, supra*, the law here is directed at a narrow class—those employers with voluntary private pension plans who either terminate the

plan or close the Minnesota office. Nor was the law intended to deal with a broad and desperate economic emergency. It did not just temporarily change the contractual rights and duties, but imposed a permanent and immediate change.

d. **Dissenting** (Brennan, White, Marshall, JJ.). The Contract Clause is simply an adjunct to the currency provisions of article I, section 10 and was intended only to prevent alteration of contracts that relieved one party of the duty to pay a debt. To "impair" a contract is not to add duties but to take away duties. Creating a previously nonexisting duty, as the Minnesota law does, is not an impairment of a contract but a valid exercise of the state's police power. The effect of the Court's adoption of these vague testing criteria, which are arguably satisfied by the statute in any case, is to invite judicial discretion to protect property interests that happen to appeal to them. The Contract Clause should simply not apply to laws that create new rights.

6. **Modern Trend.** Despite the apparent revival of the Contract Clause in *United States Trust Co.* and *Spannaus*, the Court recently has deferred to state power. In *Energy Reserves Group, Inc. v. Kansas Power & Light Co.*, 459 U.S. 400 (1983), the Court applied a three-part test. If the state substantially impairs a contractual relationship, it must have a significant and legitimate public purpose for so doing. If it does, and the contractual adjustment is reasonable and appropriate, the courts will defer to the state unless the state itself is a party to the contract. In *Exxon Corp. v. Eagerton*, 462 U.S. 176 (1983), the Court rejected a Contract Clause challenge to a law that prohibited oil and gas producers from passing through to purchasers an increase in the severance tax, thereby preventing producers from taking advantage of existing contract provisions for such a pass-through. The Court held that the alleged impairment of contractual obligations was incidental to a generally applicable rule of conduct and not a direct attack on the original contracts. The law applied to all producers, not just those with pass-through provisions in their contracts. The law was not constitutionally different from laws regulating rates, which override contractual prices.

B. **"TAKING" OF PROPERTY INTERESTS**

1. **Introduction.** The governmental power to require a private landowner to convey his land to the government for public purposes is referred to as the power of "eminent domain." Although the Constitution does not specifically grant a power of eminent domain to the federal government, the power is implied. The fifth amendment provides in part that private property may not be "taken" for "public use" without just compensation. This clause is a restriction on both the fed-

eral and state power of eminent domain. Property rights may include tangible and intangible interests. The two most troublesome constitutional issues here are the meanings of the terms "public use" and "taking."

a.   **"Public use."** Government may only exercise its power of eminent domain for a public use. This term is broadly defined by the Court. If the asserted use of the property is rationally related to a conceivable, articulated public purpose, the Court will defer to the legislative findings.

  1)   **Facilitating home ownership.** The Court's modern view of "public" use demonstrates the extent of its deference to legislative findings. In *Hawaii Housing Authority v. Midkiff*, 467 U.S. 229 (1984), the Court permitted the Hawaii legislature to use eminent domain to allow tenants who owned their homes but not the land under them to purchase the real estate. In Hawaii, the state and federal governments owned 49% of the land and 72 private owners owned another 47%, leaving only 4% of the land for all other owners.

  2)   **Disclosure of private research data.** In *Ruckelshaus v. Monsanto Co.*, 467 U.S. 986 (1984), the Court held that government disclosure of costly research and test data submitted to register a pesticide under federal law was not a taking for a "private use." Congress intended to eliminate expensive duplication of research and to promote competition among producers of end-use products by allowing applicants to use data already accumulated by others. This was a valid public use.

b.   **"Taking."** Government action may affect property rights without constituting a "taking." Mere regulation that limits the use of the property, such as zoning laws, is not normally considered a taking under the fifth amendment. The Court merely determines whether justice and fairness require that the public compensate the private owner for the loss. As the following examples illustrate, the particular facts of each case are determinative.

  1)   **Government interference not constituting a taking.** Forfeiture of property used in connection with a crime is not a taking [Calero-Toledo v. Pearson Yacht Leasing Co., 416 U.S. 663 (1974)], nor is a temporary, unplanned occupation of private property by the military during a riot [National Board of YMCA v. United States, 395 U.S. 85 (1969)].

  2)   **Regulation which is not a taking.** In *Agins v. Tiburon*, 447 U.S. 255 (1980), the Court approved a zoning plan that restricted the owners' ability to develop their land. The ordinance permitted no more than five houses on a five-acre tract. The loss in value was not a taking because the owners could still develop the land. The Court also upheld a city safety ordinance that forced the termination of a 30-year-old sand and gravel mining operation, because the

owner did not prove that the value of his land was diminished. [Goldblatt v. Hempstead, 369 U.S. 590 (1962)]

    3)   **Examples of takings.** Frequent low flights over property adjacent to a government airport [United States v. Causby, 328 U.S. 256 (1946)] or flooding caused by a government dam project [United States v. Cress, 243 U.S. 316 (1917)] have been held to be a "taking."

Pennsylvania Coal Co. v. Mahon

2.   **Compensation Requirement--Pennsylvania Coal Co. v. Mahon,** 260 U.S. 393 (1922).

    a.   **Facts.** In 1878, Mahon (P) received title to the surface rights of a parcel of land from Pennsylvania Coal Co. (D), which reserved the rights to remove the coal under the surface. P also waived all claims for damages resulting from removal of the coal. D gave notice of intent to mine. P, knowing that D's activity would cause a subsidence of the surface and of P's house, sought an injunction based on a state statute that forbids coal mining in such a way as to cause subsidence of any human habitation. The lower court denied an injunction. The state supreme court held the statute a valid exercise of police power and granted an injunction. D appeals.

    b.   **Issue.** May a state exercise its police power to destroy previously existing property and contract rights without paying compensation?

    c.   **Held.** No. Judgment reversed.

        1)   The general rule is that, while the use of property may be regulated to a certain extent, if regulation goes too far it will be recognized as a "taking." One factor is the extent of the diminution in value of the property. Here, the statute would totally divest D of his properly reserved right to mine coal. Another factor is the extent of the public interest. Here, a single private house is involved, with no threat to personal safety since adequate notice was given.

        2)   While there may be no doubt as to the need for the statute, the question is, who should pay for the changes initiated by the law? D's loss should not go uncompensated. The state may achieve its objectives properly only through eminent domain procedures. When private persons or communities take the risk of acquiring only surface rights, they ought not be given greater rights than they bought merely because their risk has become an actuality.

    d.   **Dissenting** (Brandeis, J.). Every restriction abridges property rights. Here D is merely prohibited from a noxious use.

Future events may render the use harmless; it is merely a temporary restriction and need not be compensated for by the government.

e. **Comment.** In *Miller v. Schoene*, 276 U.S. 272 (1928), the Court upheld a Virginia law that provided for the destruction of ornamental trees affected by a disease that could also damage apple orchards. Owners were compensated only for the cost of removing their trees. The state had to choose between preserving the trees or the orchards, and could properly determine that the public interest required preservation of the orchards.

3. **"Taking" Through Regulation--Penn Central Transportation Co. v. New York,** 438 U.S. 104 (1978).

a. **Facts.** Penn Central (P) owned the Grand Central Terminal in New York City (D). The terminal was designated a "landmark" under the City Landmarks Preservation Law, which prohibited destruction of designated landmarks. P was denied permission to alter the terminal solely because of the landmarks law, which P then challenged as an unconstitutional taking. The trial court granted P relief, but the higher state courts all held for D. P appeals.

b. **Issue.** May a city restrict development of individual historic landmarks, beyond applicable zoning regulations, without a "taking" requiring payment of "just compensation?"

c. **Held.** Yes. Judgment affirmed.

1) The question here revolves around two basic considerations: the nature and extent of the impact on P and the character of the governmental action.

2) The "taking" may not be established merely by showing a government-imposed inability to further develop a property, nor solely by a diminution in property value. Zoning laws have these effects yet are constitutional because they are part of a comprehensive plan for achieving a significant public purpose, as is D's law.

3) P claims the law is discriminatory and arbitrary. Yet numerous other structures are likewise under the landmark regulations. Even if P does not receive benefits to completely offset its burdens, valid zoning laws may have a similar effect. If P finds application of the law to be arbitrary, it may obtain judicial review of any commission decision.

4) The government has not taken P's airspace for its own purpose, but for the benefit of the entire public. It has done so pursuant to a legitimate interest in preserving special buildings.

5) Finally, the impact on P is mitigated by the existence of Transferable Development Rights and by the fact that P has not been prohibited from making any improvements, but only the two drastic proposals that were rejected by D. Thus P may be permitted the use of at least some portion of its airspace.

d. **Dissenting** (Rehnquist, J., Burger, C.J., Stevens, J.). A literal interpretation of the fifth amendment would clearly favor P. Even the Court's more relaxed view should result in a decision for P. Clearly valuable property rights have been destroyed. A taking need not be a physical seizure. Destruction of rights is a taking, except in two instances: prohibition of nuisances and prohibitions covering broad areas that secure an average reciprocity of advantage, such as zoning laws. Neither exception applies here. The people generally, not P individually, ought to pay the cost of the recognized public benefit of having P's property preserved.

e. **Comment.** In *Loretto v. Teleprompter Manhattan CATV Corp.*, 458 U.S. 419 (1982), the Court held that any permanent physical intrusion by the government is a taking requiring compensation. This rule applies regardless of the state's interest or the economic impact on the owner. The *Loretto* case involved a New York statute authorizing permanent cable TV installations for tenants of privately-owned apartment houses. The tenant merely had to pay a one-time fee to the landlord of $1. The dissenting Justices noted that nonphysical government intrusions often diminish the value of property more than minor physical intrusions, and that therefore a per se rule for physical intrusion was inappropriate.

Keystone Bituminous Coal Association v. DeBenedictis

4. **Extensive Limitation on Mining Rights--Keystone Bituminous Coal Association v. DeBenedictis**, 480 U.S. 470 (1987).

a. **Facts.** A Pennsylvania statute intended to prevent or minimize subsidence of surface land caused by coal mining required 50% of the coal under specified structures to remain in place for surface support. The Keystone Bituminous Coal Association (P) challenged the statute as an unconstitutional taking. P's members had acquired the mineral rights and support estates from landowners who retained only the surface estate. The statute would significantly reduce the amount of coal that could be mined. The district court found for DeBenedictis (D), and the court of appeals affirmed. The Supreme Court granted certiorari.

b. **Issue.** May a state prohibit, without compensation, the mining of coal that would have the effect of causing subsidence of surface land?

c. **Held.** Yes. Judgment affirmed.

1) A land use regulation will be deemed a taking if it: (i) does not substantially advance legitimate state interests, or (ii) denies an owner economically viable use of his land. For example, *Pennsylvania Coal Co. v. Mahon, supra*, relied on the premise that the act protected only private interests and made it commercially impracticable to mine coal in the affected areas. The statute in this case does not suffer from these deficiencies.

2) The statute has a clear public purpose—the protection of health, environment, and fiscal integrity to support the tax base. P's members' use of their coal rights is similar to a public nuisance, the control of which is supported by the notion of reciprocity of advantage. The public welfare, and in turn each individual, is benefited greatly by the restriction placed on individual use of private property.

3) P has not claimed or shown that the statute makes it commercially impracticable for its members to continue mining their coal, nor can P point to specific quantities of coal that it can no longer mine to prove a taking. Instead, the focus is on the nature of the interference with the rights in the property as a whole. When this is done, it is clear that less than 2% of P's members' coal is actually rendered unusable.

4) P also notes that Pennsylvania recognizes the support estate as a separate estate in land and claims that this estate is taken by the statute. However, the support estate has value only as it protects the value of the estate with which it is associated; it is a part of the entire bundle of rights. P's members retain the right to mine most of their coal in their mineral estates, so the value of their support estates is not taken.

d. **Dissenting** (Rehnquist, C.J., Powell, O'Connor, Scalia, JJ.). The differences between this statute and the one considered in *Pennsylvania Coal* are trivial. Both involved a public purpose. The nature of the public purpose is relevant, because a government need not pay compensation for regulation needed to prevent property owners from using their property to injure others. At the same time, labeling a regulation as a nuisance regulation does not exempt it from fifth amendment scrutiny. In this case, P's members' interests in specific coal deposits have been completely destroyed. This is different from affecting one strand of many in a bundle of interests. The statute also takes P's members' support estate interests, which were purchased to protect the mining rights.

5. **Public Access to Property Through Private Property--Nollan v. California Coastal Commission**, 483 U.S. 825 (1987).

Nollan v. California Coastal Commission

a.   **Facts.** The Nollans (Ps) purchased a beachfront lot in southern California on the condition that they replace the existing structure with a new one. Ps applied to the California Coastal Commission (D) for permission to build a home like the others in the neighborhood, but D required Ps to grant a public easement across their property along the ocean. Ps sued and won a judgment. D appealed, but meanwhile Ps build the house. The state court of appeals reversed, and Ps appeal.

b.   **Issue.** If a state may not require uncompensated conveyance of an easement over private property, may it require the conveyance as a condition to its approval of a land use permit for the property?

c.   **Held.** No. Judgment reversed.

   1)   It is clear that if D had simply required Ps to grant a public easement across their property, there would have been a taking. Such an easement constitutes a permanent physical occupation, and the right to exclude others is an essential stick in the bundle of rights that constitutes property.

   2)   A land use regulation is permissible if it substantially advances legitimate state interests and does not deny an owner economically viable use of his land. If a condition is imposed short of an outright ban on construction, it must serve the same governmental purpose as the ban would. Otherwise, the condition is not a valid land use regulation but extortion. If the condition is unrelated to the purported purpose, the true purpose must be evaluated.

   3)   In this case, D claims Ps' new house interferes with "visual access" to the beach, which in turn will cause a "psychological barrier" to the public's desire for access. D also claims Ps' house will increase the use of the public beaches. Each of these burdens on "access" would be alleviated by the easement over Ps' property. These arguments are nothing more than a play on words, however. The condition is not the exercise of the land use power for any of the stated purposes. It simply lacks any substantial advancing of a legitimate stated interest.

   4)   D's final justification is that the easement would serve the public interest, but a mere belief that the public interest would be served is insufficient. D must use its power of eminent domain to acquire the easement if it wants it.

d.   **Dissenting** (Brennan, Marshall, JJ.). The Court should defer to the state as long as the state rationally could have decided that the control used might achieve the state's objective. Instead, the majority has applied an inappropriately narrow concept of rationality. In fact, there is a reasonable relationship between the condition and the specific burden Ps' development imposes on public access. At any rate, the restriction is a minimal burden and the development increased the value of Ps' property much more than any diminution attributable to the easement.

e. **Dissenting** (Blackmun, J.). Ps knew about the easement before they bought the property, and the public had used the property for beach access for a considerable time.

f. **Comment.** Local governments have traditionally required developers to dedicate streets and utility easements within subdivisions, and frequently also require certain improvements that benefit the subdivision exclusively, such as paved streets or on-site utility facilities. However, some governments have required dedication of land for parks and schools, or a payment of money to develop parks and schools. Some courts disallow such requirements as not sufficiently attributable to the developer's activity to remove public responsibility for such improvements.

6. **Remedies for De Facto Regulatory Taking--First English Evangelical Lutheran Church of Glendale v. County of Los Angeles**, 482 U.S. 304 (1987).

First English Evangelical Lutheran Church of Glendale v. County of Los Angeles

a. **Facts.** The First English Evangelical Lutheran Church of Glendale (P) owned a campground which contained several buildings. Following a forest fire, a flood destroyed P's buildings. Due to the flood hazard, the County of Los Angeles adopted an ordinance preventing the construction of any building within the flood protection area that included P's property. About a month later, P sued D, claiming damages for inverse condemnation and loss of use of its property. The appellate court upheld the trial court's dismissal of the complaint on the ground that P could not maintain an inverse condemnation suit based on a regulatory taking. P would first have to obtain a declaratory judgment or mandamus, and then seek compensation only if D chose not to exercise its power of eminent domain. P appeals.

b. **Issue.** May a landowner obtain damages for governmental taking of his or her property before it is finally determined that the regulation constitutes a taking of the property under the fifth and fourteenth amendments?

c. **Held.** Yes. Judgment reversed.

   1) The fifth amendment does not prohibit the taking of private property, but requires the government to pay compensation for such a taking. If government action works a taking, the government has a constitutional obligation to pay just compensation. The inverse condemnation action reflects the self-executing character of the fifth amendment.

   2) It is also clear that although property use may be regulated, regulation that goes too far constitutes a taking.

Inverse condemnation results from a regulatory taking not accomplished through the normal exercise of eminent domain condemnation procedures.

3) The California Supreme Court in *Agins v. Tiburon*, 598 P.2d 25 (1979), *aff'd on other grounds*, 447 U.S. 255 (1980), disallowed damages occurring prior to the ultimate invalidation of a challenged regulation, believing that mandamus or declaratory relief, not inverse condemnation, is the appropriate relief at that stage. This holding does not comport with the fifth amendment because a temporary taking may also require payment of just compensation.

4) If the government takes land even for a limited period, it could cause a significant loss to the private owner. When such a temporary loss constitutes a taking, the fifth amendment requires the public burden to be borne by the public. This does not apply to mere fluctuations in value resulting from the process of governmental decisionmaking, which is an incident of ownership.

5) This rule that the government must compensate for temporary takings does not limit government flexibility. The government can still decide to terminate the taking regulation, or it can exercise its power of eminent domain. It cannot, however, avoid paying just compensation for property taken.

d. **Dissenting** (Stevens, Blackmun, O'Connor, JJ.). A regulation that would constitute a taking if it became permanent might not constitute a taking if it is only temporary. The majority has improperly relied on cases involving physical takings. In regulatory cases, a taking only takes place if the regulation destroys a major portion of the property's value, but the majority has ignored this difference between physical and regulatory takings. California should be permitted to require a landowner to pursue an action to invalidate an ordinance before it can bring an action for just compensation.

XI. STATE VS. PRIVATE ACTION

A. INTRODUCTION TO THE STATE ACTION DOCTRINE

1. **Basic Issue.** Both the fourteenth and fifteenth amendments prohibit certain "state action" as opposed to private, nongovernmental action. The determinative question is whether any particular conduct is state action. The response to that question has changed over the years. Early cases held that these amendments did not apply to private acts of discrimination. Distinguishing between public and private conduct became increasingly difficult as government became more intimately involved in regulating and even participating in the private sector, as will be seen in the more modern cases.

2. **Nineteenth Century Approach--The Civil Rights Cases,** 109 U.S. 3 (1883).

   a. **Facts.** The Civil Rights Act of 1875 made it unlawful for anyone to deny a person the enjoyment of accommodations at inns, on public transportation, etc., on the basis of race. Certain blacks were excluded from inns, theaters, and a railroad in five separate states. The cases were consolidated before the Supreme Court.

   b. **Issue.** May Congress prohibit private discriminatory actions by facilities generally open to the public?

   c. **Held.** No. The Civil Rights Act is unconstitutional.

      1) The fourteenth amendment permits Congress to take corrective action only against state laws or acts done under state authority. The Civil Rights Act is directed toward acts by individuals and cannot be upheld under the fourteenth amendment.

      2) The thirteenth amendment permits direct as opposed to merely corrective legislation, but it only covers slavery or involuntary servitude, or the lingering badges of such. Refusing accommodation to a black does not impose any badge of slavery or servitude. Mere racial discrimination is not a badge of slavery.

      3) Congress has no power to pass the Civil Rights Act, and Ps must seek a remedy in state law for any cause of action against private individuals or corporations that are discriminating.

   d. **Dissent.** The Court has ignored the substance and spirit of these amendments. Freedom includes immunity from and protection against racial discrimination, especially in the use of public, albeit privately-owned, accommodations and facilities licensed by the state.

e.   **Comment.** The common law of all states at the time of the Civil Rights Act of 1875 held that it was unlawful to deny the facilities of inns and carriers to any person. Therefore, Ps did have a remedy in state law. However, this case illustrates the approach to state action that permitted individuals to discriminate freely if they wanted.

B.   GOVERNMENT INACTION

1.   **Introduction.** State action exists whenever a state has affirmatively facilitated, encouraged, or authorized acts of discrimination by its citizens. States are not required to outlaw discrimination, but they cannot do anything to encourage it. The mere fact that the government permits certain commercial activity does not make that activity state action. But if enforcement of commercial rights, such as contract rights, becomes necessary, the government may decline to take action if the commercial activity is unconstitutional.

Flagg Bros.,
Inc. v. Brooks

2.   **Commercial Rights and Remedies--Flagg Bros., Inc. v. Brooks,** 436 U.S. 149 (1978).

a.   **Facts.** Brooks (P) was evicted and her possessions stored by Flagg Bros., Inc. (D). When P failed to pay storage charges, D threatened to sell P's possessions, pursuant to procedures established by the New York Uniform Commercial Code (UCC). P brought an action seeking damages, an injunction, and declaratory relief that the UCC provision was unconstitutional. The district court dismissed the complaint, but the court of appeals reversed, finding state involvement in D's action sufficient to invoke constitutional protections. D appeals.

b.   **Issue.** Does a warehouseman's sale of goods entrusted to him for storage constitute state action because it is permitted by state law?

c.   **Held.** No. Judgment reversed.

1)   P claims that the state delegated to D a power traditionally held only by the state. While many functions have been traditionally performed by governments, very few have been exclusively reserved to the states. The settlement of disputes between debtors and creditors is not traditionally an exclusive public function, so D's action is not state action.

2)   P also claims that D's action is state action because the state has authorized and encouraged it by enacting the UCC. While private action compelled by a state is properly attributable to the

state, mere acquiescence by the state is insufficient. The state here has merely refused to provide P a remedy for D's private deprivation of P's property. Therefore, D's action is not a state action.

d.   Dissenting (Stevens, White, Marshall, JJ.). The question is whether a state statute that authorizes a private party to deprive a person of his property without his consent must satisfy due process requirements. Clearly it should. Permitting only state delegation of exclusively sovereign functions to bring private action within constitutional bounds is inconsistent with prior decisions. P should be permitted to challenge the state procedure permitted by state law.

3.   Enforcement of Private Contracts--Shelley v. Kraemer, 334 U.S. 1 (1948).

Shelley v. Kraemer

a.   Facts. Shelley (D), a black, purchased residential property that, unknown to D, was encumbered by a restrictive agreement that prevented ownership or occupancy of the property by non-Caucasians. Kraemer (P), a neighbor and owner of other property subject to the restriction, brought suit to restrain D from possessing the property and to divest title out of D. The trial court denied relief, but the Missouri Supreme Court reversed. D appeals.

b.   Issue. Does the fourteenth amendment Equal Protection Clause prohibit judicial enforcement by state courts of restrictive covenants based on race or color?

c.   Held. Yes. Judgment reversed.

1)   Property rights clearly are among those civil rights protected from discriminatory state action by the fourteenth amendment. Early decisions invalidated any government restrictions on residency based on race. Here the restrictions are purely private and, standing alone, are not precluded by the fourteenth amendment.

2)   Actions of state courts are state actions within the meaning of the fourteenth amendment. Judicial enforcement of these private racial restrictions constitutes state discrimination contrary to the fourteenth amendment, and denies D equal protection.

d.   Comment. *Shelley* and other cases indicate that what is essentially a private act of discrimination may become illegal state action if the state or its officers are in any way involved in carrying out the private action. Possibly any private action that gets into court may then amount to state action.

4.   Additional Cases.

a.   Will provisions. In *Pennsylvania v. Board of Trusts*, 353 U.S. 230 (1957), the Supreme Court held that a will that had discriminatory provisions might be infused with state action when enforced by a state court. Here a private citizen willed his property to be used for a school for poor white orphan children, the city council to serve as the board of trustees.

b.   Civil damages. In *Barrows v. Jackson*, 346 U.S. 249 (1953), a case involving a damages action against a co-covenantor, the Court applied the *Shelley* reasoning to block enforcement of the restrictive covenant. The Court stated that it would not require a state to coerce a covenantor to respond in damages for failure to observe a covenant that the state would have no right to enforce.

c.   Trespass. In a three-to-three decision rendered in a case involving a restaurant sit-in, the Court reversed a trespass conviction on the basis of *Shelley*. The Court stated that the discrimination was done for business reasons and the property was associated with serving the public. The dissent, construing section 1 of the fourteenth amendment more narrowly, argued that without cooperative state action, no property owner was forbidden from banning people from his premises, even if the owner was acting with racial prejudice. [Bell v. Maryland, 378 U.S. 226 (1964)]

d.   Private school employment. In *Rendell-Baker v. Kohn*, 457 U.S. 830 (1982), the Court held that a decision to fire a teacher, made by a small private school that was publicly subsidized and regulated, was not state action.

e.   Writ of attachment. In *Lugar v. Edmondson Oil Co.*, 457 U.S. 922 (1982), the Court upheld damages under section 1983 for conduct done "under color of state law," when the creditor had attached the debtor's property in an ex parte proceeding. The Court held that this was state action because the writ was issued and executed by state officials.

C.   STATE INVOLVEMENT AND ENCOURAGEMENT

1.   **Introduction.** Private activity may also be treated as state action when the government requires, significantly encourages, or profits from the activity. This does not mean that the government's mere failure to forbid private discrimination is a constitutional violation, but if the government is closely involved in private discrimination in some way, the private discrimination is state action.

2. **Private Use of Government Property--Burton v. Wilmington Parking Authority,** 365 U.S. 715 (1961).

    a. **Facts.** Burton (P), a black, was denied service at a private restaurant (the Eagle) located within a building owned and operated by the Wilmington Parking Authority (D), a state agency. D had leased out some of its space, including the lease to the Eagle, to assist in its financing. P sued, claiming that although the Eagle was private, it had sufficient nexus to D to make its discrimination a state action. The trial court granted summary judgment for P; the Delaware Supreme Court reversed on the basis of a state law assuring restaurants of the right to refuse service to any person whose reception would injure the business. P appeals.

    b. **Issue.** Is a private lessee of state property required to comply with the fourteenth amendment if the lease furthers state interests and forms an integral part of a state operation?

    c. **Held.** Yes. Judgment reversed.

        1) Although private conduct abridging individual rights does not violate the Equal Protection Clause, if any significant state action is involved, the discrimination is unconstitutional. D is so closely involved with the Eagle that it is a joint participant, and the Eagle is not so purely private as to fall beyond the scope of the fourteenth amendment. The government has a symbiotic relationship with the Eagle and is profiting from the invidious discrimination.

        2) D clearly could have required the Eagle to agree to a binding covenant not to discriminate, but its failure to do so does not permit D to abdicate its responsibilities to prevent discrimination. D has, by its inaction, become a party to the discrimination. Lessee Eagle must therefore comply with the fourteenth amendment.

    d. **Comment.** Following the particularized approach set forth in *Burton*, the Court remanded *Gilmore v. Montgomery*, 417 U.S. 556 (1974), an action involving a federal injunction barring a city from permitting private segregated school groups and racially discriminatory non-school groups to use its recreational facilities. The Court held that although exclusive temporary use interfered with a school desegregation order, the lower court's ruling against nonexclusive use by the groups, especially the private non-school groups, was invalid without a proper finding of state action.

Blum v.
Yaretsky

3. **Private Activity Affecting Government Benefits--Blum v. Yaretsky,** 457 U.S. 991 (1982).

a. **Facts.** New York state provided Medicaid benefits to persons receiving care in private skilled nursing facilities (SNFs) and health related facilities (HRFs), which provided less medical care than SNFs. A utilization review committee (URC) of doctors would periodically evaluate the status of each patient, as required by federal regulations. When the URC decided to transfer Blum (P) and other patients from an SNF to an HRF, Ps sued for the deprivation of due process resulting from the failure to give notice and an opportunity to challenge the URC's decisions. Ps also sought an injunction requiring the state to adopt regulations to prohibit the conduct of the URCs. The lower courts found for Ps. The Supreme Court granted certiorari.

b. **Issue.** Does a decision made by a committee of private doctors, affiliated with private nursing homes that qualify for government financial assistance, constitute state action?

c. **Held.** No. Judgment reversed.

1) Generally, a state may be held responsible only for private decisions it coerces or encourages to the extent that it must be deemed a state decision. The lower courts deemed the URC decision to be state action because the level of benefits was adjusted pursuant to the decision. However, Ps complain of the transfer without adequate notice and hearings. The fact that the state responds to the decision does not make the decision itself the state's.

2) The regulations involved do require assessment of patients' needs and transfer as appropriate, but the individual URCs make the actual decisions based on medical standards not established by the state.

3) Ps also claim that because of the extensive state involvement and subsidy, this case falls within *Burton*. However, state regulation, subsidy, and licensing do not constitute joint participation in the facilities. Because there was no state action in this case, Ps' due process claim must fail.

d. **Comment.** In *Rendell-Baker v. Kohn*, 457 U.S. 830 (1982), the Court held that a private school's decision to discharge certain employees for disagreeing with school policies was not state action, even though the school received up to 99% of its budget from government funding. The Court compared the school to a private contractor that takes government contracts. It distinguished *Burton* by noting that in *Burton*, the restaurant contributed to the support of the public garage, so that the state's financial position would suffer if the restaurant did not discriminate.

4. **State Licensing--Moose Lodge No. 107 v. Irvis, 407 U.S. 163** (1972).

Moose Lodge No. 107 v. Irvis

   a. **Facts.** Irvis (P), a black, was refused service by Moose Lodge No. 107 (D). P claimed that D's action was a state action because D was licensed by the state liquor board to sell alcoholic beverages. A three-judge district court held for P on the merits. D appeals.

   b. **Issue.** Does state alcoholic licensing of a private club constitute sufficient state action to require that the club observe fourteenth amendment prohibitions against discrimination?

   c. **Held.** No. Judgment reversed.

      1) A private entity is not covered by the fourteenth amendment when it merely receives any sort of benefit or service at all from the state, or if subject to any state regulation. Otherwise the distinction between private and public would be meaningless. If the impetus for the discrimination is private, state involvement must be significant to implicate constitutional standards.

      2) Here, the state's liquor regulation in no way fostered or encouraged racial discrimination. However, those regulations did require that licensed clubs must adhere to their own constitutions and bylaws. States may not use sanctions to enforce segregative rules, and P is entitled to an injunction against the enforcement of the state regulation that would require D to enforce its own discriminatory rules.

   d. **Dissenting** (Marshall, Douglas, JJ.). The state's licensing scheme includes a complex quota system. The quota in D's area has been full for many years; no more club licenses may be issued in the city. Since private clubs are the only places that serve liquor for significant portions of each week, the state has restricted access by blacks to liquor by granting a license to D instead of to a nondiscriminatory club.

   e. **Dissenting** (Brennan, Marshall, JJ.). The state has become an active participant in the operation of D's bar through its detailed regulatory scheme, and D should be required to observe fourteenth amendment standards.

5. **Business Regulation--Jackson v. Metropolitan Edison Co.,** 419 U.S. 345 (1974).

    a. **Facts.** Metropolitan Edison Co. (D), a private utility regulated by the state, terminated Jackson's (P's) electric service for nonpayment before affording P notice, hearing, and an opportunity to pay. P sued, contending that D's action constituted state action depriving her of property without due process of law. The lower courts dismissed P's complaint. P appeals.

    b. **Issue.** Does termination of service by a heavily regulated private utility, using procedures permitted by state law, constitute state action?

    c. **Held.** No. Judgment affirmed.

        1) State regulation of a private business, even if extensive and detailed, does not by itself convert private action into state action for fourteenth amendment purposes. There must be a close nexus between the state and the actual activity of the regulated entity. D's monopoly status, by itself, fails to show such a nexus. Nor is D's service a public function, since the state has no obligation to furnish such service. The limited notion that businesses "affected with a public interest" are state actors cannot be expanded to include private utilities.

        2) The state concededly approved D's termination procedures, but not upon consideration of a specific case. The state's approval amounts merely to a finding that the procedures are permissible under state law. For these reasons, D's actions cannot be considered to be state actions.

    d. **Dissenting** (Marshall, J.). The essential nature of D's service requires that D be subject to the same standards as other governmental entities. The interests of diversity and flexibility which favor protection of private entities from constitutional standards are irrelevant in monopoly situations like D's. Finally, the majority's opinion would appear to apply to a broad range of claimed constitutional violations by the company, including racial discrimination.

D. GOVERNMENT FUNCTION

    1. **Introduction.** Some activity undertaken by private individuals or organizations replaces traditionally exclusive prerogatives of the state. In these situations, the private activity may be treated as state action on the grounds that it is a public or government function.

2.   **The Conduct of Elections.** In a series of cases called the White Primary Cases, the Court has held that the conduct of elections is an exclusively public function. Therefore, state attempts to vest in private boards or political parties any effective control over the selection of candidates or the exercise of voting rights are not valid. The Court has invalidated such state action as:

   a.   Giving authority to a political party to determine who can vote in primary elections from which the party nominee for the general election is chosen [Smith v. Allwright, 321 U.S. 649 (1944)]; and

   b.   Structuring the state's electoral apparatus to vest in a political party the power to hold a primary from which blacks are excluded, or to determine who shall run in the party primary in which blacks are permitted to participate. [Terry v. Adams, 345 U.S. 461 (1953)]

3.   **Private Company Towns.** In *Marsh v. Alabama*, 326 U.S. 501 (1946), a private corporation owned a town and posted signs prohibiting peddlers. Marsh (D), a Jehovah's Witness, distributed religious literature on the streets of the company town and was convicted of violating a state trespass law that made it a crime "to enter or remain on the premises of another" after being warned not to do so. The conviction was reversed because the town's streets, although privately owned, were in effect a public place. The Court held that neither the state nor any private owner can totally ban freedom of expression in public places; nor can state trespass laws be applied to enforce such a ban. "Ownership doesn't always mean absolute dominion. The more an owner opens up his property for use by the public in general, the more do his rights become circumscribed by the statutory and constitutional rights of those who use it." This case shows that state action includes not only any action taken directly by the state executive, legislative, or judicial branches, but also any such action taken indirectly by delegating public functions to private organizations or by controlling, affirming, or to some extent becoming involved in that private action.

4.   **Shopping Centers.** The Court has held that the "company town" rationale of *Marsh* does not extend to the passageways in a privately-owned shopping center. [Hudgens v. NLRB, 424 U.S. 507 (1976), *overruling* Amalgamated Food Employees Union v. Logan Valley Plaza, 391 U.S. 308 (1968)]

TABLE OF CASES
Page numbers of briefed cases in bold

Legalines

CONSTITUTIONAL LAW

Adaptable to Stone Casebook

Third Edition Supplement

HARCOURT BRACE LEGAL AND PROFESSIONAL PUBLICATIONS, INC.

EDITORIAL OFFICES: 176 W. Adams, Suite 2100, Chicago, IL 60603

Legalines

REGIONAL OFFICES: New York, Chicago, Los Angeles, Washington, D.C.

Distributed by: **Harcourt Brace & Company** 6277 Sea Harbor Drive, Orlando, FL 32887 (800)787-8717

SERIES EDITOR
Deirdre E. Whelan, J.D.
Attorney at Law

PRODUCTION COORDINATOR
Sanetta Hister

FIRST PRINTING—1997

Copyright © 1997 by Harcourt Brace Legal and Professional Publications, Inc.

All rights reserved. No part of this publication may be reproduced or transmitted in any form or by any means, electronic or mechanical, including photocopy, recording, or any information storage and retrieval system, without permission in writing from the publisher.

Printed in the United States of America.

Insert the following as **II., D., 3., c.** *at p.* **13:**

c. **Public interest not enough--Lujan v. Defenders of Wildlife,** 504 U.S. 555 (1992).

Lujan v.
Defenders
of Wildlife

1) **Facts.** Section 7(a)(2) of the Endangered Species Act ("ESA") requires federal agencies to insure, in consultation with the Secretary of the Interior, that any action carried out by such agency is not likely to jeopardize the continued existence of any endangered or threatened species. The Fish and Wildlife Service and National Marine Fisheries Service promulgated a joint regulation which provided that section 7(a)(2) extended to actions that were taken in foreign nations, but the regulation was later modified to require consultations only for actions taken in the United States or on the high seas. The ESA also provided that "any person may commence a civil suit on his behalf" to enjoin a government agency who is alleged to be in violation of the Act. The Defenders of Wildlife (P) brought suit against Lujan (D), the Secretary of the Interior, seeking a declaratory judgment that the more recent regulation incorrectly interpreted the ESA. Both parties moved for summary judgment. The district court granted P's motion. The court of appeals affirmed, and the Supreme Court granted certiorari.

2) **Issue.** May Congress convert the public interest in proper administration of the laws into an individual right such that all citizens may have standing to sue?

3) **Held.** No. Judgment reversed.

a) Neither P nor any of its members had any injury in fact. P's standing, if any, depends on the validity of the "citizen-suit" provision of the ESA. The court of appeals held that this provision created a "procedural right" to interagency consultation in all persons, so that anyone can file suit to challenge D's failure to follow the allegedly correct consultative procedure, even if there is no discrete injury resulting from that failure. In effect, the court held that the injury-in-fact requirement under Article III has been satisfied by congressional conferral upon all persons of an abstract, self-contained "right" to have the executive branch follow the procedures required by law.

b) Article III confers jurisdiction on the federal courts only where there is a case or controversy. This requirement is not met by a plaintiff who merely raises a generally available grievance about the government, where the harm is only to the interest of all citizens in the proper application of the Constitution and laws. Hence, a taxpayer does not have standing to challenge alleged violations of the Constitution by the executive or legislative branches where the violations would adversely affect only the generalized interest of all citizens in constitutional governance. The federal courts may only decide on the rights of individuals. Vindicating the public interest is the responsibility of Congress and the President.

c) If Congress could convert the undifferentiated public interest in an executive that complies with the law into an "individual right" to be vindicated in the courts, Congress could transfer from the President to the judicial branch his most important constitutional duty, to "take Care that the Laws be faithfully executed."

d) The fact that Congress may not eliminate the requirement of a concrete personal injury does not preclude Congress from creating legal rights, the invasion of which creates standing.

4) Concurrence (Kennedy, Souter, JJ.). Congress may define injuries and establish chains of causation that give rise to cases or controversies where none existed before, but at a minimum, Congress must identify what injury it desires to vindicate and relate the injury to the class of persons who are entitled to bring suit. The citizen-suit provisions of the ESA do not provide that there is an injury in any person by virtue of any violation. The case and controversy requirement assures both that the parties have an actual stake in the outcome and that the legal questions presented will be resolved in a concrete factual context conducive to a realistic appreciation of the consequences of judicial action. The public is entitled to know what persons invoke the judicial power, their reasons, and whether their claims are vindicated or denied.

5) Concurrence (Stevens, J.). P does not lack standing, but Congress did not intend section 7(a)(2) to apply to activities in foreign countries.

6) Dissent (Blackmun, O'Connor, JJ.). Congress granted considerable discretion to the executive branch to determine how best to attain the goals of ESA, constrained by specific procedural requirements. This does not constitute a violation of the separation of powers; nor should the separation of powers be deemed violated when Congress requires the federal courts to enforce the procedures. The citizen-suit provisions of ESA were based on the same understanding that arose from earlier cases in which the Court justified a relaxed review of congressional delegation to the executive branch because Congress provided for judicial review of the exercise of that power. [*See* Immigration & Naturalization Service v. Chadha, *infra*]

Insert the following as **II., D., 4., d.** *at p.* **15:**

Davis v.
Bandemer

d. Political party's challenge to reapportionment--Davis v. Bandemer, 478 U.S. 109 (1986).

1) Facts. The Indiana State House of Representatives consisted of 100 members serving two-year terms. Members were elected from single-member and multi-member districts. The 1981 reapportionment plan, adopted by the majority Republican party, provided for seven triple-member, nine double-member, and 61 single-member districts. The multi-member districts were primarily in metropolitan areas. Davis and other Democrats (Ps) sued, claiming that the plan was intended to disadvantage Democrats, violating their equal protection rights. Before the case went to trial, an election was held, and 43 Democrats were elected to the House. Statewide, Democratic candidates received almost 52% of the vote. In specific multi-member districts, Democratic candidates won 46.6% of the vote, but only three of 21 seats. The district court declared the reapportionment unconstitutional and ordered the legislature to prepare a new plan. Bandemer (D) appeals.

2) **Issue.** Is a claim by a political party that a legislative apportionment plan violates the party's equal protection rights a justiciable claim?

3) **Held.** Yes. Judgment reversed on the merits.

a) Equal protection claims about legislative districting have been justiciable insofar as they involve population inequalities between districts ever since *Baker v. Carr, supra*, which established the one person, one vote principle. Racial gerrymandering claims are also justiciable regardless of population equality, as are challenges against multi-member districts that diminish the effectiveness of the votes of racial minorities. Such holdings support an inference that purely political challenges are also justiciable.

b) Ps' claim is based on the proposition that all political groups in a state should have the same chance to elect representatives of their choice. It is not significant for justiciability purposes that the characteristics of Ps' group are not immutable or that Ps' group has not historically been subject to stigma. Nor does it matter that claims such as Ps' may present practical problems, for these are present in the racial cases as well. Accordingly, Ps' claim is justiciable.

c) On the merits, Ps have the burden to prove both intentional discrimination against an identifiable political group and an actual discriminatory effect on that group. The intention requirement was satisfied by the district court's findings, and at any rate is virtually inherent in the legislative process of redistricting.

d) However, the district court's findings that the plan had such an adverse effect on Ps as to constitute a violation of the Equal Protection Clause is not sustainable. The Constitution does not require proportional representation or a plan that draws lines to come as near as possible to allocating seats to the contending parties in proportion to their anticipated statewide vote.

e) Winner-take-all district-based elections inherently present the potential for disproportionate party representation when compared with the popular vote. Challenges to multi-member districts require a showing much greater than mere lack of proportional representation. One consideration is the responsiveness of elected officials to the concerns of the groups involved, because even defeated parties have influence on the winning candidate. The test is whether the electoral system is arranged to consistently degrade a voter's or a group's influence on the political process as a whole. In other words, has a group been unconstitutionally denied its chance to effectively influence the political process?

f) The district court relied primarily on the results of the 1982 election. One election is not enough to prove unconstitutional discrimination. There was no finding that the plan would render the Democrats a minority party throughout the 1980s.

g)   Justice Powell's approach focuses on various factors, including the deliberate distortion of voting district boundaries to achieve arbitrary ends. This approach would permit a finding of constitutional violation even when the only proved effect on a political party's electoral power was a disproportionate result in one election. The better approach is to require proof that the challenged plan will consistently degrade the party's influence on the political process as a whole.

4)   Concurrence (O'Connor, J., Burger, C.J., Rehnquist, J.). Partisan gerrymandering claims by major political parties are nonjusticiable political questions that should be left to the legislative branch. The Equal Protection Clause should not be used to make fundamental policy choices. Even foreseeable, disproportionate long-term election results do not constitute a constitutional violation; this approach leads toward a proportionality requirement. It also raises significant problems of implementation, such as how to account for independents who vote for one party or another in a particular election.

Insert the following as **II., D., 4., e.** *at p.* **15:**

Nixon v.
United States

e.   Justiciability of challenges to impeachment actions--Nixon v. United States, 506 U.S. 224 (1993).

1)   Facts. Nixon (P), a former federal district court judge, was convicted of making false statements before a federal grand jury. He was sentenced to prison, and refused to resign from his judicial office. The United States House of Representatives adopted articles of impeachment and presented them to the Senate. The Senate appointed a committee to hold evidentiary hearings. The committee made a report to the full Senate, which gave P three hours of oral argument to supplement the committee record. The Senate voted to convict P on the impeachment articles, and P was removed from his office. P then sued, claiming the Senate's failure to participate in the evidentiary hearings as a full body violated the Senate's constitutional authority to "try" impeachments. The lower courts held that P's claim was nonjusticiable. The Supreme Court granted certiorari.

2)   Issue. May the courts review the procedures whereby the United States Senate tries impeachments?

3)   Held. No. Judgment affirmed.

a)   A controversy is nonjusticiable when there is a "textually demonstrable constitutional commitment of the issue to a coordinate political department; or a lack of judicially discoverable and manageable standards for resolving it." [Baker v. Carr, *supra*]

b)   To apply this test, the courts must determine whether and to what extent the issue is "textually committed." In this case, Article I, section 3, clause 6 simply provides that the "Senate shall have the sole Power to try all Impeachments." This clause clearly grants the Senate the exclusive authority to try impeachments.

c)   The use of the word "try" does not require a judicial trial; it is not an implied limitation on how the Senate may try impeachments. This is made clear by the inclusion of specific provisions such as the two-thirds vote requirement.

d)   Judicial review of the Senate's trying of impeachments would be inconsistent with the system of checks and balances. Impeachment is the legislature's only check on the judicial branch, and it would be inconsistent to give the judicial branch final reviewing authority over the legislature's use of the impeachment process. The need for finality and the difficulty of fashioning relief also demonstrate why judicial review is inappropriate in this case.

4)   **Concurrence** (White, Blackmun, JJ.). The Court should reach the merits of P's claim. But on the merits, the Senate fulfilled its constitutional duty to "try" P. The Senate has wide discretion in specifying impeachment trial procedures, and the use of a factfinding committee is compatible with the constitutional requirement that the Senate "try" all impeachments. However, it is consistent with the constitution that while the Senate serves as a means of controlling a largely unaccountable judiciary, judicial review insures that the Senate follow minimal procedural standards.

5)   **Concurrence** (Souter, J.). Judicial review would be appropriate if the Senate were to act so as to seriously threaten the integrity of the results, such as by convicting based on a coin-toss.

Insert the following as **III., A., 7.** *at p.* **17:**

7.   **Limits on Congressional Power--United States v. Lopez,** 115 S. Ct. 1624 (1995).

United States
v. Lopez

a.   **Facts.** In the Gun-Free School Zones Act, Congress made it illegal for any person knowingly to possess a firearm in a school zone. Lopez (D), a 12th grade student, carried a concealed gun to his high school. D was ultimately convicted under the Act. The court of appeals reversed on the ground that Congress did not have power under the Commerce Clause to regulate this type of activity. The Supreme Court granted certiorari.

b.   **Issue.** May Congress prohibit the possession of firearms within a school zone?

c.   **Held.** No. Judgment affirmed.

1)   As business enterprises expanded beyond local and regional territories and became national in scope, the scope of the Commerce Clause as interpreted by the Court also expanded. In cases such as *NLRB v. Jones & Laughlin Steel Corp., infra,* and *Maryland v. Wirtz,* 392

U.S. 183 (1968), the Court noted that while the power to regulate commerce is broad, it does have limits.

2) There are three broad categories of activity that come within Congress's commerce power:

    a) "Congress may regulate the use of the channels of interstate commerce;"

    b) Congress may regulate the instrumentalities of interstate commerce, as well as persons or things in interstate commerce; and

    c) Congress may regulate activities that have a substantial relation to interstate commerce, meaning those that substantially affect interstate commerce.

3) The Act in this case is a criminal statute that has nothing to do with commerce. Possessing a gun in a school zone does not arise out of a commercial transaction that substantially affects interstate commerce. Neither does the Act contain a requirement that the possession be connected in any way to interstate commerce.

4) The government claims that possession of a firearm in a local school zone substantially affects interstate commerce because it might result in violent crime. This in turn imposes costs on society which are borne throughout the country through insurance rates. The government also claims that guns disrupt the educational process, which leads to a less productive society, which ultimately affects interstate commerce. If either of these propositions were adopted, there would be no limitation on federal power. The only way to find an effect on interstate commerce in this case is to pile inference upon inference, and the result would be to uphold a general police power for Congress.

d. Concurrence (Kennedy, O'Connor, JJ.). In a sense, any conduct in the interdependent world has an ultimate commercial origin or consequence. However, the Court must still determine whether the exercise of national power intrudes upon an area of traditional state concerns. Education in particular is a traditional concern of the states.

e. Concurrence (Thomas, J.). The term "commerce" as used in the Constitution is much more limited than the Court's opinions have recognized. The term referred to buying, selling, and transporting goods, as distinguished from agriculture and manufacturing. Furthermore, the Constitution does not give Congress authority over all activities that "substantially affect" interstate commerce. If it did, there would be no need for specific constitutional provisions giving Congress power to enact bankruptcy laws, to establish post offices and post roads, to grant patents and copyrights, etc.

f. Dissent (Stevens, J.). Congress clearly has power to regulate the possession of guns to some degree. This power should include the ability to prohibit possession of guns at any location. The market for possession of handguns by persons covered by the Act is sufficiently substantial to justify congressional action.

g. **Dissent** (Souter, J.). The Court seeks to draw fine distinctions between what is patently commercial and what is not, which is basically the same distinction between what directly affects commerce and what affects it only indirectly. The Court should not be placed in a position to make these fine distinctions; Congress should have to make them. The majority approach of the last 60 years should prevail.

h. **Dissent** (Breyer, Stevens, Souter, Ginsburg, JJ.). Case law recognizes that Congress can regulate even local activity if it significantly affects interstate commerce. In determining whether a local activity will have such an effect, the court must consider the cumulative effect of all instances similar to the one in the specific case. The courts are required to defer to congressional determinations about the factual basis for making this determination. In this case, Congress could rationally find that violent crime in school areas affects the quality of education and thereby interstate commerce.

Insert the following as **III., B., 9.** *at p.* **35:**

9. **Limit on Congressional Regulatory Authority--New York v. United States,** 505 U.S. 144 (1992).

New York v. United States

a. **Facts.** Low level radioactive waste is generated in substantial quantities by various industries including the medical and research industries, but in 1979 the only United States disposal site for radioactive waste was in South Carolina. In 1980, Congress enacted the Low-Level Radioactive Waste Policy Act. The Act authorized states to enter into regional compacts that, once ratified by Congress, could after 1985 restrict the use of their disposal facilities to waste generated within member states. By 1985, only three approved regional compacts had operational disposal facilities. Thirty-one states (the unsited states) were not members of these compacts. Congress amended the Act in 1985, based on a proposal submitted by the National Governors' Association, whereby sited states agreed to accept waste until 1992, collecting a graduated surcharge for waste from unsited states, and unsited states agreed not to rely on sited states after 1992. A portion of the surcharges would be collected by the Secretary of Energy, who in turn would pay them to unsited states that comply with a series of deadlines for joining a regional compact or creating their own disposal sites. States that failed to meet the deadlines could lose access to disposal sites. Finally, any state or regional compact that was unable to dispose of all waste generated within its borders by 1996 would, upon the request of the waste generator, take title to the waste and be liable for all damages incurred by such generator as a consequence of the state's failure to take possession of the waste once notified that it is available. New York (P) did not join a regional compact, but did enact legislation providing for the siting and financing of a disposal facility. The two target counties objected and joined P in suing the United States (D), seeking a declaratory judgment that the Act violates the Tenth Amendment. The district court dismissed the complaint. The court of appeals affirmed, and the Supreme Court granted certiorari.

b. **Issue.** May Congress direct the states to regulate in a particular field or a particular manner, using them as implements of regulation?

c. Held. No. Judgment reversed in part.

1) The power of Congress to legislate so as to impact state autonomy has been analyzed both by inquiring whether Congress has the power under Article I to so act and by determining whether Congress has invaded the province of state sovereignty reserved by the Tenth Amendment. But these inquiries may be mirror images, because where a power is delegated to Congress, the Tenth Amendment expressly disclaims any reservation of power to the states, and if a power is an attribute of state sovereignty reserved by the Tenth Amendment, it is necessarily one not conferred on Congress. The Tenth Amendment merely states the truism that all is retained by the states which has not been surrendered to the federal government; yet it requires the courts to determine whether an incident of state sovereignty is protected by a limitation on an Article I power.

2) P claims that Congress exceeded its powers not by regulating radioactive waste, which is interstate in character and thus falls within the Commerce Clause, but by directing the states to regulate in this field in a particular manner. The Court has long recognized that Congress cannot directly compel the states to enact and enforce a federal regulatory program. A key difference between the Constitution and the Articles of Confederation is that under the Constitution, the federal government can exercise its legislative authority directly over individuals rather than over states.

3) Congress may create incentives for states to adopt a legislative program consistent with federal interests, however. Congress has done so by attaching conditions on the receipt of federal funds and by offering states the option of regulating private activity in interstate commerce according to federal standards or having state law preempted by federal regulation. Such incentives do not compel state action. This preserves the accountability of both federal and state officials to their respective constituencies.

4) The Act in this case creates three sets of incentives. First, the surcharge provisions provide for imposition by sited states of surcharges which are partially remitted to the federal government and paid out to states that meet specified milestones. The burden on interstate commerce is within Congress's Commerce Clause authority, and the payments are within its Spending Clause authority.

5) The second set of incentives allows states that have disposal sites to increase the cost of access to the sites and eventually deny access altogether to waste that is generated in states that do not meet federal guidelines. This gives unsited states the choice of complying with federal standards for self-sufficiency or becoming subject to federal regulation that permits sited states to deny access to their disposal sites. The affected states are not thereby compelled by Congress to regulate; the incentives are a conditional exercise of Congress's commerce power, which is permissible.

6) The third set of "incentives" requires states that do not regulate according to federal standards to take title to and possession of any waste produced within their borders and become liable for all damages waste generators suffer because of the states' failure to take title promptly. But the Consti-

tution does not provide that Congress may simply transfer radioactive waste from generators to state governments, or force states to become liable for generators' damages, either of which would "commandeer" state governments into serving federal regulatory purposes. And Congress cannot require state governments to implement federal legislation. Since neither "option" is constitutional, a choice between them is not permissible either. However, this take title provision is severable from the rest of the Act.

7) No matter how great the federal interest, the Constitution does not give Congress authority to require the states to regulate. Congress must legislate directly, not by conscripting state governments. State officials cannot give Congress this authority by consenting to the federal statute.

8) Ps claim that the first two incentives violate the Guarantee Clause, but neither incentive denied any state a republican form of government.

d. **Concurrence and dissent** (White, Blackmun, Stevens, JJ.). The Act is a result of the efforts of state governments seeking to achieve a state-based remedy for the waste problem. It is essentially a congressional sanction of interstate compromises, not federal preemption or intervention. New York in particular should be estopped from asserting the unconstitutionality of the Act after the state has derived substantial benefits under the Act. The Court's opinion that the take title provision is unconstitutional does not preclude Congress from adopting a similar measure through its powers under the Spending or Commerce Clauses. Ironically, the Court gives Congress fewer incentives to defer to the wishes of state officials in achieving local solutions to local problems, all in the name of promoting federalism.

e. **Concurrence and dissent** (Stevens, J.). The Constitution enhanced the power of the federal government, and there is no history to suggest that the federal government may not impose its will upon the states as it did under the Articles of Confederation.

Insert the following as **IV., B., 2., c.** *at p.* **47:**

c. **Limits on local government control--C & A Carbone, Inc. v. Clarkstown,** 114 S. Ct. 1677 (1994).

C & A
Carbone, Inc.
v. Clarkstown

1) **Facts.** To finance construction of a "waste transfer station," Clarkstown (D) guaranteed the station a minimum flow of waste. D enacted a "flow control ordinance" which provided that all solid waste must be deposited at the station. C & A Carbone (P) was a private recycler who had a sorting facility in Clarkstown. D's ordinance increased P's costs, because P could obtain the necessary services out of state at a lower cost than D's station charged. P challenged D's ordinance. The lower courts upheld the ordinance. P appeals.

2) **Issue.** May a local government require that all solid waste within its boundaries be processed by a specific local processor?

3) **Held.** No. Judgment affirmed.

a)   Although the ordinance has the effect of directing local waste to a local facility, the economic effects reach interstate commerce. P's facility received waste from out of state. D's ordinance required P to send the nonrecycleable portion of the waste to D's local facility, which increased P's costs and hence the costs to the out-of-state sources of solid waste. The ordinance also deprives out-of-state businesses access to D's local market.

b)   D claims that its ordinance does not discriminate against interstate commerce because it applies to all solid waste, regardless of origin, before it leaves the town. However, the ordinance does discriminate because it allows only the favored processor to process waste within D's town limits. It is an example of local processing requirements that this Court has held invalid, such as the local milk pasteurizing requirement in *Dean Milk Co. v. Madison*, 340 U.S. 349 (1951). In fact, D's ordinance is even more restrictive than the one in *Dean Milk* because it leaves no room for outside investment.

c)   Any discrimination "against interstate commerce in favor of local business or investment is per se invalid," unless the municipality has no other means to advance a legitimate local interest. D has a variety of nondiscriminatory means available to address its local waste disposal problems. The objective of fundraising is not adequate to justify discrimination against out-of-state businesses.

4)   **Concurrence** (O'Connor, J.). D's ordinance is different than the ordinances the Court has previously held invalid because it does not give more favorable treatment to local interests as a group as compared to out-of-state economic interests. Thus, it does not discriminate against interstate commerce. However, the ordinance does impose an excessive burden on interstate commerce when compared with the local benefits it confers.

5)   **Dissent** (Souter, J., Rehnquist, C.J., Blackmun, J.). There is no evidence in this case that any out-of-state trash processor has been injured by the ordinance. The ordinance treats all out-of-town investors and facilities to the same constraints as local ones, so there is no economic protectionism. The only right to compete that the Commerce Clause protects is the right to compete on terms independent of one's location. The ordinance merely imposes a burden on the local citizens who adopted it, and local burdens are not the focus of the Commerce Clause.

Insert the following as IV., B., 2., d. at p. 47:

West Lynn Creamery, Inc. v. Healy

d.   **Subsidies instead of regulation--West Lynn Creamery, Inc. v. Healy**, 512 U.S. 186 (1994).

1)   **Facts.** Massachusetts adopted a milk pricing order that required every milk dealer in the state to make a monthly "premium payment" based on the amount of its sales. The funds generated by these payments were distributed to Massachusetts dairy farmers in proportion to their respective contributions to the state's total milk production. West Lynn Creamery, Inc. (P) challenged the milk order in state court. The lower courts upheld the milk order, and the United States Supreme Court granted certiorari.

2)   **Issue.** May a state impose a tax on all sales of a particular product in order to subsidize in-state producers of that product?

3)   **Held.** No. Judgment reversed.

    a)   The clearest examples of laws that discriminate against interstate commerce are protective tariffs or customs duties, which tax imported goods only and thereby make goods more expensive. Such a duty both raises revenue and benefits local producers at the expense of out-of-state producers.

    b)   The purpose for the milk order is to allow higher-cost in-state producers to compete with lower-cost producers in other states. The effect of the milk pricing order is to make milk that is produced in other states more expensive.

    c)   Even though the pricing order is imposed on milk produced in state as well as milk produced out of state, its effect on in-state producers is more than offset by the subsidy. Consequently, it functions like a protective tariff or customs duty.

    d)   The state may properly tax all milk dealers, and it may also subsidize in-state farmers (although the constitutionality of subsidies has never been squarely addressed). However, the combination of a tax and subsidy is "more dangerous to interstate commerce than either part alone." The combination impairs the state's political process because those in-state interests who would otherwise oppose the tax are mollified by the subsidy.

    e)   The fact that the taxes are paid by in-state businesses and consumers is irrelevant. The impact of the order is to divert market share to dairy farmers in Massachusetts, which hurts out-of-state farmers.

4)   **Concurrence** (Scalia, Thomas, JJ.). Nearly all subsidies, whether funded by taxes imposed on out-of-state products, in-state revenues, etc., "neutralize advantages possessed by out-of-state enterprises." Standing alone, this effect does not render a subsidy scheme unconstitutional. A state may subsidize its own industry provided that the subsidies are funded through nondiscriminatory taxes, the proceeds of which go into a general revenue fund rather than back to those in-state persons burdened by the tax.

5)   **Dissent** (Rehnquist, C.J., Blackmun, J.). The political reality is that there are other groups, namely milk dealers and consumers, who could still oppose the tax even if the dairy farmers choose not to. No precedent justifies applying the negative Commerce Clause against a subsidy funded from a lawful neutral tax.

6)   **Comment.** Both the majority and dissent (in the full opinion) cited *Bacchus Imports, Ltd. v. Dias*, 468 U.S. 263 (1984). That case involved a Hawaii liquor tax with exemptions for fruit wine manufactured in Hawaii and for a brandy distilled from a plant indigenous to Hawaii. The tax exemption was deemed a protective tariff. While the majority in *West Lynn Creamery* thought insignificant the fact that the Massachusetts milk order did not help those who paid the tax (the milk dealers), as compared to the Hawaii tax exemption which directly helped in-state producers, the dissenters thought that was an important difference that justified upholding the Massachusetts tax.

Insert the following in place of **IV., D.** *at p.* **55:**

D.   FEDERAL PREEMPTION

1.   **Introduction.** Because federal law is supreme over state law, states may not normally regulate areas already subject to federal regulation. The difficult issues arise when no federal regulation specifically preempts the state law, but the state law conflicts with federal policy. Federal law rarely occupies a legal field completely. It normally builds on legal relationships established by the states, altering or supplanting them only where necessary to accomplish a particular purpose. The Supreme Court has stated that the question of preemption is primarily one of congressional intent.

2.   **Types of Preemption.** Congress may preempt state regulation in three ways.

   a.   **Express preemption.** Many federal statutes clearly provide that they preempt state law. Even in these cases, however, the extent of the preemption may be in question.

   b.   **Conflict preemption.** When it is impossible to comply with both state and federal law, or when the state law prevents or frustrates the objectives of Congress, federal law must preempt the state law. [Hines v. Davidowitz, 312 U.S. 52 (1941)]

   c.   **Field preemption.** The scheme of federal regulation may be so pervasive as to make reasonable the inference that Congress left no room for the states to supplement it. [Rice v. Santa Fe Elevator Corp., 331 U.S. 218 (1947)]

Gade v. National Solid Waste Management Association

3.   **Application--Gade v. National Solid Waste Management Association,** 505 U.S. 88 (1992).

   a.   **Facts.** Illinois had statutes specifying the requirements for licensing workers who handle hazardous waste. The requirements included training under a program in Illinois, and the law was intended to promote job safety and to protect life. The Occupational Safety and Health Administration ("OSHA"), a federal agency, also had regulations for training hazardous waste workers that conflicted somewhat with the Illinois requirements. Federal law specifically provided that state standards could preempt federal standards, but only after approval from OSHA. The National Solid Waste Management Association (P) sought declaratory judgment that the Illinois statutes had been preempted. The lower courts found for P. Gade (D), an Illinois official, appeals.

   b.   **Issue.** Is a state statute preempted where it has dual purposes, one of which is the same purpose as that of a similar federal law?

   c.   **Held.** Yes. Judgment affirmed.

      1)   Preemption applies where a state statute is not consistent with the purpose and structure of a federal statute as a whole. In

this case, the purposes and objectives of OSHA are to subject all employers and employees to one set of regulations, whether federal or state. To have state regulations apply, the state must follow the procedures for approval set forth in the federal statute. This statutory system leads to the unavoidable implication that a state cannot enforce its own standards without obtaining approval from OSHA.

2) D claims that instead of "ousting" the federal standards by going through the approval process, Illinois may "add to" the standards without approval. However, this is inconsistent with the overall statutory scheme.

3) D also claims that the preemptive effect should not extend to state statutes that address public as well as occupational safety. States cannot avoid federal preemption simply by having a regulation that serves multiple objectives. Dual-impact state regulations are subject to preemption if one impact conflicts with federal law.

d. **Concurrence** (Kennedy, J.). The terms of the statute are clear enough to constitute express preemption. The Court should not imply preemption unless there is a direct contradiction to Congress's primary objectives.

e. **Dissent** (Souter, Blackmun, Stevens, Thomas, JJ.). The purpose-conflict preemption approach adopted by the plurality is not founded in language in the federal statute that demonstrates an intent to preempt the state law. The courts must begin with the presumption that "Congress did not intend to displace state law," especially in fields historically subject to the police power of the states. The federal law can be read to be just as consistent with a lack of intent to preempt as with an intent to preempt, and, in such cases, preemption should not be implied.

Insert the following as **V., C., 2.,** e. *at p.* **73:**

e. **Creation of sentencing commission--Mistretta v. United States,** 488 U.S. 361 (1989).

Mistretta v.
United States

1) **Facts.** In the Sentencing Reform Act of 1984, Congress established the United States Sentencing Commission to devise guidelines to be used for sentencing in criminal cases. The Act replaced the existing indeterminate sentencing process with determinate sentencing, with the Commission's guidelines binding on the courts so that judicial discretion is limited only to cases in which the judge finds specific aggravating or mitigating factors not considered by the Commission. The Act described the Commission as an independent commission in the judicial branch of the United States. All seven members are appointed by the President with the advice and consent of the Senate, and at least three of the members must be federal judges. The Commission must provide an annual report to Congress regarding the operation of the guidelines. Mistretta (D) was indicted on federal drug offenses. He challenged the constitutionality of the guidelines. The district court rejected D's challenge, and the Supreme Court granted certiorari.

2) **Issue.** May Congress create an independent judicial commission to establish sentencing guidelines that are binding on the federal courts?

3) **Held.** Yes. Judgment affirmed.

a) Congress may delegate its legislative power as long as the person or body receiving the delegated power is directed to conform to an "intelligible principle" set forth by Congress. The delegation of authority to the Commission is sufficiently specific and detailed to meet this standard. The Act includes three specific goals for the Commission to strive for, with four specific purposes of sentencing to pursue. Although the Commission has significant discretion in formulating the guidelines, developing proportionate penalties for hundreds of different crimes is an intricate, labor-intensive task that may appropriately be delegated by Congress. The Act does not give the Commission excessive legislative discretion.

b) D also claims that the Act violates the constitutional principle of separation of powers. The Commission is located within the judicial branch, but it does not exercise judicial power. The novelty of the Commission does not necessarily make it unconstitutional, however, as long as Congress has not vested in the Commission powers that (i) are more appropriately performed by the other branches, or (ii) undermine the integrity of the judiciary.

c) Despite the basic principle of three separate branches of government, there is a "twilight area" in which the activities of the separate branches merge. Judicial rulemaking tends to fall within this twilight area. Congress has previously conferred rulemaking authority on the judiciary, such as to create the Federal Rules of Civil Procedure and to establish rules for the conduct of the courts' business. Thus, Congress may delegate to the judicial branch nonadjudicatory functions that do not trench upon the prerogatives of another branch and that are appropriate to the central mission of the judiciary. These delegations, while not involving the judicial power to decide cases and controversies, share the common purpose of providing for the fair and efficient fulfillment of responsibilities that are properly the province of the judiciary.

d) The judiciary has a major role in sentencing, and the establishment of sentencing guidelines is not clearly more appropriately performed by one of the other branches. Although the Commission has a political nature, the practical consequences of placing the Commission within the judicial branch does not undermine the integrity of that branch. The Commission is independent of the members of the judicial branch and does not act as a court. Its inclusion in the judicial branch does not expand the power of that branch, which has long been responsible for sentencing.

e) The inclusion of federal judges is troublesome, but the Constitution does not specifically prohibit judges from serving on independent commissions. Participation on the Commission involves the exercise of administrative, not judicial, power. Because the Commission will only develop rules to be used by the judicial branch, participation by federal judges does not violate the Constitution. The power of the President to appoint and remove Commission members does not affect a federal judge's status as a judge and, therefore, presents no risk of compromising the impartiality of such judges.

4) **Dissent** (Scalia, J.). In effect, the Commission's guidelines are laws, since a judge who disregards them will be reversed. Congress cannot create an agency

that has no governmental power other than to make laws, because only Congress can make laws under the Constitution. The Court, by upholding a pure delegation of legislative power, has encouraged Congress to delegate its lawmaking powers more frequently in the future, particularly over "no-win" political issues. The Commission represents a new branch of government, a "junior-varsity" Congress.

Insert the following as **V., C., 2., f.** *at p.* **73:**

f. **Veto power over administrative actions--Metropolitan Washington Airports Authority v. Citizens for the Abatement of Aircraft Noise,** 501 U.S. 252 (1991).

Metropolitan Washington Airports Authority v. Citizens for the Abatement of Aircraft Noise

1) **Facts.** The Transfer Act authorized the lease of two federally-operated airports to the Metropolitan Washington Airports Authority (D), which had been created by Virginia and the District of Columbia. The lease was conditional upon the creation of a "Board of Review," comprising nine members of Congress, that would have veto power over D's decisions. The objective was to prevent local residents from shifting too much traffic from the metropolitan National Airport to Dulles, which was much further from downtown. Citizens for the Abatement of Aircraft Noise (P) challenged the constitutionality of the Board of Review's veto power as a violation of separation of powers.

2) **Issue.** May Congress appoint its members to a review board that has veto power over actions taken by a state-created administrative agency?

3) **Held.** No.

　　a)　Even though the Board of Review was created by a state and the District of Columbia, Congress played a major role and delineated the Board's powers and membership requirements. As such, the Board exercises federal power as an agent of Congress and is subject to separation-of-powers scrutiny.

　　b)　The separation-of-powers limitation on congressional power prohibits Congress from exercising either executive or judicial power, and requires Congress to follow Article I procedures when exercising legislative power. If the Board exercises executive power, Congress may not be a participant. If the Board exercises legislative power, congressional participation is invalid because it does not comply with the bicameralism and presentment requirements of Article I.

4) **Dissent** (White, J., Rehnquist, C.J., Marshall, J.). The separation-of-powers doctrine should not apply here because the Board was created by state law. If the Board does exercise federal executive power, the majority should apply the Ineligibility Clause; its failure to do so illustrates that the Board is not exercising federal power. Even if it was, though, the appointment of Board members is not substantially different from the appointments in *Bowsher* and *Mistretta, supra.*

Insert the following as **VI., C., 3.** *at p.* **86** (*and renumber subsequent section accordingly*):

Railway Express Agency v. New York

3. **Safety Regulation--Railway Express Agency v. New York,** 336 U.S. 106 (1949).

   a. **Facts.** The City of New York (P) passed a traffic regulation that prohibited advertising on vehicles except for "business notices upon business delivery vehicles," or, in other words, owner-advertising. Railway Express Agency (D), a nationwide express business, sold the space on its trucks for advertising by other businesses and was convicted for violation of P's regulation. The trial court found a reasonable basis for the regulation and upheld the conviction. D appeals.

   b. **Issue.** May a local business regulation make distinctions based on practical considerations that are theoretically discriminatory?

   c. **Held.** Yes. Judgment affirmed.

      1) D's equal protection argument is based on the allegedly irrational distinction between allowing owner-advertising but banning advertising-for-hire. However, P may have concluded that the former type of advertising is less distracting and possibly necessary for business.

      2) Equal protection questions are answered by such practical considerations based on experience rather than by purely theoretical inconsistencies.

Insert the following as **VI., C., 4.** *at p.* **86** (*and renumber subsequent section accordingly*):

Williamson v. Lee Optical of Oklahoma

4. **Deference to State Legislature--Williamson v. Lee Optical of Oklahoma,** 348 U.S. 483 (1955).

   a. **Facts.** Lee Optical of Oklahoma (P) challenged a state law that, among other things, (i) forbade an optician from fitting or duplicating lenses, even replacements without a prescription from an ophthalmologist or optometrist; (ii) prohibited advertising of eyeglass frames; and (iii) prohibited optometrists from working in a general retail establishment. The district court held these three parts of the act invalid under the Due Process Clause of the Fourteenth Amendment. Williamson (D), a state official, appeals.

   b. **Issue.** Does the Fourteenth Amendment prohibit all state business regulation that is not essential and directly related to the harm it intends to cure?

   c. **Held.** No. Judgment reversed.

      1) Although the law may exact a needless, wasteful requirement in many cases, the legislature, not the courts, must balance the advantages and disadvantages of a new requirement. There is ample reason for the legislative means adopted to correct an actual evil.

2)   The law need not be logically consistent with its aims to be constitutional. The Court will not strike down state laws regulating business and industrial conditions merely because they may be unwise, improvident, or out of harmony with a particular school of thought. The people as voters, not the courts, are the protection against legislative abuse.

Insert the following as **VI., C., 5.** *at p.* **86** (*and renumber subsequent section accordingly*):

5.   **Environmental Protection Favoring Local Industry--Minnesota v. Clover Leaf Creamery Co.,** 449 U.S. 456 (1981).

Minnesota v. Clover Leaf Creamery Co.

a.   **Facts.** Minnesota (D) banned the retail sale of milk in plastic nonreturnable, nonrefillable containers. Clover Leaf Creamery Company (P) successfully challenged D's law in the state courts under the Equal Protection and Commerce Clauses. D appeals.

b.   **Issue.** May a state enact a statute that does not on its face discriminate against interstate commerce but that does cause a shift in an industry from a predominant out-of-state location to a predominant in-state location?

c.   **Held.** Yes. Judgment reversed.

1)   Applying the familiar rational basis test, D's law is rationally related to its conservation interests and does not deny equal protection.

2)   D's ban applies to all plastic container manufacturers. While most of these are located out of state and production of the raw material for nonplastic containers is a major state industry, there is no discrimination against interstate commerce as such. There is an incidental burden on interstate commerce, but it is not "clearly excessive" in light of D's legitimate purposes in imposing the ban.

Insert the following in place of **VI., D., 1., a.** *at p.* **90:**

a.   **Discrimination on the face of the law--Strauder v. West Virginia,** 100 U.S. 303 (1880).

Strauder v. West Virginia

1)   **Facts.** Strauder (D), a black person, was tried and convicted of murder. The jury that had indicted him was composed only of whites because, under state law, blacks were ineligible to serve on grand juries. D appeals, claiming that the state law is unconstitutional.

2)   **Issue.** May a state forbid all persons of a particular race from serving on a grand jury?

3)   **Held.** No. Judgment reversed.

a)   No one has a right to have persons of his own race serve on the grand jury which indicted him, but the Fourteenth Amendment prevents the states from withholding equal protection from blacks. In other words, the law must be the same for blacks as it is for whites.

b) The law excluding blacks from grand jury service is unconstitutional discrimination. States may establish qualifications for jurors, but not racial qualifications.

Insert the following in place of **VI., D., 4., e.** *at p.* **105:**

Adarand
Constructors,
Inc. v. Pena

e. **Strict scrutiny of affirmative action--Adarand Constructors, Inc. v. Pena,** 115 S. Ct. 2097 (1995).

1) **Facts.** Adarand Constructors, Inc. (P) submitted the low bid for a guard-rail subcontract on a federal road project. The prime contract's terms provided for additional compensation if subcontractors were hired who were certified as small businesses controlled by "socially and economically disadvantaged individuals." P's competitor, Gonzales Construction Company, certified as such a business and received the subcontract, although its bid was higher than P's. Under federal law, general contractors must presume that "socially and economically disadvantaged individuals" include specified racial minorities. P sued Pena (D), Secretary of Transportation, claiming he was deprived of property without due process of law under the Fifth Amendment. The court of appeals upheld the law. P appeals.

2) **Issue.** Is the federal government's use of race-based classifications subject to strict scrutiny even for affirmative action?

3) **Held.** Yes. Judgment reversed and remanded.

a) The Fifth Amendment protects against arbitrary treatment by the federal government, but it does not guarantee equal treatment.

b) In *Croson, supra,* the Court held that the Fourteenth Amendment requires strict scrutiny of all race-based action by state and local governments. Thus, any person, of whatever race, has the right to demand that the government justify any racial classification subjecting that person to unequal treatment under the strictest judicial scrutiny.

c) In *Metro Broadcasting, Inc. v. FCC*, 497 U.S. 549 (1990), the Court held that "benign" racial classifications required only intermediate scrutiny. This holding undermined the basic principle that the Fifth and Fourteenth Amendments protect persons, not groups. Group classifications must be subject to detailed inquiry to assure that the personal right to equal protection has not been infringed. Therefore, it is inconsistent to treat "benign" racial classifications differently from other types of racial classifications, and all racial classifications shall now be subject to strict scrutiny.

d) This holding does not preclude the government from acting in response to the lingering effects of racial discrimination. When race-based action is necessary to further a compelling interest, it is permitted as long as it satisfies the "narrow tailoring" test of strict scrutiny.

4) Concurrence (Scalia, J.). There can never be a compelling interest in discriminating on the basis of race to compensate for past racial discrimination in the opposite direction. Under the Constitution, there can be neither a creditor nor a debtor race.

5) Concurrence (Thomas, J.). The government may not make distinctions on the basis of race, whether the objectives are to oppress a race or to help a race. Affirmative action programs undermine the moral basis of the equal protection principle and arouse resentment by those not benefitted. The targeted minorities are stamped with a badge of inferiority and are prompted to develop dependencies or an attitude that they are "entitled" to preferences.

6) Dissent (Stevens, Ginsburg, JJ.). There is a clear distinction between policies designed to oppress minorities and policies designed to eradicate racial subordination.

7) Dissent (Ginsburg, Breyer, JJ.). The judiciary should defer to Congress, as the political branches are better suited to respond to changing conditions.

Insert the following in place of **VI., E., 4., a.** *at p.* **110:**

a. Proof of dependency requirement--Califano v. Goldfarb, 430 U.S. 199 (1977).

Califano v. Goldfarb

1) Facts. Hannah Goldfarb worked for 25 years before she passed away. She had fully paid her Social Security taxes, but her husband (P) was told that he was not entitled to a widower's benefit because he had not been receiving at least one-half of his support from his wife. Under federal law, survivors' benefits based on a husband's earnings were payable to his widow, but a widower had to satisfy the "one-half support" requirement to collect benefits based on his wife's earnings. P challenged the law. The district court held the requirement unconstitutional under *Weinberger v. Wiesenfeld, supra.* The Supreme Court granted certiorari.

2) Issue. May Congress impose a gender-based distinction if it is intended to benefit widows as compared with widowers?

3) Held. No. Judgment affirmed.

a) Under *Wiesenfeld*, a gender-based distinction that deprives "women of protection for their families which men receive as a result of their employment" is not permitted under the Constitution. In this case, Hannah Goldfarb did not receive the same protection for her husband that a similarly situated male worker would have received for his wife. The only justification for this distinction is the overbroad generalization and assumption regarding a wife's dependency on her husband which is inadequate under the Constitution.

b) While in a sense the distinction is between widows and widowers based on a finding that widowers as a class were less likely to have been dependent upon their wives than were widows on their husbands, the gender-based distinction against wage-earning female workers is determinative.

    c)   The objective of the statute is not to provide for those who are more needy, but for those who are presumed to have been dependent on their deceased spouses. The statute is not intended to remedy the arguably greater needs of widows, but to aid dependent spouses of deceased wage earners, based on a presumption that wives are usually dependent. This assumption does not justify the gender-based discrimination against women.

    4)   **Concurrence** (Stevens, J.). P raised a claim for benefits, which is the focus of this case, and not P's wife's tax obligation. A classification that treats widows more favorably than widowers is not "invidious" discrimination. However, the discrimination against males in this case is an accidental byproduct of traditional ways of thinking about females. The discrimination can only be upheld if there is a "legitimate basis for presuming that the rule was actually intended to serve the interest" asserted by the government, and that test is not satisfied in this case.

    5)   **Dissent** (Rehnquist, J., Burger, C.J., Stewart, Blackmun, JJ.). The effect of the federal law "is to make it easier for widows to obtain benefits than it is for widowers." This requirement does not perpetuate the economic disadvantage that has previously led the Court to apply "heightened scrutiny" to gender-based distinctions. The majority incorrectly focuses on the wage earner because P's claim to benefits is not contractual. The statute simply benefits widows over widowers, and is supported by legislative judgments that widows are more likely to have greater needs than widowers. P would have had no claim had Congress required proof of dependency by widows as well as widowers. The statute is not exclusive, but overinclusive for reasons of administrative convenience. The classification merely favors aged widows and should be allowed.

Insert the following as **VI., F., 3.** *at p.* **113:**

3.   Sexual Orientation.

    a.   **Introduction.** The legal treatment of homosexuality has raised many issues. The courts have reached a variety of conclusions about what is appropriate and what is required under the Constitution. In *Bowers v. Hardwick, infra*, the Supreme Court held that there is no constitutionally protected right to commit consensual homosexual sodomy; beyond that, the Court has not clarified the issue.

Watkins v.
United States
Army

    b.   **Sexual orientation not sufficient for discharge--Watkins v. United States Army,** 847 F.2d 1329 (9th Cir. 1988), *aff'd on other grounds,* 875 F.2d 699 (9th Cir. 1989), *cert. denied,* 498 U.S. 957 (1990).

    1)   **Facts.** Watkins (P) enlisted in the United States Army (D). On his medical form, P indicated he had homosexual tendencies. P then served for 14 years, and his homosexuality was always common knowledge. D subsequently adopted new regulations that required the discharge of all homosexuals regardless of length or quality of military service. D notified P that he would be discharged because of his homosexuality. P challenged the discharge and the regulations on equal protection grounds.

2) **Issue.** May the United States Army discharge a person because the person is homosexual?

3) **Held.** No. Judgment reversed.

    a) D's regulations require the discharge of a person who is homosexual in orientation, regardless of whether the person has committed any homosexual acts. It does not require discharge of a person who commits a homosexual act as long as the person's orientation is heterosexual rather than homosexual. The regulations thus discriminate against homosexuals solely on the basis of their sexual orientation.

    b) In *Bowers v. Hardwick*, *infra*, the Supreme Court held that there is no constitutionally protected right to participate in homosexual sodomy. The Court did not hold that the state may penalize homosexuals for their orientation.

    c) Homosexuals are a suspect class. They have clearly suffered a history of purposeful discrimination. Sexual orientation bears no relevance to whether a person can perform or contribute to society. Homosexuals have been saddled with unique disabilities because of prejudice and stereotypes. The immutability requirement for a suspect class does not mean strict immutability, but it is sufficient if changing the trait would involve great difficulty. Scientific research shows that a person has little control over sexual orientation. Finally, homosexuals lack political power to obtain a remedy from the political branches of the government.

    d) D has no justification for its regulations sufficient to withstand the strict scrutiny that applies to discrimination against a suspect class.

4) **Dissent.** Under *Bowers v. Hardwick*, homosexuals cannot be considered a suspect class. A class is defined by its conduct, and in *Hardwick*, the Court held that an act done by a vast majority of class members which is fundamental to the class' very nature can be criminalized. Because of the holding in *Hardwick*, courts are not free "to describe discriminatory treatment [of homosexuals] as based on 'unreasoning prejudice.'"

c. **Sexual orientation sufficient for discharge--Steffan v. Perry,** 41 F.3d 677 (D.C. Cir. 1994).

Steffan
v. Perry

1) **Facts.** Steffan (P) enrolled in the Naval Academy. During his senior year, P told two fellow midshipmen that he was homosexual. An investigation ultimately led to P's public admission that he was homosexual. Pursuant to Navy regulations, P was discharged. P challenged the discharge. The district court upheld the regulations, and P appeals.

2) Issue. May the United States Navy discharge a person because the person is homosexual?

3) Held. Yes. Judgment affirmed.

a) P is not a member of a suspect class, because if the government can make homosexual conduct criminal, a group that is defined by homosexual conduct cannot constitute a "suspect class." Accordingly, rational basis review applies.

b) Discussing the rational basis standard of review, P concedes that the military has a legitimate governmental purpose for allowing termination of service of all persons who engage in homosexual conduct. However, P claims that the regulations do not further the legitimate purposes.

c) First, the military may reasonably assume that when a member states that he is homosexual, that member means that he either engages in or is likely to engage in homosexual conduct. P claims that an admission of homosexuality is nothing more than a declaration of "status" and not "conduct", and is therefore legally impermissible as a basis for discharge regardless of any rational relationship to the military objective. But status, such as blindness or excessive height, is a constitutional ground for finding a person unfit to serve in the military. Homosexuality is not irrelevant to homosexual conduct, which is a constitutionally permissible ground for discharge from the military.

4) Dissent. It "is inherently unreasonable to equate an admission of homosexual identity with commission of or intent to engage in homosexual conduct" that justifies discharge from the Navy.

5) Comment. Congress has since adopted a "don't ask, don't tell" policy whereby new recruits are not asked about their sexual orientation, and although homosexual acts remain a basis for rejection, sexual orientation by itself does not justify rejection. A servicemember who claims homosexual status will be discharged absent proof that the person does not engage in, intend to engage in, or have a propensity to engage in such acts.

Insert the following as **VII., C., 5.** *at p.* **117:**

Palko v. Connecticut

5. Double Jeopardy Provision Not Incorporated--Palko v. Connecticut, 302 U.S. 319 (1937).

a. **Facts.** Palko (P) was indicted for first degree murder and convicted of second degree murder. The State of Connecticut (D), based on a state statute permitting appeals by the prosecution, appealed the sentence and won a reversal and an order for a new trial. P was convicted of first degree murder in the second trial and now challenges the Connecticut statute as a violation of the Fourteenth Amendment Due Process Clause, since it placed him in double jeopardy (a violation of the Fifth Amendment if P had been tried in a federal court for a federal crime).

b.   **Issue.** Does the Fourteenth Amendment prevent a state from enacting a statute permitting double jeopardy?

c.   **Held.** No. Judgment affirmed.

1)   While it is true that the Fifth Amendment prohibits retrial against the will of a defendant once convicted, no such protection extends to prosecution by a state. P would apply all of the protections of the original Bill of Rights to state action, but there is no such general rule. Some immunities, such as those found in the First Amendment, have been extended to state action, but solely because of their indispensability to the concept of ordered liberty. Absorption of any of the Bill of Rights by the Fourteenth Amendment Due Process Clause is due solely to the belief that neither liberty nor justice would exist without them.

2)   The double jeopardy provision is not such an essential privilege; some would even say it is a mischief rather than a benefit. P has not claimed any lack of due process of law other than the Fifth Amendment claim, so his conviction is sustained.

Insert the following as **VII., C., 6.** *at p.* **117:**

6.   **Total Incorporation Rejected.** It has been argued that the Fourteenth Amendment Due Process Clause incorporates all of the Bill of Rights in full, but this view has been consistently rejected by the Court. [*See* Adamson v. California, 332 U.S. 46 (1947)] In *Adamson*, the Court decided that due process did not require reversal of a state criminal conviction where the prosecution had commented on the defendant's refusal to testify, although such a comment would be reversible error at the federal level because of the Fifth Amendment. Justices Black and Douglas dissented, arguing that the original purpose of the Fourteenth Amendment was to incorporate fully all of the Bill of Rights guarantees. They argued that failure to incorporate those specific guarantees would leave citizens without assured rights and would at the same time grant the Court an unauthorized broad power to expand or contract the scope of due process virtually at will. They also indicated a preference for selective incorporation over no incorporation at all.

Insert the following as **VII., C., 7.** *at p.* **117:**

7.   **Right to Trial by Jury Incorporated--Duncan v. Louisiana,** 391 U.S. 145 (1968).

Duncan v. Louisiana

a.   **Facts.** Duncan (D) was convicted of simple battery, a misdemeanor in Louisiana punishable by up to two years' imprisonment and a $300 fine. D was fined $150 and sentenced to serve only 60 days. D was refused a trial by jury under a Louisiana law, which he then challenged, but the state supreme court refused review. D appeals.

b.   **Issue.** May a state that provides trial by jury for all "felonies" try charges of simple battery to the court alone?

c. **Held.** No. Judgment reversed and case remanded.

1) The right of trial by jury in serious criminal cases is fundamental to the American scheme of justice and qualifies for protection under the Due Process Clause against violation by the states. The authorized penalty is of major relevance in determining whether a particular crime is serious; the possibility of two years' imprisonment clearly indicates a serious offense, so it is within due process protection. The Sixth Amendment guarantee of a right to jury trial is hereby applicable through the Fourteenth Amendment to state criminal cases which, if tried in a federal court, would be covered.

Insert the following as **VII., E., 3., c., 7)** *at p.* **132:**

Shaw v. Reno

7) **State redistricting plan designed only to separate voters on the basis of race--Shaw v. Reno**, 509 U.S. 630 (1993).

a) **Facts.** After the 1990 census, North Carolina became entitled to a 12th congressional seat. Forty of the state's 100 counties were covered by the Voting Rights Act, which required approval from a federal court or from Reno (D), the United States Attorney General, for any changes to voting districts. Black persons made up 20% of the state's population and were the majority in five of the counties. The state legislature submitted a redistricting plan that included one majority-black congressional district. After D objected to the plan, the legislature enacted a revised plan that had two majority-black districts. To include sufficient black citizens to fill the district, the second district was 160 miles long and, for much of its length, was only as wide as the freeway corridor it followed from black neighborhood to black neighborhood. Shaw (P) challenged the redistricting, claiming that the deliberate segregation of voters into separate districts on the basis of race violated the right to vote in an electoral process not tainted by racial discrimination. The district court held that P did not state a claim under the Equal Protection Clause. P appeals.

b) **Issue.** May a state legislature create a voting district that is so irrational on its face that it can be understood only as an effort to segregate voters into separate voting districts because of their race alone?

c) **Held.** No. Judgment reversed.

(1) Redistricting legislation that is so bizarre on its face that it is unexplainable on grounds other than race requires close scrutiny. A reapportionment plan that includes groups who have little or nothing in common other than their race has the appearance of political apartheid. It reinforces the stereotype that all members of a particular racial group think alike and vote alike.

(2) When a district is created solely to create a majority of one racial group, the representative from that district may believe that the primary objective is to represent only the members of that group instead of their entire constituency. Accordingly, the

courts should recognize an equal protection claim such as P's challenging the intentional creation of a majority-minority district that has no nonracial justifications.

(3) D claims that a jurisdiction covered by the Voting Rights Act may have a compelling interest in creating majority-minority districts. These states may have a strong interest in creating these districts, but they are still subject to constitutional challenges such as P's. Racial classifications of any type pose the risk of long-term harm to society by reinforcing the belief that citizens should be judged by the color of their skin.

d) Dissent (White, Blackmun, Stevens, JJ.). P has no cognizable claim, and the case should be dismissed. There are only two types of state voting practices that can give rise to a constitutional claim. The first is a direct deprivation of the right to vote and the second is that which "affects the political strength of various groups," such as where legislation unduly diminishes the group's influence on the political process. The second type, which usually arises in a gerrymandering case, is involved here. But the Court has previously required that an identifiable group show more than a mere lack of success at the polls to have a justiciable claim. In this case, P relies only on the irregular shape of the district, and this is not a sufficient ground for a claim.

Insert the following as **VII., E., 3., c., 8)** *at p.* **132:**

8) Race as a primary factor in reapportioning districts--Miller v. Johnson, 115 S. Ct. 2475 (1995).

Miller v. Johnson

a) Facts. Twenty-seven percent of Georgia's population is black. The 1990 census gave Georgia an 11th congressional district. Previously, the state had one majority-black district. After two redistricting plans were rejected by the United States Attorney General, the state legislature adopted one that included three majority-minority districts. One of the plans used narrow corridors to connect two cities containing black neighborhoods. Miller (P) challenged the reapportionment. The district court held that race was the predominant, overriding factor in designing the plan and granted relief. Johnson (D) appeals.

b) Issue. May a state use race as the primary factor in designing reapportionment districts?

c) Held. No. Judgment affirmed.

(1) The claim in *Shaw v. Reno, supra,* was not a vote dilution claim, but an equal protection claim based on allegations that the state has used race as a basis for separating voters into districts. A state may not separate its citizens into different voting districts on the basis of race any more than it may separate them on the basis of race on its parks, buses, golf courses, etc.

(2) *Shaw* does not require that the challenged district be bizarre on its face. Shape is merely circumstantial evidence of intent to use race

for its own sake. The state may not apply the stereotype that persons of the same or a particular race share a single political interest.

(3)   The distinction between being aware of racial considerations and being motivated by them can be difficult to make, and federal courts must be careful not to improperly intrude upon districting legislation. Thus, a plaintiff has the burden to show that race was the predominant factor motivating the legislature's decision to place a significant number of voters within or without a particular district. This means showing that the traditional race-neutral districting principles such as compactness, contiguity, etc., were subordinated to racial considerations.

(4)   The state's claim that it had a compelling interest in complying with the Attorney General's requirements is not acceptable to the extent that the Attorney General required more than is required by the Voting Rights Act. In this case, the Attorney General's objective was to maximize majority-black districts, which is not required by federal law. The Attorney General used the Voting Rights Act to demand the very kind of racial stereotyping forbidden by the Fourteenth Amendment.

d)   **Dissent** (Ginsburg, Stevens, Breyer, Souter, JJ.). The *Shaw* plan was not a problem because race was a factor, but because nonracial factors were virtually excluded. In this case, race did not overwhelm the other factors. The plan in this case did group people according to ethnicity, but that is a common factor for districting plans.

Insert the following as **VII., F., 3., e.** *at p.* **148:**

Planned Parenthood of Southeastern Pennsylvania v. Casey

e.   **Permissible state regulation of abortion--Planned Parenthood of Southeastern Pennsylvania v. Casey,** 505 U.S. 833 (1992).

1)   **Facts.** Pennsylvania adopted an Abortion Control Act requiring that a woman seeking an abortion must be given certain information at least 24 hours before the abortion; that the woman give informed consent prior to the abortion; that, if a minor, the woman obtain the informed consent of her parents unless a judicial bypass option is followed; that, if married, the woman certify she informed her husband; and that facilities providing abortion services must make certain reports about each abortion, including the woman's age, gestational age, type of abortion procedure, medical conditions and results, and the weight of the aborted fetus. Compliance with the requirements is not required in certain medical emergencies. Planned Parenthood of Southeastern Pennsylvania (P) challenged the Act on its face by suing Casey (D), the Governor of Pennsylvania. The district court held all the provisions unconstitutional, but the court of appeals upheld everything except the husband notification requirement. The Supreme Court granted certiorari.

2)   **Issue.** May a state impose notification and consent requirements as prerequisites for obtaining an abortion?

3) **Held.** Yes. Judgment reversed in part.

a) The three parts of the essential *Roe v. Wade, supra*, holding are reaffirmed. These are: (i) the woman's right to have an abortion before viability without undue state interference; (ii) the state's power to restrict abortions after fetal viability, as long as there are exceptions to protect a woman's life or health; and (iii) the state's legitimate interest from the outset of the pregnancy in protecting the health of the woman and the life of the fetus that may become a child.

b) Substantive due process claims require courts to exercise reasoned judgment, and the Court must define the liberty of all, not mandate a moral code. The Constitution has been interpreted to protect personal decisions regarding marriage, procreation, and contraception. Defining one's own concept of existence, meaning, and the mystery of human life is at the heart of liberty. At the same time, abortion has consequences for persons other than the woman who is pregnant.

c) *Roe* should be upheld under the principle of stare decisis because it has not proven unworkable, because people have relied on the availability of abortion, because under *Roe* women have been better able to participate equally in the economic and social life of the country, because no evolution of legal principle has left *Roe*'s doctrinal footings weaker than they were in 1973 when the decision was announced, and because there have been no changed circumstances or new factual understandings. Even if *Roe* is wrong, the error involves only the strength of the state interest in fetal protection, not the liberty of women. Overruling *Roe* simply because of a change in philosophical disposition would undermine the Court's legitimacy.

d) Although *Roe* has been criticized for drawing lines, the Court must draw specific rules from the general standards in the Constitution. The trimester approach was not part of the essential holding in *Roe* and it both misconceived the nature of the pregnant woman's interest and undervalued the state's interest in potential life. It is therefore overruled and replaced with a line drawn only at viability. Under this approach, a law that serves a valid purpose not designed to strike at the right of abortion itself may be sustained even if it makes it more difficult or more expensive to obtain an abortion, unless the law imposes an undue burden on a woman's ability to make an abortion decision. Thus, the state may further its interest in potential life but cannot place a substantial obstacle in the path of a woman's choice.

e) The state may adopt health regulations to promote the health or safety of a woman seeking an abortion. It may not prohibit any woman from making the ultimate decision to terminate her pregnancy before viability. After viability, the state may promote its interest in the potentiality of human life by regulating and even proscribing abortion except where it is necessary to preserve the life or health of the mother.

f) With regard to the specific provisions of the Act, the definition of medical emergency does not impose an undue burden on a woman's abortion right. The informed consent requirement is also permissible because it furthers the legitimate purpose of reducing the risk that a woman may elect an abortion, only to discover later, with devastating psychological consequences, that her decision was not fully informed. The 24-hour waiting period does not impose substantial obstacles, and it is not unreasonable to conclude that important decisions will be more informed and deliberate if they follow some period of reflection. The exception for cases in which a physician reasonably believes that furnishing the information would have a severely adverse effect on the woman's physical or mental health accommodates the interest in allowing physicians to exercise their medical judgment.

g) The spousal notification requirement does, however, impose an undue burden on a woman's choice to undergo an abortion and cannot be sustained. In well-functioning marriages, the spouses discuss important intimate decisions such as whether to bear a child, and the notification requirement adds nothing in such situations. However, millions of women are the victims of physical and psychological abuse from their husbands, and requiring spousal notification in these situations can be tantamount to preventing the woman from getting an abortion. The husband's interest in the life of the child his wife is carrying does not permit the state to empower him with a veto over the abortion decision. Men do not have the kind of dominion over their wives that parents have over their children.

h) The parental consent provision has been sustained before, and provided there is an adequate judicial bypass procedure, its constitutionality is reaffirmed. The recordkeeping and reporting requirements are also permissible, with the exception of whether the spouse was notified of the abortion.

4) **Concurrence and dissent** (Blackmun, J.). The Court's decision preserves the liberty of women that is one vote away from being extinguished. The Court also leaves open the possibility that the regulations it now approves may in the future be shown to impose an unconstitutional burden.

5) **Concurrence and dissent** (Stevens, J.). The Court properly follows the principle that a developing organism that is not yet a "person" does not have a "right to life." The state's interest in protecting potential life is not grounded in the Constitution, but reflects humanitarian and pragmatic concerns, including the offense taken by a large segment of the population at the number of abortions performed in this country and third-trimester abortions specifically. But the woman's interest in liberty is constitutional; the Constitution would be violated as much by a requirement that all women undergo abortion as by an absolute ban on abortions. The 24-hour delay requirement should not be upheld because it presumes that the abortion decision is wrong and must be reconsidered. The state may properly require physicians to inform women of the nature and risks of the abortion procedure and the medical risks of carrying to term, but it should not be allowed to require that the woman be provided with materials designed to persuade her to choose not to undergo the abortion.

6) **Concurrence and dissent** (Rehnquist, C.J., White, Scalia, Thomas, JJ.). *Roe* was wrongly decided, and it can and should be overruled consistent with the traditional approach to stare decisis in constitutional cases. Stare decisis is not a reason to retain *Roe*; the Court's legitimacy is enhanced by faithful interpretation of the Constitution. The Court's revised "undue burden" standard is an unjusti-

fied constitutional compromise that allows the Court to closely scrutinize all types of abortion regulations despite the lack of any constitutional authority to do so. The new "undue burden" approach is still an imposition on the states by the Court of a complex abortion code. Abortion involves the purposeful termination of potential life and is thus different in kind from the other areas of privacy recognized by the Court, including marriage, procreation, and contraception. Prohibitions on abortion have been part of the law of many of the states since before the Fourteenth Amendment was adopted; there is no deeply rooted tradition of unrestricted abortion in our history that justifies characterizing the right as "fundamental." A woman's interest in having an abortion is a form of liberty protected by the Due Process Clause, but states may regulate abortion procedures in ways rationally related to a legitimate state interest. The Act should be upheld in its entirety.

7) **Concurrence and dissent** (Scalia, J., Rehnquist, C.J., White, Thomas, JJ.). The states may permit abortion-on-demand, but the Constitution does not require that they do so. It is a legislative decision. The issue is not whether the right to an abortion is an absolute liberty or whether it is an important liberty to many women, but whether it is a liberty protected by the Constitution. It is not, because the Constitution says nothing about it and because longstanding traditions of American society have permitted it to be prohibited. Under the rational basis test, D's statute should be upheld. Instead, the Court perpetuates the premise of *Roe*, which is a value judgment, not a legal matter. The "undue burden" standard lacks meaningful content, and may be summed up by concluding that a state may regulate abortion only in such a way as to not reduce significantly its incidence. *Roe* nourished the deeply divisive issue of abortion by elevating it to the national level where it is much more difficult to resolve than it was at the state level. Political compromise is now impossible, and *Roe* has been a major factor in selecting Justices to the Court. The Court should not be concerned with predicting public perceptions but should do what is legally right by asking whether *Roe* was correctly decided and whether it has succeeded in producing a settled body of law. The answer to both questions is no, and *Roe* should therefore be overruled. The Court's reliance on value judgments instead of interpreting text has created political pressure directed to the Court, whereby various groups of people demonstrate to protest that the Court has not implemented the respective group's values.

Insert the following in place of **VIII., B., 1., a., 4)** *at p.* **163:**

4) **Intent element--Abrams v. United States,** 250 U.S. 616 (1919).

Abrams v.
United States

   a)   **Facts.** When the United States sent the Marines to Vladivostok and Murmansk in response to Russia signing a peace treaty with Germany during World War I, Abrams and other Russian immigrants (Ds) protested by distributing leaflets calling for a general strike. Ds were arrested, tried, and convicted of conspiracy to violate the Espionage Act. Specifically, they were convicted of conspiracy to urge a strike "with intent [to] cripple or hinder the United States in the prosecution of the war." Ds appeal.

b) **Issue.** May persons be convicted of criminal conspiracy as a result of urging a general strike to protest war activity?

c) **Held.** Yes. Judgment affirmed.

   (1) The convictions are sustainable under *Schenck v. United States*, 249 U.S. 47 (1919) and *Frohwerk v. United States*, 249 U.S. 204 (1919).

d) **Dissent** (Holmes, J.). While the law may punish speech that produces or is intended to produce a clear and imminent danger that the speech will bring about specific evils that the United States may constitutionally seek to prevent, there must be a present danger of immediate evil. Congress cannot simply prohibit any effort to influence public opinion. Ds' publishing of pamphlets does not present any imminent danger of Ds' opinions hindering the success of the government's war efforts. Ds' intent was to help Russia and stop American involvement in Russia, where the United States was not at war. Under the Constitution, freedom of speech must be protected unless the speech so imminently threatens immediate interference with the lawful and pressing purposes of the law that an immediate check is required to save the country. The common law doctrine of seditious libel does not survive the First Amendment.

e) **Comment.** The "clear and present danger" doctrine became highly protective of free speech as a result of Justice Holmes's dissent in this case.

Insert the following in place of **VIII., B., 3., d., 1)** *at p.* **172:**

Chaplinsky
v. New
Hampshire

1) **Classes of speech--Chaplinsky v. New Hampshire,** 315 U.S. 568 (1942).

a) **Facts.** Chaplinsky (D) was on a public sidewalk distributing literature. Certain citizens complained to the City Marshall, Bowering, that D was denouncing religion as a so-called "racket." Bowering warned D of the crowds' restlessness, although he acknowledged that D's activities were legal. Later, as D was being taken to the police station following a disturbance, he encountered Bowering again. D addressed Bowering by repeating the words "You are a God damned racketeer" and "a damned Fascist." D was convicted of violating a state law that prohibited a person from addressing "any offensive, derisive, or annoying word to any other person who is lawfully in any street or public place." The lower courts upheld the conviction, and D appeals.

b) **Issue.** May a state prohibit the use of "fighting words"?

c) **Held.** Yes. Judgment affirmed.

   (1) Under the Fourteenth Amendment, the right of free speech is not an absolute right. There are some well-defined and narrowly limited classes of speech, which can be punished under the Constitution.

   (2) Classes of speech that may be prohibited include lewd and obscene language, profanity, libel, and insulting or "fighting" words. "Fighting words" are those which "inflict injury or tend to incite an imme-

diate breach of the peace." These classes of speech are not essential to the exposition of ideas and have only a slight social value that is outweighed by a strong social interest in order and morality.

(3) The state court interpreted the statute to apply to the limited classes of speech that include "classical fighting words." So limited, the statute is constitutional.

Insert the following as **VIII., D., 6., f.** *at p.* **199:**

f. **Content of "fighting speech"--R.A.V. v. City of St. Paul,** 505 U.S. 377 (1992).

R.A.V. v. City of St. Paul

1) **Facts.** R.A.V. (D) and several other teenagers assembled a cross from broken chair legs and burned it inside the fenced yard of a black family that lived across the street from D's current residence. The City of St. Paul, Minnesota (P) charged D with disorderly conduct pursuant to an ordinance that provided: "Whoever places on public or private property a symbol, object, appellation, characterization, or graffiti, including, but not limited to, a burning cross or Nazi swastika, which one knows or has reasonable grounds to know arouses anger, alarm, or resentment in others on the basis of race, color, creed, religion, or gender commits disorderly conduct and shall be guilty of a misdemeanor." D moved to dismiss the charge on the ground that the ordinance was invalid under the First Amendment because it was overbroad and impermissibly content-based. The trial court granted D's motion, but the Minnesota Supreme Court reversed, construing the ordinance to apply only to conduct that amounts to "fighting words," *i.e.,* "conduct that itself inflicts injury or tends to incite immediate violence." The Supreme Court granted certiorari.

2) **Issue.** May the government regulate "fighting words" based on the subjects the speech addresses?

3) **Held.** No. Judgment reversed.

a) Content-based speech regulations are presumptively invalid, but, as the Court held in *Chaplinsky v. New Hampshire, supra,* there are exceptions in a few limited areas which are "of such slight social value as a step to truth that any benefit that may be derived from them is clearly outweighed by the social interest in order and morality."

b) Certain categories of expression are "not within the area of constitutionally protected speech" (*e.g.,* obscenity, defamation, etc.), which means that they may be regulated because of their constitutionally proscribable content. This does not mean they may be used to discriminate on the basis of content unrelated to their distinctively proscribable content; *i.e.,* the government may proscribe libel, but it cannot proscribe only libel critical of the government.

c) The exclusion of "fighting words" from the scope of the First Amendment means that the unprotected features of the words are essentially a "nonspeech" element of communication. But there is a "content discrimination" limitation on the government's prohibition of proscribable speech; the government may not regulate use based on hostility or favoritism toward the underlying message expressed.

d)   When the basis for content discrimination entirely consists of the very reason the class of speech at issue is proscribable, there is no significant danger of idea or viewpoint discrimination. The government may prohibit only the most patently offensive obscenity, but it cannot prohibit only obscenity that includes offensive political messages. Or, the government may regulate price advertising on one industry and not in others, because the risk of fraud is greater there, but it cannot prohibit only that commercial advertising that depicts men in a demeaning fashion.

e)   The government could properly give differential treatment to even a content-defined subclass of proscribable speech if the subclass is associated with particular "secondary effects" of the speech; *e.g.,* prohibiting only those obscene live performances that involve minors. And laws against conduct instead of speech may reach speech based on content, such as sexually derogatory "fighting words" that violate Title VII's prohibition against sexual discrimination. The key element is that the government does not target conduct on the basis of its expressive content.

f)   In this case, P's ordinance is facially unconstitutional because it applies only to "fighting words" that insult, or provoke violence, "on the basis of race, color, creed, religion, or gender." It does not apply to abusive invectives on other topics, but singles out those speakers who express views on disfavored subjects. Instead of singling out a particularly offensive mode of expression, P has proscribed fighting words of whatever manner that communicate messages of racial, gender, or religious intolerance. This creates the possibility that P hopes to handicap the expression of certain ideas.

g)   P's content discrimination is not reasonably necessary to achieve P's compelling interests; an ordinance not limited to the favored topics would have precisely the same beneficial interest.

4)   Concurrence (White, Blackmun, O'Connor, Stevens, JJ.).

a)   P's ordinance is overbroad because it criminalizes expression protected by the First Amendment as well as unprotected expression. The majority's rationale is a new doctrine that was not even briefed by the parties and is a departure from prior cases. The Court has long applied a categorical approach that identifies certain classifications of speech as unprotected by the First Amendment because the evil to be restricted so overwhelmingly outweighs the expressive interests, if any, at stake. The Court now holds that the First Amendment protects these categories to the extent that the government may not regulate some fighting words more strictly than others because of their content. Now, if the government decides to criminalize certain fighting words, it must criminalize all fighting words.

b)   The Court also refuses to sustain P's ordinance even though it would survive under the strict scrutiny applicable to other protected expression. In *Burson v. Freeman*, 504 U.S. 191 (1992), the Court applied the strict scrutiny standard and upheld a statute prohibiting vote solicitation and display or distribution of campaign materials within 100 feet of the entrance to a polling place, even though the statute could have been drafted in broader, content-neutral terms. Under the Court's decision today, the *Burson* law would have been found unconstitutional.

c)   Although the Court's analysis is flawed, the conclusion is correct because P's ordinance is overbroad. Even as construed by the Minnesota Supreme Court, the ordinance criminalizes a substantial amount of expression that is protected by the First Amendment. That court held that P may constitutionally prohibit expression that "by its very utterance" causes "anger, alarm or resentment," but such generalized reactions are not sufficient to strip expression of its constitutional protection.

5)   Concurrence (Blackmun, J.). The ordinance is overbroad.

6)   Concurrence (Stevens, J.). P's ordinance regulates conduct that has some communicative content, and it raises two questions: Is it "overbroad" because it prohibits too much speech, and, if not, is it "underbroad" because it does not prohibit enough speech? The majority and concurring opinions deal with the basic principles that (i) certain categories of expression are not protected and (ii) content-based regulations of expression are presumptively invalid. But both principles have exceptions. The majority applies the prohibition on content-based regulation to "fighting words"—speech that previously had been considered wholly "unprotected." Now, fighting words have greater protection than commercial speech, which is often regulated based on content. Assuming arguendo that the ordinance regulates only fighting words and is not overbroad, it regulates speech not on the basis of its subject matter or the viewpoint expressed, but rather on the basis of the harm the speech causes—injuries based on "race, color, creed, religion, or gender." It only bans a subcategory of the already narrow category of fighting words. It is not an unconstitutional content-based regulation of speech, and should be upheld, except that it is overbroad.

Insert the following as **VIII., E., 2.** *at p.* **199** *(and renumber subsequent section accordingly):*

2.   Viewpoint Neutral Regulations--Schneider v. State, 308 U.S. 147 (1939).   Schneider
v. State

a.   **Facts.** The State of New Jersey (P) prosecuted Schneider (D) for violating certain ordinances that prohibited all distribution of leaflets and handbills in public places. There were no provisions for licensing distribution or merely limiting distribution to a certain time, place, and manner. The Supreme Court granted certiorari.

b.   **Issue.** May a municipality prohibit any distribution of printed material in public places?

c.   **Held.** No. Conviction reversed.

1) Municipalities may adopt regulations to promote public safety, health, welfare, and convenience, but may not in so doing abridge the individual right to free speech. For example, a city may prohibit the stoppage of traffic by someone desiring to distribute literature or a city may prohibit littering. But an objective of keeping the streets clean and in good appearance is insufficient to justify an ordinance that prohibits a person rightfully on a public street from handing literature to one willing to receive it.

2) If the objective is to keep streets clean, a city may punish those who actually throw papers on the street, but it cannot ban the distribution of literature. To the extent the city must clean and care for the streets as an indirect consequence of distribution of printed material, the burden on the city is a result of the constitutional protection of the freedom of speech.

Insert the following as **VIII., E., 2., g.** *at p.* **204:**

International Society for Krishna Consciousness v. Lee

g. **Airports--International Society for Krishna Consciousness v. Lee,** 505 U.S. 672 (1992).

1) **Facts.** Members of the International Society for Krishna Consciousness (P) performed a religious ritual known as "sankirtan," which consisted of going into public places, disseminating religious literature, and soliciting funds to support the religion. P desired to perform sankirtan at the airports in the New York City area. Lee (D) was the police superintendent of the airports and was responsible for enforcing a regulation that prohibited the repetitive sale of merchandise, the solicitation of money, or the distribution of literature within the interior areas of buildings at the airport. Such activities were permitted on the sidewalks outside the terminal buildings. P challenged the regulation. The district court granted P summary judgment. The court of appeals affirmed with regard to the ban on distributing, but reversed with regard to the ban on solicitation. The Supreme Court granted certiorari.

2) **Issue.** May an airport terminal operated by a public authority prohibit solicitation in the interior of its buildings?

3) **Held.** Yes. Judgment affirmed.

a) Solicitation is clearly a form of protected speech, but the government need not permit all forms of speech on property it owns and controls. Prior cases reflect a "forum-based" approach to assess government restrictions on the use of its property. There are three categories of government property:

(1) *Traditional public forums*—property that has traditionally been available for public expression. Regulation of speech on this type survives only if it is narrowly drawn to achieve a compelling state interest.

(2) *Designated public forums*—property that the government has opened for expressive activity by part or all of the public. Regulation of speech on this type also survives only if it is narrowly drawn to achieve a compelling state interest.

(3) ***All remaining public property***. Regulation of speech on this type survives if it is reasonable, as long as the regulation is not an effort to suppress the speaker's activity due to disagreement with the speaker's views.

b) A traditional public forum exists where the property has been immemorially held in trust for the use of the public and has been used for purposes of assembly, communicating thoughts among citizens, and discussing public questions. Examples include streets and parks. Designated public forums are areas that are intentionally dedicated for use in public discourse.

c) Airports do not meet these requirements. For one thing, they have not been in existence for many years. For another, they have not historically been made available for speech activity, except when ordered to by the courts. Airports are not just "transportation nodes" like bus and rail terminals, but have special characteristics. The purpose of an airport is to facilitate travel and make a regulated profit, not to promote expression.

d) Because an airport is not a public forum, D's regulations are permissible as long as they are reasonable. P's proposed solicitation had a disruptive effect on airport travelers who are typically in a hurry and for whom a delay can mean a lost flight and severe inconvenience. Face-to-face solicitation presents a risk of duress and fraud that D can properly attempt to avoid. Therefore, D's ban on solicitation is sustained.

4) **Concurrence** (O'Connor, J.). An airport is clearly not a public forum. It could be closed to everyone except those who have legitimate business there, unlike public streets and parks, but government officials make airports open to the public as a convenience. The airport does contain restaurants, shops, newsstands, and other facilities not directly related to travel, but D's regulations are reasonably related to maintaining the multipurpose environment created by D. At the same time, the ban on leafleting cannot be upheld as reasonable, since distributing literature does not present the same problems as soliciting funds.

5) **Concurrence** (Kennedy, Blackmun, Stevens, Souter, JJ.). The areas of an airport that are outside the passenger security zones are public forums. The Court's categorical approach to classifying government property leaves no room for the development of new public forums without government approval. The traditional three-part analysis provides a better, more objective approach, based on the actual, physical characteristics and uses of the property. An airport, for example, is not much different from a street and sidewalk, since both have a principal purpose of facilitating transportation, not public discourse. As long as expressive activity would be appropriate and compatible with the actual uses of public property, the property should be considered a public forum. Under this analysis, passenger convenience would not be a sufficiently strong rationale for banning solicitation. The ban on solicitation and receipt of funds is nevertheless a proper time, place, and manner restriction. The ban does not prevent solicitation that does not involve the immediate receipt of money.

6) **Concurrence and dissent** (Souter, Blackmun, Stevens, JJ.). The traditional public forums are only "archetypes" of property from which the government may not exclude speech, and the airports involved in this case fit the archetype. The ban on solicitation is not sufficiently narrowly tailored to further a significant state interest and should not be sustained.

7) **Comment.** In *Lee v. International Society for Krishna Consciousness, Inc.*, 505 U.S. 830 (1992), the Court held that the ban on the distribution of literature was invalid, citing the concurrences above.

Insert the following as **VIII., E., 3., c.** *at p.* **206:**

Barnes v.
Glen Theatre,
Inc.

c. **Prohibition of nude dancing--Barnes v. Glen Theatre, Inc.**, 501 U.S. 560 (1991).

1) **Facts.** Glen Theatre, Inc. (P) operated a dancing establishment. P wanted to provide totally nude dancing as entertainment. Indiana had a public indecency statute that prohibited complete nudity in public places and required the wearing of pasties and G-strings. P sued Barnes (D) and other officials to enjoin enforcement of the statute. The district court held for D on the ground that P's proposed dancing is not expressive activity under the First Amendment. The court of appeals reversed, holding that non-obscene nude dancing is protected expression. The Supreme Court granted certiorari.

2) **Issue.** May a state prohibit public nudity, even if this includes nude dancing?

3) **Held.** Yes. Judgment reversed.

a) Several cases suggest that nude dancing is expressive conduct, even if it is only marginally protected by the First Amendment. Under the four-part *O'Brien* test, *supra*, D's statute is justified despite its incidental limitations on some expressive activity. The public indecency statute furthers substantial governmental interests in protecting societal order and morality, and it is within the traditional police power of a state.

b) The governmental interests are unrelated to the suppression of free expression. The statute does not proscribe nudity because of the erotic message conveyed by the dancers; erotic performances may be conducted by P as long as the performers wear a minimal amount of clothing. The law merely makes the message slightly less graphic. The state may properly prevent public nudity, even if it is combined with expressive activity.

c) The governmental interest in prohibiting public nudity is not a means to some greater end, but an end in itself. The statute is narrowly tailored because requiring the wearing of pasties and G-strings is the bare minimum necessary to achieve the state's purposes.

4) **Concurrence** (Scalia, J.). The statute is not subject to First Amendment scrutiny at all because it is a general law that regulates conduct and is not specifically directed at expression. The dissent argues that the purpose of restricting public nudity is to protect nonconsenting parties from offense, but society may prohibit activities that are immoral, regardless of whether they harm others. Examples of such prohibited activities include bestiality, drug use, cockfighting, prostitution, and sodomy. Virtually all laws restrict conduct, and virtually any prohibited conduct can be performed for an expressive purpose, including the fact that the actor disagrees with the prohibition. The First Amendment reaches expressive conduct when the prohibition applies to the communicative attributes of the conduct, but not where the impact is merely the incidental effect of forbidding the conduct for other reasons. If the law does not directly or indirectly impede speech, the First Amendment applies only if the purpose of the law is to suppress communication.

5) **Concurrence** (Souter, J.). Performance dancing is inherently expressive, but nudity per se is not; nudity is a condition, not an activity. The voluntary assumption of the condition of nudity expresses nothing more than that the condition is somehow appropriate to the circumstances, but that is the message of every voluntary act. Calling all voluntary activity expressive would reduce the concept of expression to the point of meaninglessness. The *O'Brien* test properly applies here, and the state's interest in preventing "secondary effects" such as prostitution, sexual assault, and other criminal activity is sufficient to justify enforcement of the statute against the type of adult entertainment sought by P.

6) **Dissent** (White, Marshall, Blackmun, Stevens, JJ.). Dancing is an ancient art form that inherently embodies the expression and communication of ideas and emotions. The state's general interest in promoting societal order and morality is not sufficient justification for this statute that reaches a significant amount of expressive activity. The purpose of a ban on public nudity is to protect others from offense, but that purpose is inapplicable in P's establishment, where people pay to see the dances. With regard to P's dancers, the state is simply protecting viewers from what it believes to be a harmful message. The nudity is an expressive component of the dance, not incidental conduct, and the statute is therefore related to expressive conduct. Without a compelling state interest to support the statute, P's challenge should be upheld.

Insert the following as **VIII., E., 4., e.** *at p.* **209:**

e. **Restriction on corporate political spending--Austin v. Michigan Chamber of Commerce,** 494 U.S. 652 (1990).

Austin v.
Michigan
Chamber of
Commerce

1) **Facts.** Section 54(1) of the Michigan Campaign Finance Act prohibited corporations from using corporate treasury funds for independent expenditures to support or oppose political candidates, but corporations could make such expenditures from segregated funds used solely for political purposes. The Michigan Chamber of Commerce (P) challenged the law. The court of appeals held that under the First Amendment, the law could not be applied to P. Austin (D) appeals.

2) **Issue.** May a state prohibit corporations from making independent political expenditures except from a segregated fund maintained solely for that purpose?

3) **Held.** Yes. Judgment reversed.

a) P's status as a corporation does not remove its use of funds to support a political candidate, which is "speech," from protection by the First Amendment. In *FEC v. Massachusetts Citizens for Life, Inc.*, 479 U.S. 238 (1986), the Court held that a federal statute requiring corporations to make independent political expenditures only through special segregated funds burdens corporate freedom of expression. Thus, D's restriction on such political corporate expenditures may be sustained only if they are narrowly tailored to serve a compelling state interest.

b) D claims that corporations have unique legal and economic characteristics that present a danger of corruption if their political expenditures are not regulated. State-conferred advantages make it possible for a corporation to attract capital for reasons unrelated to popular support for the corporation's political ideas. Corporate wealth can unfairly influence elections when it is deployed in the form of independent expenditures. This compelling interest in preventing corruption supports the restriction of the influence of political war chests funneled through the corporate form.

c) D's law is precisely targeted to eliminate the distortion caused by corporate spending while also allowing corporations to express their political views; thus, it is sufficiently narrowly tailored to achieve its goal.

d) P claims that even if the law is permissible with regard to for-profit corporations, it cannot be applied to a nonprofit ideological corporation such as P. The *Massachusetts Citizens for Life* case held that the federal law could not be applied to a nonprofit organization that was more like a voluntary political association than a business firm. The organization in that case was formed expressly to promote political ideas and could not engage in business activities. P, by contrast, has a nonpolitical purpose in addition to its political purpose. P's business activities are distinct from its political activities, so members who disagree with P's political agenda could still pay dues to participate in the business activities. Finally, P accepts contributions from business corporations, giving them the opportunity to use P to circumvent the Act's regulation of corporate political spending.

e) P also claims that because the Act exempts unincorporated associations and media corporations, it denies equal protection. But there are valid reasons for these exemptions.

4) **Dissent** (Scalia, J.). The majority has concluded that too much speech is an evil that the democratic majority can proscribe, but the central truth of the First Amendment is that government cannot be trusted to insure, through censorship, the "fairness" of political debate. Corporations are not the only ones that receive special advantages from the government. Other organizations and even individuals receive tax breaks, contract awards, public employment, and outright cash subsidies. But a state may not require the forfeiture of First Amendment rights as a condition to receipt of these advantages. The Court has not distinguished *Buckley v. Valeo*, *supra*, which held that independent expenditures by individuals and associations do not raise a sufficient threat of corruption to justify prohibition. The Act does not aim at preventing wrongdoing, but at preventing speech. However, in our system, there is no such thing as too much speech, and the people, not the government, must separate the wheat from the chaff.

5) **Dissent** (Kennedy, O'Connor, Scalia, JJ.). The majority upholds two forms of censorship: D's content-based law that makes it a crime for a nonprofit corporate speaker to endorse or oppose candidates for public office, and the Court's value-laden, content-based speech suppression that creates a preferred class by permitting some nonprofit corporate groups but not others to engage in political speech. D discriminates not only on the content of the speech but on the basis of the speaker's identity. D has no compelling interest to support the law, as there is no support for the assertion that corporate political expenditures present a corrosive and distorting effect on the political process. Requiring nonprofit corporations to speak politically through PACs eliminates accountability. And the media exemption ignores the reality that all corporations communicate with the public to some degree, whether it is their primary business or not, and communication is particularly important for nonprofit corporations. It is difficult to untangle the links between media and nonmedia corporations, particularly where the latter owns and controls the former.

Insert the following as **VIII., F., 1., c., 3)** *at p.* **214:**

3) **Restricted access to school district mail system--Perry Educators' Association v. Perry Local Educators' Association,** 460 U.S. 37 (1983).

Perry Educators' Association v. Perry Local Educators' Association

a) **Facts.** The Perry Local Educators' Association (P) and the Perry Educators' Association (D) both represented teachers in the school district and had equal access to the interschool mail system. D challenged P's status as bargaining representative and won election as the exclusive representative of the teachers. The labor contract negotiated by D gave it the exclusive right of access to teachers' mailboxes and to use of the interschool mail delivery system. However, during a representation contest, all involved unions had equal access under state law. P brought an action for injunctive and declaratory relief, claiming the preferential access given D violated the First and Fourteenth Amendments. The district court granted D summary judgment, but the court of appeals reversed. D appeals. (The Court treats the case as a petition for a writ of certiorari.)

b) **Issue.** May a school district restrict access to its mail system to an exclusive labor bargaining representative?

c) **Held.** Yes. Judgment reversed.

(1) The existence of a right of access to public property and the type of limitations which are allowed depend on the character of the property involved. There are three basic types:

(a) Places long devoted to assembly and debate, like parks, are generally not subject to governmental restrictions of expressive activity unless narrowly drawn to achieve a compelling state interest.

(b) Places opened for public expressive activity are usually subject to the same rules as the traditional public forum.

(c) Public property not a public forum by tradition or designation may be protected by more comprehensive restrictions to preserve its use for its primary function.

(2) The public school mail system falls within the third category. Access may be limited as long as the restriction on speech is reasonable and not an arbitrary suppression of ideas. Exclusive use by D preserves the property for the use to which it was lawfully dedicated. P has no official need to use the system, and alternative forums are available. The legitimate state interest it furthers satisfies the equal protection claim.

d) Dissent (Brennan, Marshall, Powell, Stevens, JJ.). The exclusive access given D amounts to viewpoint discrimination against P. The intent to discriminate can be inferred from the effect of the policy—which is to deny P effective communication. No substantial state interest is advanced thereby, so the restriction is unconstitutional.

Insert the following as **VIII., F., 1., f.** *at p.* **216:**

Rust v. Sullivan

f. Government subsidies to speech--Rust v. Sullivan, 500 U.S. 173 (1991).

1) **Facts.** Congress enacted Title X of the Public Health Service Act that provided federal funding for family-planning services, provided that none of the funds could be used in programs where abortion is a method of family planning. Sullivan (D), Secretary of the Department of Health and Human Services, promulgated new regulations that (i) specified that a Title X project cannot provide counseling concerning abortion or referrals for abortion; (ii) prohibited a Title X project from engaging in activities that encourage, promote, or advocate abortion as a method of family planning; and (iii) required that Title X projects be physically and financially separate from prohibited abortion activities. Rust (P) challenged the facial validity of the regulations, claiming they violated the First and Fifth Amendments. The lower courts upheld the regulations. The Supreme Court granted certiorari.

2) **Issue.** May the federal government condition the acceptance of federal funds by a particular project on the project's agreement to refrain from promoting or even discussing abortion?

3) **Held.** Yes. Judgment affirmed.

a) D's regulations do not exceed D's authority as long as they reflect a plausible construction of the plain language of the statute and do not otherwise conflict with Congress's expressed intent. The language of the statute is ambiguous and broad enough to allow D's interpretation. Courts normally must defer to the expertise of the agency charged with administering the law. The fact that the regulations are a change from the prior regulations is justified by D's experience under the prior policy.

b)   P claims that the regulations are discrimination based on viewpoint because they promote childbirth over abortion. But D has merely chosen to fund one activity to the exclusion of the other. The government has no obligation to subsidize counterpart rights once it decides to subsidize one protected right. D's regulations do not deny anyone a benefit, but merely require that public funds be spent for the purposes for which they were authorized. And they apply to the project, not to the grantee, who is left free to perform abortions and to advocate abortion in other contexts.

c)   P also claims that D's regulations violate a woman's Fifth Amendment right to choose whether to terminate her pregnancy. But Congress's refusal to fund abortion counseling and advocacy leaves a pregnant woman with the same choices as if Congress had chosen not to fund family-planning services at all. D's regulations do not affect a doctor's ability to provide information about abortion outside the context of a Title X project.

4)   Comment. The Court noted that government funding is not always sufficient by itself to justify government control over the content of expression. For example, government ownership of real property does not justify restriction of speech in such areas if they have been traditionally open to the public for expressive activity, and government payments to universities do not justify control of speech there. In this case, D's regulations do not significantly impinge upon the doctor-patient relationship because they do not apply to post-conception medical care, and the doctor can make it clear that advice regarding abortion is beyond the scope of the Title X program.

Insert the following as **VIII., F., 3., c.** *at p.* **219** (*and renumber subsequent section accordingly*):

c.   Political patronage--Elrod v. Burns, 427 U.S. 347 (1976).

Elrod v.
Burns

1)   Facts. Elrod (D), a Democrat, was elected county sheriff to replace a Republican sheriff. Burns (P) and other non-civil service employees of the sheriff's office were Republicans and were discharged by D solely because they were not Democrats. P challenged the dismissal.

2)   Issue. Does patronage hiring sufficiently advance important state interests to justify the consequent burdening of First Amendment interests?

3)   Held. No. Judgment reversed.

a)   Patronage has been practiced for a long time in American politics, but it restrains freedoms of belief and of association. Supporters claim that patronage insures effective government and efficient public employees, but there are less severe means for insuring effectiveness and efficiency. Employees may be discharged for good cause regardless of political affiliation and belief.

b) Another justification for patronage has been the need for political employees to be loyal to the prevailing party to implement the policies of elected officials. This justification is satisfied, however, by limiting patronage dismissals to those in policymaking positions.

c) A third rationale for patronage is "the preservation of the democratic process." However, political parties can clearly exist without active patronage practice.

d) For these reasons, patronage dismissals are not the least restrictive means for achieving any contribution they may make to the democratic process, and they impede the freedoms of association and speech which are essential for democratic government.

4) **Concurrence** (Stewart, Blackmun, JJ.). This case presents the sole question of whether a nonpolicymaking, nonconfidential government employee can be discharged solely because of political beliefs. He cannot.

5) **Dissent** (Powell, J., Burger, C.J., Rehnquist, J.). Ordinarily, government employment should not be conditioned on political beliefs. However, the patronage system has proven highly practical and fundamental in our political system. Patronage hiring attracts donations of time and money from supporters and strengthens party organizations. The limited role of patronage hiring in most government employment is such that the intrusion on First Amendment interests is minimal.

Insert the following in place of **VIII., F., 3., e.** *at p.* **221:**

Snepp v.
United States

e. **Contractual prior restraints--Snepp v. United States,** 444 U.S. 507 (1980).

1) **Facts.** Snepp (D), a CIA agent, had formally agreed, as a condition of his employment, not to divulge classified information and not to publish any information relating to the CIA without prepublication clearance from the CIA. Despite the agreement, D published a book about CIA activities in Vietnam without obtaining prepublication clearance. The United States (P) brought suit to enforce D's agreement by obtaining declaratory and injunctive relief and by having a constructive trust imposed on D's profits from the book. The parties agreed that the book did not contain classified material. The district court found for D, but the court of appeals reversed on the constructive trust issue, holding that, because D had published no classified information, his publication was protected by the First Amendment. P appeals.

2) **Issue.** May the CIA require, as a condition of employment, that its employees agree not to publish any agency information without first obtaining the approval of the CIA?

3) **Held.** Yes. Judgment reversed in part.

a) Whether D violated his trust does not depend on whether his book actually contained classified information. Because of the special trust given to D, he should have given the CIA a chance to approve his book prior to publication. Even if the book contains no classified information, the fact that a CIA employee freely published information, without prepublication review by the CIA, could be detrimental to vital national interests. The director of the CIA testified that as a result of D's activity and other similar publications, it has become more difficult for the CIA to develop and retain sources.

b) The court of appeals left P with no recourse except nominal and punitive damages. Such a remedy is an unreliable deterrent because of the uncertainty of proving tortious conduct justifying punitive damages. The remedy of a constructive trust is the natural and customary remedy for breach of a trust. It requires him to forfeit the fruit of his faithlessness.

4) **Dissent** (Stevens, Brennan, Marshall, JJ.). P's interest in confidentiality has not been compromised. The constructive trust is an unjustified prior restraint of criticism.

Insert the following in place of **VIII., F., 7., b.** *at p.* **228:**

b. **The "fairness doctrine"--Red Lion Broadcasting Co. v. FCC,** 395 U.S. 367 (1969).

Red Lion
Broadcasting
Co. v. FCC

1) **Facts.** The "fairness doctrine" was adopted by the FCC (D) early in the history of broadcasting. It required radio and television broadcasters to present discussion of public issues on broadcast stations and to provide fair coverage on each side of those issues. D also adopted regulations that required broadcasters to give any person who is personally attacked notice, a transcript of the attack, and a reasonable opportunity to respond. A broadcaster who chose to endorse or oppose a political candidate must also notify the opposition and allow them a reasonable opportunity to reply. Red Lion Broadcasting Company (P) challenged the rules.

2) **Issue.** May the government impose a fairness doctrine on licensed broadcasters?

3) **Held.** Yes. Judgment affirmed.

a) First Amendment protections apply to broadcasting, but the characteristics of broadcasting require special First Amendment standards. The physical realities of broadcasting limit its availability to a select few. Those who are unable to obtain licenses are barred from the airwaves. The First Amendment may not be construed to prohibit the government from restricting access to airwaves; otherwise, no one could effectively use radio or television broadcasting.

b) The First Amendment does not protect licensees more than nonlicensees. A licensee has no constitutional right to monopolize a radio frequency. The government may therefore require a licensee to act as a proxy or fiduciary with obligations to present views and voices representative of the public which would otherwise be barred from the airwaves.

c) Under the First Amendment, the right of broadcast viewers and listeners is paramount to the right of broadcasters.

d) To the extent that the fairness doctrine may prompt broadcasters to eliminate coverage of controversial issues, the doctrine may need to be reexamined, but so far it has not had such an effect.

4) Comment. In 1987, the FCC repealed the fairness doctrine on grounds that it "chilled" broadcasters' First Amendment rights.

Insert the following in place of **VIII., F., 7., c.** *at p.* **229:**

c. Other regulation of media content.

1) Right of access. The First Amendment does not require a government-regulated broadcaster to sell broadcast time to responsible parties for comment on public issues. In *Columbia Broadcasting System v. Democratic National Committee*, 412 U.S. 94 (1973), a radio station had refused to sell air time to individuals and groups who wished to express views on controversial issues. The Court held that the fairness doctrine required broadcast licensees to provide full and fair coverage of public issues, and that Congress and the FCC could appropriately give licensees the responsibility for editing.

2) Publicly-funded broadcasting. Congress cannot prohibit editorializing on the air by television and radio stations that accept federal subsidies. The Public Broadcasting Act of 1967 prohibited noncommercial educational stations that receive a grant from the Corporation for Public Broadcasting to "engage in editorializing." In *FCC v. League of Women Voters*, 468 U.S. 364 (1984), the Court held that provision unconstitutional. The government's interest in safeguarding the public's right to a balanced presentation of public issues, which justified the fairness doctrine in *Red Lion, supra*, was insufficient to justify the substantial abridgement of important journalistic freedoms that the ban imposed.

3) Cable television and "must carry" provisions. The Cable Television Consumer Protection and Competition Act of 1992 required cable television operators to carry, free of charge, the transmission of local broadcast television stations. The Court addressed a challenge to this "must carry" provision in *Turner Broadcasting System Inc. v. FCC*, 114 S. Ct. 2445 (1994). Five Justices agreed that because the cable systems do not share the physical limitations of the broadcast industry, the relaxed *Red Lion, supra*, standard should not apply. Instead, the Court applied the intermediate level of scrutiny applicable to content-neutral restrictions that impose an incidental burden on speech applied in *United States v. O'Brien, supra*. Applying this standard, four Justices remanded for further factfinding about whether the "must carry" provisions were truly necessary to protect the viability of broadcast television. Justice Stevens, concurring, would have upheld the "must carry" provisions based on deference to Congress's fact-findings. The four dissenting Justices considered the provisions to be content-based because they were based on a determination that broadcast television should be preferred over cable programmers whose access to cable channels would be reduced by the application of the "must carry" provisions.

Insert the following in place of **VIII., F., 8., c.** *at p.* **232:**

c. **Access to prisoners—Pell v. Procunier,** 417 U.S. 817 (1974).

Pell v.
Procunier

1) **Facts.** California prohibited face-to-face interviews among members of the press and individual inmates. The restriction was adopted in response to the prior practice of allowing such interviews, which created "public figures" of certain inmates and gave them disproportionate influence in the prison population, with attendant disciplinary problems. Several journalists challenged the regulation.

2) **Issue.** May a state prohibit the press from interviewing individual inmates where the general public does not have access to the inmates?

3) **Held.** Yes.

   a) The government may not interfere with the free press, but the Constitution does not require the government to give the press special access to information that is generally not available to members of the public.

4) **Dissent** (Douglas, Brennan, Marshall, JJ.). Prisons are public institutions, and the public relies on the press to provide information about its institutions. The absolute ban on press interviews is broader than necessary to protect legitimate governmental interests.

5) **Dissent** (Powell, J.). The ban impermissibly restrains the press's ability to perform its constitutional function of informing the people about their government's conduct.

6) **Comment.** If the government voluntarily grants access to prisoners, the public and the press must be treated equally. Where limitations that might be reasonable as to individual members of the public would impede effective reporting (*e.g.*, a prohibition on cameras), such limitations may not, consistent with reasonable prison rules, be used to hamper effective media presentation of what is seen by individual visitors. [*See* Houchins v. KQED, 438 U.S.1 (1978)]

Insert the following as **IX., A., 3., b.** *at p.* **235** *(and renumber subsequent section accordingly):*

b. **Prayer at graduation ceremonies--Lee v. Weisman,** 505 U.S. 577 (1992).

Lee v.
Weisman

1) **Facts.** Lee (D), the principal of a middle school, invited a rabbi to deliver prayers at a graduation exercise. He gave the rabbi a pamphlet containing guidelines that recommended public prayers be composed with "inclusiveness and sensitivity," and advised the rabbi that the prayers should be

nonsectarian. Weisman (P), one of the students, objected to the prayers' being part of the graduation ceremonies. The rabbi offered the prayers, which were nondenominational but did refer to and acknowledge God. P sued to enjoin school officials from inviting clergy members to deliver prayers at future graduations. The district court held that D's inclusion of prayers violated the Establishment Clause and granted the injunction because it violated the second *Lemon* test, *supra*; *i.e.*, it did not have a primary effect that neither advances nor inhibits religion. The court of appeals affirmed. The Supreme Court granted certiorari.

2) **Issue.** May a public school invite members of the clergy to offer prayers at graduation ceremonies?

3) **Held.** No. Judgment affirmed.

   a) At a minimum, the Constitution guarantees that government may not coerce anyone to support or participate in religion or its exercise. In this case, D, as a public official, directed the performance of a formal religious exercise at a graduation ceremony for a public secondary school. Although attendance is not a condition for receipt of the diploma, students' attendance and participation is in a fair and real sense obligatory, even for students who object to the religious exercise. Including the prayer thus violated the Constitution.

   b) The government not only decided to include a prayer and chose the clergyman, but advised the rabbi about the content of the prayer. This means that D directed and controlled the content of the prayer. But the Establishment Clause does not allow the government to compose official prayers to be recited as part of a religious program carried on by the government. The fact that D acted in good faith does not make its participation in the content of the prayer permissible.

   c) Religious beliefs and religious expression are too precious to be either proscribed or prescribed by the government. The government cannot choose to compose a nonsectarian prayer, even if were possible to devise one that would be acceptable to members of all faiths.

   d) The First Amendment protects speech and religion differently. Speech is protected by insuring its full expression even when the government participates, since some of the most important speech is directed at the government, but in religious debate or expression, the government is not a prime participant. The Free Exercise Clause is similar to the Free Speech Clause, but the Establishment Clause prevents the government from intervening in religious affairs, a prohibition with no counterpart in the speech provisions.

   e) Prayer exercises in public schools carry a particular risk of indirect coercion, particularly in the elementary and secondary public schools. Even at the graduation ceremony, there is pressure to stand and remain silent during the prayer, signifying a degree of adherence or assent. The government may not exact religious conformity from a student as the price of attending her own school graduation.

4) Concurrence (Blackmun, Stevens, O'Connor, JJ.). Under the Establishment Clause, the government may neither promote nor affiliate itself with any religious doctrine or organization, nor intrude into the internal affairs of any religious institution. In *Engel v. Vitale*, 370 U.S. 421 (1962), the Court held for the first time that a prayer selected by school officials could not be recited in a public school, even though it was "denominationally neutral." In *Abington School District v. Schempp,* 374 U.S. 203 (1963), the Court held unconstitutional a public school's opening exercises that consisted of a reading from the Bible or a recitation of the Lord's Prayer. The prayers offered at the graduation ceremonies in this case are likewise prohibited by the Constitution. Even if no one is forced to participate, mixing government and religion threatens free government because it conveys a message of exclusion to all who do not adhere to the favored belief.

5) Dissent (Scalia, J., Rehnquist, C.J., White, Thomas, JJ.). The meaning of the Establishment Clause must be determined by reference to historical practices and understandings. Yet the majority ignores history in its holding. The tradition of invocations and benedictions at graduation ceremonies is as old as the ceremonies themselves. Even the Declaration of Independence appeals to "the Supreme Judge of the world," and relies on the "protection of divine Providence." Presidents, beginning with George Washington, have included prayer in their official acts. The Court's test of psychological coercion is boundless and boundlessly manipulable, and is based on facts that are not true in any relevant sense. Even if students were coerced to stand, which they were not, such an act does not establish a "participation" in a religious exercise, any more than standing for the Pledge of Allegiance moments earlier constituted coerced approval of the political message it contains. The Establishment Clause was aimed at coercion of religious orthodoxy and financial support by force of law and threat of penalty, but P in this case faced no threat of penalty or discipline. This situation is entirely different from daily prayers in classroom settings where parents are not present, which could raise concerns about state interference with the liberty of parents to direct the religious upbringing of their children. The Court has replaced the unfortunate *Lemon* test with its psycho-coercion test, which is not at all grounded in our people's historical practice. The Constitution must have deep foundations in the historical practices of our people, not the changeable philosophical predilections of the Justices of the Court.

Insert the following as **X., B., 7.** *at p.* **258:**

7. **Complete Destruction of Property Value--Lucas v. South Carolina Coastal Council,** 505 U.S. 1003 (1992).

   Lucas v. South Carolina Coastal Council

   a. **Facts.** Lucas (P) purchased two residential lots near the seashore, intending to build single-family homes. Two years later, South Carolina passed the Beachfront Management Act, which required P to obtain a permit from the South Carolina Coastal Council (D) before changing the use of his land. This effectively barred P from building homes on his land. P sued, and the trial court found that he was entitled to compensation because his property was now valueless. The South Carolina Supreme Court reversed, and the United States Supreme Court granted certiorari.

b. Issue. Must the government compensate a private landowner if the government's regulation prohibits all economically productive or beneficial uses of the land?

c. Held. Yes. Judgment reversed.

    1) In *Pennsylvania Coal Co. v. Mahon*, *supra*, the Court held that the Takings Clause extended beyond direct appropriations of property to regulations that go "too far." There are at least two categories of regulatory action that are compensable: (i) physical invasions, *e.g.,* requiring landlords to allow television cable companies to put cable in their apartment buildings [*see* Loretto v. Teleprompter Manhattan CATV Corp., *supra*]; and (ii) denial of all economically beneficial or productive use of land.

    2) The functional basis for allowing the government, without making compensation, to affect property values through regulation is the recognition that the government could not operate if it had to pay for every change in the law that affected property values, but this basis does not apply where the government deprives a landowner of all economically beneficial uses. Such regulation really presses the private property into a form of public service under the guise of mitigating serious public harm.

    3) P claims that the finding that his property has been rendered valueless requires compensation, regardless of the reason for the regulation. Prior opinions held that harmful or noxious uses of property may be proscribed by government regulation without compensation, but this really means that land-use regulation does not effect a taking if it "substantially advances legitimate state interests." But D cannot take land without compensation merely by reciting a noxious-use or benefit-conferring rationale. D could avoid paying compensation only if the nature of P's estate shows that the proscribed use interests were not part of his title to begin with; *i.e.,* that his bundle of rights did not include an expectation that the state would not eliminate all economically valuable use.

    4) Confiscatory regulations cannot be newly legislated without compensation; they must inhere in the title itself, in the restrictions that background principles of the state's law of property and nuisance already place on land ownership. The fact that a particular use has long been engaged in by similarly situated owners, or that other landowners similarly situated are permitted to continue the use denied to P, demonstrate a lack of any common law prohibition on the use. In this case, it is unlikely that common law principles would have prevented P from building a house on the land, but this must be determined on remand.

d. Concurrence (Kennedy, J.). Where a regulation deprives the property of all value, whether it is a taking depends on whether the deprivation is contrary to reasonable, investment-backed expectations. The state supreme court erred in not evaluating P's reasonable expectations. And D did not act until after the property had been zoned for residential development and other parcels had been built on, so that the remaining lots have to bear the entire burden of the regulation.

e. **Dissent** (Blackmun, J.). The state may prevent any use of property it finds to be harmful to its citizens, and a state statute is entitled to a presumption of constitutionality. The record supports D's assessment that the building restriction is necessary to protect people and property, and the Court has departed from traditional rules by creating a new scheme for regulations that eliminate all economic value.

f. **Dissent** (Stevens, J.). The Court's new categorical rule is arbitrary since it distinguishes between a landowner whose property is diminished in value 95% and who recovers nothing, and a landowner whose property is diminished in value 100% and recovers its full value. The reliance on a common law exception prevents the states from developing the common law in response to new learning, such as the significance of endangered species and wetlands.

Insert the following as **X., B., 8.** *at p.* 258:

8. **Proportionality Requirement--Dolan v. City of Tigard,** 512 U.S. 374 (1994).

a. **Facts.** Dolan (P) owned a plumbing and electric supply store in the City of Tigard (D). P's store was on a 1.67 acre lot that bordered the Fanno Creek and was therefore in the floodplain. P applied to D for a permit to double the size of her store and pave a parking lot. D's planning commission granted P's application, subject to D's Community Development Code ("CDC"). The CDC requires property owners to comply with a 15% open space and landscaping requirement as well as to dedicate land for a pedestrian/bicycle pathway. The total dedication was 10% of P's property for the pathway and for drainage improvements on the floodplain. P sought variances, but D refused, finding that the pedestrian/bicycle pathway might offset some of the traffic on area streets, and that the required floodplain dedication was related to P's plan to intensify development, which would likely increase storm water flow into the creek. P challenged the dedication requirements, but the state courts upheld them. The Supreme Court granted certiorari.

b. **Issue.** May a city condition the approval of a building permit on the dedication of a portion of the property for public purposes?

c. **Held.** No. Judgment reversed.

1) The Takings Clause of the Fifth Amendment was intended to prevent the government from forcing some people alone to bear public burdens that should be borne by the public as a whole. If D had simply required P to dedicate her land for public use, a taking clearly would have occurred. However, land use regulation does not constitute a taking if it "substantially advances legitimate state interests and does not deny an owner economically viable use of his land." In this case, D's requirements are adjudicative in nature because they apply only to P's land, as opposed to common zoning requirements which are legislative in nature and apply to entire areas.

D's requirements also do not merely limit P's use of the land, but constitute an actual conveyance of property.

2) The two-part test for takings cases requires (i) a determination as to whether an "essential nexus" exists between the legitimate state interest and the conditions imposed; and (ii) a sufficient degree of connection between the conditions and the projected impact of the proposed development.

3) D's interests in preventing flooding and reducing traffic congestion are legitimate public purposes.

4) A variety of approaches have been adopted by courts to find the required degree of connection between the regulation and the proposed development. The best approach is an intermediate one that requires the city to show a "reasonable relationship" between the required dedication of land and the expected impact of the proposed development. However, the term is confusingly similar to the term "rational basis," so instead we will use the term "rough proportionality." This requires D to "make some sort of individualized determination that the required dedication is related both in nature and extent to the impact of the proposed development."

5) In this case, D could have satisfied its floodplain interests by simply requiring P to leave 15% of the property as open space. D never explained why a public greenway, rather than a private one, was required for flood control. D's permanent recreational easement would destroy P's right to exclude others from her property and control access to her store. D has failed to show the required reasonable relationship between the floodplain easement and P's proposed new building. D has also failed to quantify its findings that purportedly support the dedication for the pedestrian/bicycle pathway.

d.   **Dissent** (Stevens, Blackmun, Ginsburg, JJ.). Prior cases have held that a restriction on the right to exclude others is permissible unless it unreasonably impairs the value or use of the property. P has shown no adverse impact on the value of her property. The Court should merely determine whether the required nexus is present and avoid considerations of proportionality. The Court also loses sight of the fact that P has suffered no "taking." She merely challenges the terms D is offering in exchange for her building permit. As long as the government can show that the conditions it imposes in a land-use permit are rational, impartial, and conducive to fulfilling the aims of a valid land-use plan, the courts should apply a strong presumption of validity.

e.   **Dissent** (Souter, J.). If as the Court determined there is no relation between flood control and the permanent recreational easement, it is not because of lack of proportionality but because of no rational connection, which is simply the *Nollan, supra,* nexus analysis. But *Nollan* has not been properly applied here, because the Court has placed the burden of proving a relationship on D, contrary to the normal rule that the government in these cases is presumed to have acted in a constitutional manner.

Insert the following as **XI., B., 2.** *at p.* **260** (*and renumber subsequent section accordingly*):

2. **Government's Failure to Act--DeShaney v. Winnebago County Department of Social Services,** 489 U.S. 189 (1989).

   a. **Facts.** DeShaney (P), a two-year-old child, had been the victim of child abuse by his father. The incidents were reported to the Winnebago Department of Social Services (D), which investigated but took no action. One year later, after P was treated at a hospital for further abuse, D required P's father to undergo counseling and to have his girlfriend move out, but the father never fully complied with these requirements. During the next year, D's caseworker recorded additional incidents of abuse, but took no action. P's father finally beat P so badly that he suffered permanent brain damage. P sued D, claiming D had deprived him of his liberty without due process of law. The lower courts granted judgment for D. The Supreme Court granted certiorari.

   b. **Issue.** May the government's failure to protect a child from his parent's abuse constitute a violation of substantive due process?

   c. **Held.** No. Judgment affirmed.

      1) Nothing in the Due Process Clause requires the state to protect the life, liberty, and property of citizens against invasion by private actors. The clause protects people from the state; it does not require the state to protect citizens from each other.

      2) The Due Process Clause does not confer an affirmative right to governmental aid, even when necessary to secure life, liberty, or property interests. Because the clause does not impose such an obligation, the state cannot be held liable under the clause for injuries that could have been avoided had the state assumed the obligation. There is no special relationship between P and D that arose merely because D knew P was in danger. If any such relationship is desired, the people may, through their legislatures, adopt a tort law remedy.

   d. **Dissent** (Brennan, Marshall, Blackmun, JJ.). D in effect cut off private sources of help by preempting them. When D refused to help, it should not be permitted to avoid responsibility for the harm that resulted from its refusal.

Insert the following in place of **XI., D., 3.** *at p.* **267:**

3. **Private Company Towns--Marsh v. Alabama,** 326 U.S. 501 (1946).

   a. **Facts.** The Town of Chickasaw was entirely owned by the Gulf Shipbuilding Corporation. The town consisted of homes, streets, a sewage plant, and a business district which was accessible from a public highway. A notice posted in the stores stated that they were private property and that no solicitation was allowed without written permission. Marsh (D), a Jehovah's Witness, began distributing religious literature outside the post office. She refused to leave after being warned that she needed permission to distribute the literature and that no permit would be issued. D was arrested and convicted of trespassing. D appeals.

b.   Issue. May a company town forbid the distribution of religious literature in its streets?

c.   Held. No. Judgment reversed.

1)   A company town's power over its inhabitants is not the same as a homeowner's right to regulate his guests. Ownership does not always mean absolute dominion. The more a private owner extends the use of his property to the public, the more his rights must yield to the rights of those who use his property.

2)   The company cannot curtail the First Amendment rights of the people as it has done here, and any state action to enforce such a curtailment, such as prosecuting D, violates the First and Fourteenth Amendments. The constitutional rights of freedom of press and religion outweigh the constitutional rights of property owners who open their property to the public.

d.   Comment. At one time, many workers lived in houses owned by their employers, including about one-half of the miners in the United States.

TABLE OF CASES
Supplement

(Page numbers of briefed cases in bold)

Notes

Notes

Notes

Notes

Publications Catalog

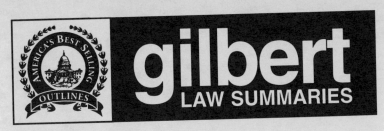

Gilbert Law Summaries are the best selling outlines in the country, and have set the standard for excellence since they were first introduced more than twenty-five years ago. It's Gilbert's unique combination of features that makes it the one study aid you'll turn to for all your study needs!

Accounting and Finance for Lawyers
TBA

Basic Accounting Principles; Definitions of Accounting Terms; Balance Sheet; Income Statement; Statement of Changes in Financial Position; Consolidated Financial Statements; Accumulation of Financial Data; Financial Statement Analysis.
ISBN: 0-15-900382-2   Pages: 136 $16.95

Administrative Law
By Professor Michael R. Asimow, U.C.L.A.

Separation of Powers and Controls Over Agencies; (including Delegation of Power) Constitutional Right to Hearing (including Liberty and Property Interests Protected by Due Process, and Rulemaking-Adjudication Distinction); Adjudication Under Administrative Procedure Act (APA); Formal Adjudication (including Notice, Discovery, Burden of Proof, Finders of Facts and Reasons); Adjudicatory Decision Makers (including Administrative Law Judges (ALJs), Bias, Improper Influences, Ex Parte Communications, Familiarity with Record, Res Judicata); Rulemaking Procedures (including Notice, Public Participation, Publication, Impartiality of Rulemakers, Rulemaking Record); Obtaining Information (including Subpoena Power, Privilege Against Self-incrimination, Freedom of Information Act, Government in Sunshine Act, Attorneys' Fees); Scope of Judicial Review; Reviewability of Agency Decisions (including Mandamus, Injunction, Sovereign Immunity, Federal Tort Claims Act); Standing to Seek Judicial Review and Timing.
ISBN: 0-15-900000-9 Pages: 300 $19.95

Agency and Partnership
By Professor Richard J. Conviser, Chicago Kent

Agency: Rights and Liabilities Between Principal and Agent (including Agent's Fiduciary Duty, Principal's Right to Indemnification); Contractual Rights Between Principal (or Agent) and Third Persons (including Creation of Agency Relationship, Authority of Agent, Scope of Authority, Termination of Authority, Ratification, Liability on Agents, Contracts); Tort Liability (including Respondeat Superior, Master-Servant Relationship, Scope of Employment). Partnership: Property Rights of Partner; Formation of Partnership; Relations Between Partners (including Fiduciary Duty); Authority of Partner to Bind Partnership; Dissolution and Winding up of Partnership; Limited Partnerships.
ISBN: 0-15-900327-X Pages: 142 $16.95

Antitrust
By Professor Thomas M. Jorde, U.C. Berkeley, Mark A. Lemley, University of Texas, and Professor Robert H. Mnookin, Harvard University

Common Law Restraints of Trade; Federal Antitrust Laws (including Sherman Act, Clayton Act, Federal Trade Commission Act, Interstate Commerce Requirement, Antitrust Remedies); Monopolization (including Relevant Market, Purposeful Act Requirement, Attempts and Conspiracy to Monopolize); Collaboration Among Competitors (including Horizontal Restraints, Rule of Reason vs. Per Se Violations, Price Fixing, Division of Markets, Group Boycotts); Vertical Restraints (including Tying Arrangements); Mergers and Acquisitions (including Horizontal Mergers, Brown Shoe Analysis, Vertical Mergers, Conglomerate Mergers); Price Discrimination — Robinson-Patman Act; Unfair Methods of Competition; Patent Laws and Their Antitrust Implications; Exemptions From Antitrust Laws (including Motor, Rail, and Interstate Water Carriers, Bank Mergers, Labor Unions, Professional Baseball).
ISBN: 0-15-900328-8   Pages: 193 $16.95

Bankruptcy
By Professor Ned W. Waxman, College of William and Mary

Participants in the Bankruptcy Case; Jurisdiction and Procedure; Commencement and Administration of the Case (including Eligibility, Voluntary Case, Involuntary Case, Meeting of Creditors, Debtor's Duties); Officers of the Estate (including Trustee, Examiner, United States Trustee); Bankruptcy Estate; Creditor's Right of Setoff; Trustee's Avoiding Powers; Claims of Creditors (including Priority Claims and Tax Claims); Debtor's Exemptions; Nondischargeable Debts; Effects of Discharge; Reaffirmation Agreements; Administrative Powers (including Automatic Stay, Use, Sale, or Lease of Property); Chapter 7- Liquidation; Chapter 11- Reorganization; Chapter 13-Individual With Regular Income; Chapter 12- Family Farmer With Regular Annual Income.
ISBN: 0-15-900245-1   Pages: 356 $19.95

Business Law
By Professor Robert D. Upp, Los Angeles City College

Torts and Crimes in Business; Law of Contracts (including Contract Formation, Consideration, Statute of Frauds, Contract Remedies, Third Parties); Sales (including Transfer of Title and Risk of Loss, Performance and Remedies, Products Liability, Personal Property Security Interest); Property (including Personal Property, Bailments, Real Property, Landlord and Tenant); Agency; Business Organizations (including Partnerships, Corporations); Commercial Paper; Government Regulation of Business (including Taxation, Antitrust, Environmental Protection, and Bankruptcy).
ISBN: 0-15-900005-X   Pages: 295 $16.95

California Bar Performance Test Skills
By Professor Peter J. Honigsberg, University of San Francisco

Hints to Improve Writing; How to Approach the Performance Test; Legal Analysis Documents (including Writing a Memorandum of Law, Writing a Client Letter, Writing Briefs); Fact Gathering and Fact Analysis Documents; Tactical and Ethical Considerations; Sample Interrogatories, Performance Tests, and Memoranda.
ISBN: 0-15-900152-8   Pages: 216 $17.95

Civil Procedure
By Professor Thomas D. Rowe, Jr., Duke University, and Professor Richard L. Marcus, U.C. Hastings

Territorial (personal) Jurisdiction, including Venue and Forum Non Conveniens; Subject Matter Jurisdiction, covering Diversity Jurisdiction, Federal Question Jurisdiction; Erie Doctrine and Federal Common Law; Pleadings including Counterclaims, Cross-Claims, Supplemental Pleadings; Parties, including Joinder and Class Actions; Discovery, including Devices, Scope, Sanctions and Discovery Conference; Summary Judgment; Pretrial Conference and Settlements; Trial, including Right to Jury Trial, Motions, Jury Instruction and Arguments, and Post-Verdict Motions; Appeals; Claim Preclusion (Res Judicata) and Issue Preclusion (Collateral Estoppel).
ISBN: 0-15-900272-9   Pages: 447 $19.95

Commercial Paper and Payment Law
By Professor Douglas J. Whaley, Ohio State University

Types of Commercial Paper; Negotiability; Negotiation; Holders in Due Course; Claims and Defenses on Negotiable Instruments (including Real Defenses and Personal Defenses); Liability of the Parties (including Merger Rule, Suits on the Instrument, Warranty Suits, Conversion); Bank Deposits and Collections; Forgery or Alteration of Negotiable Instruments; Electronic Banking.
ISBN: 0-15-900367-9   Pages: 222 $17.95

Community Property
By Professor William A. Reppy, Jr., Duke University

Classifying Property as Community or Separate; Management and Control of Property; Liability for Debts; Division of Property at Divorce; Devolution of Property at Death; Relationships Short of Valid Marriage; Conflict of Laws Problems; Constitutional Law Issues (including Equal Protection Standards, Due Process Issues).
ISBN: 0-15-900235-4   Pages: 188 $17.95

Call 1-800-787-8717 or visit our web site at http://www.gilbertlaw.com for more information.

gilbert
LAW SUMMARIES

Conflict of Laws

By Dean Herma Hill Kay, U.C. Berkeley

Domicile; Jurisdiction (including Notice and Opportunity to be Heard, Minimum Contacts, Types of Jurisdiction); Choice of Law (including Vested Rights Approach, Most Significant Relationship Approach, Governmental Interest Analysis); Choice of Law in Specific Substantive Areas; Traditional Defenses Against Application of Foreign Law; Constitutional Limitations and Overriding Federal Law (including Due Process Clause, Full Faith and Credit Clause, Conflict Between State and Federal Law); Recognition and Enforcement of Foreign Judgments.
ISBN: 0-15-900011-4   Pages: 260 $18.95

Constitutional Law

By Professor Jesse H. Choper, U.C. Berkeley

Powers of Federal Government (including Judicial Power, Powers of Congress, Presidential Power, Foreign Affairs Power); Intergovernmental Immunities, Separation of Powers; Regulation of Foreign Commerce; Regulation of Interstate Commerce; Taxation of Interstate and Foreign Commerce; Due Process, Equal Protection; "State Action" Requirements; Freedoms of Speech, Press, and Association; Freedom of Religion.
ISBN: 0-15-900265-6   Pages: 335 $19.95

Contracts

By Professor Melvin A. Eisenberg, U.C. Berkeley

Consideration (including Promissory Estoppel, Moral or Past Consideration); Mutual Assent; Defenses (including Mistake, Fraud, Duress, Unconscionability, Statute of Frauds, Illegality); Third-Party Beneficiaries; Assignment of Rights and Delegation of Duties; Conditions; Substantial Performance; Material vs. Minor Breach; Anticipatory Breach; Impossibility; Discharge; Remedies (including Damages, Specific Performance, Liquidated Damages).
ISBN: 0-15-900014-9   Pages: 326 $19.95

Corporations

By Professor Jesse H. Choper, U.C. Berkeley, and Professor Melvin A. Eisenberg, U.C. Berkeley

Formalities; "De Jure" vs. "De Facto"; Promoters; Corporate Powers; Ultra Vires Transactions; Powers, Duties, and Liabilities of Officers and Directors; Allocation of Power Between Directors and Shareholders; Conflicts of Interest in Corporate Transactions; Close Corporations; Insider Trading; Rule 10b-5 and Section 16(b); Shareholders' Voting Rights; Shareholders' Right to Inspect Records; Shareholders' Suits; Capitalization (including Classes of Shares, Preemptive Rights, Consideration for Shares); Dividends; Redemption of Shares; Fundamental Changes in Corporate Structure; Applicable Conflict of Laws Principles.
ISBN: 0-15-900342-3   Pages: 308 $19.95

Criminal Law

By Professor George E. Dix, University of Texas

Elements of Crimes (including Actus Reus, Mens Rea, Causation); Vicarious Liability; Complicity in Crime; Criminal Liability of Corporations;

Defenses (including Insanity, Diminished Capacity, Intoxication, Ignorance, Self-Defense); Inchoate Crimes; Homicide; Other Crimes Against the Person; Crimes Against Habitation (including Burglary, Arson); Crimes Against Property; Offenses Against Government; Offenses Against Administration of Justice.
ISBN: 0-15-900217-6   Pages: 271 $18.95

Criminal Procedure

By Professor Paul Marcus, College of William and Mary, and Professor Charles H. Whitebread, U.S.C.

Exclusionary Rule; Arrests and Other Detentions; Search and Seizure; Privilege Against Self-Incrimination; Confessions; Preliminary Hearing; Bail; Indictment; Speedy Trial; Competency to Stand Trial; Government's Obligation to Disclose Information; Right to Jury Trial; Right to Counsel; Right to Confront Witnesses; Burden of Proof; Insanity; Entrapment; Guilty Pleas; Sentencing; Death Penalty; Ex Post Facto Issues; Appeal; Habeas Corpus; Juvenile Offenders; Prisoners' Rights; Double Jeopardy.
ISBN: 0-15-900347-4   Pages: 271 $18.95

Dictionary of Legal Terms

Gilbert Staff

Contains Over 3,500 Legal Terms and Phrases; Law School Shorthand; Common Abbreviations; Latin and French Legal Terms; Periodical Abbreviations; Governmental Abbreviations.
ISBN: 0-15-900018-1   Pages: 163 $14.95

Estate and Gift Tax

By Professor John H. McCord, University of Illinois

Gross Estate Allowable Deductions Under Estate Tax (including Expenses, Indebtedness, and Taxes, Deductions for Losses, Charitable Deduction, Marital Deduction); Taxable Gifts; Deductions; Valuation; Computation of Tax; Returns and Payment of Tax; Tax on Generation-Skipping Transfers.
ISBN: 0-15-900019-X   Pages: 283 $18.95

Evidence

By Professor Jon R. Waltz, Northwestern University, and Roger C. Park, University of Minnesota

Direct Evidence; Circumstantial Evidence; Rulings on Admissibility; Relevancy; Materiality; Character Evidence; Hearsay and the Hearsay Exceptions; Privileges; Competency to Testify; Opinion Evidence and Expert Witnesses; Direct Examination; Cross-Examination; Impeachment; Real, Demonstrative, and Scientific Evidence; Judicial Notice; Burdens of Proof; Parol Evidence Rule.
ISBN: 0-15-900020-3   Pages: 359 $19.95

Federal Courts

By Professor William A. Fletcher, U.C. Berkeley

Article III Courts; "Case or Controversy" Requirement; Justiciability; Advisory Opinions; Political Questions; Ripeness; Mootness; Standing; Congressional Power Over Federal Court Jurisdiction; Supreme Court Jurisdiction; District Court Subject Matter Jurisdiction (including Federal Question Jurisdiction, Diversity

Jurisdiction); Pendent and Ancillary Jurisdiction; Removal Jurisdiction; Venue; Forum Non Conveniens; Law Applied in the Federal Courts (including Erie Doctrine); Federal Law in the State Courts; Abstention; Habeas Corpus for State Prisoners; Federal Injunctions Against State Court Proceedings; Eleventh Amendment.
ISBN: 0-15-900232-X   Pages: 310 $19.95

Future Interests & Perpetuities

By Professor Jesse Dukeminier, U.C.L.A.

Reversions; Possibilities of Reverter; Rights of Entry; Remainders; Executory Interest; Rules Restricting Remainders and Executory Interest; Rights of Owners of Future Interests; Construction of Instruments; Powers of Appointment; Rule Against Perpetuities (including Reforms of the Rule).
ISBN: 0-15-900218-4   Pages: 219 $17.95

Income Tax I - Individual

By Professor Michael R. Asimow, U.C.L.A.

Gross Income; Exclusions; Income Splitting by Gifts, Personal Service Income, Income Earned by Children, Income of Husbands and Wives, Below-Market Interest on Loans, Taxation of Trusts; Business and Investment Deductions; Personal Deductions; Tax Rates; Credits; Computation of Basis, Gain, or Loss; Realization; Nonrecognition of Gain or Loss; Capital Gains and Losses; Alternative Minimum Tax; Tax Accounting Problems.
ISBN: 0-15-900266-4   Pages: 312 $19.95

Income Tax II - Partnerships, Corporations, Trusts

By Professor Michael R. Asimow, U.C.L.A.

Taxation of Partnerships (including Current Partnership Income, Contributions of Property to Partnership, Sale of Partnership Interest, Distributions, Liquidations); Corporate Taxation (including Corporate Distributions, Sales of Stock and Assets, Reorganizations); S Corporations; Federal Income Taxation of Trusts.
ISBN: 0-15-900024-6   Pages: 237 $17.95

Labor Law

By Professor James C. Oldham, Georgetown University, and Robert J. Gelhaus

Statutory Foundations of Present Labor Law (including National Labor Relations Act, Taft-Hartley, Norris-LaGuardia Act, Landrum-Griffin Act); Organizing Campaigns, Selection of the Bargaining Representative; Collective Bargaining (including Negotiating the Agreement, Lockouts, Administering the Agreement, Arbitration); Strikes, Boycotts, and Picketing; Concerted Activity Protected Under the NLRA; Civil Rights Legislation; Grievance; Federal Regulation of Compulsory Union Membership Arrangements; State Regulation of Compulsory Membership Agreements; "Right to Work" Laws; Discipline of Union Members; Election of Union Officers; Corruption.
ISBN: 0-15-900340-7   Pages: 243 $17.95

Legal Ethics

By Professor Thomas D. Morgan, George Washington University

Regulating Admission to Practice Law; Preventing Unauthorized Practice of Law; Contract Between Client and Lawyer (including Lawyer's Duties Regarding Accepting Employment, Spheres of Authority of Lawyer and Client, Obligation of Client to Lawyer, Terminating the Lawyer-Client Relationship); Attorney-Client Privilege; Professional Duty of Confidentiality; Conflicts of Interest; Obligations to Third Persons and the Legal System (including Counseling Illegal or Fraudulent Conduct, Threats of Criminal Prosecution); Special Obligations in Litigation (including Limitations on Advancing Money to Client, Duty to Reject Certain Actions, Lawyer as Witness); Solicitation and Advertising; Specialization; Disciplinary Process; Malpractice; Special Responsibilities of Judges.
ISBN: 0-15-900026-2   Pages: 252 $18.95

Legal Research, Writing and Analysis

By Professor Peter J. Honigsberg, University of San Francisco

Court Systems; Precedent; Case Reporting System (including Regional and State Reporters, Headnotes and the West Key Number System, Citations and Case Finding); Statutes, Constitutions, and Legislative History; Secondary Sources (including Treatises, Law Reviews, Digests, Restatements); Administrative Agencies (including Regulations, Looseleaf Services); Shepard's Citations; Computers in Legal Research; Reading and Understanding a Case (including Briefing a Case); Using Legal Sourcebooks; Basic Guidelines for Legal Writing; Organizing Your Research; Writing a Memorandum of Law; Writing a Brief; Writing an Opinion or Client Letter.
ISBN: 0-15-900305-9   Pages: 162 $16.95

Multistate Bar Examination

By Professor Richard J. Conviser, Chicago Kent

Structure of the Exam; Governing Law; Effective Use of Time; Scoring of the Exam; Jurisdictions Using the Exam; Subject Matter Outlines; Practice Tests, Answers, and Subject Matter Keys; Glossary of Legal Terms and Definitions; State Bar Examination Directory; Listing of Reference Materials for Multistate Subjects.
ISBN: 0-15-900246-X   Pages: 210 $19.95

Personal Property

Gilbert Staff

Acquisitions; Ownership Through Possession (including Wild Animals, Abandoned Chattels); Finders of Lost Property; Bailments; Possessory Liens; Pledges; Trover; Gift; Accession; Confusion (Commingling); Fixtures; Crops (Emblements); Adverse Possession; Prescriptive Rights (Acquiring Ownership of Easements or Profits by Adverse Use).
ISBN: 0-15-900360-1   Pages: 69 $14.95

Professional Responsibility

(see Legal Ethics)

Call 1-800-787-8717 or visit our web site at http://www.gilbertlaw.com for more information.

gilbert
LAW SUMMARIES

Property
By Professor Jesse Dukeminier, U.C.L.A.

Possession (including Wild Animals, Bailments, Adverse Possession); Gifts and Sales of Personal Property; Freehold Possessory Estates; Future Interests (including Reversion, Possibility of Reverter, Right of Entry, Executory Interests, Rule Against Perpetuities); Tenancy in Common; Joint Tenancy; Tenancy by the Entirety; Condominiums; Cooperatives; Marital Property; Landlord and Tenant; Easements and Covenants; Nuisance; Rights in Airspace and Water; Right to Support; Zoning; Eminent Domain; Sale of Land (including Mortgage, Deed, Warranties of Title); Methods of Title Assurance (including Recording System, Title Registration, Title Insurance).

ISBN: 0-15-900032-7   Pages: 496 $21.95

Remedies
By Professor John A. Bauman, U.C.L.A., and Professor Kenneth H. York, Pepperdine University

Damages; Equitable Remedies (including Injunctions and Specific Performance); Restitution; Injuries to Tangible Property Interests; Injuries to Business and Commercial Interests (including Business Torts, Inducing Breach of Contract, Patent Infringement, Unfair Competition, Trade Defamation); Injuries to Personal Dignity and Related Interests (including Defamation, Privacy, Religious Status, Civil and Political Rights); Personal Injury and Death; Fraud; Duress, Undue Influence, and Unconscionable Conduct; Mistake; Breach of Contract; Unenforceable Contracts (including Statute of Frauds, Impossibility, Lack of Contractual Capacity, Illegality).

ISBN: 0-15-900325-3   Pages: 375 $20.95

Sale and Lease of Goods
By Professor Douglas J. Whaley, Ohio State University

UCC Article 2; Sales Contract (including Offer and Acceptance, Parol Evidence Rule, Statute of Frauds, Assignment and Delegation, Revision of Contract Terms); Types of Sales (including Cash Sale Transactions, Auctions, "Sale or Return" and "Sale on Approval" Transactions); Warranties (including Express and Implied Warranties, Privity, Disclaimer, Consumer Protection Statutes); Passage of Title; Performance of the Contract; Anticipatory Breach; Demand for Assurance of Performance; Unforeseen Circumstances; Risk of Loss; Remedies; Documents of Title; Lease of Goods; International Sale of Goods.

ISBN: 0-15-900219-2   Pages: 222 $17.95

Secured Transactions
By Professor Douglas J. Whaley, Ohio State University

Coverage of Article 9; Creation of a Security Interest (including Attachment, Security Agreement, Value, Debtor's Rights in the Collateral); Perfection; Filing; Priorities; Bankruptcy Proceedings and Article 9; Default Proceedings; Bulk Transfers.

ISBN: 0-15-900231-1   Pages: 213 $17.95

Securities Regulation
By Professor David H. Barber, and Professor Niels B. Schaumann, William Mitchell College of Law

Jurisdiction and Interstate Commerce; Securities Act of 1933 (including Registration Requirements and Exemptions); Securities Exchange Act of 1934 (including Rule 10b-5, Tender Offers, Proxy Solicitations Regulation, Insider Transactions); Regulation of the Securities Markets; Multinational Transactions; State Regulation of Securities Transactions.

ISBN: 0-15-9000326-1   Pages: 415 $20.95

Torts
By Professor Marc A. Franklin, Stanford University

Intentional Torts; Negligence; Strict Liability; Products Liability; Nuisance; Survival of Tort Actions; Wrongful Death; Immunity; Release and Contribution; Indemnity; Workers' Compensation; No-Fault Auto Insurance; Defamation; Invasion of Privacy; Misrepresentation; Injurious Falsehood; Interference With Economic Relations; Unjustifiable Litigation.

ISBN: 0-15-900220-6   Pages: 439 $19.95

Trusts
By Professor Edward C. Halbach, Jr., U.C. Berkeley

Elements of a Trust; Trust Creation; Transfer of Beneficiary's Interest (including Spendthrift Trusts); Charitable Trusts (including Cy Pres Doctrine); Trustee's Responsibilities, Power, Duties, and Liabilities; Duties and Liabilities of Beneficiaries; Accounting for Income and Principal; Power of Settlor to Modify or Revoke; Powers of Trustee Beneficiaries or Courts to Modify or Terminate; Termination of Trusts by Operation of Law; Resulting Trusts; Purchase Money Resulting Trusts; Constructive Trusts.

ISBN: 0-15-900039-4   Pages: 268 $18.95

Wills
By Professor Stanley M. Johanson, University of Texas

Intestate Succession; Simultaneous Death; Advancements; Disclaimer; Killer of Decedent; Elective Share Statutes; Pretermitted Child Statutes; Homestead; Formal Requisites of a Will; Revocation of Wills; Incorporation by Reference; Pour-Over Gift in Inter Vivos Trust; Joint Wills; Contracts Relating to Wills; Lapsed Gifts; Ademption; Exoneration of Liens; Will Contests; Probate and Estate Administration.

ISBN: 0-15-900040-8   Pages: 310 $19.95

Gilbert Law Summaries
FIRST YEAR PROGRAM

Includes Five Gilbert Outlines:

■ **Civil Procedure**
By Professor Thomas D. Rowe, Jr.
Duke University Law School, and
Professor Richard L. Marcus
U.C. Hastings School Of Law

■ **Contracts**
By Professor Melvin A. Eisenberg
U.C. Berkeley School Of Law

■ **Criminal Law**
By Professor George E. Dix
University Of Texas School Of Law

■ **Property**
By Professor Jesse Dukeminier
U.C.L.A. Law School

■ **Torts**
By Professor Marc A. Franklin
Stanford University Law School

Plus—

■ **Gilbert's Pocket Size Law Dictionary**
Published By Harcourt Brace

■ **The 8 Secrets Of Top Exam Performance In Law School**
By Professor Charles H. Whitebread
USC Law School

All titles are packaged in a convenient carry case with handle. $120 if purchased separately. $95 if purchased as a set. Save $25.
ISBN: 0-15-900254-0   Set $95

Gilbert's Pocket Size Law Dictionary
Gilbert

A dictionary is useless if you don't have it when you need it. If the only law dictionary you own is a thick, bulky one, you'll probably leave it at home most of the time — and if you need to know a definition while you're at school, you're out of luck!

With Gilbert's Pocket Size Law Dictionary, you'll have any definition you need, when you need it. Just pop Gilbert's dictionary into your pocket or purse, and you'll have over 4,000 legal terms and phrases at your fingertips. Gilbert's dictionary also includes a section on law school shorthand, common abbreviations, Latin and French legal terms, periodical abbreviations, and governmental abbreviations.

With Gilbert's Pocket Size Law Dictionary, you'll never be caught at a loss for words!

Available in your choice of 5 colors

■ Brown   ISBN: 0-15-900252-4 $7.95
■ Blue   ISBN: 0-15-900362-8 $7.95
■ Burgundy ISBN: 0-15-900366-0 $7.95
■ Green   ISBN: 0-15-900365-2 $7.95

Limited Edition: Simulated Alligator Skin Cover
■ Black   ISBN: 0-15-900364-4 $7.95

The Eight Secrets Of Top Exam Performance In Law School
Charles Whitebread

Wouldn't it be great to know exactly what your professor's looking for on your exam? To find out everything that's expected of you, so that you don't waste your time doing anything other than maximizing your grades?

In his easy-to-read, refreshing style, nationally recognized exam expert Professor Charles Whitebread will teach you the eight secrets that will add precious points to every exam answer you write. You'll learn the three keys to handling any essay exam question, and how to add points to your score by making time work for you, not against you. You'll learn flawless issue spotting, and discover how to organize your answer for maximum possible points. You'll find out how the hidden traps in "IRAC" trip up most students… but not you! You'll learn the techniques for digging up the exam questions your professor will ask, before your exam. You'll put your newly-learned skills to the test with sample exam questions, and you can measure your performance against model answers. And there's even a special section that helps you master the skills necessary to crush any exam, not just a typical essay exam — unusual exams like open book, take home, multiple choice, short answer, and policy questions.

"The Eight Secrets of Top Exam Performance in Law School" gives you all the tools you need to maximize your grades — quickly and easily!

ISBN: 0-15-900323-7 $9.95

Call 1-800-787-8717 or visit our web site at http://www.gilbertlaw.com for more information.

LAW SCHOOL LEGENDS SERIES

America's Greatest Law Professors on Audio Cassette

Wouldn't it be great if all of your law professors were law school legends? You know — the kind of professors whose classes everyone fights to get into. The professors whose classes you'd take, no matter what subject they're teaching. The kind of professors who make a subject sing. You may never get an opportunity to take a class with a truly brilliant professor, but with the Law School Legends Series, you can now get all the benefits of the country's greatest law professors…on audio cassette!

Administrative Law
Professor Patrick J. Borchers
Albany Law School of Union University

TOPICS COVERED: Classification Of Agencies; Adjudicative And Investigative Action; Rule Making Power; Delegation Doctrine; Control By Executive; Appointment And Removal; Freedom Of Information Act; Rule Making Procedure; Adjudicative Procedure; Trial Type Hearings; Administrative Law Judge; Power To Stay Proceedings; Subpoena Power; Physical Inspection; Self Incrimination; Judicial Review Issues; Declaratory Judgment; Sovereign Immunity; Eleventh Amendment; Statutory Limitations; Standing; Exhaustion Of Administrative Remedies; Scope Of Judicial Review.
3 Audio Cassettes
ISBN 0-15-900189-7 $45.95

Agency & Partnership
Professor Richard J. Conviser
Chicago Kent College of Law

TOPICS COVERED: Agency: Creation; Rights And Duties Of Principal And Agent; Sub-Agents; Contract Liability–Actual Authority: Express And Implied; Apparent Authority; Ratification; Liabilities Of Parties; Tort Liability–Respondeat Superior; Frolic And Detour; Intentional Torts. *Partnership:* Nature Of Partnership; Formation; Partnership By Estoppel; In Partnership Property; Relations Between Partners To Third Parties; Authority of Partners; Dissolution And Termination; Limited Partnerships.
3 Audio Cassettes
ISBN: 0-15-900351-2 $45.95

Bankruptcy
Professor Elizabeth Warren
Harvard Law School

TOPICS COVERED: The Debtor/Creditor Relationship; The Commencement, Conversion, Dismissal and Reopening Of Bankruptcy Proceedings; Property Included In The Bankruptcy Estate; Secured, Priority And Unsecured Claims; The Automatic Stay; Powers Of Avoidance; The Assumption And Rejection Of Executory Contracts; The Protection Of Exempt Property; The Bankruptcy Discharge; Chapter 13 Proceedings; Chapter 11 Proceedings; Bankruptcy Jurisdiction And Procedure.
4 Audio Cassettes
ISBN: 0-15-900273-7 $45.95

Civil Procedure
By Professor Richard D. Freer
Emory University Law School

TOPICS COVERED: Subject Matter Jurisdiction; Personal Jurisdiction; Long-Arm Statutes; Constitutional Limitations; In Rem And Quasi In Rem Jurisdiction; Service Of Process; Venue; Transfer; Forum Non Conveniens; Removal; Waiver; Governing Law; Pleadings; Joinder Of Claims; Permissive And Compulsory Joinder Of Parties; Counter-Claims And Cross-Claims; Ancillary Jurisdiction; Impleader; Class Actions; Discovery; Pretrial Adjudication; Summary Judgment; Trial; Post Trial Motions; Appeals; Res Judicata; Collateral Estoppel.
5 Audio Cassettes
ISBN: 0-15-900322-9 $59.95

Commercial Paper
By Professor Michael I. Spak
Chicago Kent College Of Law

TOPICS COVERED: Introduction; Types Of Negotiable Instruments; Elements Of Negotiability; Statute Of Limitations; Payment-In-Full Checks; Negotiations Of The Instrument; Becoming A Holder-In-Due Course; Rights Of A Holder In Due Course; Real And Personal Defenses; Jus Teril; Effect Of Instrument On Underlying Obligations; Contracts Of Maker And Indorser; Suretyship; Liability Of Drawer And Drawee; Check Certification; Warranty Liability; Conversion Of Liability; Banks And Their Customers; Properly Payable Rule; Wrongful Dishonor; Stopping Payment; Death Of Customer; Bank Statement; Check Collection; Expedited Funds Availability; Forgery Of Drawer's Name; Alterations; Imposter Rule; Wire Transfers; Electronic Fund Transfers Act .
3 Audio Cassettes
ISBN: 0-15-900275-3 $39.95

Conflict Of Laws
Professor Richard J. Conviser
Chicago Kent College of Law

TOPICS COVERED: Domicile; Jurisdiction; In Personam, In Rem, Quasi In Rem; Court Competence; Forum Non Conveniens; Choice Of Law; Foreign Causes Of Action; Territorial Approach To Choice/Tort And Contract; "Escape Devices"; Most Significant Relationship; Governmental Interest Analysis; Recognition Of Judgments; Foreign Country Judgments; Domestic Judgments/Full Faith And Credit; Review Of Judgments; Modifiable Judgments; Defenses To Recognition And Enforcement; Federal/State (Erie) Problems; Constitutional Limits On Choice Of Law.
3 Audio Cassettes
ISBN: 0-15-900352-0 $39.95

Constitutional Law
By Professor John C. Jeffries, Jr.
University of Virginia School of Law

TOPICS COVERED: Introduction; Exam Tactics; Legislative Power; Supremacy; Commerce; State Regulation; Privileges And Immunities; Federal Court Jurisdiction; Separation Of Powers; Civil Liberties; Due Process; Equal Protection; Privacy; Race; Alienage; Gender; Speech And Association; Prior Restraints; Religion—Free Exercise; Establishment Clause.
5 Audio Cassettes
ISBN: 0-15-900319-9 $45.95

Contracts
By Professor Michael I. Spak
Chicago Kent College Of Law

TOPICS COVERED: Offer; Revocation; Acceptance; Consideration; Defenses To Formation; Third Party Beneficiaries; Assignment; Delegation; Conditions; Excuses; Anticipatory Repudiation; Discharge Of Duty; Modifications; Rescission; Accord & Satisfaction; Novation; Breach; Damages; Remedies; UCC Remedies; Parol Evidence Rule.
4 Audio Cassettes
ISBN: 0-15-900318-0 $45.95

Copyright Law
Professor Roger E. Schechter
George Washington University Law School

TOPICS COVERED: Constitution; Patents And Property Ownership Distinguished; Subject Matter Copyright; Duration And Renewal; Ownership And Transfer; Formalities; Introduction; Notice, Registration And Deposit; Infringement; Overview; Reproduction And Derivative Works; Public Distribution; Public Performance And Display; Exemptions; Fair Use; Photocopying; Remedies; Preemption Of State Law.
3 Audio Cassettes
ISBN: 0-15-900295-8 $39.95

Corporations
By Professor Therese H. Maynard
Loyola Marymount School of Law

TOPICS COVERED: Ultra Vires Act; Corporate Formation; Piercing The Corporate Veil; Corporate Financial Structure; Stocks; Bonds; Subscription Agreements; Watered Stock; Stock Transactions; Insider Trading; 16(b) & 10b-5 Violations; Promoters; Fiduciary Duties; Shareholder Rights; Meetings; Cumulative Voting; Voting Trusts; Close Corporations; Dividends; Preemptive Rights; Shareholder Derivative Suits; Directors; Duty Of Loyalty; Corporate Opportunity Doctrine; Officers; Amendments; Mergers; Dissolution.
4 Audio Cassettes
ISBN: 0-15-900320-2 $45.95

Criminal Law
By Professor Charles H. Whitebread
USC School of Law

TOPICS COVERED: Exam Tactics; Volitional Acts; Mental States; Specific Intent; Malice; General Intent; Strict Liability; Accomplice Liability; Inchoate Crimes; Impossibility; Defenses; Insanity; Voluntary And Involuntary Intoxication; Infancy; Self-Defense; Defense Of A Dwelling; Duress; Necessity; Mistake Of Fact Or Law; Entrapment; Battery; Assault; Homicide; Common Law Murder; Voluntary And Involuntary Manslaughter; First Degree Murder; Felony Murder; Rape; Larceny; Embezzlement; False Pretenses; Robbery; Extortion; Burglary; Arson.
4 Audio Cassettes
ISBN: 0-15-900279-6 $39.95

Criminal Procedure
By Professor Charles H. Whitebread
USC School of Law

TOPICS COVERED: Incorporation Of The Bill Of Rights; Exclusionary Rule; Fruit Of The Poisonous Tree; Arrest; Search & Seizure; Exceptions To Warrant Requirement; Wire Tapping & Eavesdropping; Confessions (Miranda); Pretrial Identification; Bail; Preliminary Hearings; Grand Juries; Speedy Trial; Fair Trial; Jury Trials; Right To Counsel; Guilty Pleas; Sentencing; Death Penalty; Habeas Corpus; Double Jeopardy; Privilege Against Compelled Testimony.
3 Audio Cassettes
ISBN: 0-15-900281-8 $39.95

Evidence
By Professor Faust F. Rossi
Cornell Law School

TOPICS COVERED: Relevance; Insurance; Remedial Measures; Settlement Offers; Causation; State Of Mind; Rebuttal; Habit; Character Evidence; "MIMIC" Rule; Documentary Evidence; Authentication; Best Evidence Rule; Parol Evidence; Competency; Dead Man Statutes; Examination Of Witnesses; Present Recollection Revived; Past Recollection Recorded; Opinion Testimony; Lay And Expert Witness; Learned Treatises; Impeachment; Collateral Matters; Bias, Interest Or Motive; Rehabilitation; Privileges; Hearsay And Exceptions.
5 Audio Cassettes
ISBN: 0-15-900282-6 $45.95

Family Law
Professor Roger E. Schechter
George Washington University Law School

TOPICS COVERED: National Scope Of Family Law; Marital Relationship; Consequences Of Marriage; Formalities And Solemnization; Common Law Marriage; Impediments; Marriage And Conflict Of Laws; Non-Marital Relationship; Law Of Names; Void And Voidable Marriages; Marital Breakdown; Annulment And Defenses; Divorce — Fault And No-Fault; Separation; Jurisdiction For Divorce; Migratory Divorce; Full Faith And Credit; Temporary Orders; Economic Aspects Of Marital Breakdown; Property Division; Community Property Principles; Equitable Distribution; Marital And Separate Property; Types Of Property Interests; Equitable Reimbursement; Alimony; Modification And Termination Of Alimony; Child Support; Health Insurance; Enforcement Of Orders; Antenuptial And Postnuptial Agreements; Separation And Settlement Agreements; Custody Jurisdiction And Awards; Modification Of Custody; Visitation Rights; Termination Of Parental Rights; Adoption; Illegitimacy; Paternity Actions.
3 Audio Cassettes
ISBN: 0-15-900283-4 $39.95

Federal Courts
Professor John C. Jeffries
University of Virginia School of Law

TOPICS COVERED: History Of The Federal Court System; "Court Or Controversy" And Justiciability; Congressional Power Over Federal Court Jurisdiction; Supreme Court Jurisdiction; District Court Subject Matter Jurisdiction—Federal Question Jurisdiction, Diversity Jurisdiction And Admiralty Jurisdiction; Pendent And Ancillary Jurisdiction; Removal Jurisdiction; Venue; Forum Non Conveniens; Law Applied In The Federal Courts; Federal Law In The State Courts; Collateral Relations Between Federal And State Courts; The Eleventh Amendment And State Sovereign Immunity.
3 Audio Cassettes
ISBN: 0-15-900296-6 $39.95

Federal Income Tax
By Professor Cheryl D. Block
George Washington University Law School

TOPICS COVERED: Administrative Reviews; Tax Formula; Gross Income; Exclusions For Gifts; Inheritances; Personal Injuries; Tax Basis Rules; Divorce Tax Rules; Assignment Of Income; Business Deductions; Investment Deductions; Passive Loss And Interest Limitation Rules; Capital Gains & Losses; Section 1031, 1034, and 121 Deferred/Non Taxable Transactions.
4 Audio Cassettes
ISBN: 0-15-900284-2 $45.95

Future Interests
By Dean Catherine L. Carpenter
Southwestern University Law School

TOPICS COVERED: Rule Against Perpetuities; Class Gifts; Estates In Land; Rule In Shelley's Case; Future Interests In Transferor and Transferee; Life Estates; Defeasible Fees; Doctrine Of Worthier Title; Doctrine Of Merger; Fee Simple Estates; Restraints On Alienation; Power Of Appointment; Rules Of Construction.
2 Audio Cassettes
ISBN: 0-15-900285-0 $24.95

Law School ABC's
By Professor Jennifer S. Kamita
Loyola Marymount Law School, and
Professor Rodney O. Fong
Golden Gate University School of Law

TOPICS COVERED: Introduction; Casebooks; Hornbooks; Selecting Commercial Materials; Briefing; Review; ABC's Of A Lecture; Taking Notes; Lectures & Notes Examples; Study Groups; ABC's Of Outlining; Rules; Outlining Hypothetical; Outlining Assignment And Review; Introduction To Essay Writing; "IRAC"; Call Of The Question Exercise; Issue Spotting Exercise; IRAC Defining & Writing Exercise; Form Tips; ABC's Of Exam Writing; Exam Writing Hypothetical; Practice Exam And Review; Preparation Hints; Exam Diagnostics & Writing Problems.
4 Audio Cassettes
ISBN: 0-15-900286-9 $45.95

Law School Exam Writing
By Professor Charles H. Whitebread
USC School of Law

TOPICS COVERED: With "Law School Exam Writing," you'll learn the secrets of law school test taking . In this fascinating lecture, Professor Whitebread leads you step-by-step through his innovative system, so that you know exactly how to tackle your essay exams without making point draining mistakes. You'll learn how to read questions so you don't miss important issues; how to organize your answer; how to use limited exam time to your maximum advantage; and even how to study for exams.
1 Audio Cassette
ISBN: 0-15-900287-7 $19.95

Professional Responsibility
By Professor Erwin Chemerinsky
USC School of Law

TOPICS COVERED: Regulation of Attorneys; Bar Admission; Unauthorized Practice; Competency; Discipline; Judgment; Lawyer-Client Relationship; Representation; Withdrawal; Conflicts; Disqualification; Clients; Client Interests; Successive And Effective Representation; Integrity; Candor; Confidences; Secrets; Past And Future Crimes; Perjury; Communications; Witnesses; Jurors; The Court; The Press; Trial Tactics; Prosecutors; Market; Solicitation; Advertising; Law Firms; Fees; Client Property; Conduct; Political Activity.
3 Audio Cassettes
ISBN: 0-15-900371-7 $39.95

Real Property
By Professor Paula A. Franzese
Seton Hall Law School

TOPICS COVERED: Estates—Fee Simple; Fee Tail; Life Estate; Co-Tenancy—Joint Tenancy; Tenancy In Common; Tenancy By The Entirety; Landlord-Tenant Relationship; Liability For Condition Of Premises; Assignment & Sublease; Easements; Restrictive Covenants; Adverse Possession; Recording Acts; Conveyancing; Personal Property—Finders; Bailments; Gifts; Future Interests.
4 Audio Cassettes
ISBN: 0-15-900289-3 $45.95

Remedies
By Professor William A. Fletcher
University of California at Berkeley, Boalt Hall School of Law

TOPICS COVERED: Damages; Restitution; Equitable Remedies (including Constructive Trust, Equitable Lien, Injunction, and Specific Performance); Tracing; Rescission and Reformation; Specific topics include Injury and Destruction of Personal Property; Conversion; Injury to Real Property; Trespass; Ouster; Nuisance; Defamation; Trade Libel; Inducing Breach of Contract; Contracts to Purchase Personal Property; Contracts to Purchase Real Property (including Equitable Conversion); Construction Contracts; and Personal Service Contracts.
3 Audio Cassettes
ISBN: 0-15-900353-9 $45.95

Sales & Lease of Goods
By Professor Michael I. Spak
Chicago Kent College of Law

TOPICS COVERED: Goods; Contract Formation; Firm Offers; Statute Of Frauds; Modification; Parol Evidence; Code Methodology; Tender; Payment; Identification; Risk Of Loss; Warranties; Merchantability; Fitness; Disclaimers; Consumer Protection; Remedies; Anticipatory Repudiation; Third Party Rights.
3 Audio Cassettes
ISBN: 0-15-900291-5 $39.95

Secured Transactions
By Professor Michael I. Spak
Chicago Kent College of Law

TOPICS COVERED: Collateral; Inventory; Intangibles; Proceeds; Security Agreements; Attachment; After-Acquired Property; Perfection; Filing; Priorities; Purchase Money Security Interests; Fixtures; Rights Upon Default; Self-Help; Sale; Constitutional Issues.
3 Audio Cassettes
ISBN: 0-15-900292-3 $39.95

Torts
By Professor Richard J. Conviser
Chicago Kent College of Law

TOPICS COVERED: Essay Exam Techniques; Intentional Torts—Assault; Battery; False Imprisonment; Intentional Infliction Of Emotional Distress; Trespass To Land; Trespass To Chattels; Conversion; Defenses: Defamation—Libel; Slander; Defenses; First Amendment Concerns; Invasion Of Right Of Privacy; Misrepresentation; Negligence—Duty; Breach; Actual And Proximate Causation; Damages; Defenses; Strict Liability; Products Liability; Nuisance; General Tort Considerations.
4 Audio Cassettes
ISBN: 0-15-900185-4 $45.95

Wills & Trusts
By Professor Stanley M. Johanson
University of Texas School of Law

TOPICS COVERED: Attested Wills; Holographic Wills; Negligence; Revocation; Changes On Face Of Will; Lapsed Gifts; Negative Bequest Rule; Nonprobate Assets; Intestate Succession; Advancements; Elective Share; Will Contests; Capacity; Undue Influence; Creditors' Rights; Creation Of Trust; Revocable Trusts; Pourover Gifts; Charitable Trusts; Resulting Trusts; Constructive Trusts; Spendthrift Trusts; Self-Dealing; Prudent Investments; Trust Accounting; Termination; Powers Of Appointment.
4 Audio Cassettes
ISBN: 0-15-900294-X $45.95

Law School Legends Series
FIRST YEAR PROGRAM

Includes Five Law School Legends Titles:

- **Civil Procedure**
  By Professor Richard D. Freer
  Emory University Law School

- **Contracts**
  By Professor Michael I. Spak
  Chicago Kent College Of Law

- **Criminal Law**
  By Professor Charles H. Whitebread
  USC School of Law

- **Real Property**
  By Professor Paula A. Franzese
  Seton Hall Law School

- **Torts**
  By Professor Richard J. Conviser
  Chicago Kent College of Law

Plus—

- **Law School Exam Writing**
  By Professor Charles H. Whitebread
  USC Law School

All titles are packaged in a convenient carry case. $250 if purchased separately. $195 if purchased as a set. Save $55.
ISBN: 0-15-900306-7   Set $195

NEW!
Call for release dates

Antitrust
ISBN# 0-15-900341-5 $39.95

Estate & Gift Tax
ISBN# 0-15-900354-7 $39.95

Labor Law
ISBN# 0-15-900357-1 $39.95

Product Liability
ISBN# 0-15-900358-X $39.95

Securities Regulation
ISBN# 0-15-900359-8 $39.95

If you accidentally damage a tape within five years from the date of purchase we'll replace it for FREE— No questions asked!

Call 1-800-787-8717 or visit our web site at http://www.gilbertlaw.com for more information.

Legalines

Legalines gives you authoritative, detailed briefs of every major case in your casebook. You get a clear explanation of the facts, the issues, the court's holding and reasoning, and any significant concurrences or dissents. Even more importantly, you get an authoritative explanation of the significance of each case, and how it relates to other cases in your casebook. And with Legalines' detailed table of contents and table of cases, you can quickly find any case or concept you're looking for. But your professor expects you to know more than just the cases. That's why Legalines gives you more than just case briefs. You get summaries of the black letter law, as well. That's crucial, because some of the most important information in your casebooks isn't in the cases at all...it's the black letter principles you're expected to glean from those cases. Legalines is the only series that gives you both case briefs and black letter review. With Legalines, you get everything you need to know—whether it's in a case or not!

Administrative Law
Keyed to the Breyer Casebook
ISBN: 0-15-900169-2   206 pages $17.95

Administrative Law
Keyed to the Gellhorn Casebook
ISBN: 0-15-900170-6   268 pages $19.95

Administrative Law
Keyed to the Schwartz Casebook
ISBN: 0-15-900171-4   155 pages $17.95

Antitrust
Keyed to the Areeda Casebook
ISBN: 0-15-900046-7   209 pages $17.95

Antitrust
Keyed to the Handler Casebook
ISBN: 0-15-900045-9   174 pages $17.95

Civil Procedure
Keyed to the Cound Casebook
ISBN: 0-15-900314-8   316 pages $19.95

Civil Procedure
Keyed to the Field Casebook
ISBN: 0-15-900048-3   388 pages $21.95

Civil Procedure
Keyed to the Hazard Casebook
ISBN: 0-15-900324-5   253 pages $18.95

Civil Procedure
Keyed to the Rosenberg Casebook
ISBN: 0-15-900052-1   312 pages $19.95

Civil Procedure
Keyed to the Yeazell Casebook
ISBN: 0-15-900241-9   240 pages $18.95

Commercial Law
Keyed to the Farnsworth Casebook
ISBN: 0-15-900176-5   170 pages $17.95

Conflict of Laws
Keyed to the Cramton Casebook
ISBN: 0-15-900331-8   144 pages $16.95

Conflict of Laws
Keyed to the Reese (Rosenberg) Casebook
ISBN: 0-15-900057-2   279 pages $19.95

Constitutional Law
Keyed to the Brest Casebook
ISBN: 0-15-900338-5   235 pages $18.95

Constitutional Law
Keyed to the Cohen Casebook
ISBN: 0-15-900261-3   235 pages $20.95

Constitutional Law
Keyed to the Gunther Casebook
ISBN: 0-15-900060-2   395 pages $21.95

Constitutional Law
Keyed to the Lockhart Casebook
ISBN: 0-15-900242-7   348 pages $20.95

Constitutional Law
Keyed to the Rotunda Casebook
ISBN: 0-15-900363-6   281 pages $19.95

Constitutional Law
Keyed to the Stone Casebook
ISBN: 0-15-900236-2   296 pages $19.95

Contracts
Keyed to the Calamari Casebook
ISBN: 0-15-900065-3   256 pages $19.95

Contracts
Keyed to the Dawson Casebook
ISBN: 0-15-900268-0   188 pages $19.95

Contracts
Keyed to the Farnsworth Casebook
ISBN: 0-15-900332-6   219 pages $18.95

Contracts
Keyed to the Fuller Casebook
ISBN: 0-15-900237-0   206 pages $17.95

Contracts
Keyed to the Kessler Casebook
ISBN: 0-15-900070-X   340 pages $20.95

Contracts
Keyed to the Murphy Casebook
ISBN: 0-15-900072-6   272 pages $19.95

Corporations
Keyed to the Cary Casebook
ISBN: 0-15-900172-2   407 pages $21.95

Corporations
Keyed to the Choper Casebook
ISBN: 0-15-900173-0   270 pages $19.95

Corporations
Keyed to the Hamilton Casebook
ISBN: 0-15-900313-X   248 pages $19.95

Corporations
Keyed to the Vagts Casebook
ISBN: 0-15-900078-5   213 pages $17.95

Criminal Law
Keyed to the Boyce Casebook
ISBN: 0-15-900080-7   318 pages $19.95

Criminal Law
Keyed to the Dix Casebook
ISBN: 0-15-900081-5   113 pages $15.95

Criminal Law
Keyed to the Johnson Casebook
ISBN: 0-15-900175-7   169 pages $17.95

Criminal Law
Keyed to the Kadish Casebook
ISBN: 0-15-900333-4   209 pages $17.95

Criminal Law
Keyed to the La Fave Casebook
ISBN: 0-15-900084-X   202 pages $17.95

Criminal Procedure
Keyed to the Kamisar Casebook
ISBN: 0-15-900336-9   310 pages $19.95

Decedents' Estates & Trusts
Keyed to the Ritchie Casebook
ISBN: 0-15-900339-3   277 pages $19.95

Domestic Relations
Keyed to the Clark Casebook
ISBN: 0-15-900168-4   128 pages $16.95

Domestic Relations
Keyed to the Wadlington Casebook
ISBN: 0-15-900167-6   215 pages $18.95

Enterprise Organization
Keyed to the Conard Casebook
ISBN: 0-15-900092-0   316 pages $19.95

Estate & Gift Taxation
Keyed to the Surrey Casebook
ISBN: 0-15-900093-9   100 pages $15.95

Evidence
Keyed to the Sutton Casebook
ISBN: 0-15-900096-3   310 pages $19.95

Evidence
Keyed to the Waltz Casebook
ISBN: 0-15-900334-2   224 pages $17.95

Evidence
Keyed to the Weinstein Casebook
ISBN: 0-15-900097-1   241 pages $18.95

Family Law
Keyed to the Areen Casebook
ISBN: 0-15-900263-X   262 pages $19.95

Federal Courts
Keyed to the McCormick Casebook
ISBN: 0-15-900101-3   213 pages $17.95

Income Tax
Keyed to the Freeland Casebook
ISBN: 0-15-900222-2   154 pages $17.95

Income Tax
Keyed to the Klein Casebook
ISBN: 0-15-900302-4   174 pages $17.95

Labor Law
Keyed to the Cox Casebook
ISBN: 0-15-900107-2   211 pages $17.95

Labor Law
Keyed to the Merrifield Casebook
ISBN: 0-15-900177-3   202 pages $17.95

Partnership & Corporate Taxation
Keyed to the Surrey Casebook
ISBN: 0-15-900109-9   118 pages $15.95

Property
Keyed to the Browder Casebook
ISBN: 0-15-900110-2   315 pages $19.95

Property
Keyed to the Casner Casebook
ISBN: 0-15-900111-0   291 pages $19.95

Property
Keyed to the Cribbet Casebook
ISBN: 0-15-900239-7   328 pages $20.95

Property
Keyed to the Dukeminier Casebook
ISBN: 0-15-900264-8   186 pages $17.95

Property
Keyed to the Nelson Casebook
ISBN: 0-15-900228-1   288 pages $19.95

Real Property
Keyed to the Rabin Casebook
ISBN: 0-15-900262-1   208 pages $17.95

Remedies
Keyed to the Re Casebook
ISBN: 0-15-900116-1   333 pages $20.95

Remedies
Keyed to the York Casebook
ISBN: 0-15-900118-8   289 pages $19.95

Sales & Secured Transactions
Keyed to the Speidel Casebook
ISBN: 0-15-900166-8   320 pages $19.95

Securities Regulation
Keyed to the Jennings Casebook
ISBN: 0-15-900253-2   368 pages $20.95

Torts
Keyed to the Epstein Casebook
ISBN: 0-15-900335-0   245 pages $18.95

Torts
Keyed to the Franklin Casebook
ISBN: 0-15-900240-0   166 pages $17.95

Torts
Keyed to the Henderson Casebook
ISBN: 0-15-900174-9   209 pages $17.95

Torts
Keyed to the Keeton Casebook
ISBN: 0-15-900124-2   278 pages $19.95

Torts
Keyed to the Prosser Casebook
ISBN: 0-15-900301-6   365 pages $20.95

Wills, Trusts & Estates
Keyed to the Dukeminier Casebook
ISBN: 0-15-900337-7   192 pages $17.95

Also Available:

Criminal Law Questions & Answers
ISBN: 0-15-900087-4   179 pages $12.95

Excelling on Exams/How to Study
ISBN: 0-15-900098-X   101 pages $12.95

Torts Questions & Answers
ISBN: 0-15-900126-9   174 pages $12.95

Call 1-800-787-8717 or visit our web site at http://www.gilbertlaw.com for more information.

Casebriefs Interactive Software For Windows

As a law student you can't afford to waste a minute. That's why you need Casebriefs Software. With Casebriefs you simply click on the name of the case you're looking for, and you instantly have an expert brief of it at your fingertips! The facts. The issue. The holding. The rationale. Expert commentary for each and every case. You'll get everything you need, whether you're preparing for class or studying for your final exam!

When you use Casebriefs, you can focus solely on the cases covered in your casebook, or you can use the Case Library, which includes briefs of all of the major cases from every major casebook. The Case Library is ideal for researching cases for writing assignments, Moot Court briefs, Law Review and other periodicals.

With Casebriefs, searching for cases is a breeze. You can search by topic. You can search alphabetically. You can search the cases in the order in which they appear in your casebook. You can even enter the date you'll cover different cases in class, and sort them by those dates. No matter how you want to look for a case, Casebriefs will help you find it instantly!

For each brief, you can add your own notes, or leave it "as is." Whether you customize the briefs or not, you can print them out and take them to class with you. You can even configure Casebriefs to access Lexis/Nexis and Westlaw directly from the Casebriefs screen (with Lexis/Nexis or Westlaw software and account). Whether you want to compare your own briefs to expert briefs, fill in gaps in your class notes, or research cases for your legal writing class, moot court, law review or other periodicals—Casebriefs is the source you'll turn to, over and over again!

■ Administrative Law
Includes briefs of all of the major cases from the Breyer, Gellhorn and Schwartz casebooks, many of the major cases from the Bonfield and Mashaw casebooks, plus a Case Library.
ISBN# 0-15-900190-0 $27.95

■ Civil Procedure
Includes briefs of all of the major cases from the Cound, Field, Hazard, Rosenberg and Yeazell casebooks, many of the major cases from the Marcus and Freer casebooks, plus a Case Library.
ISBN# 0-15-900191-9 $27.95

■ Conflict Of Laws
Includes briefs of all of the major cases from the Cramton and Reese casebooks, many of the major cases from the Brilmayer casebook, plus a Case Library.
ISBN# 0-15-900192-7 $27.95

■ Constitutional Law
Includes briefs of all of the major cases from the Brest, Cohen, Lockhart, Rotunda and Stone casebooks, plus a Case Library.
ISBN# 0-15-900193-5 $27.95

■ Contracts
Includes briefs of all of the major cases from the Calamari, Dawson, Farnsworth, Fuller, Kessler and Murphy casebooks, many of the major cases from the Crandall, Hamilton, Knapp, Murray, Rosett and Vernon casebooks, plus a Case Library.
ISBN# 0-15-900194-3 $27.95

■ Corporations
Includes briefs of all of the major cases from the Cary, Choper, Hamilton and Vagts casebooks, many of the major cases from the O'Kelley and Solomon casebooks, plus a Case Library.
ISBN# 0-15-900195-1 $27.95

■ Criminal Law
Includes briefs of all of the major cases from the Boyce, Dix, Johnson, Kadish and La Fave casebooks, many of the major cases from the Dressler, Foote, Kaplan and Weinreb casebooks, plus a Case Library.
ISBN# 0-15-900196-X $27.95

■ Criminal Procedure
Includes briefs of all of the major cases from the Kamisar casebook, many of the major cases from the Allen, Haddad and Saltzburg casebooks, plus a Case Library.
ISBN# 0-15-900197-8 $27.95

■ Evidence
Includes briefs of all of the major cases from the Waltz, Sutton, and Weinstein casebooks, many of the major cases from the Strong, Green, Lempert and Mueller casebooks, plus a Case Library.
ISBN# 0-15-900198-6 $27.95

■ Family Law
Includes briefs of all of the major cases from the Areen casebook, many of the major cases from the Clark, Ellman, Krause and Wadlington casebooks, plus a Case Library.
ISBN# 0-15-900199-4 $27.95

■ Income Tax
Includes briefs of all of the major cases from the Andrews, Freeland and Klein casebooks, many of the major cases from the Graetz casebook, plus a Case Library.
ISBN# 0-15-900200-1 $27.95

■ Property
Includes briefs of all of the major cases from the Browder, Casner, Cribbet, Dukeminier and Rabin casebooks, many of the major cases from the Donahue, Haar and Kurtz casebooks, plus a Case Library.
ISBN# 0-15-900201-X $27.95

■ Remedies
Includes briefs of all of the major cases from the Re and York casebooks, many of the major cases from the Laycock, Leavell and Shoben casebooks, plus a Case Library.
ISBN# 0-15-900202-8 $27.95

■ Torts
Includes briefs of all of the major cases from the Epstein, Franklin, Henderson, Keeton and Prosser casebooks, many of the major cases from the Dobbs and Shulman casebooks, plus a Case Library.
ISBN# 0-15-900203-6 $27.95

■ Wills, Trusts & Estates
Includes briefs of all of the major cases from the Dukeminier casebook plus a Case Library.
ISBN# 0-15-900204-4 $27.95

Welcome to gilbertlaw.com

 Pre-Law Center

 Bookstore

 Past Exam Library

 Links to Law Sites

 Welcome Center

 Employment Center

 Wanted! Student Marketing Reps

 1st Year Survival Manual

 Taking the Bar Exam?

GilbertLaw.com is the site that helps law students study smarter. Shop for study aids in the bookstore or get ready for your first year with the 1st Year Survival Manual.

http://www.gilbertlaw.com

Dictionary of Legal Terms

Gilbert's Dictionary Of Legal Terms Software:
Features over 3,500 legal terms and phrases, law school shorthand, common abbreviations, Latin and French legal terms, periodical abbreviations, and governmental abbreviations.
Includes Free Pocket Size Law Dictionary!

ISBN: 0-15-900250-8   Macintosh $27.95
ISBN: 0-15-900249-4   Windows $27.95

Call 1-800-787-8717 or visit our web site at http://www.gilbertlaw.com for more information.

Employment Guides

A collection of best selling titles that help you identify and reach your career goals.

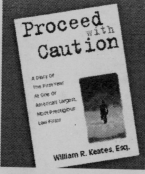

The National Directory Of Legal Employers
National Association for Law Placement

The National Directory of Legal Employers brings you a universe of vital information about 1,000 of the nation's top legal employers— *in one convenient volume!*

It includes:

- Over 22,000 job openings.
- The names, addresses and phone numbers of hiring partners.
- Listings of firms by state, size, kind and practice area.
- What starting salaries are for full time, part time, and summer associates, plus a detailed description of firm benefits.
- The number of employees by gender and race, as well as the number of employees with disabilities.
- A detailed narrative of each firm, plus much more!

The National Directory Of Legal Employers has been the best kept secret of top legal career search professionals for over a decade. Now, for the first time, it is available in a format specifically designed for law students and new graduates. *Pick up your copy of the Directory today!*
ISBN: 0-15-900248-6   **$39.95**

Proceed With Caution: A Diary Of The First Year At One Of America's Largest, Most Prestigious Law Firms
William R. Keates

Prestige. Famous clients. High-profile cases. Not to mention a starting salary approaching six figures.

In *Proceed With Caution*, the author takes you behind the scenes, to show you what it's really like to be a junior associate at a huge law firm. After graduating from an Ivy League law school, he took a job as an associate with one of New York's blue-chip law firms.

He also did something not many people do. He kept a diary, where he spilled out his day-to-day life at the firm in graphic detail.

Proceed With Caution excerpts the diary, from his first day at the firm to the day he quit. From the splashy benefits, to the nitty-gritty on the work junior associates do, to the grind of long and unpredictable hours, to the stress that eventually made him leave the firm — he tells story after story that will make you feel as though you're living the life of a new associate.

Whether you're considering a career with a large firm, or you're just curious about what life at the top firms is all about — *Proceed With Caution* is a must read!
ISBN: 0-15-900181-1   **$17.95**

Guerrilla Tactics for Getting the Legal Job of Your Dreams
Kimm Alayne Walton, J.D.

Whether you're looking for a summer clerkship or your first permanent job after school, this revolutionary book is the key to getting the job of your dreams!

Guerrilla Tactics for Getting the Legal Job of Your Dreams leads you step-by-step through everything you need to do to nail down that perfect job! You'll learn hundreds of simple-to-use strategies that will get you exactly where you want to go. You'll Learn:

- The seven magic opening words in cover letters that ensure you'll get a response.
- The secret to successful interviews every time.
- Killer answers to the toughest interview questions they'll ever ask you.
- Plus Much More!

Guerrilla Tactics features the best strategies from the country's most innovative law school career advisors. The strategies in *Guerrilla Tactics* are so powerful that it even comes with a guarantee: Follow the advice in the book, and within one year of graduation you'll have the job of your dreams… or your money back!

Pick up a copy of *Guerrilla Tactics* today…and you'll be on your way to the job of your dreams!
ISBN: 0-15-900317-2   **$24.95**

Beyond L.A. Law: Inspiring Stories of People Who've Done Fascinating Things With A Law Degree
National Association for Law Placement

Anyone who watches television knows that being a lawyer means working your way up through a law firm — right?

Wrong!

Beyond L.A. Law gives you a fascinating glimpse into the lives of people who've broken the "lawyer" mold. They come from a variety of backgrounds — some had prior careers, others went straight through college and law school, and yet others have overcome poverty and physical handicaps. They got their degrees from all different kinds of law schools, all over the country. But they have one thing in common: they've all pursued their own, unique vision.

As you read their stories, you'll see how they beat the odds to succeed. You'll learn career tips and strategies that work, from people who've put them to the test. And you'll find fascinating insights that you can apply to your own dream — whether it's a career in law, or anything else!

From Representing Baseball In Australia. To International Finance. To Children's Advocacy. To Directing a Nonprofit Organization. To Entrepreneur.

If You Think Getting A Law Degree Means Joining A Traditional Law Firm — Think Again!.
ISBN: 0-15-900182-X   **$17.95**

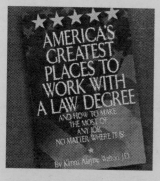

America's Greatest Places To Work With A Law Degree
Kimm Alayne Walton, J.D.

"Where do your happiest graduates work?" That's the question that author Kimm Alayne Walton asked of law school administrators around the country. Their responses revealed the hundreds of wonderful employers profiled in *America's Greatest Places To Work With A Law Degree.*

In this remarkable book, you'll get to know an incredible variety of great places to work, including:

- Glamorous sports and entertainment employers – the jobs that sound as though they would be great, and they are!
- The 250 best law firms to work for between 20 and 600 attorneys.
- Companies where law school graduates love to work and not just as in-house counsel.
- Wonderful public interest employers – the "white knight" jobs that are so incredibly satisfying.
- Court-related positions, where lawyers entertain fascinating issues, tremendous variety, and an enjoyable lifestyle.
- Outstanding government jobs, at the federal, state, and local level.

Beyond learning about incredible employers, you'll discover:

- The ten traits that define a wonderful place to work…the sometimes surprising qualities that outstanding employers share.
- How to handle law school debt, when your dream job pays less than you think you need to make.
- How to find – and get! – great jobs at firms with fewer than 20 attorneys.

And no matter where you work, you'll learn expert tips for making the most of your job. You'll learn the specific strategies that distinguish people headed for the top…how to position yourself for the most interesting, high-profile work…how to handle difficult personalities… how to negotiate for more money…and what to do now to help you get your next great job!
ISBN: 0-15-900180-3   **$24.95**

Presented by The National Law Journal

The Job Goddess column is a weekly feature of the *National Law Journal's Law Journal Extra*, and is written by Kimm Alayne Walton, author of the national best seller *Guerrilla Tactics For Getting The Legal Job Of Your Dreams*. View recent columns or e-mail the Job Goddess with your job search questions on the Internet at www.gilbertlaw.com

Call 1-800-787-8717 or visit our web site at http://www.gilbertlaw.com for more information.